A Allgemeiner Teil

1 Didaktisch-methodische Konzeption

1.1 Allgemeine Grundlagen

Learning English - Green Line New 3 baut systematisch und kontinuierlich auf *Green Line New 2* auf; es ist konzipiert als Lehrwerk für Englisch als erste Fremdsprache an Gymnasien. *Green Line New 3* ist der dritte einer Reihe von sechs Jahrgangsbänden, die bis zum Abschluss der Sekundarstufe I zu einer grundlegenden sprachlichen Handlungsfähigkeit in der Fremdsprache Englisch und damit zu einer wichtigen Basisqualifikation für den Beruf sowie für die Vorbereitung auf die Arbeit an der gymnasialen Oberstufe beitragen.

Entsprechend der Klassenstufe 7 findet gegenüber *Green Line New 2* eine Erweiterung der Übungs- und Lernformen, der Textsorten sowie eine Intensivierung im Bereich der Lern- und Arbeitstechniken statt. Insbesondere im Bereich der Lern- und Arbeitstechniken sowie der Lernstrategien wird in *Green Line New 3*, entsprechend dem fortgeschrittenen Alter und der damit einhergehenden kognitiven Entwicklung der Lernerinnen und Lerner, ein zusätzliches, stark erweitertes und nach den einzelnen Fertigkeiten differenzierendes Angebot gemacht. Dieses Angebot wird konsequent in fertigkeitsbezogene *Workshops* umgesetzt. Die *Workshops* stehen als gleichwertige Teile zwischen den *Units*. Dies führt zu einer Umstrukturierung des bisherigen Buchaufbaus: Während *Green Line New 1* und *2* vor allem von den *Units* getragen werden, kommt es nun bei *Green Line New 3* (und auch beim Folgeband *Green Line New 4*) erstmals zum alternierenden Vorkommen von *Units* <u>und</u> *Workshops*.

Die *Workshops* stellen eine logische und konsequente didaktische Umsetzung neuester Erkenntnisse der Fremdsprachenforschung und -didaktik, der pädagogisch-psychologischen Unterrichtsforschung und der Psycholinguistik in der Unterrichtspraxis dar. Somit wird das besondere Anliegen der neuen *Lines*-Generation, die Schülerinnen und Schüler zunehmend zum autonomen und selbstverantwortlichen Lernen zu führen, auch im dritten Lernjahr Englisch voll und ganz fortgeführt. Dieses übergreifende Lernziel kommt auch in den neuen Richtlinien und Lehrplänen zum Ausdruck. Es wird in *Green Line New 3* realisiert durch die *Workshops*, die speziell auf die verschiedenen Fertigkeiten bezogen und auf deren jeweils korrespondierenden, kontextbezogenen und bereichsspezifischen Lernstrategien hin konzipiert sind; weiterhin wird dieses Ziel verwirklicht durch ein entsprechendes Übungsangebot innerhalb der *Units*, durch auf *Green Line New 3* abgestimmte **Materialien zur Freiarbeit** und durch abgestimmte Lernmedien, so z.B. durch ein ständig aktualisiertes Internetangebot auf den Web-Seiten **Klett Online-News** (http://www.klett.de/), durch die zum Buch gehörende Software sowie durch CDs und Kassetten, durch systematisch integrierte Hinweise zu den Lern- und Arbeitstechniken innerhalb der unterschiedlichen sprachlichen Fertigkeiten, durch übungsimmanente Hinweise und durch den Lernberater Monny. Der genaue Aufbau von *Green Line New 3* wird unter 2.1 dargestellt.

Angebote in *Green Line New 3*	Autonomisierung durch	Zusatzmaterialien zu *Green Line New 3*
– Lernberater Monny, der die Lernenden weiterhin beim Lernen begleitet und sie berät – Ein schülergerechtes, transparentes Inhaltsverzeichnis mit verständlichen Symbolen – Vier *Workshops* mit kontext- und bereichsspezifischen Lerntechniken und Lernstrategien – Fünf themenbezogene *Units* mit vielfältigem, motivierendem Text- und Übungsangebot – Ein umfangreiches Hörtextangebot mit unterschiedlichen Ideolekten, Dialekten und Registern – Eine *Extra Line* mit Textangeboten zum fächerübergreifenden Lernen und zur Projektarbeit – Ein den unterschiedlichen Lernertypen gerecht werdender Vokabel- und Grammatikanhang. – Gelbe Vokabellerntippboxen vor jeder *Unit* – Graue Vokabelboxen vor jeder *Unit* zum Neulernen (beim Wechsel von *Orange Line New* zu *Green Line New*) bzw. zur Revision (für bisherige *Green-Line-New*-Nutzer). – Eine alphabetische Wortschatzliste, die den gesamten Wortschatz der ersten drei Lernjahre Englisch umfasst und die jeweilige Fundstelle angibt.	*Explizites und implizites Training von Lernstrategien, Lerntechniken und Kommunikationsstrategien anhand unterschiedlichster Kontexte und Themen sowie durch differenzierte Herangehensweisen und unterschiedliche Abstraktionsniveaus*	– **Workbook** (mit weiteren HV-Übungen) – Didaktisch-methodische Hinweise für die Lehrenden im **Begleitbuch für den Unterricht** – **Materialien zur Freiarbeit** mit zunehmend höherem Anteil an authentischen Texten – **Kontrollaufgaben** für die Hand der Lehrenden – **Begleitkassetten** und **CDs zum Schülerbuch** und **zum Hörverstehen** – **Skriptheft** zu Hörtexten – **Bildfolien:** Transfer – **Klett Online News:** Angebot ständig aktualisierter Texte im Internet

Wichtigstes Ziel des Buches ist, wie auch bei *Green Line New 2*, ein Angebot zu machen, das es erlaubt, Schülerinnen und Schüler sowohl unterschiedlicher Lernstile und -profile einerseits als auch diverser kultureller und sozialer Hintergründe andererseits gleichermaßen im Fremdsprachenlernen zu fördern, zu unterstützen und dafür auch besonders zu motivieren.

1.2 Entwicklungspsychologische Grundlagen

Gerade im Hinblick auf die Motivation muss jedoch die Übergangsphase vom „‚nicht mehr Kind' und ‚noch nicht Erwachsener'" (Oerter & Dreher 1995, S. 310) besonders betrachtet werden. Dieser Phase wird hier insbesondere deshalb ein kurzer Abschnitt gewidmet, weil der Englischunterricht in jeder Hinsicht von der Veränderungsdynamik dieser entwicklungsbedingten Zwischenposition der Schülerinnen und Schüler betroffen ist. Diese Phase hat direkte und indirekte Auswirkungen, die sich zum Beispiel an einem oft zu Beginn oder Mitte der siebten Klasse einsetzenden Motivations- und Lustverlust am Englischlernen ablesen lässt. Dieser Motivationsverlust lässt sich in der Tat auch empirisch nachweisen (vgl. Finkbeiner 1995).

Dieser Motivationsverlust kann darauf zurückgeführt werden, dass sich ein Großteil der Schülerinnen und Schüler beim Übergang der Klassenstufe 6 in die Klassenstufe 7 in einer Phase innerhalb ihres Lebenszyklus befindet, die starke biologische, soziale und intellektuelle Veränderungen mit sich bringt. Die Entwicklungsphase der Transeszenz, das heißt das

Jugendalter vom Übergang der Kindheit (11./12. Lebensjahr) in die frühe Adoleszenz (14. Lebensjahr), fordert von den Schülerinnen und Schülern stark veränderte Verhaltensformen: diese sind einerseits mit einer Aufgabe von Privilegien der Kindheit verbunden, andererseits führen sie zur Entwicklung von Merkmalen und Kompetenzen, die sie auf die zukünftige Rolle als junge Erwachsene vorbereiten. Körperlich ist dieser gesellschafts- und kulturinvariante Prozess durch die eintretende Geschlechtsreifung und den Wachstumsschub gekennzeichnet; dieser kann bei den Mädchen bis zu zwei Jahre früher einsetzen. Darüber hinaus ist jedoch diese Lebensspanne durch wesentliche Veränderungen in der Sozialisation gekennzeichnet. Der Jugendliche konstituiert sich zunehmend selbst und eigenverantwortlich in Relation zu seiner Umwelt und seinem direkten Lebenskontext (Freunde, *peer group*, Familie und Schule). Er übernimmt mehr und mehr Verantwortung, insbesondere für seinen eigenen Entwicklungsverlauf, für den Stellenwert verschiedener Aktivitäten und für seinen eigenen Lernprozess. In der oft konflikthaften Auseinandersetzung mit seiner unmittelbaren Umwelt und innerhalb seines direkten Lebenskontextes bewegt sich der Jugendliche meist auf einem Kontinuum zwischen *adjustment* und *turmoil*. Dieses entwicklungsbedingte, veränderte Sozialisationsverhalten kann von ebenfalls entwicklungsbedingten, veränderten Lernvoraussetzungen begleitet sein.

1.3 Lernpsychologische Grundlagen und Schlussfolgerungen für Zielsetzungen in *Green Line New 3*

Diese veränderten Lernvoraussetzungen lassen sich dadurch charakterisieren, dass zumindest ein Teil der Jugendlichen nicht länger allein zu konkret-operationalen sondern auch mehr und mehr zu formal-operationalen Denkprozessen in der Lage ist. Dieser Übergang zum formal-operationalen Denken kann nicht bei allen Schülerinnen und Schülern gleichermaßen vorausgesetzt werden, das heißt, im Unterricht werden immer auch anschauliche Beispiele, zum Beispiel zur Bedeutungserhellung herangezogen werden müssen. Über diese anschaulichen Beispiele hinaus müssen nun aber insbesondere im gymnasialen Bereich vermehrt auch solche Themen- und Aufgabenstellungen angeboten werden, die es den Schülerinnen und Schülern erlauben, operationale Prozesse der Hypothesenbildung, der Kombination von Fakten, des logischen und des transitiven Denkens durchführen zu können.

Da eine veränderte Lernvoraussetzung jedoch nicht automatisch zu einem veränderten Lernverhalten führt, und Lernende heute weniger als Produkt als vielmehr als Produzent der oben beschriebenen Entwicklung gesehen werden, ergibt sich für die Schule und somit auch für den Fremdsprachenunterricht eine veränderte Aufgabenstellung. Aus lernpsychologischer Sicht lässt sich diese Aufgabenstellung aus den Theorien zum „Autonomen Lerner" und zur „Autonomen Lernerin" ableiten: sie haben das stete und immanente Ziel, Schüler und Schülerinnen zur Selbständigkeit im Lernen zu führen, um dadurch ein lebenslanges Lernen zu ermöglichen. In *Green Line New 3* wird diese Aufgabenstellung durch ein entsprechendes Übungsarrangement, durch ein kontextbezogenes Lernstrategien- und Lerntechnikangebot in den *Workshops*, im Vokabular und in der Grammatik sowie durch das lehrwerksbegleitende Material zielstrebig umgesetzt. Sie lässt sich wie folgt beschreiben:

- Simultane gezielte Förderung und Ausbildung der fremdsprachenspezifischen <u>und</u> kognitiven sowie affektiven und sozialen Handlungsfähigkeit der Schülerinnen und Schüler.
- Aufbau einer Handlungskompetenz, welche langfristig konstruktive Formen der Selbstregulation im Lernprozess ermöglicht.
- Förderung der unterschiedlichen Lerntypen durch ein Übungsangebot auf den unterschiedlichen Ebenen menschlichen Handelns, um Schülerinnen und Schüler sowohl auf der rein praktischen als auch der abstrakten Handlungsebene herauszufordern. Dabei kommt es nun jedoch beim Übergang von der Orientierungsstufe in die Klassenstufe 7 zu einer für den gymnasialen Bereich notwendigen, stärkeren Betonung des kognitiven Lernens.
- Anknüpfung an Vorwissen der Schülerinnen und Schüler durch Beibehaltung von Bekanntem und Vertrautem, z.B. Monny als Lernberater, Charaktere der Lehrwerkspersonen, *vocabulary boxes*, Spielwiesen, „Waschzettel", grammatischer Anhang, alphabetische Wortschatzliste u.s.w.
- Ausgehend vom Vorwissen der Schüler ein stark erweitertes, neues Angebot an Situationen, die den aktiven und bewussten Umgang mit Lernstrategien und Lerntechniken fordern und fördern und somit auch zur Ausbildung einer metakognitiven Fähigkeit für die Schülerinnen und Schüler beitragen können (vgl. *Workshops*).
- Ein motivierendes Zusatzangebot an narrativen und authentischen Texten, um dem eingangs beschriebenen Motivationsverlust entgegenzuwirken und Schülerinnen und Schüler positive, gemeinsame Leseerlebnisse zu ermöglichen, z.B. durch das gemeinsame Planen, Erproben, Aufführen und Evaluieren eines Theaterstücks (vgl. ***Green Line New 3***, S. 88ff.).
- Ein Themenangebot, das sich an dem gegenwärtigen Lebenskontext und an den Interessen der Schülerinnen und Schüler orientiert, z.B. an lebensweltlich relevanten Themen wie *computer, video conference, e-mail* (vgl. ***Green Line New 3***, S. 32ff.) oder auch an Identitätsprobleme von sich in der Migration befindenden und im Exil lebenden Jugendlichen (vgl. ***Green Line New 3***, S. 60).
- Da sich dieser Lebenskontext immer schneller, häufiger und kurzfristiger ändert, wird zusätzlich zu den Printmedien ein ständig aktualisiertes Zusatzangebot auf den Klett-Webseiten im Internet angeboten.

2 Zum Schülerbuch *Green Line New 3*

2.1 Zum Buchaufbau von *Green Line New 3*

In *Green Line New 3* gibt es fünf *Units* und vier *Workshops* mit jeweils unterschiedlichen Themen. (Siehe Seite 3.) Die *Units* sind wie in den ersten Bänden aufgebaut: sie vermitteln ganz konkrete, auf die Themenkomplexe abgestimmte, Kommunikationsstrategien. Die *Workshops* wurden dazu konzipiert, bestimmte Arbeitstechniken und Lernstrategien auf konkrete Fertigkeiten zu beziehen und anzuwenden. Auf Seite 88 beginnt die *Extra Line* mit weiteren interessanten Geschichten, einem Theaterstück und ab Seite 97 mit Übersetzungsübungen. Auf Seite 100 beginnt dann der Anhang für die Grammatik, das Vokabular und die alphabetische Wortschatzliste.

2.2 Von *Green Line New 2* zu *Green Line New 3*

Auf der Grundlage der Erfahrungen mit mehreren traditionsreichen Lehrwerksgenerationen von Klett sowie aufgrund der völlig veränderten gesamtgesellschaftlichen und schulischen Anforderungssituationen, werden mit den Bänden von ***Green Line New*** neue unterrichtliche Wege beschritten und alternative Prinzipien berücksichtigt. Wichtigste handlungsleitende Kriterien bei der Weiterentwicklung der Neukonzeption sind dabei die oben beschriebenen autonomen Lerner auf der lernpsychologischen Seite, und die sprachliche, landeskundliche und soziokulturelle, d.h. multikulturelle Authentizität des jeweiligen Handlungsschauplatzes und der Charaktere auf der sprachdidaktischen Seite. Unter Beibehaltung der in ***Green Line New 2*** aufgezeigten Grundprinzipien kommt es, auch wegen der kognitiven, affektiven und psychosozialen Veränderungen der Jugendlichen in der Klassenstufe 7, zu einer weiteren Differenzierung bzw. einem Neuangebot in den bereits im **Begleitbuch** für ***Green Line New 2*** aufgelisteten folgenden Bereichen:

- Lern- und Arbeitstechniken/Lernstrategien
  - Kontextbezogene und bereichsspezifische Arbeitstechniken innerhalb der verschiedenen Fertigkeiten in den *Workshops*.
  - Kontextbezogene und bereichsspezifische Kommunikationsstrategien innerhalb bestimmter thematischer Schwerpunkte in den *Units*.
- Textauswertung: bei der Textarbeit treten nun auch mehr elementare Formen des *creative writing*, z.B. als Versprachlichung von Erzählhandlungen und dem Entwurf von Dialogrollen in den Vordergrund.

Units/Steps Topics	Nr.	S.	Arbeitstechniken und Lernstrategien	Kommunikationsstrategien
Workshop Let's talk	A	7	• Telefongespräche beginnen, Anrufe entgegennehmen. • Vortrag anhand von Notizen vorbereiten und durchführen. • Sprechtechniken	• Kontakt aufnehmen • korrekte Ausdrucksformen und Höflichkeitsfloskeln lernen • Übernachtung in einer Jugendherberge buchen/absagen • Urlaubserlebnisse berichten
Unit A trip to London	1	14	• Wortabstammungen erkennen	• über Sehenswürdigkeiten sprechen • über fremde Kulturen und Bräuche berichten • Wegbeschreibungen machen, Anweisungen für öffentliche Verkehrsmittel geben • über Begabung und Interessen sprechen • seinen Geschmack äußern • den Verlauf einer Geschichte fortsetzen und diese als Dialog erzählen
Workshop Working with words	B	26	• Erschließungstechniken für neuen Wortschatz • Wörter ordnen, Wortfelder erstellen • Begriffe umschreiben; neue Lexik aus Hörtext erschließen • Wortbildung mit Hilfe von Suffixen	• Dinge auf verschiedene Art und Weise ausdrücken
Unit Trouble at school	2	32	• intelligent guessing	• über das britische Schulsystem, über Zeugnis sprechen • über Fotos sprechen • Schulprobleme diskutieren • eine Verabredung mit jmd. treffen, absagen • Hilfe anbieten; jmd. ermahnen • Vermutungen begründen
Unit Welcome to Wales	3	44	• Informationen ordnen • Wortfamilien bilden	• eine Region beschreiben • über die Vergangenheit erzählen • Ratschläge geben • sich vergewissern • Gefühle beschreiben
Workshop Let's read	C	56	• Texte thematisch und nach Textart einordnen; Erwartungen an den Text formulieren • extensives, intensives und selektives Lesen • Reaktionen auf einen Text analysieren • Analogien zwischen Lateinisch, Englisch, Deutsch erkennen	• einen Text lesen und darauf reagieren lernen
Unit The environment	4	62		• Wegbeschreibungen mit einer Karte machen • über Umweltprobleme diskutieren • über Umweltveränderungen sprechen • Argumente abwägen • über die Zukunft nachdenken
Workshop Let's write	D	74	• den Aufbau einer Rezension erarbeiten; einen Text gliedern • Ideen strukturieren; Adjektive für stilistische Verbesserung eines Textes sammeln • eine Checkliste für Fehler erstellen	• Ideen sammeln und in schriftlichen Text umsetzen lernen
Unit Great Britain and the sea	5	78	• Stimmungen aus Texten und Bildern entnehmen • über irreale Situationen mutmaßen	• über irreale Situationen mutmaßen • Ratschläge geben • Tipps für ein Flugblatt zusammenstellen • über den Verlauf einer Geschichte anhand von Vorinformationen spekulieren • eine Geschichte als *report* wiedergeben

- Vermittlung landeskundlichen Wissens und interkulturelles Lernen
  - *Units*: Landeskundliches Wissen wird durch Texte, über Bilder, Graphiken und durch begleitendes Medienmaterial vermittelt. Da die Bildungspläne den landeskundlichen Schauplatz über die Klassen 5 und 6 hinaus auch in Klasse 7 in Großbritannien ansiedeln, wird die Figurenkonstellation und der geographische Schauplatz in den *Units* zum Teil beibehalten. Dies soll den Schülerinnen und Schülern eine Identifikationsmöglichkeit mit bereits Vertrautem ermöglichen, um auf dieser Basis zu einer Erweiterung ihres Wissen in folgenden Bereichen zu ermöglichen: Geographie und Bevölkerung Londons, England, Wales, Schottland, *Great Britain and the sea*, Verkehr und Umwelt, Schule, Geschichte (Spuren aus römischer Zeit etc.).
  - *Workshops*: Innerhalb der *Workshops* wurde jedoch auf eine Thematisierung unter Bezugnahme auf die Lehrwerkspersonen verzichtet. Dies ist insofern günstig, als die Schülerinnen und Schüler mit dem völlig veränderten Schwerpunkt „USA" in der Klassenstufe 8 völlig neuen Schauplätzen und Charakteren begegnet werden und somit eine gewisse Kontinuität bis zur Klassenstufe 7 angezeigt ist.
  - Übungen zum interkulturellen Lernen: Da der Inhalt des gesamten **Green Line New** 3 den Themeninhalt *Great Britain* fokussiert, wurde aus Gründen der zu hohen Redundanz auf die Seiten *Looking at the UK* verzichtet. Deren Funktion wird voll und ganz durch ständiges *Unit* begleitendes Bild- und Textmaterial abgedeckt. Der interkulturellen Perspektive kommt auch in Band 3 eine herausragende Rolle zu. Während die Schülerinnen und Schüler in den Bänden 1 und 2 vor allem ihre eigene Situation reflektierten, Analogien zwischen Heimatstadt und Zielstadt suchten, Perspektiven der Charaktere übernahmen und Vergleiche zwischen ähnlichen institutionellen Einrichtungen zogen, werden sie nun auf einer abstrakteren und detaillierten Ebene für interkulturell relevante Unterschiede hingeführt:
  Beispiel 1: Unterschiedliche Kommunikationsabsichten innerhalb des Englischen zum Ausdruck bringen: *Use different words for different people* (vgl. **GLN 3**, S. 8)
  Beispiel 2: unterschiedliche Differenzierungen im deutschen und englischen Sprachsystem, um gleiche Sachverhalte auszudrücken: *Saying things in different words* (vgl. **GLN 3**, S. 29)
  Beispiel 3: Übungen zur Perspektivenübernahme aus verschiedenen Blickpunkten und durch Übernahme verschiedener, auch konträrer Rollen (vgl. **GLN 3**, S. 60ff)

2.3 Lern- und Arbeitstechniken in den verschiedenen sprachlichen Fertigkeiten

Aufgrund von Untersuchungen zum guten und erfolgreichen Lernen nimmt man heute an, dass eigentätiges, selbstreflexives, selbstmotiviertes und interessegeleitetes Handeln zu einer tieferen Art der Verarbeitung und zu einer höheren Behaltensrate führt. Deshalb ist es ein Ziel des Englischunterrichts in der Klassenstufe 7, dem oben beschriebenen Motivations- und Interessenverlust am Fremdsprachenlernen entschieden entgegen zu steuern: In **Green Line New 3** sind zahlreiche Übungen zu finden, die die Schülerinnen und Schüler selbsttätig fordern und Eigenbezüge *(Your turn)* zulassen.

Wortschatzarbeit

Wie in **Green Line New 1** und **2** auch werden im **Vocabulary** (S. 118ff.) weiterhin systematisch Lerntipps vermittelt. Diese Tipps stehen in den gelben Kästchen vor den *Units*, die Spielwiesen *Let's play with words* stehen vor den *Workshops*. Außerdem fassen *Vocabulary boxes* Wörter und Wendungen zusammen, die in inhaltlichem oder kontextuellem Zusammenhang miteinander stehen (Wortfelder und Wortfamilien): sie dienen den Lernenden dazu, Wortschatz strukturiert, assoziativ und in Gruppen lernen und wiederholen und dadurch langfristig die Behaltensleistung verbessern zu können.

Einführung in die Arbeit mit der Tilde (~): Zu den in **Green Line New 1** und **2** üblichen Konventionen und Verfahren der Vokabelsemantisierung und -erklärung wird in **Green Line New 3** die Tilde (~) neu eingeführt. Die Tilde ersetzt in der Mittelspalte das neue englische Wort, das in der linken Spalte abgedruckt ist. Dadurch ergibt sich für die Lernenden eine zusätzliche Möglichkeit des Selbstlernens, bzw. Selbstabfragens: Dazu müssen sie mit einem Streifen die linke Wortschatzspalte zudecken und dann aus dem Kontext heraus das in der Tilde indizierte Wort herausfinden. Sie können jedoch auch die rechte Spalte mit einem Streifen abdecken, haben dann das Lösungswort vorgegeben und versuchen nun aus dem Kontext heraus, die deutsche Bedeutung dieses Wortes zu erschließen. Die Arbeit mit der Tilde stellt eine höhere kognitive Anforderung an die Schüler dar. Diese erhöhte kognitive Leistung sollte in ihrer Schwierigkeit, insbesondere zu Beginn der Klasse 7, nicht unterschätzt werden. Deshalb sollte das „Lesen" der Tilde im Englischunterricht geübt, ihre Funktion besprochen und an konkreten Beispielen erläutert werden. Beispielen, bei denen an die Tilde keine Flexionen angehängt sind, sind dabei von den Schülern leichter zu meistern: hier muss nur das Wort „eingelesen" werden. Schwieriger wird es jedoch, wenn die Tilde mit einer Flexion versehen ist. Hier wird also eine grammatikalische Struktur mitgeliefert und die Struktur ist beim Einsetzen des Wortes zu übernehmen. Den Schülerinnen und Schülern sollte klar gemacht werden, dass in dem „Mitliefern" der Flexionen kein Nachteil, sondern im Gegenteil ein Vorteil zu sehen ist. Dieser Vorteil kann jedoch von den Lernenden nur genutzt werden, wenn die Arbeit mit der Tilde entsprechend vorbereitet und im Unterricht thematisiert worden ist.

Alphabetical word list:
In der *Alphabetical word list* (S. 156ff.) ist das Vokabular von **Green Line New** 1 bis 3 enthalten. Die Zahlen hinter den Wörtern verweisen auf das erstmalige Vorkommen der Wörter. Dies kann wiederum als Tipp an die Schülerinnen, Schüler und Eltern für das häusliche Lernen weitergegeben werden: Wörter, hinter denen eine I und II steht, werden für die Klasse 7 vorausgesetzt, sie wurden in **Green Line New** 1 und 2 eingeführt und behandelt. Wörter mit einer III werden im Laufe des 7. Schuljahres behandelt und eingeführt.

2.4 Zusatzangebote zum Übergang von *Orange Line New* 1 und 2 zu *Green Line New* 3

Graue Vokabelboxen: Als Zusatzangebot sind in **Green Line New** 3 die grauen Vokabelboxen zu sehen: sie sind für Lernende aus den Bundesländern vorgesehen, die in Klassenstufe 5 und 6 die Orientierungsstufe besucht und mit *Orange Line New* gearbeitet haben. Diese grauen Boxen gehen den *Units* und *Workshops* voran und enthalten genau den Wortschatz, den die Lernenden, die bislang mit *Orange Line New* gearbeitet haben, noch nicht kennen. Dieser Wortschatz sollte vor Beginn der *Unit* gelernt werden. Die Lerner, die bereits in Klassenstufe 5 und 6 mit **Green Line New** gearbeitet haben, können diese Boxen zur Revision nutzen.

Grammar revision: Zusätzlich zum Grammatikanhang gibt es in **Green Line New** 3 zwei Seiten *Grammar Revision*. Diese Seiten befinden sich direkt vor dem Grammatikanhang (S. 100-101) und sind insbesondere für Lernende gedacht, die bislang mit *Orange Line New* gearbeitet haben. Es wird davon ausgegangen, dass diese Seiten gleich zum Schuljahresbeginn gemeinsam mit den Lernenden erarbeitet werden. Übungen befinden sich auf **Schülerbuch**-Seite 114 und in diesem **Begleitbuch** auf S. 57.

Zur Entwicklung von Handlungsfähigkeit durch Sprache wird auf die diesbezüglichen Ausführungen im **Begleitbuch für den Unterricht** Band 2 verwiesen.

Literatur

Finkbeiner, Claudia. (1995). *Englischunterricht in europäischer Dimension. Zwischen Qualifikationserwartungen der Gesellschaft und Schülereinstellungen und Schülerinteressen. Berichte und Kontexte zweier empirischer Untersuchungen.* Bochum: Brockmeyer.

Oerter, Rolf &, Dreher, Eva. (Hrsg.). (1995). Jugendalter. In: Montad, Leo. *Entwicklungspsychologie.* 3., vollständig überarbeitete Auflage. Weinheim: Beltz Psychologie Verlags Union, S. 310-395.

B Zu den Workshops und Units

Schülerbuch Seite 7

Workshop A Let's talk

Allgemeiner Hinweis zu Workshop A
Die vier Workshops des SB wenden sich, grob gesprochen, den *four basic skills* zu, nämlich den Fertigkeiten des Hörens, Sprechens, Lesens und Schreibens. Während diese Grundfertigkeiten allgemein als methodisches Prinzip beim Erlernen (Akquisition) neuer Pensen beim Sprachenlernen verstanden werden, die auch in der chronologischen Abfolge beachtet werden müssen, so wollen die *Workshops* in diesem Band im jeweiligen Bereich besondere Fertigkeiten sichern, schulen und weiterentwickeln. In zunehmenden Maße werden Arbeitstechniken geübt und bewusst gemacht, die dann als Grundlagen für alle weitere Tätigkeiten im sprachlichen Bereich dienen.
Workshop A hat den Aspekt ‚Sprechen' zum Thema und setzt einen deutlich handlungsorientierten Akzent: Interkulturelle Kommunikation (Sprechen über fremde Länder und Sprachen) in *Part 1*, Versprachlichung zwischenmenschlicher Kontakte in Höflichkeitsfloskeln in *Part 2*, der Umgang mit dem Medium Telefon in *Part 3*, Bericht über Ferienerlebnisse in *Part 4* stehen im Mittelpunkt.
Der Gebrauch des Telefons ist in einer Fremdsprache erfahrungsgemäß besonders schwierig wegen der Reduzierung der Kommunikation auf rein akustische Verständigung, die häufig noch durch zusätzliche Geräuschquellen gestört wird. Idiomatische Ausdrucksweisen bei der Telefonsprache müssen als Lexeme eingeübt werden. Eine für Schüler lebensnahe Situation zu Beginn des neuen Schuljahres – der Austausch von Urlaubserlebnissen in unterrichtsgebundener Form – legt das Einüben des Referathaltens nahe. Gerade letztere Fertigkeit wirft einen Gewinn für alle anderen Schulfächer ab, in denen auf dieser Klassenstufe Referate gehalten werden können. Eine Abstimmung mit anderen Kollegen, die in der Klasse unterrichten, ist sehr zu empfehlen.
Die Sprachübungen der *Practice page* (S. 13) sind fakultativ und können während der Erarbeitung des *Workshop*-Materials nach Bedarf punktuell eingesetzt werden.

1 New friends

Ziel: Kontakt aufnehmen; über fremde Länder und Sprachen reden.

Neu: *workshop, crossing, phew!, alive, to meet, international; Rotterdam, Hull*

Unterrichtsempfehlungen
Semantisierung: *workshop:* Da die Denotation des Wortes im Sinne der ‚Werkstatt' eines Handwerkers weder der Bedeutung der *Unit* noch dem im Deutschen längst gebräuchlichen Anglizismus entspricht, sollte den S in mehreren Sätzen auf deutsch erklärt werden, worin der Sinn der *Workshops* und des Wortes selbst liegt, im Kern etwa so: „Ihr lernt hier, euch in besonderen Gesprächssituationen mit anderen Leuten auf englisch zu sprechen, besonders, wenn ihr nach GB reist. Und wir üben das, wir machen es. Und wir schauen, wie wir es gemacht haben und halten diese Methoden und Techniken fest."
Es wird den S – mit Ausnahme des *Part 4*, der wieder eine *classroom situation* vorstellt, ein Kommunikationsszenario vorgestellt, das sie selber authentisch auf einer Reise in das Land der Zielsprache erleben können. *crossing:* When you take the ferry from France to Great Britain, you must cross (gestisch verdeutlichen) the sea. The crossing (gestisch verdeutlichen) can be an adventure. *phew!* als Ausruf der Überraschung und Erleichterung wird im Kontext verstanden; *alive:* not dead; *to meet:* to see s.o. for the first time and get to know them. *Rotterdam:* (die Aussprache kontrollieren!) da *port* noch unbekannt ist, auf deutsch erklären: Hafenstadt im Norden der Niederlande; *Hull:* auf deutsch: Hafenstadt im Nordosten Englands – evtl. den S die Position auf der Landkarte vorne im SB erläutern: *It lies between ... and ..., next to....*
Szenisches Spiel mit verteilten Rollen ist sehr zu empfehlen. Auch eine Bildbeschreibung ist sinnvoll. Vorschlag: L kann die unbekannten Vokabeln problemlos einbringen: *Sarah is tripping over Ellen's bag. Sarah is falling against Florian and pushing him* (neu, erst in III, 2 eingeführt, erklären durch Vormachen). *Ellen is watching the accident. They are all very surprised. In the background* (*back* und *back door* sind bekannt) *you can see a boat* (Fähren sind *boats* und nicht *ships*) *through one of the windows.* Zu beachten ist der interkulturelle Akzent der Szene, in der Englisch als lingua franca von einem Deutschen und einer „Holländerin" (= dt. Umgangssprache, korrekt: „Niederländerin") benutzt wird.
Es lohnt ferner, folgende Wendungen ganz zum Schluss übersetzen zu lassen, um die idiomatische Differenz zwischen beiden Sprachen zu verdeutlichen: D: Mensch, paß doch auf! – E: *Hey, mind where you're going.;* E: *I left it in a silly place.* – D: Ich hab sie blöderweise mitten im Weg stehen lassen.; E: *Hey, what a way to meet ...* – Mensch, ist das 'ne lustige Art sich kennenzulernen ...

Bildfolie 1

1 Collect ideas for your own dialogue

Ziel: Festigung der Redemittel und Transferübungen zur Szene 1, *New friends*.

Neu: *typical, to revise, tense, to imagine*

Unterrichtsempfehlungen
Semantisierung: *typical:* an die Tafel schreiben und S das dt. Wort nach dem Hinweis: *The German word is almost the same.* nennen lassen. Nur bei Bedarf/auf Anfrage den Unterschied der kollokativen Verwendung erklären: typisch für = *typical of.* Die Wiederholungsübung 1 auf S. 13, auf die Monny verweist, nur dazwischenschalten, falls S Fehler bei den Verbformen machen. *To revise* lässt sich mit *to practise again* erklären. L: *German „Zeit" can be two words in English: the simple present is a* tense*, the simple past is a tense,too. We use the word tense, when we talk about grammar. In other cases we use the word time.* to imagine: *to make a situation, person or thing in your mind.* c) Man kann die S ähnliche Situationen (vgl. Bildfolie 2) entwerfen lassen wie in der Szene *New friends* und die allgemeine Arbeitsaufforderung spezifizieren, z. B. *On a German train; at a Spanish beach; in an Italian restaurant* etc; .
Lösungen: a) *Do you speak English, too? – er – a bit; Where are you from? – I'm ..../– I come from ...; My name is ... – And you?*

Revision: S. 13 Part 5, Practice page, ex. 1, Ferry dialogues

Bildfolie 2

2 Talk about countries and languages

Ziel: Ländernamen, Sachenbezeichnungen, Nationalitätenadjektive richtig verwenden und aussprechen können.

Neu: *language, lots of, tip, perfect*

Unterrichtsempfehlungen
Semantisierung: *language: German and English are languages; lots of: = a lot of; tip:* in dieser Bedeutung ist das Wort ein *cognate* und wird von S sofort verstanden: *Monny gives you a lot of tips, they help you to speak and write good English; perfect:* Der Satz *Nobody is perfect.* ist den S bekannt, außerdem ist das Wort ein unmissverständliches *cognate.*

Für diese Übung kann man gekaufte oder selbstgefertigte Nationalitäten-Kennzeichen verwenden. Man kann auch S vor Durchnahme der gesamten SB-Seite 7 den Auftrag geben, Schilder entsprechend denen in *ex. 2* anzufertigen. Einige S halten die Zeichen, andere S versprachlichen. L kann steuern: *Where's he/she from? What language does he/she speak?* S übernehmen das Fragen. Diese „Inszenierung" entspricht den Teilübungen a) und b), die man natürlich dem SB folgend durchnehmen kann, auch bevor man sie „in Szene" setzt. Wichtig ist der Hinweis für die S (auf deutsch), dass das Nationalitätsadjektiv in der Regel gleich der im betreffenden Land gesprochenen Sprache ist. In dieser Übung gibt es als Ausnahme: *Switzerland – Swiss*, da die Schweiz bekanntlich viersprachig ist. Manch S überrascht auch der Wortwurzelwechsel in *Netherlands – Dutch*, da ja meist dieselbe Wortwurzel für Land und Nationalitätenadjektiv verwendet wird. Auch die Kombinationen *Britain – British* (nur Nationalitätenadjektiv) – *English* (Sprache), *England – English* (Nationalitätenadjektiv und Sprache) sollte man bewusst machen und mit kurzen Stimuli üben. Warnung ist geboten vor dem Umgang mit dem Nationalitätenadjektiv, wenn S vom Deutschen her denken: Zu verdeutlichen ist also: *He/she is English.* ist nicht „Englisch", sondern „Engländer/Engländerin".usw. Die angegebenen Nationalitätskennzeichen sind nicht identisch mit den in der *box* vorgestellten Ländern und Sprachen. Es fehlen – aus Platzgründen – die Kennzeichen GR (= *Greece*) und CH (= lat. Confoederatio Helvetica) mit *Swiss* als Nationalitätenadjektiv; zu E (von Espana) gehören: *Spain – Spanish*, zu F: *France – French*. Die S könnten noch nennen: A = *Austria*, CDN = *Canada*, B = *Belgium*, AND = *Andorra*, YU = *Yugoslavia*, HUN = *Hungary*, CZ = *Czech Republic*. Es ist nicht nötig, die S hier, das System ergänzend, etwas aufschreiben zu lassen. Verwiesen sei auf die komplette Übersicht in der *box* zu Beginn des *Part 1: New friends* im Vokabelanhang, S. 120, die am besten mit den S durch lautes Lesen erarbeitet werden sollte. L kann insbesondere die „Problemfälle" in den 3 Kolumnen üben. Um solche Fälle handelt es sich, wenn Sprache und/oder Nationalitätenadjektiv vom Ländernamen relevant abweichen. L kann sie auch in den 3 Kolumnen je variierend auf einer Fotokopie tilgen, eine Folie anfertigen und zur Wiederholung/Auffrischung die Schüler die richtigen Länder- und/oder Sprachennamen und/oder Nationalitätenadjektive nennen und selber am Tageslichtprojektor eintragen lassen. Natürlich ist die Vorlage auch als Arbeitsblatt geeignet.

Die „Problemfälle" sind: *America ..., Australia ..., Austria ..., Belgium ..., Britain ..., India ..., Ireland ..., Scotland ..., Switzerland ...;* zusätzlich noch: *the Netherlands* (wegen *Dutch*).

Eine Tabelle, die vergrößert und dann als Folie gefertigt werden kann, könnte so aussehen:

country	language	national adj.
		American
Australia		
Austria		
		Belgian
		British
	a lot of different languages	
		Irish
Scotland		
	German, French, Italian, Romansh	
	Dutch	

Nationalitätenschilder besorgen, oder anfertigen (lassen)

Übersicht: Vocabulary S. 120

WB S.1, 1.1a) b)

Kopiervorlage: Arbeitsblatt oder Folie

WB S.1, 1.2

Schülerbuch Seite 8

2 The right words

Ziel: korrekte Ausdrucksweise und Höflichkeitsformen kennen lernen; Einführung von Sätzen mit *object complement*.

Neu: *deck, on deck, round, to go crazy, to call, to upset, object; Edinburgh*

Unterrichtsempfehlungen

Die Unterscheidung verschiedener Kommunikationsformen *(formal-informal/colloquial)* ist inzwischen auch im Deutschen ein erzieherisches, nicht mehr nur ein fremdsprachlich pragmatisches Ziel. Daher wäre es auch wichtig, evtl. als Vorbereitungsgespräch mit den S auf deutsch zu besprechen, wie Jung und Alt, bzw. Bekannte und Fremde sprachlich im Deutschen miteinander umgehen, welche Begrüßungsfloskeln sie wählen. In Anlehnung an das englische *hello* ist im deutschen Sprachgebrauch ein „Kompromiß-Hallo!" zu registrieren, das Jugendliche unterschiedslos in ihrer Altersgruppe und Erwachsenen gegenüber verwenden. Ein „guten Morgen/Tag/Abend!" ist immer seltener zu hören. Auch für *ex. 2* lohnt sich aus erzieherischen Gründen ein vorbereitendes Unterrichtsgespräch auf deutsch zu der Frage „Warum sollten Menschen miteinander höflich umgehen?" Dass man im Umgang mit Ausländern in deren Heimatland (das ist die Kommunikationssituation des *Workshop, Parts 1 & 2*) sich in besonderem Maße zu Höflichkeit verpflichtet fühlen sollte – aus reinem „Selbsterhaltungstrieb" und aus Respekt vor den „anderen" – sind Aspekte, die S dieses Alters noch nicht recht erfassen können. Der *tip* will dennoch auf diesen Sachverhalt behutsam aufmerksam machen.

Semantisierung: *deck: part of a ship; we use the same word in German. on deck: When you are on deck on a ship, you are in the open air. Edinburgh: a beautiful city in Scotland.* Aussprache sollte intensiv geübt werden. *round:* diese Präposition ist aus GLNI als „um...herum" bekannt. Die neue Bedeutung „rund, durch ganz" sollte auf deutsch erklärt werden. *to go crazy:* Da das Adjektiv *crazy* bekannt ist, wird der Satz *I could go crazy! My sister/brother never brings back my CDs.* verstanden. Evtl. sollte man den S auf deutsch erklären, dass *to go* + Adj. „werden" bedeutet bzw. einen Vorgang bezeichnet wie z. B. im bereits gelernten *to go wrong*. Nützlich wäre es, S. darauf hinzuweisen, dass *to go* Basis für viele idiomatische Wendungen ist; ein Blick auf den entsprechenden Eintrag in der *alphabetical word list*, S. 163, belegt das eindrucksvoll. Diese Kollokationen kann man insgesamt lernen lassen (als Hausaufgabe aufgeben); *to call s.b. s.th.:* Da den S die neue Bedeutung von *call* in Verbindung mit der neuen grammatischen Struktur *(object + complement)* erklärt werden muss, empfiehlt sich die Bewusstmachung durch gemeinsame Lektüre des Grammatikparagraphen § 1. Diese Struktur ist prinzipiell vom deutschen Sprachgebrauch nicht unterschieden, ist also eigentlich nur ein lexisches Problem.

Allerdings zeigt der Beispielsatz in der *box: Don't laugh at Dad's French. You'll make him angry.* gleichzeitig auch wieder die idiomatische Andersartigkeit der beiden Sprachen auf. *To make s.o. angry* lässt sich im Deutschen eben nicht in derselben Struktur ausdrücken – „Du wirst ihn verärgern. Du wirst bewirken, dass er sich ärgert."
Die dazu passende Übung 2 der *Practice Page*, S. 13, ist leicht, kann als Hausaufgabe zusätzlich gegeben werden, wenn nicht im Unterricht (ohne Zeitaufwand). *to upset s.b.: If you don't do your homework, you'll upset your teacher, you'll make him angry.* Kontrollieren, dass die S. den Akzent korrekt auf die 2. Silbe setzen [-'-]. *object:* Das deutsche „Objekt" ist für S zu abstrakt, wird in der neuen Bedeutung „Objekt, Gegenstand" nicht als *cognate* erkannt. Als *cognate* wird es eher irreführend erkannt, weil den S eher der grammatische Objektbegriff vertraut ist, also deutsche Bedeutung „Gegenstand"

GR §1

Revision: S. 13 Part 5, Practice page, ex. 2, All about Scotland

geben, wenn Sätze wie: *A pen is an object, a desk is an object, too. A boy or a girl, living things, aren't objects.* nicht verstanden werden sollten.
Nach Semantisierung des neuen Vokabulars Präsentation des Textes, Lesen mit verteilten Rollen und Spielen der Szene.

WB S.2, 2.1
WB S.2, 2.2

1 Use different words for different people

Ziel: höfliche Ausdrucksformen kennenlernen, einfache informelle und formelle Sprechsituationen unterscheiden und sprachlich angemessen reagieren lernen.

Neu: *see you tomorrow!, formal, situation, difference*

Unterrichtsempfehlungen
Semantisierung: *see you tomorrow!:* deutsch: „Bis morgen!", *formal:* die deutsche Bedeutung „formal, formell" ist für S dieser Altersstufe nichtssagend. Die deutsche Bedeutung des Wortes bedarf der weiteren ausführlichen deutschen Erklärung im Sinne von „höflich" vs. „weniger höflich, flapsig, unhöflich", auch mit Beispielen für deutschen Sprachgebrauch: z.B. „Guten Morgen / Tag / Abend" vs. „Hallo", „Auf Wiedersehen" vs. „Tschüs!", (neudeutsch) „Ciao!"; *situation:* als *cognate* leicht zu erklären: *We have the same word in German. difference: What's an important difference between a city and a village? – There are more people in a city.*
Die Termini *informal/colloquial* können hier sinnvollerweise eingeführt werden als Gegenbegriff zu *formal*. Die Aufgaben sind einfach: a) ist eine Verifikation von Textstellen, b) ist eine Differenzierung *formal/informal (colloquial)*.
Lösungen: *a) Hi, Sarah. – Good morning, Mr Dixon. He wants to be polite to Mr Dixon.* b) als Tafelanschrieb darstellen: (Raster mit Überschrift vorgeben, S die Sätze einschreiben lassen.)

WB S.3, 2.4a)

Tafelanschrieb

for friends/ colloquial	formal situations
1. Bye. See you tomorrow.	1. Goodbye. Have a nice evening.
2. What have you got to drink? Lemonade?	2. Excuse me. Can you bring me a glass of lemonade, please?
3. Hey, that's my bag!	3. I'm sorry, but I think that's my bag.

WB S.2, 2.3

2 Be polite

Ziel: unhöfliche Ausdrucksweisen in höfliche umwandeln, Herstellen von dialogischen Texten mit höflichen Ausdrucksmitteln.

Unterrichtsempfehlungen
a) Um die hier vorgestellten Kommunikationsmuster zu habitualisieren, sollten sie nach Möglichkeit in mehreren Phasen erarbeitet und „inszeniert" werden: 1. In Partnerarbeit werden die Sätze umgeformt und schriftlich notiert. 2. L – oder S in Kettenspiel – geben unhöflichen Impuls, S geben auf Basis der schriftlich notierten richtigen Fassungen die höfliche Korrektur. Zum Schluss Spielen von Miniszenen mit jeweils 2 S, die pantomimisch Szenen darstellen, wobei S1 und S2 jeweils gestisch/mimisch/sprachlich den höflichen Satz evozieren bzw. auf den höflichen Satz gestisch / mimisch oder sprachlich angemessen reagieren.

Möglichkeiten für Miniszenen	
Impuls	Reaktion
1. (Geste)/ Would you like some...?	No sugar in my tea, thank you.
2. Do you mind if I open the window?	Of course not.
3. I'd like a map of this town. Can I help you?	No problem. Here you are. I'd like a map of this town.
4. Can you pass me that pen over there?	Yes, of course. Which one do you mean? This one or that one?

5. Excuse me, where's the station, please?	Just go straight on, then turn right at the next crossing. The station is on the left.
6. Could I have a ticket to London, please?	Yes, of course./Here you are.

b) Auf der Basis der gründlichen Übung wie oben in a) ein machbarer, sinnvoller Transfer mit freien Inhalten.

WB S.3, 2.4b)
WB S.3, 2.5

Schülerbuch Seite 9

3 Check your geography

Ziel: über verschiedene Teile der Britischen Inseln reden können.

Unterrichtsempfehlungen
Die Übungen 3 und 4 sind landeskundlich-lexikalisch orientiert, werden dem kommunikativen Titel dieses Abschnitts aber insofern gerecht, als Kommunikation im Land/auf dem Weg ins Land der Zielsprache eine geographisch-politische Anfangsorientierung voraussetzt.
Die drei Karten stellen geographisch-politische Teile der Britischen Inseln vor. In zwei Schritten erfolgt die Progression vom Teil zum Ganzen. Als Orientierungshilfe bei der Analyse der Karten kann den S noch der Tipp gegeben werden: *Look at the red lines.*
Als mnemotechnische Hilfe für den sicheren Umgang mit den verschiedenen Ländernamen/Regionalbezeichnungen erweist sich das Prinzip der Rechenaufgabe, wie es in der *box* im Vokabelanhang S. 121 vorgeführt ist. Nach der Analyse der Karten kann die Beantwortung der Fragen dementsprechend als Tafelanschrieb notiert werden. Anschließend, mit Tafelbild und dann ohne Stütze, kann das Prinzip der „Rechenaufgabe" zur Festigung noch einmal durchgespielt werden, auch in Subtraktions-Varianten (auch durcheinander, auch mit den „Additionen" gemischt):
The British Isles – (minus) the UK = ? [Republic of Ireland]
The British Isles – (minus) the Republic of Ireland = ? [the UK]
The UK – (minus) Great Britain = ? [Northern Ireland]
The UK – (minus) Northern Ireland = ? [Great Britain]
Hinweise auf die politische Problematik Nordirlands nur bei Bedarf und dann nur auf deutsch. Die komplizierte politische Situation lässt sich in dieser Alters- und Lernstufe nur schwer erklären. Grundlegende landeskundliche Information ist Sinn. Evtl. noch der Hinweis auf die keltische Verwandtschaft von Schottland, Wales und Irland, als Vorgriff auf *Unit 3 B*, und auf die keltische Bezeichnung für Irland: *Eire* [ˈeərə]. Sinnvoll wäre auch noch die traditionelle Zuordnung der Teile Großbritanniens zu ihren Nationalblumen: *Scottish thistle, English rose, Welsh daffodil and leek, Irish shamrock* (eine Art Klee) oder ein Rätsel mit Bildfolie 3.
Lösungen: *1. 3 countries: Scotland, England, Wales 2. GB +Northern Ireland = UK 3. the Republic of Ireland*

WB S. 4, 2.6

Bildfolie 3

4 Listening practice: Find out about different parts of the UK

Ziel: über verschiedene Teile der Britischen Inseln sprechen können.

Neu: *accent, recording; Snowdon, Luton, Glenarm*

Text
1. *Megan (Welsh accent):*
I'm Megan. I live on a sheep farm in North Wales. It's lovely in the hills here. In good weather you can see Snowdon, the highest mountain in Wales. The only problem is – it often rains! I usually speak English with my friends. But at home we speak Welsh, too. A lot of families here speak two languages.

2. Asim (North London accent):
I'm Asim. What can I say about Luton? I don't love it here – it isn't the most exciting place in England – but it's OK. Luton is famous for its cars, of course. I don't know how many cars they make here – but it's a lot! And then there's the airport. Thousands of people use Luton Airport because it's near London – but they never stay in the town.

3. Ryan (Northern Irish accent):
My name is Ryan. Glenarm is where I live. If you aren't from here, you've probably never heard of it. It's just a little place near the sea. You get to it if you drive north from Belfast – but it's very different from Belfast. There you have the biggest city in Northern Ireland, but in Glenarm you just have the sea on one side of you, and green hills on the other side.

4. Kate (Edinburgh accent):
I'm Kate. I'm from Edinburgh. It's a beautiful city. Maybe you've seen pictures of the famous castle here. And there are a lot of interesting old streets and houses. In the summer Edinburgh is full of visitors from everywhere in the world. They come for the Edinburgh Festival, the music, the films and the drama – I think it's great!

Unterrichtsempfehlungen
Diese HV-Übung basiert auf den in *ex.* 3 vermittelten landeskundlichen Kenntnissen. Es kann sein, dass manche S noch mehr geographische Details kennenlernen wollen, oder eigene Kenntnisse einbringen wollen. Daher empfiehlt es sich, für die Stunde eine Landkarte der Britischen Inseln im Klassenzimmer aufzuhängen. Weniger aufwendig ist die Benutzung der Karte vorne im SB. Die S werden ein erstes Mal systematisch an unterschiedliche britische Varietäten des Englischen herangeführt. Die Übung ist progressiv in 3 Lernschritte unterteilt.
In Teil a) geht es nach einem ersten Hören um die Benennung der jeweiligen Landesidentität der 4 Jugendlichen und die entsprechende Zuordnung der Bildinformationen – entsprechend der HV-Fertigkeit *listening for gist*. In Teil b) wird die Sozialform des Arbeitens geändert – Partnerarbeit – und beim zweiten Hören entsprechend der HV-Fertigkeit *listening for detail* nach genaueren Inhalten gefragt. In Teil c) schließlich wird der inhaltliche Aspekt über die HV-Übung hinaus weiterverfolgt. Lohnend wäre es auch, zum Zwecke der Materialbeschaffung sich an The British Council, Hahnenstr., Köln, zu wenden. Allerdings müßten das L zeitig vor Durchnahme dieses *Part* tun, womit die Eigeninitiative der S bei der Materialbeschaffung unterbunden wäre. Material, das L vom British Council erhalten, sollte also prinzipiell nur ergänzend hinzugezogen werden. Pädagogisch unmotiviert wäre es sicherlich, die S selber an den British Council sehr zeitig im Vorgriff auf diesen Textteil schreiben und um Material bitten zu lassen.
Semantisierung: <u>accent:</u> dieser linguistische Begriff ist im Deutschen als ‚Akzent' weniger gebräuchlich als ‚Dialekt' oder ‚Aussprache'. ‚Akzent' ist im Deutschen dann das übliche Wort, wenn man sagen will, dass jemand eine Sprache mit dem Akzent einer anderen Sprache überlagert. Nach einem Beispielsatz wie: *People in Karlsruhe and Berlin have different accents.*, wobei L je nach gewähltem Stadtbeispiel evtl. den Dialekt nachmachen kann, sollte man auf deutsch die Problematik des Wortgebrauches ‚Akzent' wie oben geschildert kurz bewusst machen. Wichtig ist, die vom Deutschen unterschiedene Silbenbetonung richtig einzuüben: Ak-'zent vs. 'accent; <u>recording:</u> Da den S ein dt. Rekorder bekannt ist, kann das engl. Wort hierfür gleich mit eingeführt werden. Ein oder zwei Anwendungssätze schaffen sofort Klarheit: *You find recordings on your cassettes. You put the cassettes in a recorder, if you want to listen to them. On a CD you have recordings, too.* <u>Snowdon:</u> der höchste Berg in Wales; <u>Luton:</u> eine Stadt nördl. von London; <u>Glenarm:</u> Kleinstadt in Nordirland. Bei allen drei geographischen Namen ist auf die richtige Aussprache zu achten.

Lösungen:
a) Megan – Wales, picture D; Asim – England, picture B; Ryan – Northern Ireland, picture A; Kate – Scotland, picture C.
b) Edinburgh: is beautiful, famous castle, old streets and houses, in the summer a lot of visitors, Edinburgh Festival (music, films, drama). – Luton: not very exciting, but OK, famous for cars, airport near London. – Glenarm and Belfast: little place near the sea, north of Belfast (to drive north from ...) the biggest city in Northern Ireland, between the sea and green hills. – North Wales: sheep farm in North Wales, not far from Snowdon (highest mountain in Wales), lot of rain, people speak two languages: Welsh and English.

Schülerbuch Seite 10

3 On the telephone
Auslandsreisen sind heute für junge Menschen selbstverständlicher denn je. Im europäischen Ausland wird Englisch immer wichtiger als lingua franca. Gespräche, auch am Telefon, werden immer häufiger auf Englisch geführt. Das Telefon als wichtiges Kommunikationsmittel gerade für den Touristen im Ausland stellt für den Englischlerner häufig eine besondere Schwierigkeit dar: Das Fehlen von Mimik und Gestik des Gegenübers, formelhafte Redewendungen (die in den verschiedenen europäischen Sprachen z.T. unterschiedlich ausfallen und somit echte idiomatische Wendungen sind), Ablenkung durch den (im Ausland ungewohnten) Umgang mit dem technischen Medium sowie störende Hintergrundgeräusche oder technisch schlechte Verbindungen bauen psychologisch eine hohe Hürde auf, sich überhaupt des Telefons zu bedienen. Daher soll dieser Teil des *Workshop*, wenn er schon die Realsituation nicht komplett imitieren kann, zumindest pragma-linguistisch auf die Realsituation des Telefonierens auf englisch und in England vorbereiten. – Monnys Anregung in Frageform macht im übrigen deutlich, dass die Erschwernisse der telefonischen Kommunikation z.T. auch für das Telefonieren in gewohnter Umgebung in der Muttersprache gelten: *lack of body language, background noises, bad connection, technical problems* wäre die Antwort auf Monnys Frage. Es ist sinnvoll, über die Probleme des Telefonierens in einer fremden Sprache zu Hause und im Ausland auf deutsch zu sprechen, dabei einige wichtige englische Lexeme (s.o.) einzuführen und ins Vokabelheft aufnehmen zu lassen. Die Verwendung alter, ausgedienter Telefongeräte kann eine Annäherung an eine Realsituation bedeuten.

1 Practise telephone language

Ziel: Telefongespräche beginnen, Anrufe entgegennehmen können.

Neu: *face to face, message, machine, answering machine, tone, call, to make a call*

Unterrichtsempfehlungen
Die Übung verfolgt zwei Ziele: In Teil a) geht es um die Zuordnung von jeweils zwei zusammengehörigen Dialogteilen, die den Beginn eines Telefongesprächs ausmachen. Die 6 Teile, A-F, ergeben drei Kurzdialoge. Nach einer kurzen Stillarbeitsphase sollte man die S die 3 Kurzdialoge sprechen lassen: *You take part A, you part ..., please./Who wants to speak part ...? etc.* In Teil b) wird durch das aufgelistete Sammeln von Ausdrucksmitteln in den Dialogteilen A-F das Bewusstsein dafür geschärft, mit welchen sprachlichen Mitteln man ein Telefongespräch beginnt, mit welchen man darauf reagiert. Hier sollte ein Tafelanschrieb gefertigt werden, der über ein bloßes Abschreiben aus dem SB hinausgeht, indem (engl. Spiel- oder Phantasie-) Namen und Telefonnummern

Tafelanschrieb

von Schülern eingesetzt werden. S nennen die richtigen Antworten und schreiben sie selber in das Raster. Es sind auch – ohne Veränderung – die Redemittel aufgeführt, die in der nachfolgenden *Listening practice* enthalten sind. Semantisierung: <u>face to face:</u> *face* ist bekannt. L zeigt auf 2 S: *A & B can see their faces, because they're here, together. They can speak together face to face.* <u>message:</u> Nachricht; <u>answering machine:</u> Anrufbeantworter. Für *machine* im D. außer ‚Maschine' unbedingt das deutsche Äquivalent ‚Automat' geben, das häufig richtiger ist als ‚Maschine' (*washing machine*: Waschmaschine; *dishwasher*: Spülmaschine, aber: *drinks-machine; slot-machine*: ‚Getränkeautomat; Automat'. *cigarette machine* sollte man, trotz allgemeiner Kenntnis dieser Einrichtung bes. in Deutschland aus pädagogischen Gründen nicht als Beispiel wählen); <u>tone:</u> nach Anschreiben des Wortes: *We have almost the same word in German.*; <u>to make a call:</u> *When you phone s.o. you make a call.* gestisch mit Hand am Ohr unterstützen.

to answer the telephone	*to make a call*
7-1-double 4-3-6-3, Tom Smith speaking.	Hi, Judy, It's Caroline. I'm back again from London.
Hello. Who's speaking, please?	This is Roger. Tom, can you phone me when you get home? Bye.
Sorry, the MacTavishes aren't at home. But you can leave a message.	Oh sorry, I've got the wrong number. I wanted 7 - 5- double o - two - nine.
Ex 2: Hello. Sue Croft speaking.	**Ex 2:** Hello....It's David here.
Hello. This is Simon Burton. Who's speaking?	... Can I speak to Robert, please?
6 - 7 - 2 - 5 - 0 - 6	... she **must** phone me when she gets back ...
Can I take a message?	I'll write the message down.

2 Listening Practice: Take messages

Ziel: Training der Informationsentnahme bei ankommenden Telefonaten.

Neu: *to take a message*

Text

1. *(Phone rings, sound of receiver being picked up.)*
Mrs Croft: Hello. Sue Croft speaking.
David: Hello, Mrs Croft. It's David here. Can I speak to Robert, please?
Mrs Croft: Robert isn't here at the moment, David. Can I take a message?
David: Yes, please. You see, we wanted to play cricket after tea, but now I can't. I have to go to my grandma's house after tea. So I'll see Robert tomorrow.
Mrs Croft: OK. I'll tell him.
David: Thanks, Mrs Croft. Bye.

2. *(Phone rings, sound of receiver being picked up.)*
Simon: Hello. This is Simon Burton. Who's speaking, please?
Jenny: It's Jenny, Simon. Is Becky there, please?
Simon: No, she's gone for a walk with Maxi.
Jenny: Hm. Do you know when she'll be back?
Simon: No, but she won't be long, I'm sure.
Jenny: Well, please tell her she must phone me when she gets back. I want to tell her something.
Simon: Oh? Anything interesting?
Jenny: You'll find out later. Don't forget, Simon. Tell her it's very important.
Simon: Don't worry. I'll write the message down – in big letters!
Jenny: Great. Thanks a lot. Bye

3. *(Phone rings, sound of receiver being picked up.)*
Sarah: 967 2506.
Boy: Kim! Oh, I'm so glad you're back from the Netherlands! Two weeks without you has been ...
Sarah: Er, sorry, but it's Kim's sister Sarah here. Kim isn't at home.
Boy (embarrassed): Oh, I thought – I – well, this is Martin Best. Can you give Kim a message, please?
Sarah: Yes, of course.
Boy: Can you tell her I phoned. And I'll phone again at 10 o'clock.
Sarah: All right. Martin West is the name, right?
Boy: No. It's Best. B–E–S–T. Thank you. Goodbye.
Sarah: Bye. *(puts phone down)* Hm. Lucky I didn't tell him that Kim's out with another boy.

Unterrichtsempfehlungen

Semantisierung: <u>to take a message:</u> da *message* in ex. 1 eingeführt wurde, reicht hier ein kurze Erklärung: *Mrs Dixon isn't at home, but when the phone rings Sarah can take a message: She can write it down and give it to her mother later.*

Die Gesprächssituation des Telefonierens in der Fremdsprache ist allein schon sprachlich schwierig. Die Schwierigkeit wird durch die Kommunikationssituation zusätzlich erhöht. S können – in der Wirklichkeit – das Gespräch nur ein Mal hören bzw. müssen bei Nichtverstehen nachfragen, was sie wieder an neue Grenzen ihrer Verstehens- und Ausdrucksfähigkeit führen kann; gleichzeitig müssen sie Aufzeichnungen – in Stichwörtern – machen. In der Unterrichtssituation muss bei Schwierigkeiten sicherlich wiederholt werden. Das Sammeln weiterer *telephone language* in Übungsteil b wird mehrfache Präsentation der Gespräche nötig machen.
Es wäre sicher sinnvoll, wenn L mit Partner(in) noch weitere „Telefontexte" auf eine Kassette spricht, möglichst auch mit Zunahme von Hintergrundgeräuschen, um den Trainingseffekt noch weiter zu erhöhen. Sehr empfehlenswert sind Imitation der präsentierten und freie Sprechszenen in der Klasse mit alten Telefongeräten.

Lösungen: *Call no 2: Becky – Jenny phoned – must call Jenny back. Call no 3: Kim – Martin Best phoned. – Will phone you again at 10 o'clock!*

3 Sound practice

Ziel: Unterscheidung und richtige Aussprache der labialen (p, b), alveolaren (t, d) und velaren (k, g) Plosivlaute, sowie der labio-dentalen Frikativa (f, v).

Unterrichtsempfehlung:

Nach der üblichen Präsentation, Teil a), und Übung, Teil b), von/mit Kassette oder CD kann die semantische Füllung der einzelnen Konsonanten auch so geübt werden, indem L die relevanten englischen Wörter aus Teil a) und b) vorspricht und die S – auch im Wettspiel mit zwei Gruppen – die deutsche Bedeutung nennen lässt. Weitere Beispiele für schwierige Wortpaare (mit z.T. noch nicht* bekannten Wörtern): [b/p]: *bull*- pull, bad – pad*, bear – pair*, [k/g]: *dog – dock* [t/d]: *ride - write/right, sad – sat, had – hat*, [f/v]: *safe* – save, life – live*, sollen den S bewusst machen, wie breit die phonologisch-semantische Fehlerquelle sprudelt. Es sind ja auch andere Konsonanten betroffen, z.B. in: *rise – rice, thick – sick*, auch verwandte Vokale, z.B. in: *pin – pen – pan – pun*.

Schülerbuch Seite 11

4 Some useful telephone tips

Ziel: handlungsorientierte Anwendung der bisher in *Part 3* gelernten Fertigkeiten beim Buchen einer Übernachtung.

Neu: *youth hostel, to book, warden, to cancel, to check in; Lake District, Ambleside*

Unterrichtsempfehlungen
Semantisierung: *Lake District: a part of England in the Northwest. It has a lot of mountains and lakes and is famous for its beautiful scenery* [= Landschaft]. *Have a look at the map on the inside cover; Ambleside: a small town in the Lake District; youth hostel: a kind of simple hotel for young people; to book: when you book a room in a hotel you tell people there that you want to have it for one or more nights; warden: a warden's job in a youth hostel is to look after the hostel and its guests; to cancel: Sometimes people change their plans and don't want to stay at the hostel after they've booked. So they must say they don't want their rooms any more: they cancel them. to check in: When you arrive at a hotel or youth hostel, you must tell the warden that you are there. People will show you your room etc.*

Mit den Übungen 4 und – der nachfolgenden – 5 werden die S progressiv in Situationen geführt, die sie selber so im Ausland, speziell in England erleben können. In Übung 4 werden die S zu genauer Beobachtung und damit Verinnerlichung sinnvoller Schritte angeleitet: sich Notizen zu machen, dabei schwierige, aber unentbehrliche Wörter, die man möglicherweise nicht „draufhat", zu notieren, die Notizen während des Telefonats zur Hand zu haben. Die Übung ist eine kombinierte Hörverstehens- und Mitlese-Übung, vermeidet also den Schwierigkeitsgrad eines reinen *listening practice*. Die Aufgaben 1.–3.) sind demzufolge kombinierte *pre-listening* und *while-listening activities*.

Nach dem üblichen Semantisieren, Präsentieren, Lesen des Telefonats ist, auch als Vorbereitung auf die folgende Übung 5, ein Rollenspiel angezeigt. Auch Auswendiglernen als Hausaufgabe mit mehrfacher Inszenierung durch mehrere Schülerpaare in der nächsten Stunde wären eine gute Vorbereitung für *ex 5*.

WB S.5, 3.4

Lösungen:
1. *Ellen/she makes notes. It is a good idea: she can write down what she wants to say; she can write down difficult, but important words. Her call will be easier for her.*
2. *She tells the warden what she wants and when. The note 'check in?' tells her that she must ask when they have to be at the youth hostel.*
3. *– I'm sorry, I didn't understand ..., Can you say it again, please?*
   – you can spell your name

Hierbei ist es sinnvoll, die S auch andere Wörter buchstabieren zu lassen, die die „schwierigen" Buchstaben beinhalten. z. B.: **June, July, dirty, zoo, January, grumpy.** Die Buchstabenpaare j-g, a-r , i-e sowie h und die „Schlusslichter" des Alphabets x, y, z sind die üblichen Stolpersteine. Auch die eigenen Namen und vielleicht Heimat- und Geburtsort auf englisch buchstabieren zu lassen, ist sinnvoll, weil Realsituationen antizipierend.

5 Call a youth hostel
Ziel: Anwendung der in *Part 3* vermittelten Kenntnisse und Fertigkeiten beim Telefonieren in der Zielsprache, im Land der Zielsprache.

Neu: *Lake Windermere, Scarborough, York, Malham*

Unterrichtsempfehlungen
Semantisierung: alle Erklärungen der geographischen Namen auf deutsch; *Scarborough* und *York* auf der Karte des vorderen Umschlags verifizieren lassen. Die sachlichen, für S im Unterrichtsprozess etwas sterilen Erläuterungen zu den geographischen Begriffen im **Vocabulary**, Seite 122, sollten etwas weiter ausgeführt werden: *Lake Windermere:* See im *Lake District; Scarborough:* Küstenstadt in Ostengland, an der Nordsee; *Scarborough Fair* ist ein berühmter Song von Simon & Garfunkel. *York*: Stadt im Norden Englands, in North Yorkshire, geschichtlich wichtige Besiedlung durch die Römer und Dänen/ Wikinger (volkskundlich interessantes, museumspädagogisch vorbildliches *Viking Museum*); *Malham:* Dorf in Yorkshire, der Grafschaft *(county)*, die nach York benannt ist.

Für die Durchführung der Übung a) ist es unerlässlich, S erst Stichwörter *(notes)* machen zu lassen (entsprechend dem letzten Teil der Aufgabenformulierung). S sollten auch angeleitet werden, gestisch durch Halten der Hand am Ohr die Realsituation des Telefonierens zu imitieren. L sollte bei mehreren S-Paaren nacheinander genügend lange verweilen, um die S zu einer echten Dialoggestaltung zu veranlassen: Kontrolle und Korrektur/Hilfe sind unerlässlich.

Übungsteil b) verlangt die Realisierung (Schreiben und szenische Gestaltung) eines inhaltlich bisher nicht geübten Telefonats – die Absage/Stornierung einer Buchung. Dieser – schwierige – Transfer bedarf der besonderen Aufmerksamkeit der L. L sollten während der schriftlichen Arbeitsphase besonders aufmerksam kontrollieren, korrigieren und beraten. Die Vorführung der Telefonate vor der Klasse ist wichtig, um die S zur Konzentration zu zwingen, wie sie ja auch in der Realsituation unbedingt erforderlich wäre. Man kann den Rest der Klasse vor der Inszenierung auch auffordern, zu notieren/darauf zu achten, was besonders geschickt gelungen ist, was fehlerhaft war.

> Schülerbuch Seite 12

4 A short talk
Ziel: Referat, Kurzvortrag halten können.

Neu: *talk, to give a talk, experience, key, to lock, to lose/lost/lost*

Unterrichtsempfehlungen
Dieser letzte *Part* führt aus der Welt der inszenierten Ferien-/Reiseerfahrung direkt zurück in das deutsche Klassenzimmer, in den Englischunterricht. Die Ferienerfahrung soll sprachlich im Englischen gefestigt werden. Ferien in anderen Ländern könnten ebenso thematisiert werden – im Sinne einer Öffnung des Englischunterrichts über die traditionelle landeskundliche Bindung an englischsprachige Länder hinaus. Gleichzeitig aber leistet die Auswertung in Form eines Referats einen methodischen Beitrag zur Förderung dieser allgemeinen, in fast allen Schulfächern erwünschten Fertigkeit. Eine Absprache mit anderen Fachlehrern der Klasse wäre außerordentlich sinnvoll. Eine gleichzeitige Einübung in das Referathalten in mehreren Schulfächern würde eine Habitualisierung dieser Fertigkeit natürlich enorm fördern.

Semantisierung: *talk; to give a talk: to talk about* ist bekannt, das Substantiv ist neu. *When people talk about s.th. they have a talk. But when only one person talks to other people, he or she gives a talk, the others just listen. experience:* dt.: Erfahrung, Erlebnis; *key:* Schlüssel (am Schlüsselbund) zeigen; *to lock:* am besten demonstriert L mit einem Schlüssel für das Klassenzimmer, wie er/sie die Tür verschließt und wieder öffnet. Es sollte sinnvollerweise das Begriffs- bzw. Antonymenpaar *to lock – to unlock* eingeführt werden. Evtl. auch Kurzübung zu Wortbildung mit prefix *un-*, z.B.: *friendly/unfriendly, tidy/untidy, happy/unhappy, lucky/unlucky* einstreuen; *to lose:* L geht durchs Klassenzimmer, lässt scheinbar zerstreut Schlüssel/Schlüsselbund oder etwas anderes auf einem S-tisch liegen und fragt anschließend – gespielt-verwirrt, unter Einbeziehung der *irregular form* und des *opposite 'find': I always lose my keys. Where are they? I've just lost them. I hope I'll find them again.*

Nach Semantisierung der neuen Wörter Präsentation des Textes durch L, danach lesen S den Text mehrfach laut vor.

1 How you can use notes

Ziel: a) Erkennen und unterscheiden von inhaltlichen Stichwörtern und nützlichen Satzstellungs- und ‚Transport'-Vokabulars.
b) Anfertigen von Stichwörtern.
c) Erkennen von Satzverknüpfungsmitteln, hier: *conjunctions.*

Unterrichtsempfehlungen
Mit dieser Übung erfolgt eine Grundsteinlegung in einem wichtigen, nicht immer gepflegten Bereich der Sprachproduktion. Bis zum Abitur leiden viele schriftliche Englischtexte deutscher Englischlerner unter dem sogenannten ‚Primitivstil'. Die Unfähigkeit, komplexe Aussageabsichten lexikalisch nuanciert im Englischen umzusetzen, ist der Grund dafür. Variabler Satzaufbau durch *conjunctions* (Terminus und Beispiele eingeführt in Band II, *Unit 7*, S. 69), *sentence connectives* und satzwertige Konstruktionen wie *gerund* und *participle constructions* bedürfen einer progressiven Einführung und kontinuierlicher Pflege durch Anwendung und Kontrolle. Eine hervorragende Palette von Übungsmaterial, Übungstypen zu diesem Arbeitsgebiet findet sich in: Leo Jones, *Use of English. Grammar practice activities for intermediate and upper-intermediate students* (Cambridge, 51988), pp.70-75. – Cambridge University Press. Für das dritte Lernjahr sind die Übungen selbst jedoch zu anspruchsvoll und nicht in Gänze zu übernehmen.
Es ist wichtig, den S den Sachverhalt und die Bedeutung dieser Übung für die zukünftige mündliche und schriftliche Textproduktion auf deutsch bewusst zu machen. Semantisierung: *full: full of* ist bekannt, nützt aber zur Erklärung nichts. Daher: *The 'full text' means the 'text from the beginning to the end'. On page 12 from "I want to tell you ..." to "... went crazy!"*

Lösungen:
a) inhaltliche Stichwörter vs. deren Einbindung in komplette Sätze mit finiten Verbformen und Konjunktionen
b) *no car keys – Dad to information desk – Mum crazy – Kim – keys inside car – car unlocked – Mum crazy*
c) *I want ... – while – when – well – because – suddenly – before – when*

2 Make a talk from notes

Ziel: a) und b): Ausformulieren eines Berichts auf der Basis vorgegebener Stichwörter.
c): Hörverstehen eines Berichts und Vergleich mit der eigenen schriftlichen Fassung.

Neu: *to cycle, picnic, rainstorm, bus shelter, Newstead Abbey*

Text
I am going to tell you about my "travel experience". It happened last month when I was with David. One day we were cycling to Newstead Abbey. We wanted to have a picnic there. But on the way there, a terrible rainstorm began. I've never seen rain like it in my life! It was raining so hard that we had to stop under a bus shelter to keep dry. While we were waiting there, someone else on a bike arrived. He was a nice boy from Leipzig in Germany and he was spending his holidays in England. After some time the rain stopped, so we could go on. We said goodbye to the German boy, but before we left, I gave him my address. Yesterday I got a postcard, it comes all the way from Leipzig, Germany.

Unterrichtsempfehlungen
Semantisierung: *to cycle:* to ride a bike; *picnic:* We use the same word in German: A picnic is a meal in the open air, not in a house/building; *rainstorm:* a lot of rain and wind; *bus shelter:* the place at a bus stop where you can wait for the bus and don't get wet when it rains; *Newstead Abbey:* Kloster in der Nähe von Nottingham.
Es ist sinnvoll, den Text zwei Mal mit zwei unterschiedlichen Teilaufträgen zu präsentieren. Zunächst soll darauf geachtet werden, welche Lexeme, grammatische Formen, Füllwörter, Adverbien zu beachten sind *(progressive forms; I am going to ... – one day – we wanted – but – after some time – but – yesterday)*. In einem zweiten Durchgang sollen S nur auf *conjunctions* achten *(when – so...that – while – so – before)*. Wichtig ist der Hinweis, dass die *conjunctions* meist zwei verschiedene Positionen im Satzgefüge einnehmen können: vor und nach dem Hauptsatz. Lehrer sollte das an drei oder vier unterschiedlichen Sätzen üben lassen, z.B.: *When we went back to our car, Dad couldn't find the car keys. – Daddy couldn't find the car keys when we came back to our car.* Dass solche Umstellungen semantische Unterschiede bewirken können, kann hier außer Acht gelassen werden.
Sollte sich eine Wiederholung der *past tense* als nötig erweisen, können Übung 4.1 im WB und *ex.3a* der *Practice page* eingesetzt werden.

WB S.6, 4.2

WB S.6, 4.1
Revision:
S. 13 Part 5,
Practice page,
ex. 3 On holiday in Wales a)

3 Make your own talk

Ziel: Notizen für einen Bericht/Vortrag verfertigen; in Gruppenarbeit Vortrag ausarbeiten und vortragen.

Neu: *own, to divide*

Unterrichtsempfehlung
Semantisierung: *own: Betty doesn't ask her brother for his CD player. She's got her own. to divide: For group work I must divide the class into groups.*
Vor Beginn der Gruppenarbeit soll festgelegt werden, wer in der jeweiligen Gruppe den Bericht vorträgt. Das verpflichtet die Gruppenmitglieder, im Interesse des Vortragenden konzentrierte Arbeit zu leisten. L sind gehalten, die Gruppen intensiv zu beraten und bei Fragen oder Problemen zu helfen. Das Engagement der Gruppen könnte noch durch Aufnahmen der Präsentation durch die „Gruppensprecher" mit Kassettenrekorder oder Camcorder gesteigert werden, die dann zum Schluss von allen angehört/angesehen und prämiert werden.

Aufzeichnung, Wettbewerb

Schülerbuch Seite 13

5 ⟨Practice Page⟩

1 Ferry dialogues

Ziel: Wiederholung des differenzierenden Gebrauchs des *simple present* und *present progressive* in Aussage- und Fragesätzen.

Lösungen: *2. Who is Sarah talking to? – Our Sarah always talks to everyone. 3. Do ferry cinemas show good films? – Let's go and ask what they're showing on this ferry today. 4. Are you travelling to England alone? – We always travel together. 5. How many cars does this ferry usually carry? – Well, at the moment we're carrying 360.*

2 All about Scotland

Ziel: Wiederholung des *object complement* nach Verben wie *make, call, find, like.*

Neu: *to make s.o. welcome*

Unterrichtsempfehlung:
Die Struktur ist im Deutschen und Englischen identisch. Dieses sollte auf deutsch bewusst gemacht werden. Nur aus lexikalischen Gründen ist – wie in der idiomatischen Wendung *to make s.o. welcome* – gelegentlich Vorsicht geboten: das *make* heißt im Deutschen eben nicht

'machen'. Die Wendung in der dt. Bedeutung geben: ‚jdn willkommen heißen, mit offenen Armen aufnehmen'.

Lösungen: *2. You call them lochs. 3. I find the idea interesting/exciting/ silly. 4. They call their skirts kilts. 5. ... but I find it terrible. 6. Good weather always makes a holiday nice/great.*

3 On holiday in Wales

Ziel: a) Wiederholung des *simple past*.
b) Wiederholung von kontrastiven Sätzen im *present perfect* und *simple past*.

Neu: *one day, dragon*

Unterrichtsempfehlung:
Semantisierung: <u>one day:</u> dt. 'eines Tages, an einem Tag'; Hinweis geben, dass im Gegensatz zum E im D ein Genitiv bzw. präpositionaler Ausdruck nötig ist. <u>dragon:</u> Hinweis auf die Figur im SB, S. 13, reicht zur Erläuterung. Kontrastierung Drache *(dragon)* – Drachen *(kite)* ist sinnvoll.
Wichtig ist die Beachtung der Dreiteiligkeit der Übung: 1. Die Anfangsfrage wird im *present perfect* gestellt mit entsprechendem *signal word: ever*. 2. Die negative Antwort beinhaltet eine Kurzantwort und eine inhaltliche Korrektur im ganzen Satz: beides im *present perfect*. Im Falle einer positiven Antwort: nur Kurzantwort im *present perfect*. 3. Eine zeitlich spezifizierte Zusatzantwort, die das *simple past* notwendig macht.

Schülerbuch Seiten 14-15

Unit 1 A trip to London

Allgemeiner Hinweis zur Unit 1
Diese Unit ist mit London, mit seinen Sehenswürdigkeiten und einigen historischen Informationen über 1066 befaßt. L haben hier die Möglichkeit, über die sprachlichen Lernziele hinaus mit ihrer Klasse längerfristige landeskundliche Lernziele mit handlungsorientierten Methoden anzustreben. Über den auf S.16 beginnenden Lehrgang hinaus könnten Aktivitäten angestrebt werden wie etwa:
1. Organisation einer Ausstellung über London (im Klassenraum/im Schulflur o.ä., evtl. zusammen mit der/den Parallelklasse(n), geordnet etwa nach Themen wie *Parts of London, London's river, Royalty, Parliament, The city, Cultural London, Shops and markets, London transport.*
2. Herstellung von interessanten, informativen Postern/ Collagen zu einzelnen Sehenswürdigkeiten (Bilder und Texte).
3. Planung alternativer *Round London Sightseeing Tours by Bus, starting from Tower Hill or Victoria, the Houses of Parliament...* – bzw. *Five interesting London walks.*
4. *What's on in London?* Veranstaltungskalender für eine Woche in London herausfinden und im Klassenraum präsentieren. Darauf aufbauend: *What I would like to do if I had a week in London.*
5) S sammeln Material zu *Swinging London*.
6) Statistische Informationen über London zusammentragen. Evtl. Vergleich zu einer deutschen Großstadt. Die Fakten tabellarisch darstellen und versprachlichen lassen.
Für welche dieser Aktivitäten sich L und S auch entscheiden – im Unterricht müsste hinreichend Zeit und Raum gegeben werden für Beratung und vor allem

sprachliche Unterstützung (erst 3. Lernjahr!) bei der Produkterstellung. Die Arbeit ist aber in jedem Fall lohnend, relevant und motivierend.
Zur Materialbeschaffung: S und L können sicherlich eine erhebliche Menge diesbezüglicher Materialien aus Eigenbeständen beitragen. Hilfreich bei der Beschaffung sind darüber hinaus der British Council in Hamburg (Rothenbaumchaussee 34,20148 Hamburg, Tel.040/446057), in Köln, Berlin, München und Leipzig, Reisebüros (für Prospekte), das London Tourist Board, die British Tourist Authority (Neue Mainzer Str. 22, Frankfurt/M.), das Official Handbook 'Britain 97' des Central Office of Information, *sold by HMSO*, britische Tages- und Sonntagszeitungen (Veranstaltungspläne), das Internet (z.B. http://www.yahoo.com/), CD-ROMs (z.B. Encarta 97) etc.
Britische Fremdsprachenassistenten und -innen – so vorhanden – sollten hier dringend hilfreich, verantwortlich, den L auch entlastend, eingesetzt werden.

Als direkte Einstimmung in die *Unit 1* wäre ein Tourismus-Videofilm über London motivierender als alternative Einstiegsmöglichkeit. Aber auch Songs wie *'The Streets of London'* (Ralph McTell) sind hier hilfreich.

Step A Famous sights

Ziel: – Einführung in das Thema 'London':
– sich in der Stadt orientieren können;
– Lage einiger Sehenswürdigkeiten erkennen;
– sich auf einem Stadtplan orientieren können;
– Wege beschreiben können (Wiederholung).

Neu: *sight, queue, carnival, square, palace, queen, circus, taxi, attraction, Egyptian, Roman, pigeon, double decker bus, cathedral, tower, bridge, bit, Hindu, temple.*

Unterrichtsempfehlungen
Semantisierung: Problematisch können hier die Namen der Straßen, Plätze, Brücken, Sehenswürdigkeiten sein. Am schnellsten ist wohl eine gemeinsame Ausspracheerarbeitung (L und S) der Box auf S.124. Eine andere Möglichkeit wäre, in der Mitte der Karte anzufangen, etwa bei Piccadilly Circus, und mit Hilfe der Himmelsrichtungen mit L-Frage: *Where's Leicester Square/The Mall/... ?* und S-Antwort *Leicester Square is north of Piccadilly / The Mall is south of Piccadilly / ...* weiterzuarbeiten.
<u>carnival, palace, queen, circus, taxi, Egytian, cathedral, Hindu temple</u> werden von den S über das Laut- bzw. Schriftbild direkt erschlossen und bedürfen keiner speziellen Semantisierung (aber lautl. Sicherung!). <u>sight:</u> *famous place that tourists often visit;* <u>queue:</u> *people standing in a long line at a bus-stop, for instance;* <u>square:</u> *Zeichnung an der Tafel. Beispiel aus dem Heimatort (‚Berliner Platz' o.ä.);* <u>attraction:</u> *a sight in a town that is very interesting and popular;* <u>Roman:</u> *adj. of Rome – of the Rome just before and after the time of Jesus Christ;* <u>pigeon:</u> *a grey bird with short legs that you mostly find in towns and cities. People like to feed them when they are sitting in parks or city squares;* <u>double decker bus:</u> *a bus with stairs in it so that you can sit upstairs or downstairs. SB S. 14 oder auf der Folie zeigen;* <u>tower:</u> *a very high house. Churches have towers with bells in them;* <u>bridge:</u> *you can get from one side of a river to the other through a tunnel under it or over it on a bridge;* <u>bit:</u> *a small part.*

Vocabulary S. 124

Bildfolie 5

1 What do you know about London?

Ziel: Erste Eindrücke von London bekommen.

Unterrichtsempfehlungen
Die S sollten sich einige Zeit allein mit dem Stadtplan beschäftigen dürfen. Sie könnten hier Straßen, Gebäude etc. erkennen, von denen sie gehört haben, die sie selbst evtl. besucht haben, über die sie etwas wissen. Bei der Verbalisierung ihrer Vorerfahrungen über die Stadt,

WB S.7, A1

zusammen mit der Identifizierung einiger *sights* auf dem Stadtplan (*in the middle of page..., at the top/bottom of page ..., on the left/right, next to ...*) werden die ersten korrekten Aussprachen der Namen gesichert und Vokabeln semantisiert.

Anschließende Aktivitäten anhand des Stadtplans: Bildfolie 5
– *Let's go on some tours of London on foot. We'll start off at (Baker Street/Tower Bridge...). How do we get to (the London Dungeon, ...)? (straight on, turn left/right, there is ...).* Dabei immer wieder Aussprachen sichern (vgl. S.124: gemeinsamer Durchgang durch die Liste).
– *Right/wrong questions, z.B. At Covent Garden there are hundreds of pigeons. In Regent's Park you can learn about the history of London ....*
– Make a list

train to Paris	Waterloo Station
pigeons	Trafalgar Square
nice shops	....
horror	London Dungeon
the Queen	....
etc.	

– *Bridges and parks in London*: Hier aufgeführte Brücken ab Tower Bridge westwärts: *London Bridge, Southwark Bridge, Blackfriars Bridge, Waterloo Bridge, Westminster Bridge, Lambeth Bridge, Vauxhall Bridge, Chelsea Bridge* (die Straße, die von dieser Brücke nördlich führt, heißt *Buckingham Palace Road*). Parks östlich vom *Hyde Park: Green Park, St James's Park*.

Schülerbuch Seite 16

Step A The exchange visit

2 Listening practice: Arriving in London

Ziel: Üben des Hörverstehens; Festigen des landeskundlichen Wissens über London.

Neu: *exchange visit, flight, to land*

Text
Airline pilot over PA system:
This is Captain Johns speaking again. In a moment we will land at London's Heathrow Airport. We're just flying over London on our way to Heathrow. If you look out of the windows on the right of the plane you can see Tower Bridge. It's a nice, sunny day in London, so you can see lots of the famous sights.
We're flying along the Thames now. Those of you on the right of the plane can see the Houses of Parliament and Big Ben. We can't see the time on Big Ben but I can tell you that it's ten past three in London now. People on the right of the plane can see Hyde Park and, yes, that's Buckingham Palace.
We will land at Heathrow in a minute. We hope you have enjoyed your flight with us and wish you a safe journey if you have to travel on from London.

Unterrichtsempfehlungen
Semantisierung: *exchange visit: one person visits another one and later that one then visits the first one*; *flight*: noun of 'to fly'; *to land: You fly in a plane; when the plane comes back to the ground, it lands.*
L liest die Einleitung vor und spielt anschließend die Aufnahme ein. Die S haben ihre SB auf S. 14/15 geöffnet und verfolgen jede/r für sich die Route des Flugzeugs gemäß den Ausführungen des Flugkapitäns. Sie identifizieren den Tower, die Themse, Big Ben etc. Dann Frage: *Where is Heathrow Airport in London?* (weit links auf dem Plan, im Westen, auf der Karte nicht enthalten. L erläutert dies). Dann L: *How do you think one can get from Heathrow to the city? (bus, taxi, underground). How else can one get to London from Kiel? How does one find an exchange partner? (school, teacher, pen-pal).*

3 Samira's family

Ziel: erste Eindrücke von London als multikultureller Stadt erfahren; Hörverstehen verbessern.

Neu: *African, most of them, to take place, West Indian, she was born, festival, to take part in sth., Londoner; Bethnal Green, India, West Indies, Caribbean, Pakistan, Coventry, Muslim*

Unterrichtsempfehlungen
Semantisierung: Mit Hilfe einer Weltkarte aus dem Erdkundefundus lassen sich <u>West Indies</u> (adj. <u>West Indian</u>), <u>Caribbean</u> (auf Rechtschreibung achten!), <u>Pakistan</u>, <u>Africa</u> (adj. <u>African</u>) leicht semantisieren. <u>Coventry</u> findet sich auf der Karte auf der Innenseite des SB. <u>Bethnal Green</u> ist auf dem U-Bahn-Plan S.18 ganz rechts auf der *Central Line* zu finden. *Bethnal Green is a part of London in the east.* <u>Londoner:</u> *a person who lives in London.* <u>Most of them:</u> *the greater part of a group of people;* <u>to take place:</u> *to happen;* <u>she was born:</u> *she first saw the light of the world as a baby;* <u>Muslim:</u> deutsch erläutern; <u>festival:</u> *a long fete where they play music, have plays, or show films in the cinemas;* <u>to take part in s.th.:</u> *to join s.th.*
Situation des Dialogs vorbereiten: L erzählt über Bethnal Green: *in the east of London, east of the Tower; Katrin Hoffmann's exchange family lives in this part. At the moment Katrin and Samira are taking the underground to Bethnal Green:*
– L verliest den Dialog oder spielt die Aufnahme vom Tonträger vor, S lesen im SB mit.
– L klärt Vokabeln und Aussprachen.
– S lesen Text jeder für sich und mit leiser Stimme noch einmal.
– S identifizieren die Fotos *(Notting Hill Carnival, Hindu temple)* und finden diese auf S. 14.
– S lesen mit verteilten Rollen.
– L: *What do we learn about London and about Samira's family?* Tafelanschrieb: Tafelanschrieb:

London:	Samira's family
....	....
....	....

– *Why is it that Samira calls herself a Londoner and British and not Indian?* (Partnerarbeit, dann Plenum).

Vorschläge für weitere Aktivitäten *(post-reading-activities)*:
– Katrin schreibt einen ersten Brief heim nach Kiel.
– Samira und Katrin kommen in Bethnal Green an: Katrin formuliert ihre ersten Eindrücke in ihrem Tagebuch. (S lesen ihre Ergebnisse in Partner oder Gruppenarbeit vor und vergleichen.)
– S versuchen Zusatzinformationen zu Hindus/Moslems zu bekommen.

4 People from other countries   WB S.7, A2

Ziel: Berichten über fremde Kulturen; Transfer der Situation in London auf den eigenen Heimatort.

Neu: *Ramadan*

Unterrichtsempfehlungen
Semantisierung: <u>Ramadan:</u> *the 9th month of the Muslim year. No food or drink may be taken between the beginning and the end of the day.* (In vielen Klassen gibt es S, die moslemischen Glaubens sind. Sie können hier hilfreich sein.)
Dies könnte als Hausarbeit eine lohnende Aufgabe sein. Kommunikativer wäre eine Umsetzung im Unterricht: Die S der Klasse befragen ihre Mitschüler/innen aus anderen Ländern. Weiterführung: Die S befragen Mitschüler/innen aus den Parallelklassen bzw. der ganzen Schule, sammeln Informationen. Verschriftlichung: *In*

our school we've got ... pupils from ... . have got ... parents/... were born in ... . Some of their festivals are ...; their food is ...; how they feel in Germany, etc.
Relevant wäre auch eine etwa 1 Woche dauernde Sammlung von Zeitungsausschnitten (deutsch) über Ausländer in Deutschland/ im Bundesland. Eine daran anschließende längere Diskussion über die Berichterstattung (deutsch, da erst 3. Lernjahr) ist hier dann unumgänglich.

Schülerbuch Seiten 17-18

Step A What you can see in London

Ziel: Weitere landeskundliche Informationen über London erhalten.

Neu: *disappointed, whole*

Unterrichtsempfehlungen
Semantisierung: *disappointed: unhappy because s.th. is not like one had hoped; whole: the complete parts of s.th.* L führt die neuen Vokabeln kurz ein, danach lesen die S den Text einmal still. L liest den Text einmal vor, S lesen mit. Anschließend lesen die S den Text mit verteilten Rollen.

Vorschläge für *post-reading-activities:*
– Text als Rollenspiel organisieren: Darrens Gedanken als ‚asides‘; den Schluss um mindestens 3-5 Dialogsätze erweitern. Schlusssatz vorgeben (etwa: *OK, let's visit ... first thing tomorrow morning*).
– Gespräch der Familie Taylor *later that evening* über ihren Gast aus Kiel *(to be lucky, good at history, helpful perhaps, books, polite boy, too quiet ...)*
– Christophs Eindrücke von seinem ersten Tag bei den Taylors: S schreiben einen ‚inneren Monolog' *(beautiful, my room is ..., brochures, clean house, enjoy stay, excited, fantastic family, Darren seems disappointed, ...).*
– Adjektivsammlung mit Hilfe der SB-Seiten 165 ff. Welche Adjektive treffen die Stimmung Darrens/Christophs/Mrs Taylors am besten? *(angry, disappointed, bad, difficult, friendly, frightening, miserable, nasty, boring, worried, scared, ...)*

5 What is it?

Ziel: Identifizierung von Sehenswürdigkeiten.

Neu: *underground, waxwork, king, they are crowned, royal, prison*

Unterrichtsempfehlungen
Semantisierung: *underground: a train that travels under the ground; waxwork: A candle is made of wax. Waxworks are forms, animals, people made of wax; King: Today Queen Elizabeth is the first woman in the UK. If a man is in her place, he is called 'king'; they are crowned: they are made king or queen.* (auch Tafelzeichnung bzw. Gestik); *royal: of the king/queen; prison: place where burglars and killers must stay when the police have caught them.*
Die S arbeiten mit ihren Nachbarn bzw. in Gruppen. Da die Bilder und Texte nicht mit Nummern versehen sind, muss ihr Standort versprachlicht werden. Dann sollen die Lösungen verlesen. Zur Erhöhung des Übungseffektes kann L ähnliche Texte / Bilder fotokopieren und zur Zuordnung eingeben *(British Museum, London Dungeon ...).*
Die S identifizieren dann auf S. 14/15, wo die *sights* sind *(north/ west of ..., next to ..., on the left ...).*
In häuslicher Arbeit könnten die S versuchen, mehr über diese und andere *sights* zu erfahren (CD-ROM, Internet – Suchadresse s.o. – Nachschlagewerke, Prospekte, Befragung des/der Fremdsprachenassistenten/in, etc.).

Bildfolien 7a und 7b

Empfehlenswert ist weiterhin die Fortsetzung der Liste oben: Vorschlag 3 zu S. 14/15.

Lösungen: *At the top on the right is a ticket to Madame Tussaud's. It goes with the second photo on the right: there are waxworks and people in the picture. The text in the middle of the page on the left goes with this picture, too. The text in the middle of the page goes with the photo on the left. That's the Tower of London. Below the photo is a ticket to the Tower. The text on the left at the top of the Tower photo goes with the picture at the bottom of the page. That's Buckingham palace. The text at the bottom of the page on the right goes with the picture at the top on the right. That's Westminster Abbey.*

6 Eastbound or westbound?

Ziel: Eindrücke bekommen vom Londoner Untergrundbahn-System.

Neu: *eastbound, westbound, stop*

Unterrichtsempfehlungen
Semantisierung: *eastbound, westbound: travelling to the east / west; stop* ist durch *bus stop* schon bekannt. Das Problem hier ist die Aussprache vieler Stationsnamen. Ein erschöpfender Durchgang durch alle Namen dieses Teil-U-Bahn-Planes ist sicherlich nicht lohnend, evtl. könnte aber zu Beginn die *box* auf S. 124 zur Kenntnis genommen und geübt werden. Weitere Aussprache-probleme sollten dann nicht isoliert, sondern eher aus den Notwendigkeiten von Situationen (z.B. Wegbeschreibungen) heraus geklärt werden.
Mögliche Aktivitäten anhand des Plans (auf Folie) etwa:
– *Follow the (Piccadilly)-Line from Earl's Court in the west to King's Cross and say where the train stops and where you can change to other lines.*
– *You want to go from (Notting Hill Gate) to (Blackfriars). Which is the best way to go?*
– *Say which Lines the following stations are on: Aldgate East, Euston Square, ...*
– Auch als Rollenspiel in Kleingruppen möglich, etwa: deutsche S fragen englischen Polizisten nach dem Weg. Dabei Übung vieler *helpful phrases: Excuse me, can you help us, please?/Thank you very much for your help./You're welcome./Could you say that again, please?/Could you please speak more slowly?*

Vocabulary S. 124

Bildfolie 6

7 Find the station

Ziel: Festigung der Eindrücke vom Londoner U-Bahn-System.

Neu: *to change, northbound; Paddington, Victoria*

Unterrichtsempfehlungen
Semantisierung: *to change:* bekannt, muss nur als *change trains* erweitert werden; *Paddington, Victoria: train and underground stations in London* (vgl. Plan S. 18).
In Partner- oder Gruppenarbeit spielen die S das Spiel wie vorgesehen. L hilft bei Bedarf mit der Aussprache. Die Übung macht S Freude und kann daher intensiv (viele Beispiele) durchgeführt werden. Zum Schluss einige ‚Testaufgaben' im Plenum (durch L oder S).

8 Your trip to London

Ziel: Weitere Übung mit dem U-Bahn-Plan und Festigung des bisherigen Wissens über Sehenswürdigkeiten.

Neu: *trip*

Unterrichtsempfehlungen
trip: in their holidays many people go on trips to other countries, that is: they travel to other countries. Die Übung bietet sich als Hausarbeit an, da einige Ruhe und Konzentration nötig sind. In Gruppenarbeit werden die Texte verlesen, einige zur Kontrolle auch im Plenum.
Alternative im Unterricht: S zählen auf (Tafelbild), was

WB S.8, A3
WB S.8, A4

sie gern sehen würden und formulieren kurz warum. Dann gemeinsames Suchen, wie man ab *Leicester Square* dorthin kommt. Tafelbild etwa:

| Tower | because I want to see the old prison | Northern Line southbound, change onto Circle Line eastbound at Embankment |
| Mme Tussaud's | because I like waxworks | Piccadilly Line to Green Park then Jubilee Line northbound |

Schülerbuch Seite 19

Step A At the Tower

Ziel: Einige Fakten aus der (Sprach-)Geschichte Englands erfahren.

Neu: *to go sightseeing, guard, to build/built/built; Beefeater, the White Tower, William the Conqueror*

Unterrichtsempfehlungen

Semantisierung: *beefeaters: men in red uniforms who watch out that everything is OK at the Tower. They also help tourists; guard: the beefeaters are guards: they see to it that everything is OK; to build: to put pieces together. You build a house of many stones.*
Um konkrete Eindrücke vermitteln zu können, sollten dringend Zusatzmaterialien zum Tower in der Klasse gesammelt und verfügbar gemacht werden, etwa: *leaflets*, die herumgereicht werden, Bilder, Fotos, auf Poster geklebt und ausgestellt (Der Tower als *castle/fortress*, als *royal palace*, als *prison (Traitor's Gate)*, als *mint (place where money is made)*, als *museum (today)*. Informationen können von S nach Kräften und Möglichkeiten auch in Hausarbeit gesammelt und beigebracht werden (Reisebüros, Nachschlagewerke, Bildbände, Internet ...).
Der einführende Text *(Darren and Christoph ...)* kann dann vom L vorgelesen werden. Anhand des Fotos können die Wörter *beefeater, guards* und *to build* bei Bedarf leicht semantisiert werden. Ausgehend von Christophs Frage *Who was William the Conqueror?* Übergang zu:

WB S.9, A5

9 1066

Ziel: Informationen über den *Norman Conquest* erarbeiten.

Neu: *however, to become/became/become, Norman, army, coast, battle, to fight/fought/fought; Edward the Confessor, Normandy, Hastings, Christmas Day*

Unterrichtsempfehlungen

Semantisierung: *to become: to be s.th. or s.o. in the future; to fight: you fight with an enemy if you hurt him or he hurts you; however: but; army: people in the Bundeswehr are our German army; coast: the seaside; battle: a fight between armies; Christmas Day: Dec. 25.* Die Namen situativ aus dem Text heraus erläutern.
Eine Landkarte aus der Erdkundesammlung, auf der Nordfrankreich (Normandie) und Südengland (bis London) zu sehen sind, sollte während dieses historischen Exkurses im Klassenraum aufgehängt sein. Alternative: die Klasse zeichnet selbst im Unterricht (Tafel, großes Poster, Tapetenrolle, ...) eine solche Karte, die dann während der *Unit* ständig sichtbar bleibt.
Zu 1066 gibt es natürlich unendlich viele Materialien, bis hin zu diesem Ereignis in Zeitungsform (mit Leitartikel, Kommentaren, Werbung ...). Da es sich hier jedoch nur um eine 7. Klasse (mit noch beschränkter L2-Kompetenz) handelt, sollte L sich darauf beschränken, die S. 19, die Basisinformationen enthält, für die S verständlich zu machen.
– Die S studieren die 7 *boxes*, mit L als Helfer bei Sprachfragen. Anschließend ordnen die S diese *boxes* in Partnerarbeit, die entstehende Geschichte wird dann verlesen, die Orte werden auf der Landkarte gesucht. (Zur Begründung des Thronanspruchs durch William – Text B – : sein Cousin Edward the Confessor (1002-1066, Text A) hatte ihm den Thron versprochen.)
– Beschreibung des Hintergrundbildes durch die S, Erläuterungen durch L, etwa: *Bayeux tapestry, 11th century, scenes show the events leading to the Battle of Hastings and the Battle, 70 m long, 49.5 cm high, 1512 figures, 72 scenes.* Zur Beschreibung: King Harold greift nach einem Pfeil, der ihn im Auge getroffen hat. Kurz danach wird er mit einem Schwert erschlagen (*Harold the King* – HAROLD. REX – *is killed* – INTERFECTUS EST). Wer weitere Bilder aus dem Teppich von Bayeux (die eigentlich eine Stickerei ist) besitzt, kann hier auf andere Details der Invasion und Schlacht eingehen. Auch in diesem Bild sind interessante Kleinigkeiten zu beobachten, z.B: der Mann in der unteren Bordüre, der die Schwerter der Gefallenen einsammelt.
– Möglich ist natürlich auch ein längerfristiges 1066-Projekt. Materialien sind leicht erhältlich. Bequemster Zugriff: CD-ROM (z.B. Encarta 96 oder 97) bzw. Internet. Über die Suchhilfen http://www.yahoo.com/ und http://webcrawler.com/ sind Informationen reichhaltig zu bekommen.

Lösungen: A, C, B, D, G, F, E

10 Looking at English

Ziel: Wortabstammungen erkennen und zuordnen.

Neu: *religion, spy*

Unterrichtsempfehlungen

religion: durch das Schriftbild klar – aber Aussprache üben; *spy:* bekannt als Verb (GL2-1/7). *A person who spies for a country.* Eine Semantisierung ist aber eigentlich überflüssig.
a) Im Anschluss an Text E aus Übung 9 versuchen die S in Partnerarbeit Ordnungsmöglichkeiten für die Wörter zu finden und sie dann zu ordnen. Vorschlag: *food; government; army, church; clothes.*
b) Herauszufinden ist, daß die Wörter fast alle fertige Produkte bezeichnen eher als Rohmaterialien, oder aber mit der Regierungsschicht von Staat (Armee) und Kirche zu tun haben: Französisch wurde hauptsächlich von der herrschenden Klasse gesprochen.

Lösungen: *Food: sausage, cream* (als Speise), *biscuit,, fruits, sugar, salad, roast, beef; dinner, plate. Government: royal, parliament, spy, army: army, guard, officer, battle, prisoner. Church: religion, charity, abbey. Clothes: coat, lace, blue, cream* (als Farbe)

Schülerbuch Seite 20

Step B What do you like doing?

Ziel: Einführung in das *gerund* als Subjekt bzw. Objekt im Satz; über *hobbies*, Vorlieben, Abneigungen sprechen lernen.

Neu: *stupid, to ski, to dance, to hate, past*

Unterrichtsempfehlungen

Semantisierung: *stupid: s.th. that you don't like; to ski, to dance:* werden über das Schrift- bzw. Lautbild klar; *to hate: opposite of 'to love'; past:* S kennen den grammatischen Begriff. Auch: *opposite of 'future'*; Die 4 Sprechblasen sind eine situative Bereitstellung eines Corpus, mit dem sich in Übung 1 dann die Funktion *gerund as subject* und *gerund as object* hinreichend darstellen läßt. L erläutert das neue Vokabular, liest die Sprechblasen vor, oder spielt die Tonaufnahme ein, klärt evtl. Fragen der S.
– Beim nochmaligen Hören lesen S still mit.
– Rollenlesen (4 S).

1 Looking at English

Ziel: Das *gerund* kennenlernen und als Subjekt bzw. Objekt erkennen können.

Neu: *gerund, subject*

Unterrichtsempfehlungen

gerund, subject: werden bei der Grammatikvermittlung erklärt. *subject* ist ohnehin evtl. noch aus GL 1, S. 144 bekannt. Ansonsten müsste dies hier im Vorfeld geklärt werden (Wie erkennt man ...?)
a) Am Beispiel wird gesichert, ob alle S Subjekt/Objekt im Satz erkennen können. Evtl. Einhilfe durch L. In Partnerarbeit machen die S dann die 2 Listen – gleichzeitig je ein S hinter verdeckter Tafel schreibt Liste 1 bzw. Liste 2. Dann gemeinsamer Durchgang durch die Listen an der Tafel, evtl. Korrektur derselben, dann Korrektur der Partnerarbeits-Leistungen (S selbst).
Schwierigkeiten sind höchstens zu erwarten in Samiras Text : *My favourite hobby is going to the cinema*.
b) Auf der Tafelliste *gerund as object* können dann die Verben der Vorliebe und Abneigung mit Farbkreide hervorgehoben werden *(love, can't stand, like, enjoy, hate)*.
Der erreichte Bewusstseinsstand kann an dieser Stelle durch einen gemeinsamen Durchgang durch **Grammar** § 2/1, 2 (S 103) gefestigt und in Details ergänzt werden.

GR §2

2 What do you know about them?

Ziel: Übung des *gerund* als Subjekt.

Neu: *to agree*

Unterrichtsempfehlungen

Semantisierung: *to agree: to say 'yes' to s.th*. Die Übungen 2 und 3 stellen viel Sprachmaterial für alle S bereit. Vorschlag: L überträgt das Wortmaterial des grünen Kastens in Übung 3 auf Folie (Alternative: S übertragen sie auf die Mitteltafel), ergänzt durch die restlichen Beispiele aus den Sprechblasen oben *(find out about people from the past, take photos, repair things ...)*. Die Mitte bleibt frei. Diese dann mit den Adjektiven der Übung 2 überdecken (*overlay*-Folie) oder eintragen.

go to museums visit friends swim do homework ...	silly fun terrible easy great fantastic difficult	work in the garden dance read history books play the guitar

Aufgabe: Dialog mit dem Nachbarn:
S1: *Playing football is fantastic*.
S2: *No, it isn't, playing football is terrible. Skiing is fun*.
S1: *No, it isn't, skiing is too difficult. Dancing is easier*.
S2: ...

eigene Folien oder Tafelbild

WB S.9, B1

3 I like ...

Ziel: Übung des *gerund* als Objekt.

Unterrichtsempfehlungen

Dann neue *overlay*-Folie (oder an der Tafel ersetzen) mit den Verben *like, hate ...* von Übung 1b. Tafelbild etwa:

eigene Folien oder Tafelbild

go to museums visit friends dance swim do homework	love hate enjoy can't stand	work in the garden read history books play the guitar

Aufgabe: *Say what you (or Samira, or pupils ...) like or hate doing*. Dann zügiges, übungsdichtes Üben aller S im Plenum oder in Gruppenarbeit.

WB S.10, B2

Schülerbuch Seite 21

Step B Getting around

Ziel: das *gerund* nach Adjektiv + Präposition.

Neu: *to be interested in, clown, waiter, fly, soup, to be tired of s.th., Crown Jewels, crown*

Unterrichtsempfehlungen

Semantisierung: *to be interested in: to find s.th. interesting; clown* muß nicht semantisiert werden; *waiter: s.o. who works in a restaurant and brings you your drinks etc.; fly: a small dark insect; soup:* bekannt aus GL new 2, S. 56). *You eat it with a spoon from a plate or large cup, often before a meal; to be tired of s.th.:* (tired ist bekannt) *to find s.th. very boring; crown:* über *they are crowned* (Step A). Tafelzeichnung, Gestik; *Crown Jewels: the Queen's /King's crown and other expensive, rich things, like wonderful rings. You can see them in the Tower of London.*
L und S gehen gemeinsam die 3 *jokes* durch. Wichtig: der Motivationscharakter: Die neuen Vokabeln hier sind leicht und z.T. durch die S sofort selbst erschließbar. Daher eher eine Vokabeleinführung vermeiden und erst im kurzen Unterrichtsgespräch über die *boxes* beiläufig erläutern.
S identifizieren die *gerunds*. Diese werden an die Tafel geschrieben. Dazu: *What do we find in front of them?* Die S finden: *adjective plus preposition*. Diese vor die entsprechenden *gerunds* an die Tafel schreiben, durch Farbkreide hervorheben. Die S bilden dann einige Sätze analog, etwa: *Katrin is good at skiing. She is not interested in playing football ...* . Dann Übergang zu:

4 Doing things

Ziel: Festigung der Struktur *adjective + preposition + gerund*.

Neu: *to fill in s.th., Wembley Stadium,*

Unterrichtsempfehlungen

Semantisierung: *to fill in s.th.: to put s.th. in where there is nothing; Wembley Stadium: football stadium* im Nordwesten von London.
Zunächst individuell schriftlich anfertigen lassen, dann Verlesen im Plenum.

Lösungen: 1. good at reading 2. tired of seeing 3. good at remembering 4. interested in watching 5. tired of walking 6. interested in seeing

5 What are you good at?

Ziel: Weitere Festigung der Struktur in Übung 4.

Neu: *to paint*

Unterrichtsempfehlungen

Semantisierung: *to paint: to make a picture with colours*.
Alle S machen ihre eigenen 3 Listen (Vorschlag: auch in Hausarbeit). Dann übungsdichtes Verfahren: alle S bewegen sich frei im Raum (oder in Gruppenarbeit) und befragen einander im Sinne der Sprechblasen. Sie schreiben von 3–5 Mitschülern auf, was sie von ihnen erfahren haben. Dann sprechen sie im Plenum anhand ihrer Notizen über ihre Mitschüler. Etwa:

Miriam is | interested in | learning the gerund.
Amina is | good at | cooking porridge.

Zur Sicherung : Grammar § 3 (S. 104) gemeinsam studieren. Bewußtmachung und Überblick über die neu eingeführten Verwendungen durch ein Tafelbild, etwa

WB S.10, B3

WE USE THE GERUND AFTER ADJECTIVES AND PREPOSITIONS
I am | interested in | learning about people from the past.
We are | good at | understanding grammar problems.
         | tired of | singing this old song.

GR §3
WB S.10, B4
Tafelanschrieb

```
           AND
AS SUBJECT              AS OBJECT
Skiing    │ is very difficult.   I   │ enjoy │ learning about the
Playing   │ is great fun.        We  │ love  │ gerund.
football  │                          │ like  │ reading.
                                     │ hate
              THE GERUND
```

Step B Going out for a meal

Ziel: Adjektiv nach Verben der sinnlichen Wahrnehmung.
Neu: to go out for a meal, Murgh, to smell/smelt/smelt, hot

Unterrichtsempfehlungen

Semantisierung: <u>Murgh</u>: chicken in an Indian language; <u>to smell</u>: good food tastes good and it smells good; your nose says: I like this; <u>hot</u>: 'Hot' food can be cold, but if it tastes 'hot' you may need bread or rice, or something to drink with it. Deutsch: scharf.
Die Übung deutlich abgetrennt von den *gerund*-Übungen durchführen. Indische Restaurants waren wegen der Verbindung aus der Kolonialzeit viel eher in Großbritannien bekannt als in Deutschland. Die Küche variiert von mild bis sehr scharf.

6 What does it taste like?

Ziel: Übung der Struktur ‚Verb der sinnlichen Wahrnehmung + Adjektiv'.

Unterrichtsempfehlungen

Die S kennen seit langem das *pattern*-Verfahren wie hier vorgeschlagen. Sie bilden zur Übung viele Sätze aus dem *switchboard*.
Anschließend mit Hilfe des Strukturmusters im „Waschzettel" (Bewußtmachung) finden S das außergewöhnliche der Struktur (Adjektiv statt Adverb) – evtl. Einhilfe durch L: *Bob speaks angrily* danebensetzen – identifizieren dann die Verbart (Wahrnehmung durch unsere Sinne. L: *in English 'perception'*). Danach Regelformulierung, z.B.

GR §4

> AFTER VERBS OF PERCEPTION *(smell, look, taste ...)*
> WE USE AN ADJECTIVE,
> NOT AN ADVERB.

S nehmen anschließend den einleitenden Text *(Going out ...)* zur Kenntnis und identifizieren im Unterrichtsgespräch die neue Struktur noch einmal.

WB S.11, B5

Schülerbuch Seiten 22-23

Step C A trip to the British Museum

Ziel: Schulung des Lese- und Hörverstehens: *pre-, while and post-reading activities* durchführen.

Neu: to whisper, Pardon?, Cheer up!, all the way, afterwards, worksheet, to go inside, quite, mummy, Hurry up!, across, cyclist, to cross, to fall off s.th., front, to bend/bent/bent, along, to catch up with s.o., scarf/scarves, to act normal, to copy, husband, to notice

Unterrichtsempfehlungen

Semantisierung: <u>to whisper</u>: to speak very quietly; <u>Pardon?</u>: sorry, what did you say?; <u>Cheer up!</u>: forget your problem; <u>all the way</u>: the whole way; <u>afterwards</u>: after something has finished; <u>worksheet</u>: a piece of paper with exercises and questions on it; <u>to go inside</u>: to step in (*inside* ist bekannt); <u>quite</u>: almost; <u>mummy</u>: deutsch geben, bzw. mit den leicht verständlichen Wörtern versuchen wie: *Egypt, pyramid, kings and queens who died, lie for thousands of years ...*; <u>hurry up!</u>: be quick, we haven't got much time; <u>across, to cross</u>: you cross a road if you walk from one side to the other. If you do that you are walking across the road; <u>cyclist</u>: s.o. who rides his or her bike; <u>to fall off</u>: to fall from s.th. that you were on: to fall off a bike/a horse/ a wall; <u>front</u>: opposite of 'back' (front door, back door); <u>to bend</u>: to bend down ist bekannt. Hier: *a wheel is bent=* it is no longer really round; <u>along</u>: L macht vor: *walk along the classroom walls. You walk from one end to the other*; <u>to catch up with s.o.</u>: if you run behind s.o. and later come close to him or her (Gestik-Unterstützung oder Linien an der Tafel); <u>scarf</u> (pl. scarves): Realgegenstand mitbringen; <u>to act normal</u>: to do things like all the others do them; <u>to copy</u>: to write down s.th. that s.o. else has worked out, and then say it is your own work; <u>husband</u>: father is mother's husband in a family; <u>to notice</u>: to suddenly see.

Realie

Die Liste der unbekannten Vokabeln ist sehr lang. Daher Vorschlag: statt langer Semantisierung studieren die S 5 Minuten lang die Vokabelliste S. 127/128. L liest die Vokabeln dabei einmal deutlich vor. S versuchen sich so viele neue Wörter wie möglich einzuprägen. Evtl. daran anschließend ein kurzer, mündlicher Abfragedurchgang im Plenum *(How many do we remember in our class?)*

WB S.11, C1

a) *pre-reading activities:*
– *Is the British Museum an interesting or boring place? Find information about what you can see and do there.*
– *Is a trip to the British Museum a nice plan for Darren and Christoph? Explain.*

Text: L spielt den Text in Teilen (s. Text und CD-Tracks) vom Tonträger vor. Alternative: L liest selbst.

b) *while-reading activities:*
– Z. 1-10: Rollenspiel: S reden mit Darren über die Behandlung seines Gastes Christoph.
– Z. 10-15: S improvisieren ein Gespräch Katrin-Samira, ob sie zum Videospielen gehen – und ob sie Christoph mitnehmen.

WB S.12, C2

– Z. 15-30: Klasse erörtert Christophs Wahl, lieber mit den beiden Mädchen Videospielen zu gehen als ins Museum und diskutiert das Verhalten aller 3 Kinder (Freundlichkeit, Mitgefühl – Interesse am Museum; Verantwortlichkeit, Täuschung, billiges Interesse, Lernchancen ...)
– Z. 46-68 : Was halten wir vom Wegrennen Christophs und der Mädchen?
– Z. 69-77: *Copying from others. How do the other pupils probably feel when Samira asks them for their worksheets in order to copy them?*

c) *post-reading activities:*

1 What do you think?

Ziel: S führen eine Geschichte zu Ende.

Unterrichtsempfehlungen

Partnerarbeit oder Gruppenarbeit. Ergebnisse im Plenum vortragen.

2 How do they feel?

Ziel: Beantworten von Fragen zum Text im Unterrichtsgespräch.

Unterrichtsempfehlungen

L oder S verlesen die Fragen, Klasse beantwortet mündlich.

Schülerbuch Seite 24

3 Christoph's story

Ziel: Erstellen eines Dialogs

Unterrichtsempfehlungen

Vorschlag: in Partnerarbeit durchführen lassen, als Dialog dann vorlesen.

4 Listening practice: A visit to the British Museum

Ziel: Hörverstehen schulen und Informationen zum British Museum erarbeiten.

Neu: *checklist*

Text
Telephone information line:
Information about the British Museum:
The Museum is open Mondays to Saturdays from 10 in the morning to 5 in the afternoon.
It is not open on Sunday mornings. On Sunday the museum opens at 2.30 and closes at 6 in the evening.
The Museum is not open on Christmas Day.
The nearest underground stations are Holborn, Tottenham Court Road, Goodge Street and Russell Square. You can also get to the Museum by bus. The number 1, 14, 24, 68, 77 and 196 buses stop near the museum. Only numbers 77a and 77b run on Sundays.
You can buy books, postcards and other interesting things at the museum shop.
You may take photos in the Museum but please do not take photos of other people and do not use a video camera.
The museum snack bar is open from 10.30 to 4.30 every day from Monday to Saturday. On Sunday afternoons it is open from 3 to 5.15.
Thank you. If you need more information please call ...
(fade out)

Unterrichtsempfehlungen
checklist: *check*, *list* und *shopping-list* sind bekannt. Die S arbeiten allein, lesen die Fragen, präparieren die *checklist* und hören die Tonaufnahme. Lösungen dann im Plenum vergleichen.

Lösungen: *1. No 2. Yes 3. Yes 4. At the museum shop. 5. Yes, but not of other people. No video cameras. 6. In the Museum snack bar.*

Weitere *post-reading activities*:
– Welche Person ist dir am sympathischsten? Warum? (S schreiben Stichpunkte, dann Gespräch in Gruppenarbeit oder im Plenum.)
– Die S schreiben ein persönliches Urteil über die Geschichte bzw. über einen sie interessierenden Aspekt.
– Training der Lesekompetenz: L kopiert einen Textteil auf Folie und lässt dabei alle Vokale weg (außer, wenn ein Vokal ein Wort konstituiert: *I, a*). Die S rekonstruieren beim Lesen den Text. Ziel: Zügigkeit.

5 Sound practice

Ziel: Hör- und Schreibübung: *words that sound similar.*

Neu: *missing*

Unterrichtsempfehlungen
missing: *not there. Who is missing today?* Die S hören die Tonaufnahme (oder L-stimme) Satz für Satz und schreiben in Individualarbeit die Wörter auf. Ein S schreibt auf einer verdeckten Tafelseite. Dann Korrektur des Tafelbildes und der S-Leistungen.

Lösungen: *2. aunt, aren't 3. nose, knows 4. their, there 5. see, sea 6. hear, here 7. no, know 8. write, right 9. threw, through 10. read, red.*

6 London thoughts

Ziel: Üben der Struktur *verbs of perception + adjective.*

Unterrichtsempfehlungen
Zur Erreichung hoher Übungsdichte mit den wenigen Sätzen die Übung zunächst in Partnerarbeit machen lassen, dann Kontrolle im Plenum.

Lösungen: *1. taste 2. look 3. feels 4. smell 5. sounds 6. seem*

Schülerbuch Seite 25

Step D Let's check

1 London questions

Ziel: Festigung des *gerund* nach Verben der Vorliebe und Abneigung: *love, hate, enjoy, can't stand.*

Unterrichtsempfehlung
Diese Übung soll von allen S individuell gelöst und dann vom L kontrolliert werden. Aus dem *questionnaire* sind 24-30 Sätze möglich, dazu kommen noch einmal 6 durch die Zusatzfrage *What about you?* Die S sollten nicht überfordert werden. Vorschlag: Jeder S schreibt 6–10 Sätze in häuslicher Arbeit auf. Diese werden dann im Unterricht verlesen und schließlich noch viele andere hier mögliche mündlich durch möglichst viele S hinzugefügt.
Lösungen nach dem vorgegebenen Schema.

2 What are they good at?

Ziel: Festigung des *gerund* nach Adjektiv + Präposition. WB S.12, C1 / WB S.13, C2

Unterrichtsempfehlung
Die 4 Sätze schriftlich anfertigen und dann im Unterrichtsgespräch bei Bedarf korrigieren. Adjektive – Präpositionen – *gerunds* unterschiedlich farbig unterstreichen lassen.

Lösungen: *Darren is good at playing football, but he isn't good at taking photos.*
Katrin is good at skiing, but she isn't good at cooking.
Christoph is good at rowing, but he isn't good at running.
Samira is good at playing the piano, but she isn't good at painting pictures.

3 Travelling in London

Ziel: Wortschatzübung. WB S.13, C3

Unterrichtsempfehlungen
Die S führen die Übung jeweils abwechselnd in Partnerarbeit durch, damit möglichst viele von ihnen drankommen können. Jede(r) S sagt also 4 Sätze. Kurzer Abruf dann im Plenum.

Lösungen: *1. car 2. taxi 3. underground 4. street 5. flight 6. stops 7. line 8. bus.0*

Schülerbuch Seite 26

Workshop B Working with words

1 Understanding new words

Ziele: Die Aufgabe dieses Workshops ist es, verschiedene Techniken der Wortschatzarbeit exemplarisch vorzuführen, bewusst zu machen, und zu trainieren. Damit sollen S aus der öfters beobachtbaren Hilflosigkeit gegenüber unbekannten Wörtern herausgeführt werden, indem ihnen Strategien an die Hand gegeben werden, die sie in die Lage versetzen, unbekanntes Vokabular über verschiedene Wege und Kanäle zu erschließen.

1 Find the picture

Ziel: Einübung der Lesetechnik *reading for gist.*

Neu: *Sports Day, court, to compete in, to mend, goal-*

keeper, match, sportsfield, athletics, high jump, gym, jazz dance, rugby, to train, metre, to jog; Selby School

Unterrichtsempfehlungen

Semantisierung: Die im SB-Text nicht blau hervorgehobenen neuen Vokabeln *(match, metre, jogging)* bedürfen als *cognates* bzw. als in deutscher Form bekannte Wörter keiner Semantisierung.

S ordnen die vier Aussagen den Fotos zu. Danach sollte durch Nachfragen bei den S diese Erschließungstechnik bewusst gemacht werden: *How do you know? How did could you find out?* Beispielantwort: *Picture C goes with Darren, because I know football is his hobby. He uses the words 'football team' and 'football match'. In picture A we can see a football match.*

Lösungen: *Jackie McCarthy – photo D; Darren Taylor – photo A; Samira Sheikh – photo C; Lee Jones – photo B.*

2 Can you guess?

Ziel: Erschließung der Bedeutung unbekannter Vokabeln durch Hinweise aus dem Kontext und den Fotos.

Neu: *to guess, context*

Unterrichtsempfehlungen

Semantisierung: *to guess* + *context*: *If you don't know a word, you can look at the whole sentence and try to find out the meaning of the word. The sentences around this word are the context of the new word.*

Der Kasten mit den Tipps zur Lösung dieser Aufgabe führt an den Beispielen in den Sprechblasen vier Möglichkeiten zur Bedeutungserschließung vor.

Die Erklärungen der S mögen für die einzelnen blau markierten Wörter aus 1 unterschiedlich sein, doch dürfte die zweite Begründung der *tip-box (a word is like one in German)* am häufigsten als Erschließungshilfe gegeben werden, zumal die *items jazz dance, match, rugby, court* (als *Centre-Court*) und *jogging* als Lehnwörter aus dem Englischen bereits ihren Platz in der deutschen Sprache gefunden haben.

Die auf dieser Seite neu eingeführte Vokabel *match* kann als Anlass genommen werden, diese mit *game* zu kontrastieren:

game: allgemein: Spiel *game of cards*, im Sport als Sportart,

match: der einzelne Sportwettkampf. Bei *match* wird der Wettbewerbscharakter des Spiels betont.

Bei Interesse der S können noch die die anderen Sprungarten im Sport als *vocabulary items* eingeführt werden. Ihre Semantisierung ist durch einfache Strichmännchenzeichnungen möglich.

Hochsprung: *high jump*, Weitsprung: *long jump (AE broad jump)*, Dreisprung : *triple jump*, Stabhochsprung: *pole-vaulting.*

WB S.15, 1.1
WB S.15, 1.2

3 Listening practice: What's the situation?

Ziel: Einüben der parallelen Hörtechnik *listening for gist.*

Text

1.
Boy 1: Have you got the tickets, Pete?
Boy 2: Yeah, they're here, in my pocket.
Boy 1: Cor – this queue is worse than last Saturday. It goes on for miles.
Boy 2: Well, it's a big match this afternoon, isn't it?
Boy 1: It's a pity Kevin Lawson isn't playing today.
Boy 2: Yeah. He hurt his leg after that foul by Thatcher last week.
Boy 1: Yes, he needs a knee operation now. Anyway, Steve Jobson isn't a bad goalkeeper. We've still got a chance.
Boy 2: Of course, we have!
Boy 1: When's the kick-off – 2.30?
Boy 2: Yeah. 2.30!

2.
Girl 1: That was boring. It didn't scare me one little bit. What about you? You look as white as a sheet.
Girl 2: Well, I didn't like it when that ghost cut the man's head off. All that blood! Yuk!
Girl 1: It was only tomato ketchup! Come on, let's get some hot dogs – I'm starving! Then we can have another go on the dodgems.
Girl 2 (feebly): Do you really want to? I'm feeling a bit sick after all those rides.

3.
Girl: Excuse me. There are some skates in the window. Can I try them on, please?
Shop assistant: Yes, of course. Which ones do you want?
Girl: I'll show you. Look, there they are. The ones at the front.
Shop assistant: The roller skates? The ones in front of the golf clubs?
Girl: No, sorry, the ice skates. See? They're on the right, next to that squash racket.
Shop assistant: Oh, those. I'll get them for you. Just a minute.

Unterrichtsempfehlungen

Es empfiehlt sich eine zweimalige Darbietung des Hörtexts. Die erste Darbietung sollte ohne große Einführung *(Just listen and try to understand as much as possible.)* bei geschlossenem Buch erfolgen. Danach werden die Schüler mit der Aufgabenstellung in b) vertraut gemacht. Bei der Besprechung der Lösungen kann nochmals auf die Verständnishilfen aus dem Kontext eingegangen werden. 1. *tickets – queue – big match – goalkeeper – kick-off* 2. *scare – ghost – blood – hot dogs – dodgems – rides* 3. *skates – window – try on.*

Lösungen: b) *1. They're standing in a queue in front of a football field/stadium. They're going to watch a match. 2. Two girls are at a fair and have just had a ride on the ghost train. They're going to get some hot dogs after that. 3. A girl is in a sports shop. She asks the assistant if she can try on some ice skates from the shop window.*

WB S.15, 1.3

Schülerbuch Seite 27

2 Organizing words

Ziel: Der zweite Teil von *Workshop B* will anhand eines semi-authentischen Textes aufzeigen, wie das individuelle (Er)Arbeiten mit einem Vokabelheft (oder auch einer Vokabelkartei) organisert werden kann.

Neu: *express, national, pitch, to weigh, kilo, tall, size, to tackle, to move, second, past, opponent; New Zealand, Tonga, All Blacks, World Cup, South Africa*

Unterrichtsempfehlungen

Die Aufgabenstellung bezieht den zugehörigen Vokabelteil auf Seite 130/131 mit ein, so dass ein Semantisieren der neuen Vokabeln nicht notwendig ist. Ein stilles „Erlesen" des Textes in Partnerarbeit (ein S mit aufgeschlagenem Vokabelteil, sein Partner oder seine Partnerin mit aufgeschlagenem Text) bereitet die Folgeaufgabe vor.

Vocabulary S. 130f.

WB S.16, 2.1

1 Collecting and organizing words

Ziel: Vorführung der verschiedenen Möglichkeiten, neues Vokabular z.B. im Vokabelheft zu notieren.

Neu : *vocabulary*

Unterrichtsempfehlungen

Der Kasten mit den Tipps führt fünf verschiedene Möglichkeiten vor, neue Vokabeln zu notieren. Damit könnte von L der Hinweis verbunden sein, dass derartige Einträge in ein Vokabelheft (oder eine Lernkartei) eine bessere Lernhilfe darstellen, wenn der einzelne Lerner

WB S.16, 2.2

erkannt hat, welche Art der Eintragung für ihn die beste und hilfreichste ist.
Der Tipp-Kasten führt folgende Möglichkeiten vor:
1. Wortgleichung englisch – deutsch
2. Erklärung durch *synonym* (=)
3. Erklärung durch Beispielsatz
4. *opposite* ↔
5. Bild.
Die Arbeit mit dem Vokabelteil kann dazu noch zum Anlass genommen werden, die Wörterbucharbeit des folgenden Schuljahrs vorzubereiten, indem auf die Abkürzungen und Zeichen auf S. 118 hingewiesen und ihre Funktion als sinnvolle zusätzliche Informationsträger verdeutlicht wird.

2 Your turn – Writing about a person

Ziel: Schreiben über eine Person, Darstellung von Themen eigenen Interesses in der Fremdsprache.

Neu: *star, fact*

Unterrichtsempfehlungen
Diese Aufgabe stellt ein kleines handlungsorientiertes Projekt dar und ist wegen der nötigen Zeit für die häusliche Vorbereitung durch S längerfristig angelegt. Gerade für leistungsstärkere Schüler ist diese Aufgabe eine Herausforderung. Weniger leistungsstarke S oder scheue S, denen die persönliche Darbietung vor der Klasse weniger liegt, können stattdessen ein Poster mit englischem Text über ihren Star an die Wand des Klassenzimmers hängen und so in überlegene Konkurrenz – da selbst hergestellt – zu den doch eintönigen Star-Postern aus den Musikzeitschriften für Jugendliche treten. Dabei kann der Star aus Sport, Unterhaltung oder einem anderen Bereich kommen.

Bildfolie 8

3 Word banks

Ziel: a) Sammeln und Ordnen von Vokabular eines Wortfelds mit Unterkategorien.
b) Spielerisches Sammeln von bereits bekanntem Vokabular zu verschiedenen Wortfeldern.

WB S.16, 2.3

Neu: *event, board*

Unterrichtsempfehlungen
Lösungen a): (Die Lösungen berücksichtigen die Vokabeln bis einchl. Teil 2 des Workshops)
<u>sports:</u> football, athletics, badminton, climbing, cricket, high jump, jazz dance, rugby, tennis, table tennis
<u>places:</u> pitch, court, gym, ice rink, playground, swimming pool, riding school, sports centre, sportsfield
<u>people:</u> player, club, cyclist, dancer, fan, goalkeeper, kid, member, non-swimmer, queue, skater, swimmer, team
<u>things:</u> ball, bike, cup, goal, helmet, skates, skateboard, swimming things, ticket, trainers
<u>events:</u> match, accident, activity, competition, game, jump, PE, practice, race
<u>verbs:</u> to play, to cancel, to clap, to cycle, to be fun, to have fun, to give s.th. up, to go swimming, to jog, to jump, to lose, to practise, to row, to shout, to start, to tackle, to train, to trip
b) In größeren Klassen kann die Spielanweisung variiert werden, indem daraus eine Art Kettenübung gemacht wird, bei der 6–8 Gruppen jeweils ca. 20 Sekunden Zeit bekommen, ein zum jeweiligen Wortfeld gehörendes *vocabulary item* zu benennen.

Schülerbuch Seite 28

4 Word partners

Ziel: Festigungsübung von Kollokationen zur Vermei-
dung von Interferenz-Fehlern zur deutschen Entsprechung „machen".

Unterrichtsempfehlungen
Bei Bedarf kann nach der Lösung die Aufgabenstellung noch erweitert werden, z.B. durch eine Wendung mit *have*, die auch einer Wendung mit „machen" entspricht. *(to have a break).* Dabei kann auf die verschiedenen deutschen Entsprechungen der bekannten Wendungen mit *have* eingegangen werden:

WB S.17, 2.4

to *have a bath/...*	ein Bad nehmen
to *have fun*	Spaß haben
to *have a look*	sich etw. ansehen
to *have on*	(Kleidung) anhaben
to *have a ride on the dodgems*	Boxauto/Autoskooter fahren
to *have breakfast/tea/...*	frühstücken / ...

Lösungen: <u>to make</u>: *a cake, a mistake, a request, a plan, a cup of tea. sandwiches, money, a poster*
<u>to do</u>: *homework, nothing, athletics, the washing-up, a test, an exercise, housework,*

5 Verbs with prepositions

Ziel: Festigung von bekannten *phrasal verbs*.

WB S.17, 2.5
WB S.17, 2.6

Unterrichtsempfehlungen
Die Aufgabenstellung macht deutlich, dass es hier um die Beschreibung von Einzelbildern geht *(present progressive),* wobei möglichst viele bereits bekannte *phrasal verbs* zum Einsatz kommen sollten. In einem zweiten Durchgang kann dann die Aufgabenform gewechselt werden: *Samira explains what the other children must do in that crazy race. (simple present: First ..., then ..., after that ...)* Die nicht verwendeten Verben lassen sich im alphabetischen Verzeichnis aufsuchen und prüfen.

Lösungsmöglichkeit: *1. The teams are putting on funny costumes. 2. One child is picking up a racket, the other child is getting on a skateboard. 3. The child with the racket is pulling the child on the skateboard. One child is falling off the skateboard. The other team is coming to some buckets. 4. The children are putting down the rackets and skateboards and picking up a bucket of water. 5. They are running on the flowerpots to the finishing line. They are taking off their costumes at the finishing line.*

6 ⟨Just for fun⟩

Ziel: Fun element,

Neu: *to try harder, cup*

Unterrichtsempfehlungen
Das Erzählen des Witzes *(One fly says to the other fly: ...)* wird mit dem Hinweis verbunden, dass ein englisches Wort durchaus zwei verschiedene Bedeutungen im Deutschen haben kann. (Weiteres Beispiel: *letter:* Brief; Buchstabe). Damit ist zugleich eine Überleitung zum dritten Teil des Workshops möglich, dessen Einleitungstext genau das umgekehrte Phänomen (ein Wort im Deutschen – mehrere Wörter im Englischen) thematisiert.

Schülerbuch Seite 29

3 Saying things in different ways

Ziel: Bewusstmachung des Phänomens, dass es für ein deutsches Wort mehrere, nicht austauschbare englische Entsprechungen gibt.

Neu: *racket, bat, string, hockey stick*

Unterrichtsempfehlungen
Semantisierung: Einzelne Anhänger der drei Sportarten aus der Klasse können ihre „Schläger" mit in den Unterricht bringen. Alternative: Illustrationen im Vokabelteil auf S. 131.

Vocabulary
S. 131

1 In other words

Ziel: Vorführung von vier Verfahren, andern unbekannte Vokabeln auf englisch zu erklären.

Unterrichtsempfehlungen

a) Die drei Erklärungsmöglichkeiten, die hier benutzt werden, lehnen sich eng an die bisher im Vokabelteil verwendeten Symbole an. Das mögliche Tafelbild könnte diese Symbole als Kurzzeichen verwenden und so für einen zweiten Durchgang dieser Übung genutzt werden, da die Kurzzeichen in Sprache umgesetzt werden müssen:

... is the opposite of : ↔
... is a kind of : ≈ ((Doppeltes Ungefährzeichen))
... means the same as: =

WB S.18, 3.1

			Tafelanschrieb
fast, to win, big	↔	slow, to lose, small	
helmet, pitch, gym, kilt, to jog, racket	≈	hat, sportsfield, sports room, skirt, to run, bat	
to cycle, match, to practise	=	to ride a bike, competition, to train	

Lösungsvorschlag: (Andere Zuordnungen sind durchaus möglich)

2 Listening practice: What does it mean?

Ziel: Erschließung der Bedeutung unbekannter Vokabeln durch gehörte Umschreibungen und Erklärungen, Training der Technik des *note-taking*.

Neu: *changing room, referee, to dive*

Text

1.
Katrin: Mrs Grant said that we should meet in the changing room. What's that?
Samira: It's in the gym.
Katrin: And what do you do there?
Samira: You change your clothes.
Katrin: Oh, I see.
2.
Boy 1: I'm going to be the referee at the match next week.
Katrin: Referee? What's that?
Boy 1: It's a kind of player ...
Girl: But he doesn't really play, he watches the others.
Boy 1: He checks that the players keep the rules and in football matches he usually wears black.
Katrin: Oh, now I understand.
3.
Samira: Do you like diving at the swimming pool?
Katrin: Diving? What does that mean?
Samira: 'To dive' means to jump into the water.
Katrin: Ah, so it's like 'springen'.
Samira: But you don't jump with your feet first, your head and arms go in the water first.
Katrin: OK. Yes, I like diving.

Unterrichtsempfehlungen

Nach Hinweis auf die Aufgabenstellung im Schülerbuch sollten die Schüler ihre Übungshefte entsprechend vorbereiten, dass sie während der Darbietungen des Hörtexts zu jeder der drei unbekannten Vokabeln entsprechende Notizen machen können. Eine Semantisierung der unbekannten Vokabeln ist nicht im Sinne der Aufgabenstellung. Nach der Besprechung der Lösungen kann noch darauf eingegangen werden, dass *to dive* noch eine zweite Bedeutung besitzt (s. **Vocabulary** S. 131).

Vocabulary S: 131
WB S.18, 3.2

Lösungen: *1. A changing room is a room where you change your clothes. 2. A referee watches the players during a match. He checks that they keep the rules. In football matches he usually wears black. 3. To dive is to jump into the water. But your head and arms go into the water first.*

3 ⟨A song⟩

Ziel: Genaueres Erschließen des Textes eines an sich bekannten Liedes

Neu: *champion, dues (pl.), time after time, to do one's sentence, to commit a crime, to do one's sentence, share, to keep on doing s.th., till, loser, 'cause, I've taken my bows, curtain, I've taken my curtain calls, fame, fortune, rose, pleasure cruise, to consider, challenge, human race, I ain't gonna lose, refrain*

Unterrichtsempfehlungen

Die Erschließung des Liedtextes mit Hilfe des Vokabelverzeichnisses kann auch als vorbereitende Hausaufgabe gestellt werden. Diese Aufgabenstellung an sich kommt der Interessenlage der Schüler sehr entgegen, da sie in ihrer Freizeit sich oft aus eigenem Interesse der gleichen Aufgabe stellen. Als Unterschied dazu könnte bei der Besprechung herauskommen, dass diese private Wörterbucharbeit wesentlich mühsamer ist, da nicht gleich die erstgenannte Bedeutung im Wörterbuch eine sinnvolle Übertragung ins Deutsche ermöglicht. Oft kommen auch Wendungen vor, die in dieser Form gar nicht im Lexikon zu finden sind. Ein Beispiel in diesem Lied findet sich in Zeile 3 der 1. Strophe mit dem Satz *I've done my sentence* – ich habe meine Strafe „abgesessen", wo man normalerweise *to serve a (prison) sentence* erwarten würde. Inhaltlich ist das Lied sicherlich nicht allein oder gar in erster Linie auf Sport bezogen, sondern benutzt dieses Bild, um allgemein über das Bedürfnis zu sprechen, sich im Leben durchzusetzen. Gliederung: *The past: hard work, mistakes and problems. Refrain: go on training, working. Winning: fame and money, but hard work again to stay champions.*

Schülerbuch Seite 30

4 Words in grammar

(a)

Ziel: Einführung der *reflexive and reciprocal pronouns*.

Neu: *myself, yourself, himself, herself, itself, ourselves, yourselves, themselves*

Unterrichtsempfehlungen

Die Präsentation über die Bilderleiste kann durch die Heranziehung von §§ 5 und 6 des Grammatikteils ergänzt werden. Die Pluralformen der Reflexivpronomen lassen sich durch Analogiebildung zu den Sonderpluralen *-ves* wie z.B. in *knife – knives* plausibel machen.

1 Reflexive verbs

Ziel: Einübung der *reflexive pronouns* und des *reciprocal pronoun*.

Neu: *reflexive*

Unterrichtsempfehlungen

Vorschlag für Tafelbild / Lernposter zur evtl. nötigen Verdeutlichung kann aus den Illustrationen aus § 6 abgeleitet werden (Die Pfeile symbolisieren den Regelwortlaut):

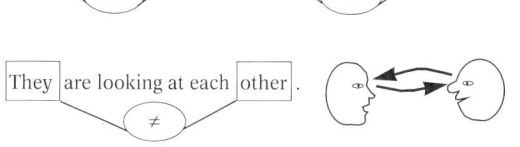

GR § 6

He is looking at her. ≠ They are looking at themselves. =

They are looking at each other. ≠

Lösungen: *1. themselves 2. each other 3. themselves 4. themselves 5. each other 6. himself – each other 7. herself 8. myself*

b

Ziel: Unterschiedliche Häufigkeit des Gebrauchs des Reflexivpronomens im Englischen und Deutschen.

Neu: *to concentrate, to scream*

Unterrichtsempfehlungen

Nach der textsortenentsprechenden Einführung des Textes als Stilllektüre übersetzen die S den Text. Dabei kann in zwei Spalten die unterschiedliche Häufigkeit des Reflexivpronomens an der Tafel festgehalten werden: Tafelbildvorschlag: *Tafelanschrieb*

reflexives Verb nur im Deutschen	
to meet	sich treffen
to feel (nervous / ... / ...)	sich ... fühlen
to concentrate	sich konzentrieren

Die Heranziehung des Tipps auf der gleichen Seite und § 5 des Grammatikteils können diese Tabelle vervollständigen. Diese sollte als Hausaufgabe auswendig gelernt werden. *GR § 5 WB S.18, 4.1*

2 Watch out: -self/ -selves or nothing

Ziel: Überprüfung der auf dieser Seite erworbenen Kenntnisse. *WB S.18, 4.2*

Unterrichtsempfehlungen

Die Aufgabe ist auch als Hausaufgabe möglich.

Lösungen: *1. – 2. yourself 3. myself 4. – 5. herself 6. ourselves 7. –*

Schülerbuch Seite 31

5 Word building

Ziel: Kenntnis einzelner Wortbausteine und Training der Möglichkeit, an sich unbekannte Ableitungsformen zu erkennen, zu nutzen und anzuwenden und so den verfügbaren Wortschatz stark zu erweitern.

Neu: *word building, newspaper, article, thief, bench, ground, Ms, careless, helpful; Elf Row, Shadwell, East Cheam*

Unterrichtsempfehlungen

Bei diesem Text empfiehlt es sich, ihn textsortengerecht still erlesen zu lassen. Eine ausführliche Semantisierung jedes neuen *vocabulary items* sollte unterbleiben. Einzig und allein *bench* ließe sich durch eine Strichzeichnung (s. **Vocabulary** S. 132) semantisieren.
Bei einem zweiten Durchgang könnte auf folgende Einzelheiten eingegangen werden: *Vocabulary S. 132*
thief → plural : *thieves*; dt. „Bank" = engl. 1. *bank* 2. *bench*
<u>Ms:</u> Kontrastierung mit *Miss* und *Mrs*: *You use Ms – especially in written English – when you can't or don't want to say if a woman is married or not.* Ein Verweis auf den anderen Gebrauch im Deutschen könnte als interkultureller Hinweis dies abschließen.

1 Looking at English

Ziel: Kennenlernen der Suffixe *-ful* und *-less* in ihrer Grundbedeutung.

Unterrichtsempfehlungen

Die vier im Text vorkommenden Adjektive lassen sich durch die Gegenteil-Formen *useless* und *helpless* erweitern und so die Folgeübung vorbereiten.
Eine vertiefte Betrachtungsmöglichkeit stellt die abschließende Übertragung ins Deutsche dar. Ein Ergebnis könnte die Erkenntnis sein, dass die unten in eckigen Klammern angegebene Bedeutung nur eine Grundbedeutung ist und im Deutschen verschiedene Suffixe möglich sind.

careless – sorglos, unachtsam   *careful* – sorgsam, sorgfältig
useless – nutzlos, unnütz   *useful* – nützlich, brauchbar
helpless – hilflos,   *helpful* – hilfreich, hilfsbereit

Lösungen: *useful, careful, helpful   careless*   *Tafelanschrieb*
   suffix -ful   suffix -less
   [WITH]   [WITHOUT]

2 Word endings

Ziel: Anwendung der Suffix-Formen *-ful* und *-less* bei der Wortbildung von Adjektiven.

Neu: *helpless, useless, sleepless*

Unterrichtsempfehlungen

Die Lösung von Satz Nr. 6 könnte zum Anlass genommen werden, S darauf aufmerksam zu machen, dass nicht immer beide Suffix-Formen beim gleichen Ausgangsverb möglich sind und dass diese Suffixe auch mit Substantiven kombinierbar sind. Beispiele: *WB S.19, 5.1*
meaningful, meaningless, beautiful (Rechtschreibung!), *timeless, lawless, lawful*

Lösungen: *1. useful 2. helpless 3. careless 4. useless 5. careful 6. sleepless 7. helpful*

3 Making nouns

Ziel: Suffix *-er* als Wortbaustein.

Neu: *worker, rider, runner, learner, swimmer, dancer, writer, reader*

Unterrichtsempfehlungen

Die Ähnlichkeit dieses Wortbildungsphänomens mit dem Deutschen macht eine Einführung problemlos. Auf die Besonderheiten bei der Rechtschreibung macht Monny aufmerksam: *winner, runner, swimmer*. Des weiteren ist auf den Wegfall des stummen *e* bei *rider, writer, dancer, driver* hinzuweisen. (Die dt. Entsprechung von *learner* war bis vor wenigen Jahren als terminus technicus auf die Sprachwissenschaft beschränkt.) Als Erweiterungsmöglichkeit bietet es sich an, weitere Verben suchen zu lassen, die ebenfalls nach der Regel *verb + er = person* den bekannten Wortschatz erweitern. Beispiele: *to teach, to review, to send, to lose etc.* *WB S.19, 5.2 WB S.20, 5.3 WB S.20, 5.4*
Als Vertiefungsmöglichkeiten kann auf die leichte Bedeutungsverschiebung bei *to wait – waiter* und auf die lat. Endung *-or* bei *doctor* und *actor* hingewiesen werden. Des weiteren könnten Ausnahmen bei dieser Art Wortbildung wie bei *folder, football player* vs. *CD player, (food) mixer etc.* zur Sprache kommen, bei denen nicht immer eine Person gemeint ist.

Lösungen: *reader, worker, rider, learner, writer, runner, driver, swimmer, dancer*

4 Adjectives from verbs

Ziel: Bildung von Adjektiven mit dem Suffix *-able*.

Neu: *washable, washing machine, breakable, understandable, readable, changeable*

Unterrichtsempfehlungen

Zusätzlich zu den Hinweisen im Schülerbuch können die dt. Übersetzungen der gefundenen Adjektive verdeutlichen, dass nicht nur die dt. Nachsilbe *-bar* diesem engl. Suffix entspricht (*breakable* – zerbrechlich, *changeable* – wechselhaft). Bei den Lösungen sollte auf die Beibehaltung des stummen *e* bei *changeable* hingewiesen werden. *WB S.20, 5,5*

Lösungen: *1. breakable 2. changeable 3. understandable 4. readable*

Schülerbuch Seite 32

Unit 2 Trouble at school

Step A The video conference
Ziel: Erweiterung des aus Band 2 *(Unit 1)* bekannten Themas und Wiederholung des Wortfelds ‚Schule'.

1 Questions and answers
Ziel: Zuordnung von Fragen und Antworten.

Neu: *trouble, conference course, in town, library, detention, packed lunch*

Unterrichtsempfehlungen
Semantisierungshinweise: <u>trouble</u>: *problems;* <u>conference</u>: *A conference is a meeting of people where they talk about things and problems. At a video conference these people aren't in the same room. Here a class in Karlsruhe is talking with pupils from a German class (= course) at Haywood School about school life in Britain;* <u>in town</u>: *in the city centre;* <u>library</u>: *room or building where you can read books;* <u>packed lunch</u>: *sandwiches for lunch time in a lunch box;* <u>detention</u>: kleine Tafelskizze. Gesicht hinter Gefängnisgittern.
Die Lösung der Aufgabe a) sollte durch die Besprechung des Tipps am oberen Rand der Seite vorbereitet werden. Nach dem (in Partnerarbeit möglichen) Herausfinden der Frage-Antwort-Paare können die Fragen mit der jeweils richtigen Antwort partnerweise vorgelesen werden. Die Aufgabe b) frischt das aus Band 2 bekannte Wortfeld ‚Schule' auf. Die in der Aufgabe geforderte Liste kann sich u.U. auf die Unterschiede zum deutschen oder lokalen Schulleben beschränken, z.B.: *What's different at Haywood School? What can you remember?*

Lösungen: a) *Paul – Emma, Sebastian – Wayne, Leonie – David, Daniel – Becky, Amelie – Edward, Anna – Sarah, Markus – Robert*
b) *Subjects: Technology, Drama, Science, Humanities (= History + Geography)*
Activities: piano lessons, guitar lessons, sports (cricket, badminton, table tennis), clubs: table tennis, bird watchers, climbing, computer club, drama group
And: no school on Saturdays, only activities sometimes, lunch in the canteen, school uniform, 3 terms

Schülerbuch Seite 33

2 Karlsruhe questions
Ziel: Partnerarbeit: Stellen von Fragen zu vorgegebenen Antworten. Transferaufgabe: Beschreiben des deutschen Schullebens.

Neu: *e-mail = electronic mail, exam, to test s.b. on s.th, primary school, secondary school, comprehensive, to take an exam, GCSE = General Certificate of Secondary Education, 'A' level, mark, special help, to repeat a year, grammar school, boarding school*

Unterrichtsempfehlungen
Semantisierung: <u>e-mail</u> = *electronic mail. You can send messages from one computer to another.*
Es empfiehlt sich, die weiteren neuen Vokabeln in den Antworten aus Nottingham in einer anderen Bündelung erklärend als Tafelbild zu präsentieren. Der kleine Mark Penrose kann hierbei als Beispielschüler dienen.
Which school did Mark go to first? ...

SCHOOLS in ENGLAND and WALES

STATE SCHOOLS

| **nursery school** 2-5 years | **primary school** 5-11 years |

secondary school (11- 16/18 years)
Most secondary schools are **comprehensive**, a few (app. 3%) are secondary modern and 4% are secondary **grammar** schools
There are a few state **boarding** schools but most are day schools and most are mixed (girls and boys).

PRIVATE SCHOOLS (independent schools)
Of the 26,441 schools in England and Wales in 1995, 2,325 were independent.

prep(aratory) school 7-13 years (boarding and day schools)

Independent schools (13-18)
Some private schools are called **"public schools"**. Many are for boys or girls only. Some boys' schools let girls into the "sixth form" (the last two years). Some of these schools are boarding schools which also take day pupils. Many are day schools.

SCHOOLS in SCOTLAND and NORTHERN IRELAND
Both have their own school system and exams.

EXAMS
There are national tests at intervals in primary and secondary school and public exams at 16 and 18:
GCSE exams → 'A'-Level (in 2 or 3 subjects) after 2 years (AS level after one year also possible).
Schools may set internal tests and exams as they like and usually do so every year for all pupils.

BAD EXAMS = BAD MARKS: special help by teachers, pupils can go on to next year, needn't do a year again = repeat a year.

Im Anschluss daran können die Schüler (in Partnerarbeit) die Antworten des *e-mail*-Briefs lesen und die dazugehörigen Fragen schriftlich festhalten. Die als Abschluss vorgesehene Transferaufgabe kann als Hausaufgabe (auch in normaler Briefform an eine Brieffreundin oder an einen Brieffreund) erfolgen. Dabei sollten sich die S an den Satzstrukturen der abgedruckten *e-mail*-Antworten orientieren. Die Beschreibung des deutschen Schulwesens hängt von den örtlichen/regionalen Gegebenheiten ab. Diese Aufgabenstellung kann auch erst nach der Behandlung der nachfolgenden Übung 3 schriftlich erledigt werden.
Auf eine Übersetzung der Bezeichnungen für die deutschen Schularten im Sekundarbereich sollte verzichtet werden.
Landeskundlicher Hinweis: Anders als bei den deutschen Schulabschlüssen wie Abitur und Mittlere Reife wird der britische Abschluss GCSE in jeweils einzelnen Fächern erworben *(I've got a GCSE in Maths. / I'm going to take my GCSEs next year.)* 'A'- Level steht für *Advanced Level*.

Lösungsmöglichkeiten: *A: Do you do all your subjects*

together? B: Do you have tests during the term? / How many tests do you have during the term? C: When do children in Britain start school? D: What exams do you take? When? E: How much time do you spend on homework? F: What happens if pupils get bad marks in the exams (at the end of the term)? G: Are there any other secondary schools?

3 Right or wrong

Ziel: *Reading for details / testing knowledge of everyday life in British schools.*

Unterrichtsempfehlungen

Die Bearbeitung dieser Aufgabe kann auch als schriftliche Hausaufgabe erfolgen. Bei der Besprechung der Lösung für Aussage 6. kann als ergänzender Aspekt die Information über die Privatschulen *(independent schools)* in Großbritannien eingeflochten werden. Berühmte und oft sehr alte Schulen dieser Art sind King's School in Canterbury (gegr. 600), Winchester (1394), Eton (1440), ferner beispielsweise in Harrow (1571), Rugby (1567), Westminster (1560). Für Mädchen: Cheltenham Ladies' College (1853), The Red Maids' School, Bristol (1634), North London Collegiate School (1850). Interessant sind villeicht auch die Kosten: *"annual boarding fee"* in Eton 1996 war £13,410, Rugby £13,290, für Tagesschüler £10,440 im Jahr.

Lösungsvorschläge: Die Aussagen 2, 5 und 7 sind richtig. *1. Children in Britain go to primary school for six years. 3. Pupils don't have to / needn't repeat the year if they get bad marks in the exams. 4. Children are allowed to take sandwiches for lunch. (Or they can have lunch in the canteen.) 6. Not all secondary schools are comprehensives. (There are grammar schools and boarding schools, too.)*

4 ⟨Just for fun⟩

Ziel: *fun*-Element zur Auflockerung.

Neu: *to be excused, brain*

Unterrichtsempfehlungen

Die Frage *May I be excused?* ließe sich am besten mit „Darf ich mal raus?" übertragen.

Schülerbuch Seite 34

5 Sound practice

Ziel: Bedeutungsunterscheidung zwischen Wörtern mit langem und kurzem i: [ɪ] / [iː]

Unterrichtsempfehlungen

Die nur auf den ersten Blick banal erscheinende Unterscheidungsübung sollte die S dazu anregen, präzise zwischen langen und kurzen Vokalen zu differenzieren, bzw. bei Diktaten genau darauf zu achten.

Lösungen: [ɪ]: *sit, will, chip, this, it his, live*
[iː]: *seat, we'll, cheap, these, eat, he's, leave*

6 Edward's report

Ziel: Landeskunde: Kennenlernen eines britischen *school report.*

Neu: *school report, comment, to do well, to be pleased with, progress, experiment, lazy, interest in s.th., project, to put work into s.th., to get better, weak; St. John's School for Boys*

Unterrichtsempfehlungen

Eine Alternative bei der Behandlung ist der Einstieg über die bewusst unvollständige Notenskala am unteren rechten Ende der Seite *(A = very good, E = very bad = very weak // B is good, C is not so good, D is weak)*, um dann als nächstes nur die Fächer und die erteilten Fachnoten zu betrachten.

(Wenn das Zeugnis auf eine OHP-Folie kopiert wurde, *eigene Folie* lässt sich der Kommentarteil abdecken und später bei der Semantisierung/Besprechung der Lehrerkommentare schrittweise aufdecken. Die Umsetzung der Buchstaben-Noten in leistungsbeurteilende Adjektive ist eine schulinterne Angelegenheit, z. B: *C= fair/average, D = satisfactory, E = very weak/poor;* dazu kommen noch manchmal *unsatisfactory, unclassified, incomplete.*

What is Edward's favourite subject – probably? Which subjects is he good at? In which subject did he get the worst mark? ...

Danach wird für die S neu sein, dass jeder Fachlehrer die Leistungen kommentieren kann.
Semantisierungshinweise: <u>to be (very) pleased with:</u> *to like very much;* <u>progress:</u> *getting better and better* (s.a. Hinweis im *unit*-begleitenden Vokabular); <u>lazy:</u> *Edward is lazy = he doesn't want to do anything in R.E.;* <u>(have / show) interest in:</u> *to be interested in.*

Die Aufgabe a) schließt diese Betrachtungen ab. Dabei können die Schülerantworten stichwortartig in einer zweispaltigen Tabelle an der Tafel festgehalten werden. Daran vorgenommene Tilgungen ermöglichen gerade in großen Klassen einen zweiten Durchgang. Die Aufgabe b) kann auch als schriftliche Hausaufgabe gestellt werden. Dabei kann eine Wortfeldsammlung von Wendungen aus den Lehrerkommentaren als Vorbereitung dienen. Tafelbildvorschlag:

Comments for good pupils
learn easily, do (very) well in tests, have interesting ideas, enjoy one's work, be good at..., be (very) pleased with ..., put a lot of work into ...,

Comments for not so good pupils
could do better, not work hard enough, should try to ..., be (very) careless with ..., be (too) lazy, should show more interest in ..., do badly in ..., not like ..., must try harder, make some progress, get better

Schülerbuch Seite 35

Step B The new boy

Ziel: Einführung der *defining relative clauses.*

Neu: *show-off, Dracula*

Unterrichtsempfehlungen

Ein Blick auf die Sprachwirklichkeit macht deutlich, dass bei bestimmten Relativsätzen (auch: notwendige Relativsätze/*defining relative clauses*) der Satztyp ohne Relativpronomen *(contact clause)* häufiger vorkommt als der Satztyp mit Relativpronomen. Dies legt den methodischen Schritt nahe, mit den *contact clauses* zu beginnen und die Verwendung des Relativpronomens bei jenen Relativsätzen einzuführen, bei denen der Gebrauch der Pronomen grammatisch notwendig ist, d.h. bei Relativsätzen, in denen das Relativpronomen das Subjekt des Relativsatzes darstellt. (S.a. Grammatik § 7). *GR § 7*
Nach der Darbietung des Textes vom Tonträger sollten die S vor dem eigenen Lesen des Dialogs auf die Intonation der Sätze mit Relativsätzen hingewiesen werden. Die fehlenden Kommas und die fehlenden Sprechpausen könnten u.U. eine Lesefalle darstellen.
Der Merkzettel stellt an zwei Beispielen die Entstehung dieser komplexen Satzstruktur dar. Dabei dürften die ggf. im Deutschunterricht vermittelten Kenntnisse über den Relativsatz als ein an einem Substantiv eingehängtes Attribut – deshalb auch Attributsatz genannt – hilfreich sein. Bei dieser Darstellung werden S gleich erkennen, dass hier das Englische ohne Relativpronomen auskommen kann.
An der Tafel können dann die weiteren Sätze aus dem Präsentationstext herausgeschrieben werden. (Alternative: vorbereitete OHP-Folie). Dabei bietet sich folgende

Präsentation als Alternative an:
We all know about

	the horse	he got for his birthday.
	the house	he lives in.
	the countries	his mum and dad have lived in.
	the famous people	they know.
The photos		they took in China were great.

1 The photos everyone saw

Ziel: a) *Matching clauses*, Überprüfung des Textverständnisses; b) Erste Andeutungen zum in der *Unit* thematisierten Problemfeld „Freundschaft".

Lösungen: a) 2. *The present Edward got for his birthday was a horse. 3. The photos Mr and Mrs Clark took in China are interesting. 4. The boarding school Edward went to is very old. 5. The house the Clarks live in now is very big.*

2 Talking at break

Ziel: Einübung der *contact clauses*.

Unterrichtsempfehlungen
Die Aufgabe ist auch als schriftliche Hausaufgabe möglich.

Lösungen: *2. Have you seen the photos I took in Scotland? 3. Did you like the postcard I sent from Fort William? 4. The report Edward got from his old school looks quite good. 5. I can't stand the new teacher we've got for Maths. 6. I enjoyed the new experiments we did in Science on Monday. 7. The book Robert brought to school yesterday is good.*

Schülerbuch Seite 36

Step B Wayne gets into trouble

Ziel: Bestimmende Relativsätze mit *who, which* und *that*.

Neu: *to get into trouble, back, to spray, graffiti, wall, spray, to get rid of s.th., case, chance, to settle s.th, to shut/shut/shut, Shut up!*

Unterrichtsempfehlungen
Semantisierungsvorschläge: L zeichnet eine Farbsprühdose an oder bringt eine Dose in den Unterricht. *What can do with that spray? You can spray graffiti on a wall.* (gestisch) *What's the problem then? If the spray is washable, you can get rid of it. But if it is not washable, it will be a problem. It may be a case for the police. What would your parents do if they found graffiti on the wall of your garage?*
Nach der Darbietung des Textes vom Tonträger wird der Text von S gelesen. Bei dem letzten neuen *vocabulary item 'Shut up!'* sollten S darauf hingewiesen werden, dass dessen Gebrauch sehr unhöflich ist.

Realie

3 School words

Ziel: Verständnisfragen unter Verwendung von Relativsätzen.

Neu: *writing*

Unterrichtsempfehlungen
Zur Vorbereitung auf die Bearbeitung der Folgeaufgabe können die 5 Fragen an die Tafel oder auf eine Folie geschrieben werden. Sollte L vorhaben, dabei auf den zweiten Teil von § 7 des Grammatikanhangs einzugehen, empfiehlt sich folgende Schreibweise: GR § 7

What is a school meeting
  which takes place at the beginning of the day?

What do you call the person
  who usually speaks at assembly?

What do you call a boy or girl
  that has lessons at school?

What do you call the writing
  that was all over the wall of the gym?

What do you call the people
  who come if someone has done something wrong?

Tafelanschrieb oder eigene Folie

Lösungen: *1. assembly 2. headteacher 3. pupil 4. graffiti 5. police*

4 Looking at English

Ziel: Herleitung der Regel für den Gebrauch der drei Relativpronomen.

Neu: *relative pronoun*

Unterrichtsempfehlungen
Obiger Tafelanschrieb / Folienaufschrieb kann noch mit den Sätzen aus dem Eingangstext ergänzt werden. Dabei können die Substantive vor den Relativsätzen farblich hervorgehoben werden (*persons* z.B. blau, *things* grün). Danach lässt sich mit Hilfe der vorgeschlagenen Tabelle die Regel für den Gebrauch der Relativpronomen herleiten. Der entsprechende Teil von § 7 des Grammatikanhangs kann zur Ergänzung herangezogen werden. GR § 7
Bei obiger Darstellungsweise lässt sich – vorgreifend auf Übung 7 der Folgeseite – auch leicht demonstrieren, dass bei einer Weglassung des Relativpronomens der Relativsatz sein Subjekt verlieren würde und somit kein Satz mehr wäre. Mit der Übersetzung der gesammelten Relativsätze ins Deutsche sollte auf die im Deutschen vielfältigen Kasus- und Genus-Formen hingewiesen werden. Weitere Übungsmöglichkeiten ergeben sich im Zusammenhang mit Bildfolie 9

Bildfolie 9

Lösungen: *We use 'which' with things. We use 'who' with people. We use 'that' with people and things.*

5 'who' or 'which'?

Ziel: Unterscheidung des Gebrauchs von *who* und *which*.

Unterrichtsempfehlungen
Diese Aufgabe ist auch als Hausaufgabe möglich.

Lösungen: *1. who 2. which 3. who 4. which 5. who*

Schülerbuch Seite 37

Step B A meeting on the stairs

Ziel: Kontrastierung von Sätzen mit und ohne Relativpronomen, Einführung von *whose*.

Neu: *stairs, to steal/stole/stolen*

Unterrichtsempfehlungen
Der kurze Dialog führt das in der Bedeutung von ‚wessen' schon bekannte *whose* als weiteres Relativpronomen ein und mischt Sätze mit und ohne Relativpronomen. Die neue Funktion von *whose* kann auch durch eine kontrastierende Übersetzung ins Deutsche verdeutlicht werden, zumal umgangssprachlich das Wort ‚dessen/deren' selten verwendet wird und regional unterschiedlich andere Konstruktionen Anwendung finden.

6 Matching the parts

Ziel: Bildung von Relativsätzen mit *who, which, whose, that.*

Neu: *clause, relative clause*

Unterrichtsempfehlungen

Ergänzend sollte der § 8 des Grammatikanhangs besprochen werden. GR § 8

Lösungen: *1. ...who / that enjoy bothering other people. 2. ... whose skin is green and slippery. 3. ... which/ that comes from Asia. 4. ... who / that knows everything 5. ... which / that English people often find difficult. 6. ... which / that has a very long nose.*

7 Looking at English

Ziel: Herleitung der Regel für die Bildung der *contact clauses.*

Neu: *to think of*

Unterrichtsempfehlungen

Ergänzend kann die für *ex. 3* vorgeschlagene Darstellungsweise eingesetzt werden. Ebenso kann die Darstellung der Vorgängerübung als *switchboard exercise* genutzt werden. Hier beginnen die Relativsätze mit der zweiten Spalte. Ein Blick auf die Satzfortsetzungen in der dritten Spalte macht deutlich, dass nur der unterste Satz zu einem *contact clause* werden kann, da er in der dritten Spalte das Subjekt *English people* besitzt. Bei der Regelfindung kann der § 7.2 als Ergänzung herangezogen werden. GR § 7.2

8 ⟨A limerick⟩

Ziel: Einführung der Gedichtform *limerick*, Einführung des heutzutage relativ seltenen Relativpronomens *whom*, *fun*-Element zur Auflockerung.

Neu: *limerick, creature, whom*

Unterrichtsempfehlungen

Der Limerick sollte nach der Semantisierung unbedingt vom Tonträger zu Gehör gebracht werden. Die Einführung von *whom* in dieser wahlfreien Übung entspricht der heutigen Bedeutung dieses Relativpronomens. (s.a. letzte Anmerkung § 7). Die Form *whom* kommt allerdings häufiger im amerikanischen als im britischen Englisch vor. GR § 7

9 Who is who

Ziel: Bildung von Sätzen mit *whose*

Unterrichtsempfehlungen

In leistungsschwächeren Klassen empfiehlt sich ein zweischrittiges Vorgehen. Dabei werden die Notizen in zwei Sätze verwandelt, bevor dann in einem zweiten Schritt der zweite Satz als Relativsatz mit *whose* an den ersten angehängt wird. Beispiel: *Becky is a nice girl. Her poster won a prize.* → *Becky is that nice girl whose poster won a prize.*

Lösungen: *2. Mario is that Italian boy whose jokes are so funny. 3. Robert is that friendly boy whose mother works for Radio Nottingham. 4. Daniel is that clever boy whose father is our Science Teacher. 5. Maggie is that Irish girl whose sister is a pop star. 6. Thomas is that crazy boy whose dad takes him to school in a tractor. 7. Jenny is that really pretty girl whose parents come from Germany.*

Schülerbuch Seite 38

Step B A busy week

Ziel: Das *present progressive* (mit Zeitangabe) zur Wiedergabe der Zukunft.

Neu: *tonight, Romeo and Juliet*

Unterrichtsempfehlungen

Semantisierungsvorschlag: *7.00–12.00: this morning, 12.00–17.00: this afternoon, 17.00–19.00: this evening, 19.00– ...: tonight.* L kann S darauf hinweisen, dass in GB die mit *tonight* ausgedrückte Tageszeit früher beginnt als die ableitbare deutsche Bedeutung.
Nach dem Lesen mit verteilten Rollen können zur Vorbereitung der Folgeaufgabe die Sätze mit *present progressive* + Zeitangabe herausgesucht werden.
– *What are you doing tonight?*
– *I'm going to the youth club.*
– *I'm playing in a hockey match after school.*
– *I'm meeting Robert at 6 o'clock.*
– *We're acting 'Romeo and Juliet' at the end of the term.*
– *We're practising a difficult part tonight.*

10 No time for Edward

Ziel: Verständnisüberprüfung mit Anwendung der neuen Struktur.

Unterrichtsempfehlungen

Nach der Verständnisüberprüfung sollte die Aussage Monnys durch die Besprechung von § 9 ergänzt werden. GR § 9
Der an letzter Stelle stehende Hinweis (mit der Taschenlampe) verweist nochmals auf die Anwendungsunterschiede des *present progressive*. Bei einer mündlichen Bearbeitung oder Kontrolle dieser Übung sollte auf die Verwendung der passenden Kurzformen der Aussprache geachtet werden: *she's, they're.*

Lösungen: *1. She is playing in a hockey match after school. 2. She is meeting Robert at six o'clock. 3. They are acting 'Romeo and Juliet' at the end of the term. They are practising a difficult part tonight..*

11 Jenny's diary

Ziel: Übung der neuen Struktur.

Neu: *arrangement, flower*

Unterrichtsempfehlungen

Die Aufgabe kann auch als Hausaufgabe gestellt werden. Beim Einsatz dieser Übung im Unterricht kann ein zusätzlicher Spielanreiz dadurch erreicht werden, dass S sich den Zeitplan Jennys 1–2 Minuten lang einprägen und dann die Fragen und Antworten aus dem Gedächtnis gestellt und beantwortet werden.

Lösungen: (Beliebige Reihenfolge) *What is Jenny doing after school on Monday? – She's playing hockey. What is she doing on Monday at 6 o'clock? What is she doing on Tuesday at 4 p.m.? – She is visiting / going to see Aunty Pat in hospital (And she mustn't forget flowers for her.) – What is she doing on Wednesday at 5.45 p.m.? She is having a haircut at Victoria Centre. What is she doing on Thursday at 5 p.m.? – She is going with Becky to the sports centre / She is going swimming with Becky. What is she doing on Friday at 5 p.m.? – She is going with Emma to Victoria Centre. They are buying Fiona's birthday present, a CD. What is she doing on Saturday? She is going on a theatre trip. / She is seeing 'Romeo and Juliet' at the theatre. What is she doing on Sunday at 3.30 p.m.? She is going to Fiona's party.*

12 A fantasy diary

Ziel: Anwendung des *present progressive with a future meaning.*

Neu: *fantasy, V.I.P. (= very important person), to leave free*

Unterrichtsempfehlungen
Als vorbereitende Hausaufgabe für a) kann das Abfassen der VIP-Tagebucheinträge gestellt werden. In b) können dann S die Struktur spielerisch stets mit Blick in ihren eigenen Terminkalender anwenden.
Lösungen: Freie Schülerlösungen.

Schülerbuch Seite 39

Step B Emma

Ziel: Vorbringen eines Vorschlags mit *shall* (§ 10), Ausdruck eines Wunsches oder einer Bitte mit *will you* (§ 11). GR § 10, 11

Neu: *So do you!, shall, way*

Unterrichtsempfehlungen
Die auf dieser Seite behandelten Kurzpensen stellen keine so großen Anforderungen an die S. Zusammen mit der Besprechung der §§ 10, 11 lässt sich diese Seite flott behandeln. Die Übungen 13 und 14 lassen sich auch als schriftliche Hausaufgabe stellen.

13 Shall I help?

Ziel: Vorbringen eines Vorschlags mit *shall*.
Lösungsmöglichkeiten: *2. Shall I close the window? 3. Shall we mend it together? 4. Shall I call an ambulance? 5. Shall I get the book for you? 6. Shall I lend you some money? 7. Shall I show you the way (to the toilet)?*

14 A teacher

Ziel: Ausdruck eines Wunsches oder einer Bitte mit *will you?* (§ 11). Es gibt weitere Übungsmöglichkeiten mit Bildfolie 10.   GR § 11
Bildfolie 10

Neu: *noisy*

Lösungsmöglichkeiten: *1. Will you be quiet, please? 2. Will you clean the board, please? 3. Will you close the door, please? 4. Will you give me your homework, please? 5. Will you carry some of the books, please? 6. Will you pick up that sweet paper, please?*

15 ⟨Just for fun⟩

Ziel: *Fun*-Element zur satirischen Umsetzung der an sich höflichen Wendung *Will you?*

Schülerbuch Seite 40

Step C A thief in the school

Ziel: Kombinierter Hör- und Lesetext

Unterrichtsempfehlungen
Für diese gelungene Kombination zwischen Hörtext und Lesetext sollte nach Möglichkeit eine Doppelstunde vorgesehen werden. Es ist aber auch ohne weiteres die Verteilung auf zwei Einzelstunden hintereinander möglich, da selbst geübte „Vorausleser" unter den Schülern die Lösung der Geschichte nicht vorwegnehmen können, da diese erst über den Tonträger bzw. von L präsentiert wird.

1 Listening practice: In assembly

Ziel: Einstimmung in die Situation

Neu: *advice*

Text
(The last chorus of 'All things bright and beautiful' fades away.)

Mrs Benson:
Now, everybody, I've got something to tell you that is very serious.
Three pupils in Year 9 have lost money. Now, it sometimes happens that pupils think someone has stolen something and then the next day they find their money again! But it's also possible that we have a thief at Haywood. The thief may be in your tutor group. If you are quite sure that someone has stolen something of yours, you must tell your tutor right away. And if you find something which you think someone has lost, maybe a purse or some money, please don't keep it. Give it to your tutor. Don't wait! And remember: Never leave any money in the classroom at breaktimes. Always be very careful with your things. Don't give the thief a chance!

Unterrichtsempfehlungen
Erweiterung der Kontrollfragen im SB nach der ersten Darbietung des Hörtextes: *Some pupils have lost money. How can you explain this? Who can be the thief? What must the pupils be, before they go and tell their tutor about the thief?*

2 Find the clues

Ziel: Fortsetzung des Hörtextes als Lesetext

Neu: *clue, to appear, to be in a hurry, to pay s.o. back, to promise, to be annoyed, free, dinner lady, tomato, after all, to push, against, to cry, jealous of, to tell lies, safe, bell, to ring/rang/rung, while*

Unterrichtsempfehlungen
Als Alternative zur üblichen Vorgehensweise kann L den Text vor der Präsentation vom Tonträger selbst (bei geöffneten Büchern) vorlesen und die neuen Vokabeln dabei erläutern *(Read-and-Explain Procedure)*. *Find the clues: Find ideas and facts that can be answers to the question. Who is the thief?* appeared: came up; *I'm in a hurry:* I haven't got any time; *pay ... back:* When are you going to give me my money back?; *promise:* gestisch; *annoyed:* very angry; *free lunches:* he and his parents don't have to pay for the lunches; *dinner lady:* the lady at the counter in the canteen; *tomato:* tomato soup, ketchup; *not so bad after all:* dt.: doch nicht so schlecht; *pushed against:* gestisch; *cried:* shouted; *jealous of me:* dt: eifersüchtig auf; *tell lies:* dt. lügen; *in a safe place:* where nobody can take it away; *the bell rang:* imitatorisch; *for a while:* for some time.
Danach kann der Text vom Tonträger präsentiert und anschließend mit verteilten Rollen *(Narrators 1–3, Jenny, Robert, Emma, Wayne, dinner lady, Edward, Becky, Mr Stuart)* gelesen werden.

Schülerbuch Seite 41

3 Who did it?

Ziel: Verständnisüberprüfung durch *sensible guessing.*

Unterrichtsempfehlung
Da sich der Verdacht der S auf wenige Personen konzentriert, empfiehlt es sich, die Vermutungen und Begründungen der S an der Tafel in Form einer Tabelle festzuhalten.
Tafelbildvorschlag: Tafelanschrieb

Emma	Wayne	Edward Clark
clues: jealous of Jenny, tells lies, is always there when money is missing	**clues:** free lunches, poor parents, no money, can't pay Robert back	**clues:** is always there when money is missing, lends money

4 Listening practice: Who is the thief?

Ziel: Hörtext zur Auflösung der Geschichte.

Text

Robert: So it's you! And we thought the thief was Wayne!
Jenny: And I thought it was Emma!
Edward: But you don't understand. I …
Robert: You took Jenny's purse, and Becky's too, right? You thief, Edward! How could you …?
Edward (beginning to cry): I'm really sorry. But I didn't keep the money. I was going to give yours back, too.
Robert: What do you mean, give it back? I don't understand.
Edward (sobbing): I … you … you'll never understand!
Jenny: Look, just sit down here. Tell us why you stole the money.
Edward: Well, it's like this. I didn't have any friends at my old school. I don't know why. And nobody likes me at this school! Nobody wants to talk to me or do things with me.
Robert: That's not true, Edward! But I still don't understand. Nobody likes a thief!
Edward: Well, Jenny and Becky were really happy when I gave them money.
Jenny: But you took our money!
Edward: I know it's crazy. I just wanted to help you somehow. Then …
Robert: You can't buy friends, Edward.
Edward: I know. *(sob)* W-what are you going to do now? Please don't tell anyone, Robert! Please!

Unterrichtsempfehlungen

Das affektiv berührende Ende der Geschichte sollte nach der Darbietung des Hörtextes durch behutsames Nachfragen aufgearbeitet werden: *Why did he steal the money? Can you remember his words? Edward: You'll never understand. … I didn't have any friends at my old school. I don't know why. … Nobody likes me at this school. Nobody wants to talk to me. Nobody wants to do things with me.*
(Aus Gründen der Zeitökonomie könnte es sich im Anschluss daran empfehlen, die Stunde mit dem Beatles-Song von *ex. 6* abzuschließen und *ex. 5* etwas abgewandelt als schriftliche Hausaufgabe zu stellen. *(Write a short ending for the story.)*

5 What should they do next?

Ziel: Fortführung der inhaltlichen Auswertung der Geschichte.

Neu: *possible*

6 ⟨A song: Can't buy me love⟩

Ziel: Wiederkennen der Thematik der Geschichte in einem Song.

Neu: *Can't buy me love, diamond, to care for, satisfied*

Schülerbuch Seite 42

7 The most interesting film I've ever seen

Ziel: Übung zu *contact clauses*.

Unterrichtsempfehlungen

Die S erstellen mit Hilfe der Fragen in Partnerarbeit ein Blatt mit Aussagen ihres Partners in Stichworten (Aufgabe a) und stellen ihn damit der Klasse vor (Aufgabe b). In größeren Klassen kann dies noch durch die Variante *Who is it?* abgewandelt werden. Dabei werden die Blätter mit den Aussagen der S ohne Namensangabe an andere weitergereicht.

8 A word game

Ziel: Einüben der Relativsätze mit oder ohne Pronomen.

Neu: *definition*

Unterrichtsempfehlungen

Als Erweiterung bietet sich folgende Alternative an: *Let's play Jeopardy*. Jeder S bereitet für das klasseninterne „Jeopardy"-Spiel als Hausaufgabe 5–10 Definitionen auf Fragekärtchen vor.

9 Nice or nasty?

Ziel: Wortschatzübung mit Komparativ- und Superlativformen.

Unterrichtsempfehlungen

Die Aufgabe a) kann als Vorbereitung für eine Hausaufgabe in Partnerarbeit (Aufgabe b) dienen, bei der die Partner ihre *Nice-Nasty-List* z.B. als Poster auf einem Stück Tapete präsentieren und vor der Klasse in Sprache umsetzen. Eine weitere Übungsgrundlage bieten die Bilder der Bildfolie 11.

Bildfolie 11

Schülerbuch Seite 43

Step D Let's check

1 At school

Ziel: Wortfeld ‚Schule'.

Unterrichtsempfehlungen
Lösungen: 1. LIBRARY 2. COMPREHENSIVE 3. EXPERIMENT 4. ASSEMBLY 5. DETENTION 6. BELL

2 At Haywood

Ziel: *Relative clauses, contact clauses.*

Unterrichtsempfehlungen
Lösungen: a) 1. *who / that* 2. *which / that* 3. *who/that* 4. *whose* 5. *whose* 6. *who / that* 7. *which / that* 8. *which / that* 9. *who / that*
b) Contact clauses möglich in Satz 2, 8, 9;
missing pronouns: 2. *which / that* 8. *which / that* 9. *who / that*

3 About me

Ziel: Anwendung des *present progressive with a future meaning*.

Unterrichtsempfehlungen
Diese Aufgabe eignet sich auch als schriftliche Hausaufgabe.

Lösungen: Individuelle Schülerlösungen

4 Helping each other

Ziel: Anwendung von *shall* und *will* zum Ausdruck eines Vorschlags, Erfragen eines Wunsches, Ausdruck eines Wunsches oder eine Bitte.

Lösungsmöglichkeiten: *1. Shall I try it with this bottle opener? 2. Will you be quiet, please? 3. Will you feed them, please? 4. Shall I drive for you?*

Schülerbuch Seite 44-45

Unit 3 Welcome to Wales

Step A Country and people

Allgemeiner Hinweis: In diesem *Step* steht die Vorstellung von Wales im Vordergrund mit dem zur Ortsbeschreibung notwendigen Vokabular. Grammatik wird nicht vermittelt. Es empfiehlt sich, die neuen Wörter der Übung 1 bei der Betrachtung der Photos gleich zu berücksichtigen.

Landeskundliche Informationen
500–100 v. Chr. besiedeln die Kelten das Gebiet von Wales und leisten 43 v. Chr. erbitterten Widerstand, als die Römer unter Kaiser Claudius in Britannien einfallen. 78–84 n. Chr. wird Wales von den Römern unterworfen, Festungen (Caerleon) und Straßen, die teils heute noch existieren, werden gebaut. Nachdem die Römer Britannien ab ca. 400 n. Chr. verlassen, bekriegen sich die Volksstämme. Im Jahre 784 errichtet König Offa von Mercia, ein Sachse, einen Grenzwall zwischen England und Wales, den *Offa's Dyke*. Wales entwickelt sich zu einer Nation mit einer für die Zeit sehr fortschrittlichen Gesetzgebung. Als die Normannen auf die Insel kommen (1066, *William the Conquerer*), versuchen sie, die Waliser einzunehmen, weitere Befestigungsburgen entstehen. Als der letzte walisische Prinz Llywelyn II (Llywelyn ap Gruffydd ap Llywelyn) 1282 stirbt, wird das Land von den Briten annektiert. König Edward I. baut den *iron ring of castles*: Caernarfon, Beaumaris, Conwy, Harlech und Criccieth sind heute Touristenattraktionen. Seinen ältesten Sohn, den späteren König Edward II of Caernarvon, ernennt er 1301 zum *Prince of Wales* und begründet damit die bis heute anhaltende Tradition. Unter Henry VIII wird Wales mit den *Acts of Union 1535–6* vollständig politisch mit England vereinigt. Erst 1900 wird es den ersten Abgeordneten für Wales im Unterhaus geben, 1925 wird die walisische Nationalpartei, *Plaid Cymru*, gegründet, dessen erster Vertreter 1966 ins Londoner Parlament gewählt wird. Seit 1955 hat Wales eine eigene Hauptstadt, Cardiff, regiert wird Wales von Westminster aus. Das *Welsh Grand Committee* berät das Unterhaus in walisischen Angelegenheiten und es gibt einen *Secretary of State for Wales*. Viele Waliser hegen einen Groll gegen die zentralistische Regierung in London und streben die walisische Unabhängigkeit an. 1997 findet eine Abstimmung über den Vorschlag für eine eigene *Welsh assembly (Cynulliad i Gymru)* statt.

Wales war stets ein armes, landwirtschaftliches Gebiet, doch im 19. Jahrhundert mauserte es sich zu einer reichen Industrieregion. Grund dafür waren die reichen Kohle- und Eisenerzvorkommen in Südwales, die für die Industrielle Revolution Großbritanniens so wichtig waren. Die Industrialisierung veränderte Wales grundlegend. Die Bergwerke und Fabrikschornsteine verwandelten das Land in eine schwarze Hölle, die ausbeuterischen Arbeitsverhältnisse beim Kohleabbau in Südwales und in den Schieferbergwerken des Nordens führten zu erbärmlichen Lebensbedingungen. Aber schon zur Jahrhundertwende begann es, mit dem walisischen Bergbau abwärts zu gehen, da Frankreich und Deutschland immer größere Marktanteile erkämpften. Während es 1913 noch 620 Zechen in Wales gab, in denen 232.000 Bergleute arbeiteten, gab es 1995 nur noch lediglich 30 private Zechen, die 9.000 Bergarbeiter beschäftigen. Nach einer gewaltigen wirtschaftlichen Depression vor allem auch in den 80er Jahren, gibt es in Wales heute wieder einen Aufschwung. Neue Industriezweige wie die Computerbranche und der Tourismus verändern die „schwarzen Täler" von Wales positiv. Einige Bergwerke wurden in Touristenattraktionen verwandelt, die ebenso beliebt sind wie die Burgen des Mittelalters.

Informationen über Wales:
Wales Tourist Board
2 Fitzalan Road
Cardiff
CF2 1UY (Tel.: 00 44-12 22-49 99 09)

1 All about Wales

Ziel: Einen ersten Eindruck von Land und Leuten bekommen.

Neu: *to go with, strong, to conquer, century, prince, capital, heavy, industriy, million, video recorder, factory, railway, choir, valley, coal, mine, visitor, B&B (=bed and breakfast), village, one in five, camp, wild, countryside; King Arthur, Camelot; Aberystwyth, Caerleon, Caernarvon, Cardiff, Fishguard, Holyhead, Snowdonia National Park, Swansea, Tenby*

Unterrichtsempfehlungen
Man kann mit der Aussprache der Ortsnamen beginnen, zunächst die einfacheren Wörter wie Cardiff, Tenby, Swansea, Fishguard, Holyhead ermitteln lassen, die schwierigeren Namen wie Snowdonia National Park, Aberystwyth, Caernarvon, Caerleon, Camelot entweder vorsprechen oder anhand der Lautschrift im Vokabelanhang herausarbeiten lassen. Im Zusammenhang mit den Ortsnamen können eingeführt werden: *Wales and the Prince of Wales, Cardiff = capital of Wales, Snowdonia – Snowdon = mountain – valley*. Dann werden die Photos versprachlicht und der entsprechende Wortschatz eingeführt: *1. This castle was built in the 13th century, 2. What are these people doing? 3. What does this sign mean? 4. What can you see in this picture? 5. Who knows what this is? It's an old coal mine. What can you see in the background? A village. 6. What is this woman doing? She works in a factory. 7. Do you know what they are playing? People often sing together at Rugby matches, it's like a choir. 8. What can you see in this picture?* Die restlichen Wörter werden bei der anschließenden Lektüre der Fragen erschlossen. Die S lesen die Abschnitte und ordnen sie dem Beispiel entsprechend den Photos zu.

WB S.29, A1

Lösungen: *b) goes with 6; c) with 2; d) with 7; e) with 5; f) with 3; g) with 9; h) with 4; i) with 8.*

1 A ticket to Llanfairpwllgwyngyllgogerychwyrndrobwllllantysiliogogogoch

Ziel: Vorstellung der walisischen Sprache.

Neu: *for short*

Unterrichtsempfehlungen
Der Name wird vom Tonträger präsentiert. Versuche, den Namen nachzusprechen, machen Spaß, werden aber kaum von Erfolg gekrönt sein.

Landeskundliche Informationen
Das Dorf mit dem längsten Namen Großbritanniens – und vielleicht der Welt? – befindet sich auf der Insel Anglesey. Der Name bedeutet: „Kirche St. Mary bei der weißen Haselnussquelle über dem wilden Strudel und der Kirche St. Tysilio an der roten Höhle". Weitere schöne walisische Namen finden sich auf der Karte von Wales auf Bildfolie 12.

Bildfolie 12

Weitere Informationen zur Walisischen Sprache s. Hinweise zu Schülerbuch Seite 50, **Step B The Celts and their language.**

Schülerbuch Seite 46

3 Describing Wales

WB S.29, A2

Ziel: Umwälzung und Wiederholung von Wortschatz.

Neu: *mind, mind map*

Unterrichtsempfehlungen

Zur Gestaltung der *mind map* kann entweder der hier vorgeschlagene Anfang herangezogen werden, oder neu begonnen werden, wobei wahrscheinlich Wales zumeist im Zentrum stehen wird, aber auch *Great Britain* als Ausgangspunkt vorstellbar ist.

4 Your area

Ziel: Interkulturelles Lernen.

Neu: *area*

Unterrichtsempfehlungen

Diese Aufgabe kann in Partner- oder Gruppenarbeit bis zu 4 Personen ausgeführt werden. Die S werden mit Vorlauf von ein paar Tagen aufgefordert, Photomaterial und Prospekte einer ausgewählten Region oder Sehenswürdigkeit mitzubringen, entweder alle zum gleichen oder zu verschiedenen Themen. Für die Erstellung der Poster sollte eine Unterrichtsstunde vorgesehen werden. Gegebenenfalls können die fertigen Seiten an die englische – oder amerikanische– Partnerschule zur Vorbereitung eines Austausches geschickt werden.

5 Listening practice: Arriving at the Snowdon Hotel

Ziel: Schulung des Hörverstehens.

Neu: *inside, huge*

Text:
Mrs Pritchard: Good afternoon. Can I help you?
Mrs Walker: We've booked two rooms for the weekend. Two doubles. Walker is the name.
Mrs Pritchard: Ah yes. Here we are. Rooms 10 and 24.
Mrs Walker: Are the rooms both on the same floor?
Mrs Pritchard: No, they aren't. Room 10 is on the first floor, and Room 24 is on the second. Sorry about that, Mrs Walker. Are your children very young?
Mrs Walker: No, they're twelve and fourteen. It'll be quite all right.
Mrs Pritchard: That's fine then. Here are the keys, Mrs Walker.
Mrs Walker: Thank you. – Er, can you give us any tips for our stay here? We aren't quite sure yet what we want to do.
Mrs Pritchard: Well, there's a lot of wild countryside round here, if you like walking. And of course there are some very famous castles. Caernarvon Castle is the nearest. Look, here's a brochure about it.
Mrs Walker: Oh, thank you. Yes, we really must see Caernarvon. Maybe we'll go there tomorrow morning.
Mrs Pritchard: Do you want to go up Snowdon while you're here? Most of our visitors do.
Mrs Walker: I'm not sure about that. We've never done much climbing!
Mrs Pritchard: Well, you needn't walk up, you know. You can go up by railway, too.
Mrs Walker: Really? That sounds like a good idea.
Mrs Pritchard: Of course you need good weather for the trip. It's no good going if the weather's bad.
Mrs Walker: What's the forecast like for tomorrow?
Mrs Pritchard: Very good. It'll be quite sunny and warm. But I don't think it'll be so good on Sunday...
(Sound of hotel entrance door opening as Mr Walker and the two children come in, laughing...)

Unterrichtsempfehlungen

Semantisierung der neuen Wörter: *Mrs Walker goes into the hotel* = *she goes inside; very big* = *huge*.
Nach ein- oder zweimaligem Anhören ergänzen die S die Dialoge in Stillarbeit und tragen sie dann vor.

6 Sound practice

Ziel: Üben der Aussprache und Diskriminierung von [f], [v] und [w].

Unterrichtsempfehlung

Das Gedicht eignet sich zum Auswendiglernen, der Vortrag kann zeilenweise erfolgen. Wenn die Klasse spielerisch veranlagt ist, kann zu jeder Zeile eine passende Geste oder ein Geräusch gefunden werden, z.B.:
1. marschieren, 2. mit den Fingern 7 zeigen, 3. herzliches Armeausbreiten, 4. Händeschütteln, 5. Huuuhhh (Windgeräusch), 6. Splish-splash (Regengeräusch), 7. + 8. Geste des Wasserabschüttelns, 9.+ 10. Schirmaufspannen, 11. Halbkreisgeste für aufgehende Sonne, 12. Winke, winke! für Abschied.

Schülerbuch Seite 47

Step B The Pritchards

Ziel: Dinge über die eigene Vergangenheit erzählen.

Neu: *penfriend, since, out of work, to move*

Unterrichtsempfehlungen

Semantisierung: *A friend you write letters to is a penfriend;* die restlichen Wörter nach der ersten Lektüre durch L aus dem Kontext erschließen: *since* = seit; *out of work* = they haven't got a job; *to move* = to go and live in a new place. Dann lesen die S den Text, anschließend Klären des Textverständnisses durch Fragen: *What did Michelle write about in her letter? Where is Gwen from? Why did they move to North Wales? What do her parents do there? What else do we learn about Gwen?*

1 Gwen and her family

Ziel: Bildung des *present perfect progressive* (**Grammar** § 12).

Neu: *up here, to teach/taught/taught*

Unterrichtsempfehlungen

Semantisierung der neuen Wörter: *up here:* aus dem Kontext; *to teach* – a teacher teaches. In leistungsstärkeren Gruppen dürfte die Bildung der neuen Form kein großes Problem sein, so dass die Übung direkt mündlich erarbeitet werden kann. In schwächeren Gruppen kann es sich empfehlen, zunächst ein Paradigma für alle Personen an der Tafel zu erstellen:

I you	have been	
he she it	has been	working
we you they	have been	

Dann die Aufgabe in Stillarbeit lösen und anschließend vortragen lassen.

Lösungen: *1. have been working, have been looking; 2. has been living; 3. have been speaking, have been doing; 4. have been learning, has been speaking, have been listening, has been working.*

2 Looking at English

Ziel: Bewusstmachung des Gebrauchs des *present perfect progressive* (**Grammar** § 12).

Neu: *present perfect progressive*

Unterrichtsempfehlungen

Zur Bewusstmachung des neuen Pensums zunächst Detailfragen zum Text stellen: *Since when have they been living in North Wales? How long have Mr and Mrs Pritchard been working at the Snowdon Hotel? Since when have Gwen and Hugh been going to the new school? How long has Gwen been learning Welsh?*

Dabei entsteht folgendes Tafelbild: **Tafelanschrieb**

Since when?	How long?
They have been living there <u>since</u> last August.	They have been working there <u>for</u> six months.
They have been going there <u>since</u> September.	She has been learning Welsh <u>for</u> three years.

In lernstärkeren Gruppen kann die jeweilige Überschrift nachträglich ergänzt werden, indem man die entsprechenden Fragen von der Klasse abruft. Nun kann die Regel zum Gebrauch von *for* und *since* erarbeitet werden. Zur Überprüfung der eigenen Regel wird der Grammatische Anhang herangezogen. **GR § 12**

Schülerbuch Seite 48

3 How long?

Ziel: Fragen und Aussagen zur Vergangenheit formulieren; Kontrastierung von *for* und *since* (**Grammar** § 12). **GR § 12**

Unterrichtsempfehlungen
In lernschwächeren Gruppen kann der Klarheit halber die unterschiedliche Fragestellung wie in Übung 2 beibehalten werden. Nach der Partnerarbeit sollten die Ergebnisse im Plenum kontrolliert werden. Weitere Übungsmöglichkeiten ergibt Bildfolie 13   **WB S.30, B2**   **Bildfolie 13**

4 Facts about you

Ziel: Über die eigenen Lebensumstände, Hobbys etc. sprechen.   **WB S.30, B3**

Neu: *instrument, to interview*

Unterrichtsempfehlungen
Semantisierung der neuen Wörter über das entsprechende deutsche Wort.
Alternativ zu der im Buch vorgeschlagenen Vorgehensweise können die S die Angaben über sich selbst auch auf Zettel schreiben, die eingesammelt und beliebig wieder verteilt werden. Dann berichten die S über ihren „Partner": *My partner lives in ...; he/she has been living there since ...* etc. Anschließend muss der/die Vortragende raten, wessen Zettel er/sie hat.

5 People at the hotel

Ziel: Sich über etwas beschweren; Gebrauch von *for* und *since*.

Neu: *sir*

Unterrichtsempfehlungen
Um die Übung lebendig zu machen, sollte auch der Erwiderung besondere Beachtung geschenkt werden. Dem Einfallsreichtum der S im Hinblick auf Entschuldigungen sollten keine Grenzen gesetzt werden!
In lernstärkeren Gruppen können die S sich weitere Situationen ausdenken und Dialoge dazu entwickeln.

Schülerbuch Seite 49

Step B Tips for visitors

Ziel: Ratschläge geben; Infinitiv nach Fragewörtern (**Grammar** § 13).   **GR § 13**

Neu: *to wonder, whether, roadside, to park, service, choice, to fish, golf, route*

Unterrichtsempfehlungen
Die Informationsbroschüre über den *Snowdonia National Park* kann zum selbständigen Erschließen eingesetzt werden. Außer *to wonder whether* (= *to ask yourself*) sind alle neuen Wörter über das Deutsche, bekannte englische Wörter oder den Kontext erschließbar. Die S lesen den Text in Stillarbeit und beantworten anschließend folgende Fragen: *How can you get there? What's the problem? – Where would you like to stay? Why? – How would you like to spend your time there?* Zur Sicherung des neuen Wortschatzes kann anschließend ggf. noch besprochen werden, welches der neuen Wörter wie erschlossen wurde, dabei wird auch die Aussprache geklärt.
Die Bewusstmachung sollte bis Übung 6 zurückgestellt werden, da erst dann das neue Pensum in ganzen Sätzen vorliegt.

6 Very useful!

Ziel: Übung und Bewusstmachung des Infinitivs nach Fragewörtern (**Grammar** § 13).   **GR § 13**

Neu: *farmer, to milk*

Unterrichtsempfehlungen
Auch der neue Wortschatz dieser Übung kann von den S erschlossen werden. Vorbereitung der Satzverknüpfungen des Teils a) in einer kurzen Stillarbeitsphase, Besprechung in der Klasse, dann Bewusstmachung des neuen Pensums. Tafelanschrieb:

	how often	to take
... you'll know	how	to milk ...
... you're not sure	which	train to take
... he will tell you	where	to get off
	when	to be back
	whether	to go climbing

Der Zusammenhang zwischen Fragewort und Infinitivkonstruktion wird so deutlich, die Redeabsicht kann besprochen werden. Zur Konkretisierung dient § 13 im Grammatischen Anhang.   **GR § 13**
Nun wird Teil b) der Aufgabe im Plenum mit möglichst vielen Variationen gelöst.   **WB S.31, B4**

Lösungen: a) 1. *which way to go.* 2. *which train to take.* 3. *where to get off.* 4. *how often to take your medicine.* 5. *when to be back in the evening.* 6. *whether to go climbing or not.* 7. *how to milk a cow.*
b) 8. *where to go/how to get there/which hotel to choose;* 9. *what to cook/how to cook spaghetti (etc.)/ how to make a cake;* 10. *what to buy*.

7 They don't know

Ziel: Indirekte Fragen stellen (**Grammar** § 13).   **GR § 13**

Unterrichtsempfehlungen
Die S sollten auch auf Variation bei den einleitenden Verben achten.   **WB S.31, B5**

Lösungsmöglichkeiten: 1. *She is wondering what to do.* 2. *He doesn't know how to get home.* 3. *example* 4. *He isn't sure whether to walk or to take the railway.* 5. *He wants to know where to get a good map of Snowdon* 6. *They are wondering which poster to buy.*

Schülerbuch Seite 50

Step B The Celts and their language

Ziel: Informationen über die keltische – und walisische Geschichte – kennenlernen.

Neu: *BC, AD, to invade, to settle, to exist, official, status, land; Celts, Celtic, Angles, Saxons, Britons*

Unterrichtsempfehlungen
Vor der Präsentation des Textes sollten folgenden Wörter semantisiert werden: <u>BC</u> = *before Christ,* <u>AD</u> = *anno domini, after Christ;* <u>to invade</u> *a country* = *to come into a country with an army;* <u>to settle</u> *in a place* = *to build a house and live there.* Die übrigen Wörter können von

den S erschlossen werden. Die erste Textpräsentation sollte von L erfolgen, wegen der Aussprache der Namen, dann lesen die S. Fragen zur Überprüfung des Textverständnisses: *Who were the first people to speak Welsh in Britain? Who conquered them? What did they call their country? Where did the Britons move? Did they all speak the same language? Where are Celtic languages spoken today? What is the difference between them and Welsh?*

Alternativ kann eine handlungsorientierte Auswertung erfolgen. Dazu paust man die Umrisse des UK, Skandinaviens, Deutschlands, der Niederlande, Belgiens und Frankreichs von der Europakarte hinten im Buch ab und kopiert sie für die S. Diese können nun mit unterschiedlichen Farben die Einwanderungswellen eintragen und anschließend versprachlichen.

WB S.32, B6

Landeskundliche Informationen

Welsh is the oldest of all the languages spoken in Europe today, and it is related to Irish, Scottish and Breton. Today, only about 19% of the population speak Welsh. With the Acts of Union in 1536 English had become the official language in Wales. Since then, fewer and fewer people living in Wales speak Welsh. Since the 1960s, however, there have been activities to bring back the Welsh language. Nowadays all street signs are bilingual, people can ask for Welsh defence in court, there are Welsh TV and radio stations and newspapers and even schools which teach most subjects in Welsh. You can study Welsh at the University of Aberystwyth. At the University there is also a centre which translates new words like "nuclear power plant" or "computer screen" from English into Welsh. There are 28 letters in the Welsh alphabet with j, k, q, v, x and z missing. All words are stressed on the penultimate syllable.

*Rules for pronunciation: **c** is hard, as English **k**. **ch** as in Scottish lo**ch**, or German na**ch**. **dd** similar to English **th** [ð] as in **th**is. **f** as English **v**. **ff** as English **f**. **g** is hard as English **g**ate. **ll** as the Swiss German sound **chl**. **ph** as in English tele**ph**one. **r** is rolled, as in Scots. **rh** is the same sound followed by an aspirate. **s** is hard [s] as in English **s**ea; never soft as in tho**s**e. **th** [θ] as in **th**ing. **u** is like the **y** in English m**y**stery. **w** is a short vowel as in c**oo**k, or long as in m**oo**n. **y** can be a long **e** as in t**e**a, a short **a** [ʌ] as in g**u**n or an **i** as in t**i**n.*

8 ⟨A song: Bachgen bach o dincer / The little tinker lad⟩

Ziel: Ein walisisches Lied kennenlernen.

Neu: *tinker, lad, to sling, slung, slung, hammer, trifle, pipe, whiskers, 'neath, pitcher, pot, frying pan, to heat, iron, to cover, solder, flaw, none, to seek/sought/sought, to vanish, to miss, on every hand*

Unterrichtsempfehlungen
Dieses Lied in walisischer Sprache soll einen Eindruck vom Klang der Sprache geben. Vor der Präsentation den englischen Text erarbeiten, damit das Sujet des Liedes bekannt ist und die S sich beim Vorspielen des Liedes ganz auf den Klang der Stimmen konzentrieren können. Der englische Text ist eine reine Übersetzung, er stimmt im Versmaß und Rhythmus nicht mit dem Original überein und lässt sich daher nicht singen.

Schülerbuch Seite 51

Step B Plans for the weekend

Ziel: Eine Verabredung treffen; sich versichern, *question tags* (**Grammar** § 14)

GR § 14

Unterrichtsempfehlungen
Die S lesen den Dialog mit verteilten Rollen zwei Mal vor, dann untersuchen sie das neue Pensum. Zuerst werden die Sätze auf den gelben Merkzetteln analysiert, dann werden die Beispiele aus dem Dialog den entsprechenden Zetteln zugeordnet:

+/–: *We're going to the cinema tonight, aren't we? That'll be early enough, won't it.*
–/+: *You don't want to go anywhere, do you? That's OK, isn't it?*

Für die Klärung der Bedeutung empfiehlt sich eine Wiedergabe der Sätze auf deutsch mit den im Deutschen möglichen Nuancen: oder? nicht (wahr)? ja? (oder schwäbisch auch: gell?).

9 These are easy, aren't they?

Ziel: Nachfragen; Übung der **question tags** (**Grammar** § 14).

GR § 14

Unterrichtsempfehlungen
Mit den Sätzen des Teils a) kann die beim Dialog begonnene Liste in Stillarbeit fortgesetzt werden. Teil b) bietet sich als Hausaufgabe an.

Lösungen:

+/–	–/+
1. doesn't she?	3. will it?
2. isn't he?	4. do you?
5. can't I?	6. is he?
7. haven't you?	8. are they?

10 Knights of Camelot

Ziel: Festigen der *question tags* (**Grammar** § 14).

GR § 14

Neu: *knight, question tag*

Unterrichtsempfehlungen
Die Übung wird in der Klasse mündlich durchgearbeitet – auch wiederholt – dann kann der Dialog in einem weiteren Durchgang so verändert werden, dass aus negativen Äußerungen jeweils positive werden und umgekehrt, mit der entsprechenden Veränderung der *question tags*, z.B. *You weren't at the cinema, were you? It wasn't about King Arthur, was it?* etc.

WB S.32, B7
WB S.32, B8

Schülerbuch Seite 52-53

Step C The sword in the stone

Ziel: Einen Teil der keltischen Arthus-Sage kennenlernen.

Neu: *sword, to follow, to take over, kingdom, handle, true, wizard, miracle, tournament, inn, What a piece of luck! till, look, to miss, to fetch, to believe, wife, danger, cheer; King Uther, Merlin, New Year's Day, Sir Ector, Queen Igrayne*

Unterrichtsempfehlungen
Vor der Präsentation des Textes werden die wichtigsten Wörter semantisiert, evtl. in einem neuen Kontext: *The Celts always had kings. A king has a kingdom; the queen is the wife of the king. When a king died, usually his son followed him as King, he was the true King. Sometimes there was no son, so someone else had to take over the kingdom. It was important to have a strong king, so sometimes the King was chosen at a tournament, when all the knights fought against one another and the best one won. The knights fought with swords* (anzeichnen); *this is the handle of the sword* (anzeichnen). *The Celts did not have our God, they didn't believe in our God, they had wizards, a very famous wizard was Merlin* (ist den S evtl. bekannt), *and they believed in miracles. Sometimes when they were in danger and did not know what to do, they got the wizard, they fetched the wizard to help them.* Zur Vorbereitung des Textverständnisses empfiehlt es sich auch, die Namen: *King Uther, Sir Ector, Kay, Arthur, Queen Igrayne* an die Tafel zu schreiben.

Tafelbild

Je nach Leistungsstärke der Lerngruppe wird der Text dann ganz oder abschnittsweise vom Tonträger präsentiert.
Fragen Zl. 1-19: *Who was Uther, what do you know about him? How could the knights find out, who was the true king after him? What did Merlin tell them?*
Zl. 20-67: *Who are Sir Ector, Kay and Arthur? What are they doing? Why must Arthur ride back to the inn* (übersetzen)? *Then what happens? How does Kay react when he gets the sword? Why? And his father? Why did they go down on their knees?*
Zl. 68 - Ende: *What do we learn about Arthur? How do the knights react to him?*
Anschließend wird der Text mehrmals, evtl. mit verteilten Rollen, gelesen.

WB S.33, C1

Schülerbuch Seite 54

1 The characters and their feelings

Ziel: Gefühle beschreiben.

Neu: *feeling*

Unterrichtsempfehlungen
Je nach Leistungsstärke und vorhandener Zeit kann die Übung entweder in der Klasse vorbereitet und dann im Unterrichtsgespräch erarbeitet werden, oder man arbeitet in Gruppen. Jede Gruppe untersucht eine Person, bzw. Personengruppe, also *the knights, Arthur, Kay* oder *Sir Ector*. Außer den im Buch genannten Situationen können weitere untersucht werden, die Ergebnisse werden auf Postern festgehalten. Z.B.:
The knights:
When King Uther died they were
– *sad, because he had been a good king*
– *afraid, because there was no one to take over the kingdom*
– *jealous of one another, because everyone wanted to follow him as King*
– ...
When they couldn't move the sword
– ...
When Merlin talked to them
– ...
On New Year's Day when they waited for the tournament
– ...
In the evening when they stood in the Cathedral Square
– ...
When they saw what Arthur could do
– ...
So machen die S sich über die verschiedenen Situationen des Textes Gedanken und entwickeln ein tieferes Verständnis für den Ablauf der Handlung sowie die Sage an sich.

2 Kay and Arthur

Ziel: Personen charakterisieren.

Neu: *statement*

Unterrichtsempfehlung
Im Unterrichtsgespräch werden die Personen und ihre Handlungsmotive untersucht, wobei durchaus unterschiedliche Meinungen zugelassen werden sollten, vor allem z.B. bei 3., 5. und 6. Wichtig ist, dass jede Meinung mit einer Textstelle belegt werden muss.

WB S.33, C2

3 Families

Ziel: Wortschatzarbeit

Unterrichtsempfehlungen
Teil a) erarbeiten die S in Partnerarbeit ohne Vorbereitung durch L, wodurch der Reiz erhöht wird, weil zunächst das Lösungsprinzip herausgefunden werden muss. Evtl. können die S anschließend aufgefordert werden, Überbegriffe für ihre Wortgruppen zu finden. Als Hausaufgabe können die S eine *mind map* zu einem Überbegriff ihrer Wahl erstellen.
Teil b) kann auch als Wettspiel angelegt werden: jede/r S versucht in einer vorgegebenen Zeit (ca. 2 Minuten) zu jedem Wort so große Familien wie möglich zusammenzustellen. Wer am meisten hat, hat gewonnen.

WB S.34, C3
WB S.34, C4

Lösungen: a) 1. valley, mountain, hill 2. golf, rugby, climbing 3. inn, hotel, youth hostel 4. route, road, path 5. Romans, Saxons, Britons 6. village, city, town 7. English, Scottish, Welsh.

4 Listening practice: Sir Ector remembers

Ziel: Schulung des Hörverstehens.

Neu: *real*

Text
Arthur: Tell me about the night when Merlin brought me to you, Father. I can still call you Father, can't I?
Sir Ector: Of course, my boy! I'll always think of you as my son, you know that. – Well, that night there was a terrible storm. Your mother and I couldn't sleep, with the nowse of the thunder. Just after midnight we heard somebody at the door. "Who can that be – at this time of night?" your mother wondered. Well, I opened the door – and there in the rain stood Merlin, with a little baby in his arms. You were so small then, Arthur!
Arthur: But – but what did you and Mother say when Merlin brought me? It was a shock to you, wasn't it?
Sir Ector: No, not really. We knew that King Uther had enemies. Some were even at the court. Some weeks before you were born, Merlin told us his plan. We were glad we could help. So your life was no longer in danger.
Arthur: And what about Kay? What did he say when a little baby brother suddenly appeared in the house?
Sir Ector: Well, he was jealous at first. Small children often are. Of coursse he had no idea who you really were, Arthur.
Arthur: I still can't quite believe you aren't my father!
Sir Ector: Well, I still feel you're my son, Arthur! When I heard about the sword in the stone, I didn't really want to take you with me to the tournament. I didn't want to lose you as my son. But you wanted to come – and of course it had to happen sooner or later. And now you will be King...
Arthur: What happened to my real father and mother?
Sir Ector: Your father died when you were two. One of his enemies killed him. Your mother is still alive, I believe, but I don't know where you can find her. Her life was in danger when King Uther died, and she left the court.
Arthur (slowliy, thoughtfully): Perhaps Merlin knows where to look for her.

Unterrichtsempfehlungen
Zunächst werden die Aufgabenstellung sowie die Fragen gelesen und geklärt, bevor der Text vom Tonträger präsentiert wird. Nach der ersten Textpräsentation sollen die S sich stichwortartige Antworten notieren, bevor der Text ein zweites Mal vorgespielt wird.

Schülerbuch Seite 55

Step D Let's check

1 Gosh! So long?

Ziel: Festigung des *present perfect progressive*.

Unterrichtsempfehlungen
Die Übung kann in Partnerarbeit vorbereitet, dann in der Klasse vorgetragen werden. Außerdem können die S, ggf. als Hausaufgabe, weitere Situationen finden, in denen vergangene Zeiträume ausgedrückt werden. WB S.35, D1

Lösungen: *2. They have been driving for nearly seven hours. / ... since 9.30. 3. It has been raining for an hour. 4. They have been living there for twelve years. 5. He has been watching TV since 6 o'clock. / ... for some hours.*

2 I don't know ...

Ziel: Festigung des Infinitivs nach Fragewörtern. WB S.35, D3

Unterrichtsempfehlungen
Erarbeitung der Übung in der Klasse. Anschließend können als Erweiterung in Stillarbeit die Satzenden verändert werden, so dass neue Situationen entstehen. Die S tragen jeweils ihre Situationen vor, neue Schlussfolgerungen müssen gefunden werden, z.B.: *2. You need a new film for your camera, but you haven't got any money*. Situationen, die keinen Infinitiv nach Fragewort verlangen, sind natürlich auch zuzulassen.

Lösungsmöglichkeiten: *2. You don't know where to buy one. / ... where to find a shop. 3. You're not sure what to wear. / ... how to dress. 4. You have no idea when to go. / ... what time to be there. 5. You don't know how to ride. / ... whether to go. 6. ... whether to see it. / ... who to go to the cinema with. 7. ... which one to read first. / ... when to read them.*

3 Not sure

Ziel: Festigung der *question tags*. WB S.35, D2

Unterrichtsempfehlungen
Nach der mündlichen oder schriftlichen Durchnahme der Übung empfiehlt sich evtl. die Übersetzung der Sätze. Zur Erweiterung können positive Sätze wieder in negative umgeformt werden und umgekehrt.

Lösungen: *1. isn't it? 2. are we? 3. didn't you? 4. isn't there? 5. doesn't it? 6. have they? 7. won't it? 8. don't they?*

Schülerbuch Seite 56

Workshop C Let's read

Allgemeiner Hinweis zu Workshop C
Im Zentrum dieses *Workshop* steht eine Einführung in die wesentlichen Lesetechniken, dazu das Analysieren von Leseerwartungen und von Reaktionen auf Gelesenes.
Diese Lesetechniken werden eingeführt und geübt anhand von Material zum Thema *Hadrian's Wall / The Romans in Britain*. Es wird ein hohes Maß an historisch-landeskundlicher Information vermittelt, die ihren eigenen Stellenwert auf diesen Seiten hat, die in der Regel hohen Motivationswert aufweist und die zu erarbeiten und zu sichern sich lohnt.
Hier eine stichwortartige Zusammenfassung von Fakten, die zur Einordnung und Beantwortung von Fragen in diesem *Workshop* wichtig sind:
a) 55 v.Chr.: Caesars erste Landung in Britannien. Die Römer treffen auf keltische Stämme. Spätere Landung Caesars: Unterwerfung einiger weniger Stämme im Süden. Danach ca. 100 Jahre kaum militärische Aktivitäten.
b) 43 n.Chr.: Eigentliche Eroberung unter Kaiser Claudius. Britannien wird römische Provinz. Hauptstadt: das heutige Colchester (lat.: Camulodunum).
c) 60 n.Chr.: Iceni-Rebellion unter Königin Boudicca (s. S. 58). Die 3 zerstörten Städte waren Londinium (London), Camulodunum (Colchester), Verulamium (St. Albans). Boudicca wurde Thema verschiedener literarischer Werke, z.B. John Fletcher, *Bouduca*, Lord Tennyson *Boadicea*. *Iceni*: keltischer Stamm im heutigen Suffolk /Norfolk.
d) ca. 84 n.Chr.: Agricola besiegt die Caledonier im Norden.
e) Anlage von Straßennetzen durch die Römer. Urbanisierung wird vorangetrieben. Einbezug auch eines Teils der keltischen Bevölkerung in die Verwaltung der römischen Organisation. Der keltische Adel, die Reichen, die Stadtbevölkerung übernehmen z.T. den römischen Lebensstil (Kleidung, Bäder, ...) und die lateinische Sprache. Die Landbevölkerung bewahrte ihre keltische Tradition.
f) ca.122–133 n.Chr. unter Kaiser Hadrian: Gedanke einer festen Begrenzung des Römischen Reiches im Norden: *Hadrian's Wall*: 117 km lang von (Ost nach West) Wallsend/Newcastle–Benwell–Rudchester–Halton–Chesters–Carrawburgh–Housesteads–Great chesters–Carvoran–Birdoswald–Castlesteads–Stanwix/Carlisle–Burgh by Sands–Drumburgh–Bowness. Hinweis: nicht die heutige Grenze zu Schottland (vgl. Karte am Anfang von **Green Line New** 3). Die Mauer war 3m dick, 4,6 m hoch. Davor auf der nördl. Seite ein Graben: 10 m breit, 3 m tief. Südseite: Versorgungsstraße parallel zur Mauer. Nach jeder Meile ein *milecastle* (kleines Fort), besetzt mit 6–32 Soldaten. Dort Durchgänge (Grenzübergänge für die Bevölkerung und Handel). Zwischen den *milecastles* je 2 *turrets* (Beobachtungstürme). Garnisonsleben in 16 größeren Forts /Siedlungen entlang des Walls. Erbaut als Abgrenzung gegen die Picten und Scoten im Norden. Kämpfe hier während der gesamten Besatzungszeit. Grenze der römischen Jurisdiktion.
g) ca. 400–450 n.Chr.: Rückzug der Römer aus Britannien wegen der Bedrohung des Reiches durch die Westgoten. *Hadrian's Wall* danach bedeutungslos, zerstört. Ruinen sind geblieben. Die Steine z.T. zum Häuser- und Straßenbau benutzt. Seit Mitte des 19. Jh. systematische Ausgrabungen durch *National Trust* und *English Heritage*.
h) Aus der römischen Besatzungszeit geblieben: Mauerreste / Mosaikböden / einige sprachliche Einflüsse / Bäder (Bath) / Straßennetzanlagen (heutige M1; A1, A4) / Trennung Schottland–England / Städtenamen (<u>Chester</u> /<u>Leicester</u> / Col<u>chester</u> /...) / Einflüsse auf das Rechtssystem und politische Strukturen.

Informationsquellen sind reichlich vorhanden.
English Heritage, 429 Oxford Street, London W1R 2HD; tel.: 0044-171-973 3434. (Internet: www.english-heritage.org.uk) Handbook 1997: £4.95 (kann mit Kreditkarte direkt über Tel. Nr. 0044-1604-781163 bestellt werden.)
The National Trust, Bromley, Kent BR1 1UG; tel. 0044-181-315-1111 (Internet: http.//www.ukindex.co.uk/ nationaltrust) Handbook 1997: £4.50 (Kann über 0044-1225-790800 bestellt werden).
Über das Internet ist z.B. über folgende Adressen Zusatzinformation, Material und Hilfe zu beziehen:
(zu Iceni/Boudicca)
http://celt.net/wwwboard2/messages/47.html
http://travesti.geophys.mcgill.ca/~ olivia/BOUDICA
(= *County Tourism Guide*):
http://www.demon.co.uk/tynedale
(Museum of Antiques; spezialisiert auf *Hadrian's Wall*):
http://www.ncl.ac.uk/~nantiq/moremus.html

Schülerbuch Seite 56-57

1 Starting off

Ziel: Arbeitstechnik: Erwartungen an einen Text formulieren; den Inhalt eines Textes feststellen; Vorwissen über die Römer formulieren und durch neue Information ergänzen.

Neu: *to start off, wind, to blow/blew/blown, to have a cold, sky, soldier, to decide, to defend s.th.; Kent.*

Unterrichtsempfehlungen
Am Anfang der Arbeit an diesem *Workshop* sollte ein Hinweis auf den Vokabelkasten im *Vocabulary* auf Seite 144 stehen. Hier sind die Wörter zu finden, die nur vorübergehend für die Lektüre der (authentischen und semiauthentischen) Texte dieses *workshop* gebraucht werden. Der Lernwortschatz ist unter den einzelnen Übungen angegeben. [Vocabulary S. 144]
Gegenstand der Übungen 1–4 sind alle Texte und Illustrationen der oberen Seitenhälften der Doppelseite 56-57. Es empfiehlt sich, das Text- und Bildmaterial anhand der Fragen in Übung 1 zu erarbeiten.
Semantisierung: *Kent:* auf der Landkarte zeigen. *to start off: to begin s.th.; wind:* wird aus dem Schriftbild deutlich; *to blow: the noise the wind makes.* L bläst Stück Papier auf dem Tisch; *to have a cold: in winter one often has a temperature and does not feel well. Throat and nose are sore; sky: the air above you, where you can see the clouds; soldier: a member of an army; to decide: to choose to do s.th. after careful thinking; to defend s.th.: to keep bad things away from s.th./s.o.*

1 The subject

Ziel: Das Thema eines Textes herausfinden; Leseerwartungen formulieren; vorhandenes Wissen über die Römer reaktivieren.

Neu: *complete, to expect, subject*

Unterrichtsempfehlungen
Semantisierung: *complete: full* (wird durch Schriftbild deutlich); *to expect: to think that s.th. will happen; subject: s.th. that one talks about in a lesson or discussion.* Am Anfang der Textarbeit steht die vermeintlich einfache Frage *What is the text about?* Das man auch bei dieser Feststellung manchmal Hilfe aus anderen Quellen als nur der Wortlaut des Textes gewinnen kann, wird im Laufe dieser und der folgenden Übungen den S bewusst gemacht. Ein erster Schritt in diese Richtung stellen die beiden Fragen im *tip box* dar. Damit diese Grundlagen der Textarbeit nicht mit der Abgabe des 3. Bandes verlorengehen, empfiehlt es sich, die Inhalte der *tip boxes* nach der Erarbeitung der jeweiligen Übung von den S im Heft notieren zu lassen.
In lernstarken Klassen kann die Erarbeitung der einzelnen Textfragmente anhand von Fragen 1 und 2 in Gruppenarbeit erfolgen. In lernschwächeren Klassen empfiehlt sich eine gemeinsame Erarbeitung im Klassengespräch und Festhaltung der Ergebnisse an der Tafel oder auf Folie. Frage 3 kann in Gruppen- oder Partnerarbeit bearbeitet werden. Als Verfahren bieten sich entweder ein *brainstorming* (mit anschließendem Vergleich und Zusammenstellung an der Tafel) oder eine *mindmap* von jedem S. Später Sammlung an der Tafel. Etwa: [Tafelbild]

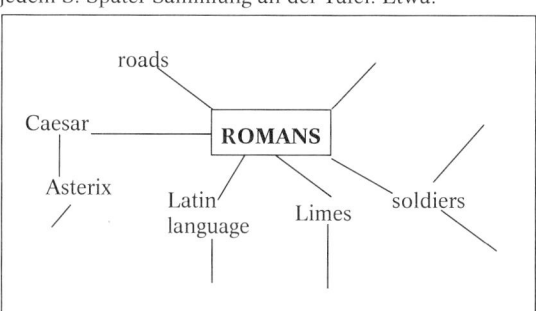

```
            roads
Caesar ─────┐
            │
            ROMANS ──── soldiers
Asterix ────┤
         Latin    Limes
       language
```

In den meisten Bundesländern weisen die Lehrpläne Geschichte für die 6. bzw. 7. Klasse die Beschäftigung mit den Römern aus. Es bestehen also gute Chancen, dass gesichertes Vorwissen vorhanden ist und die Aufgabe zufriedenstellend gelöst werden kann. Fächerübergreifende Arbeit evtl. mit dem Geschichtslehrer oder in Klassen mit Latein als 2. Fremdsprache ist hier möglich und empfehlenswert. **Green Line 3 neu** liefert neu den britischen Aspekt zum Thema.
Frage 4 fördert die Phantasie und bringt zunächst auf der affektiven Ebene ein Gefühl für die unterschiedliche Art der drei Textfragmente.
Um das Formulieren von Leseerwartungen weiter zu trainieren, könnte der L weitere Anfänge von Kurzgeschichten/Romanen/... als *handout* verteilen mit der Aufforderung, die Erwartungen an die Fortsetzung der Texte zu formulieren, etwa:
– *Colly Babcock was shot (dead) on the night of September 9.* (B.Pronzini, *It's a Lousy World*)
– *I think that I (hated) Dr. Fischer more than any other man ... just as I loved his daughter more than any other woman.* (Graham Greene, *Dr. Fischer of Geneva*)
– *It was Sunday. Chance was in the garden. He moved slowly ...* (Jerzy Kosinski, *Being There*)

Lösungsmöglichkeiten: 1. *Roman Wall Blues:* 1. It's about a soldier on a wall where it's cold and wet. He doesn't feel happy about his job. *The Romans conquer ...:* It says how the Roman army under Claudius invaded Britain. *It was a warm evening:* A woman is watching the Roman army as they march past. She must be a British woman.
2. *Roman Wall Blues:* That it was not nice for the soldiers on this wall. *The Romans conquer ...:* That the Roman army landed in Kent and fought against the Britons. The Romans under Claudius came in AD 43. They wanted Britain to be part of their empire. 40,000 soldiers landed in Kent. They were the strongest army in the world but they didn't conquer Britain quickly: it took 17 years. *It was a warm evening:* The Britains could not do much against the Roman army
3. S. oben
4. *Roman Wall Blues:* The soldier could say that he wants to go home. Or there could be a battle against the people north of the wall. *The Romans conquer ...:* ... and the Britons had no chance against them. In time the Roman soldiers conquered the whole country. *It was a warm evening:* The soldiers go past and the woman's husband comes back. He and his friends are going to get together to fight the Romans.

2 More clues

Ziel: Weitere Informationsquellen bewusst nutzen lernen.

Neu: *sun, to shine/shone/shone, gold, blues, no-one, to protect; Rome*

Unterrichtsempfehlungen
Semantisierung: *sun: the hot star in the sky that gives us light; to shine:* durch das Lautbild in Verbindung mit *sun* deutlich. *The sun isn't shining today; gold:* durch Schrift- und Lautbild deutlich; *no-one:* nobody; *to protect: if a guard keeps s.th. safe, he protects it; Rome = capital of Italy* (Karte); Texte und Bilder auf diesen Seiten unterstützen sich gegenseitig in ihrem Informationsgehalt. Aus dem Bildmaterial sind Bestätigung und Erweiterung der Textaussagen zu gewinnen. Im Unterrichtsgespräch werden die Antworten auf Fragen 1 und 2 der *ex. 1* nochmals im Zusammenhang mit dem Bild- und Kartenmaterial untersucht.

Lösungsmöglichkeiten: 1. *A photo, two maps and a cartoon.*
2. *There's a photograph of Hadrian's Wall. It's a long stone wall across the hills. People are walking along it. On the little map below you can see a line across the country in the north near Scotland, so that's probably the wall. Hadrian's Wall is on the map at the front of the book, too. You can see it better there. It goes across*

35

the north of England. The small map shows how the Romans landed in the southeast and marched to the southwest, the west and the north. The larger map shows how big the Roman empire was. Rome was in the middle and Britain was a long way from Rome. The cartoon shows the soldiers, who like fighting. The weather is not as good as the weather in Italy.
3) Individuelle SS-Lösungen.

3 Different kinds of text

Ziel: Textsortenidentifizierung und Formulierung von Leseerwartung an die Textsorten.

Unterrichtsempfehlungen
L und S erarbeiten dann gemeinsam an der Tafel eine Liste von Textsortenbezeichnungen (Vorschlag: L hat je ein Beispiel mitgebracht): *story, report, brochure, letter, play/drama, poem, history book, geography book, map, picture story, comic, prescription, newspaper article, comment, summary, notice, picture...*
Die S ordnen dann die Texte von Seiten 56 und 57 den Textsortenbezeichnungen zu und besprechen die 2. Frage dieser Übung. Hier ist die Möglichkeit, die S auf einige hilfreiche *classroom phrases* (S. 182f) hinzuweisen. SB S. 182f.
Relevanter Wortschatz zur Formulierung der Erwartungen ist bereits reichhaltig vorhanden, z.B. *action, adventure, beautiful, boring, clever, to conquer, crazy, dangerous, dead, difficult, enemy, exciting, facts, famous, fantasy, frightening, funny, ghost, to imagine, information, interesting, to invade, to laugh, country, city, to learn, opponent, outlaw, police, rescue, spy, rhyme...*
Die gewaltige Ausdehnung des Römischen Reiches sollte den S anhand der *map* (S. 57) bewusst gemacht werden. WB S.37, 1.1 / WB S.38, 1.2, 1.3

Lösungen: *1. poem, picture, history book, map, comic, story.*

4 Talk about it

Ziel: Fächerübergreifender Ansatz: Mauern und Wälle. Aktivierung von S-Wissen.

Unterrichtsempfehlungen
1) Als fächerübergreifendes Miniprojekt denkbar: S sammeln Beispiele (etwa *Berlin Wall, Limes, Great Wall of China, Belfast,* ...). Dann in arbeitsteiligen Gruppen: Bildfolie 14
Informationen sammeln zu den Beispielen, Intergruppen bilden (neue Gruppenzusammensetzung, so dass in jeder neuen Gruppe Vertreter der ursprünglichen Gruppen sitzen) und gegenseitige Information über die Arbeitsergebnisse. L stellt Lexika, Bildbände, Internetzugang zur Verfügung. Auf die Möglichkeit der Befragung von Geschichts- und Geographielehrern der Schule müssen die S hingewiesen werden. Diese 2. Frage kann in diesem Zusammenhang mitbeantwortet werden. Sachliche Information siehe **Allgemeiner Hinweis** auf S. 34.

Schülerbuch Seite 58

2 How to read a text

1 Getting the gist

Ziel: Einführung in extensives Lesen; Erweiterung des Informationsstandes über die Römer

Neu: *to get the gist, main, heading, paragraph, to welcome s.o., border, field, false, tooth/teeth, rebellion, to lead/led/led, to burn/burnt/burnt, fort*

Unterrichtsempfehlungen
Semantisierung: <u>to get the gist</u>: *to understand the most important thing;* <u>main</u>: *most important;* <u>heading</u>: *the title of a text;* <u>paragraph</u>: *part of a text;* <u>to welcome s.o.</u>: *welcome* ist bekannt, muß nur nur in Kontext gebracht werden; <u>border</u>: *the line between two countries;* <u>field</u>: *a farmer works in the field;* <u>false</u>: *not correct;* <u>tooth:</u> zeigen. *You need your teeth if you want to eat;* <u>rebellion:</u> wird durch das Schriftbild klar; <u>to lead:</u> *to be number one person in s.th.;* <u>to burn:</u> *to put fire to s.th.;*
Zunächst noch keine Vokabelsemantisierung. Die S erarbeiten in Partnerarbeit oder Gruppenarbeit, was ihnen hilft, das Wesentliche eines Textes zu erschließen (vgl. auch S. 56/2). Konkretion: *What information and help do we get from headings, pictures, beginnings of paragraphs...?*
Weitere Vorschläge: Zu *keywords*:
a) S erhalten den Text als *handout*. Aufgabe für Individualarbeit: Markiere (mit Textmarker) im Text so, dass Information über *Hadrian's Wall* sichtbar wird.
b) Markiere im Text so, dass Reaktionen der Menschen auf die Römer sichtbar werden.
c) Finde und markiere schnell folgende *keywords*: *welcome, plans for a great wall, rebellion, burned 3 cities, poison, central heating, straight streets, Latin language ...*
Zum *extensive reading:* an diesem und an anderen Texten Lesetraining: Mit Bleistift/Finger o.ä. und mit wachsender Geschwindigkeit in schlangenförmiger Bewegung die Zeilen des Textes verfolgen, mit den Augen dabei den Text wahrnehmen. Allmählich ausgiebigere Schlangenlinien (mehr als 1 oder 2 Zeilen pro Bewegungsrichtung). Auf diese Weise Vergrößerung des Blickfeldes und der Wahrnehmung durch das Auge. Temposteigerung. L erfragt dann, wieviel vom Text nach einmaligem Durchgang auf diese Weise verstanden wurde. WB S.39, 2.1
Vorschläge zum landeskundlichen Bereich: a) den Verlauf des *Hadrian's Wall* auf einer Karte genau nachvollziehen; b) Informationen zu Boudicca sammeln (siehe **Allgemeiner Hinweis** auf S. 34).

Schülerbuch Seite 59

2 Understanding the details

Ziel: Einführung in intensives Lesen.

Neu: *to get s.th. right, to translate*

Unterrichtsempfehlungen
Semantisierung: <u>to get s.th. right</u>: *to understand s.th. correctly;* <u>to translate:</u> *to put a text into another language.*
Die S erhalten Gelegenheit, den Text S. 58 noch einmal in Ruhe zu lesen (vgl. *tip 1*, S. 59). Dann im Sinne der Aufgabe: Jede/jeder S schreibt 3 Fragen zu Textdetails auf, die dann dem Nachbarn zwecks Beantwortung gestellt werden. Etwa: *How big was Boudicca's army? In which year did she kill herself? What is said about Roman clothes in the text? Where did young Britons have to call if they wanted to help build the wall?...* WB S.40, 2.2

3 Picking out information

Ziel: Einführung in selektives Lesen

Neu: *to pick out, to function, personal*

Unterrichtsempfehlungen
Semantisierung: <u>to pick out</u>: *to choose;* <u>to function:</u> *to work well.* <u>personal:</u> dt.: *persönlich. Can I ask you a personal question?*
Die S finden in Einzel- oder Partnerarbeit heraus, auf welcher Seite der Broschüre zu *Hadrian's Wall* sie die Informationen finden würden, die in den Fragen gesucht werden. Als Wettkampf: Wer findet als erster die Antworten auf alle Fragen? Im Unterrichtsgespräch: *Explain how you found out so quickly. What did you look for?*
Vorschlag: selektives Lesen an einigen weiteren Texten üben: Text vorgeben, Frage(n) vorgeben, knappe Zeitvorgaben (z.B. *Find in 45 seconds what* ...).
Landeskundlicher Hinweis: Zu den Antworten hier siehe auch **Allgemeiner Hinweis** auf S. 34.

Noch zu a) *soldiers' personal and military life:* Siehe auch Workbook Seite 39. Dienst auf dem Wall, Leben in *barracks* in den Forts, Aufgaben waren: Sicherung der Nachschubtransporte, Patrouillengänge, Wachdienste, Säuberungsarbeiten, Militärübungen, Leibesertüchtigung, Durchgänge im *milecastle* kontrollieren. Nach 25 Jahren Kriegsdienst gab es Niederlassungsmöglichkeit (z.B. Landbesitz). Es bestanden auch Kontakte zur Zivilbevölkerung.

Zu b) Einfluss auf die Einheimischen: recht enger Kontakt. Sprache, Kleidung, Luxus ... wurden z.T. von den Einheimischen übernommen. Einige halfen beim Mauerbau. Insgesamt: Koexistenz.

Mögliche Aktivitäten hier:
- Ausstellungsprojekt *Hadrian's Wall* organisieren *(The Roman army/ the Wall/ traces of the Romans/ Iceni/ ...)*
- Broschüre im Sinne der S. 59 erstellen *(Special features* bearbeiten und mit Material füllen) oder *newspaper page* wie Seite 58.
- S erarbeiten in Partnerarbeit den fiktiven Tagesablauf eines römischen Soldaten am *Hadrian's Wall* (etwa: *At 6 o'clock in the morning he ...*).

Lösungen: *1: p. 16; 2: pp. 11,13; 3: p. 13; 4: p. 18; 5: p. 15*

4 Talk about it

Neu: *remains*

Unterrichtsempfehlungen

Semantisierung: *remains: what is left over.*

> Schülerbuch Seite 60

3 Reacting to a text

1 Reacting while you read

Ziel: Reaktionen auf einen Text formulieren *(while-reading activity)*; Einflüsse des Lateinischen auf das Englische und Deutsche ansatzweise erkennen.

Neu: *to react to s.th., author, next door, thin, though, everyday life, room, to wish, to pretend, outside, tongue, change*

Unterrichtsempfehlungen

Semantisierung: *to react to s.th.:* deutsch geben. Ähnlichkeit zum Deutschen; *author: the person who has written a book or s.th. else; next door: in the house next to yours; thin: opposite of fat; though: although; everyday life: normal life as it happens every day; room:* hier: Platz. Deutsch geben, gegen Zimmer abgrenzen; *to wish: to want, hope that s.th. will happen; to pretend: to act as if s.th. was true; outside:* opp. of inside; *tongue:* another word for 'language'; *change:* noun of 'to change'

Unterrichtsempfehlungen

Als Wiederholungsübung der *Workshop*-Teile 1 und 2 zunächst z.B.:
- *Decide quickly what kind of text this is.*
- *What do you expect from a text like this?*
- *What is the text probably about? How did you find out?*
- *You've got 45 seconds. Find information about Aunt Valaria.*
- *Underline words you don't know. Look at the tip on p. 26. Guess what the words mean. If you can't, look them up or ask your teacher.*

L erläutert dann die Zielrichtung: *reacting while you read.*
L liest dann den Text langsam vor, hält nach den markierten Stellen ein, bezieht sich auf die erläuterte Zielrichtung. Im Unterrichtsgespräch werden die Fragen/ Aufträge am Rand bearbeitet.
Dieses *reacting* sollte an mehreren Texten bzw. auch später im Lehrwerk (pp. 69, 84, 85 etwa) geübt werden.

> Schülerbuch Seite 61

2 The characters

Ziel: auf einen Text reagieren; Übung des intensiven Lesens und der tabellarischen Darstellung von Fakten.

Neu: , *to feel sorry for s.o.*

Unterrichtsempfehlungen

Semantisierung: *to feel sorry for s.o.: sorry* ist bekannt. Kontext: *We felt sorry for him when he heard the bad news.*
Die Charaktere sind: *Cottia, her father, her mother, her brother, Marcus, Aunt Valaria, the hunter.*
Die S arbeiten in 3 arbeitsteiligen Gruppen und sammeln jeweils Informationen über a) *Cottia,* b) *Marcus,* c) *Valaria, mother, father, brother, the hunter.* (z.B. *Marcus: Roman soldier / 2nd century / is staying at his uncle's house west of Londinium / feels in exile; Valaria: Iceni / tries to be as 'Roman' as possible / has no children / brings up Cottia).* – Jede Gruppe fertigt eine Ergebnisfolie an.
Anhand dieser Ergebnisse (OHP-Bild) Übergang zu: *eigene Folie*

3 Reacting to the text

Ziel: auf einen Text reagieren, Partei ergreifen; Meinung durch Textstellen belegen.

Unterrichtsempfehlungen

1) Die S bleiben in ihren Gruppen und diskutieren die einzelnen Charaktere mit Hilfe des hier angegebenen Sprachmaterials (s. auch S. 183 als Hilfe) und des OHP-Bildes. Dann kurze Darstellung im Plenum: L fragt: *Who talked about Valaria/Marcus/Cottia ...? What were your arguments? Do you like/feel ...?'*
2) L: *Let's take Cottia, for example. You said you ... her. Let's find out what made you feel like this ...* Den Text durchgehen und Belege suchen für positive bzw. negative Leserreaktionen. (Z.B.: *my father was killed, my real name is ..., there was no room ... for me, I hate – hate – hate – ..., I did not wish to live in that hunter's home.)* *WB S.41-42, 3.1-3*

4 Comparing situations

Ziel: auf einen Text reagieren; einbringen des eigenen Umfeldes.

Neu: *to remind s.o. of s.th.*

Unterrichtsempfehlungen

Semantisierung: *to remind s.o. of s.th.: to tell s.o. to remember s.th.*
Der erste, persönliche, Teil der Aufgabe sollte in Partnerarbeit gelöst werden. Die S berichten einander über einschlägige persönliche Erfahrungen (wenn vorhanden).
Der 2. Teil (gezielt zur Fremdenproblematik) kann von den S gemeinsam als *cluster* an der Tafel gelöst werden, etwa: *Tafelbild*

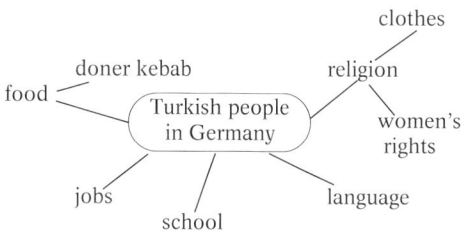

```
                              clothes
          doner kebab        religion
    food  ─┐    ┌─────────────┐    
          └──┤ Turkish people ├──
             │   in Germany   │    women's
          ┌──┤                ├──  rights
    jobs ─┘    └─────────────┘    
                 │         │     language
              school
```

Verfahren etwa: S1 z.B.: *They have language problems.* S2: *But Turkish people who have been to school .... I'm sure it was the same with ...*
Als Hausarbeit könnten die S anhand des Tafelbildes einen Text zum Thema schreiben.

5 Looking at language: The Romans in Europe

Ziel: Einflüsse des Lateinischen auf die englische und deutsche Sprache erkennen.

Unterrichtsempfehlungen
a) Ein S an der Tafel erstellt auf Zuruf der anderen die lateinische Spalte. Danach werden von zwei weiteren S – ebenfalls auf Zuruf neben die lateinischen Wörter die englischen und deutschen geschrieben.
Lösung:

Latein	Englisch	Deutsch
turris	tower	Turm
Augustus	August	August
vallum	wall	–
castellum	castle	–
strata	–	Straße
Januarius	January	–
tabula	–	Tafel
fructus	fruit	–
carota	–	Karotte
familia	–	Familie

Die fehlenden Wörter werden gemeinschaftlich ergänzt.
Englisch: *street, table, carrot, family.*
Deutsch: Wall, Kastell, Januar, Frucht.
In Lateinklassen bzw. mit Hilfe von Lateinlehrern an der Schule kann die Liste erweitert werden.
b) Herauszufinden wären hier: *food / calendar / streets / houses.*
Am Ende des *Workshop* sollte eine gezielte Zusammenfassung über das stehen, was zum Thema ‚Lesetechniken' gelernt wurde. Alle einzelnen Techniken müssen im Folgenden ständig wiederholt und geübt werden.
Zur Sicherung der landeskundlichen Aspekte s. oben: Broschüre / Ausstellung / Tafelbilder.

Schülerbuch Seiten 62–63

Unit 4 The environment

Allgemeine Hinweise
Hauptthema dieser *Unit* ist der Einfluss des Straßenverkehrs auf die Umwelt, ein Thema, das sich besonders für die Projektarbeit im fächerübergreifenden Unterricht anbietet. Dabei werden verschiedene Probleme des ständig zunehmenden Straßenverkehrs aufgezeigt und besprochen.
Sprachliches Hauptthema ist die Einführung und Anwendung des Passivs, das zunächst im typischen Gebrauch ohne *by-agent* vorgestellt wird:

"... *when the agent is unknown,* or difficult to specify, the passive is the normal construction [...] The passive is also used when, for some reason or other, it is necessary or desirable to *leave the agent unspecified.*"
(P. Christophersen & A.O. Sandved. *An Advanced English Grammar.* London: Macmillan, 1969. p. 227).

Das Thema Umwelt und Umweltverschmutzung eignet sich besonders gut als Kontext für den Passivgebrauch, da es oft sehr schwer ist festzustellen, wer letzten Endes an Verschmutzung schuld ist. Statt viele Sätze mit *"They"* oder *"People"* anfangen zu lassen, lernen S im Laufe der *Unit,* in solchen Fällen das Passiv zu verwenden. So kommen sie gar nicht erst in die Versuchung, sinnlose Passivsätze mit *by-agent* zu konstruieren, wo ein Aktivsatz natürlicher wäre. Der *by-agent* wird erst dann eingeführt, und zwar in *Step C,* nachdem das Passiv schon im normalen Gebrauch gefestigt wurde.

Step A A trip to a theme park
Ziel: Einführung in das Thema Straßenverkehr.

Neu: *environment, theme park, mile, traffic, motorway, roadworks, traffic jam, service station, petrol, roundabout, traffic lights; Alton Towers*

Unterrichtsempfehlungen
Im Mittelpunkt dieser Doppelseite steht die Straßenkarte, mit der unter *ex. 1* gezielt gearbeitet wird. Zunächst aber sollte man zur Orientierung das übrige Bildmaterial auf der Seite besprechen und dabei den neuen Wortschatz einführen. Die S ordnen die neuen Wörter den Bildern auf Seiten 62–63 zu. Der Auftakt bietet die L-Frage: *Have you ever been to a theme park like Phantasialand/Euro-Disney/...* (entsprechende Anlage aus der näheren Umgebung)? *What can you do there?* (S: *go on rides – ride on a train – eat/drink ... – see animals/...*) Alton Towers *is a theme park like that. Look at the poster on the left. What can you do there? ... If you drive to a theme park you could go on a fast road: a* motorway. *In Germany the motorways have numbers with A for "Autobahn", in Britain they have numbers with M for "motorway".* (Sign, bottom of page 62.) *You can drive fast on a motorway, up to 70* miles *an hour, that's 110 kilometres an hour, a mile is 1.609 (one point six-o-nine) kilometres. Sometimes there are too many cars on the motorway, then the traffic stops and nobody can move, there's a* traffic jam. *Which photo shows a traffic jam?* (P. 62, top) *Sometimes there's a traffic jam on the roads when they're repairing the road. They put up a sign:* road works. *If you want to get something to eat or drink or you need* petrol *for the car you can stop at a* service station. *(P. 63 top) When you drive a car in town you have to stop sometimes at a corner with a stop sign or at* traffic lights. *When the traffic lights are red you have to stop. Then they go yellow and green and you can go on. Where three or more roads meet you sometimes have a* roundabout. *You have to go round it* (Gestik – gegen den Uhrzeiger). *(P. 63 bottom). Where else can you see a roundabout on this page?* (Sign, bottom of p. 62)
Anschließend lesen S still die Texte zu den Photos und beantworten dabei folgende Fragen. — WB S.43, A1
1. *Why can you get stuck in a traffic jam?*
2. *You can get petrol at a service station. What else can you get there?*
3. *Why are roundabouts better than traffic lights?*
4. *Look at the roundabout on the sign. If you have come from Penderton and you take the first road out of the roundabout, where are you going to?*
Lösungen: *1. When there are roadworks or if there has been an accident. 2. Food / A meal / Something to eat and drink. 3. You don't have to wait. 4. Birmingham, Bourne and the M15. (You go left round a roundabout.)*

1 The way to Alton Towers
Ziel: Eine Route anhand einer Straßenkarte planen. — WB S.43, A2; WB S.50, Tandem Activity 4

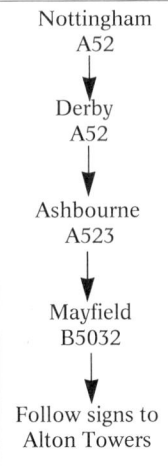

Neu: *Derby, Mayfield, Ellastone, Uttoxeter, Sudbury, Ashbourne*

Unterrichtsempfehlungen
Zur besseren Orientierung sollten die S kurz die hier gezeigte Straßenkarte mit der GB-Karte am Anfang des Bandes vergleichen. Danach sichert man Anfang (Sherwood, wo die Penroses wohnen, liegt im Westen von Nottingham) und Ziel der Fahrt (Alton Towers, bzw. der gelbe Pfeil an der Straße B5032 in der Nähe von Ellestone) und Aussprache der Ortsnamen und bespricht mögliche Routen. Sinnvoll wäre eine schematische Darstellung der Route, etwa als Flussdiagramm, die als Vorlage für Übung 2 dienen kann.

Tafelbild:
Nottingham
A52
↓
Derby
A52
↓
Ashbourne
A523
↓
Mayfield
B5032
↓
Follow signs to Alton Towers

Landeskundlicher Hinweis: Neben den *motorways*, von denen die erstgebaute, die M1, von London nach Norden führt, gibt es noch zwei weitere Straßenklassifizierungen: die *A roads* sind in der Regel gute Straßen, teilweise fast bis zum *motorway*-Standard ausgebaut. Die *B roads* sind kleinere, in ländlichen Gegenden teilweise sehr schmale Straßen. Die Ausschilderung ist in Großbritannien in der Regel gut. Alle *motorway exits* sind nummeriert. Die Angaben in Klammern auf einem Verkehrsschild (siehe Schild unten auf S. 62) bedeuten, dass die Straße zwar nicht diese Nummer trägt aber zur angegebenen Straße führt.

Lösungsmöglichkeiten: *They should take the A52 from Nottingham to Derby. Then they can stay on the A52 to Ashbourne or they can take the A516 to Sudbury and the A515 to Ashbourne, but that's a longer road. At Ashbourne they should take the A523 to Mayfield, and turn onto the B5032, then follow the signs to Alton Towers.*

2 Listening practice: Traffic news

Ziel: Hörverstehen. Relevante Informationen heraushören und notieren.

Neu: *light*

Text
This is the traffic news from the AA. Let's look at the traffic to the west of Nottingham. On the A52 to Derby there's light traffic. However, there's a problem on the A52 after Derby: an accident just to the east of Ashbourne. So there's a traffic jam over 5 miles long – and it's getting longer.
If you want to go west, it's best to use the A38 after Derby and then the A516 – but be careful if you want to go north again because there's heavy traffic on the A515, too. So take a B road if you can, and … *(fade)*

Unterrichtsempfehlungen
Semantisierung: <u>light</u>: opposite of 'heavy'. Beim Hören verfolgen die S ihre aufgezeichnete Route auf der Karte im Buch oder auf ihrem Flussdiagramm. Dabei schreiben sie die Informationen als Notizen auf, die für ihren Weg wichtig sind, revidieren ihr Flussdiagramm und formulieren die Beschreibung der neuen Route.

Lösungen: a) *A52 Nottingham to Derby OK – 5-mile traffic jam on A52 east of Ashbourne. – After Derby: A38 – not A515 – B road better*
b) *As ex. 1 but take the A38 after Derby and then the A516. Do not take the A515 at Sudbury because of heavy traffic. Go on past Uttoxeter and take the B5030.*

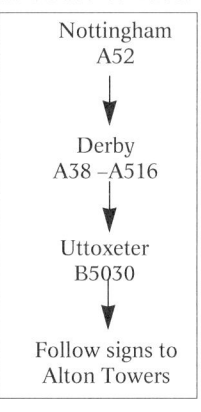

Tafelbild:
Nottingham
A52
↓
Derby
A38 – A516
↓
Uttoxeter
B5030
↓
Follow signs to Alton Towers

Schülerbuch Seite 64

Step A In the car

Ziel: Einführung in die Rahmenhandlung der *Unit*; Einführung in die Problematik des Autofahrens; Wiederholung von *should/shouldn't*.

Neu: *copy, It says …, to pollute, to cause, pollution, air, to switch off*

Unterrichtsempfehlungen
Semantisierung: <u>copy</u>: zusätzlich zur naheliegenden Entsprechung ‚Kopie' hat *copy* auch die Bedeutung ‚Exemplar einer Auflage', die am besten anhand von Zeitungen oder Zeitschriften oder Exemplaren vom SB oder WB zu demonstrieren ist. L: *Here are two copies of the Green Line 3 workbook. How many copies are there in the classroom? Hold up your copy.* <u>It says …</u>: *What does it say on the front of the book? It says: (Learning English 3 – Green Line new – workbook). What does it say at the top of page 50? (Tandem Activity)*; <u>to pollute</u>: *to make s.th. dirty*; <u>to cause:</u> *to make s.th. happen*; <u>pollution</u>: *making dirty*; <u>air:</u> *We need air to live, so do other animals, we take it in* (demonstrativ einatmen) *all the time. The air is all around us but we can't see it and birds and planes fly in the air;*
L liest die Einleitung vor, um kurz die Ausgangssituation zu klären, bevor der Dialog vom Tonträger eingespielt wird. S sollten danach hören, was über Autos und Umweltverschmutzung gesagt wird und welche Schlussfolgerung Mrs Penrose nach Marks Einwand zieht. L: *What do David and Mark say about cars? What does Mrs Penrose think?*

3 What should we do?

Ziel: Lesen einer Anzeige.

Neu: *to switch off, energy, to waste, to recycle, to destroy, to give s.th. up, light, plastic*

Unterrichtsempfehlungen
S erschließen sich den Inhalt der Anzeige selbst mit Hilfe des Vokabelverzeichnisses, wie sie es in einer realen Situation auch tun müssten. L kann kurz mit Fragen das Verständnis überprüfen und Beispiele abrufen: *1. What does the ad tell us? 2. What can you turn off to save energy? 3. What can you turn down? 4. What should you avoid?* S finden mit Sicherheit anhand der Materialliste noch viele weitere Beispiele. Interessant wäre auch die Aufgabe: *What do we do for the environment in school? Could we do more?*

WB S.44, A3

4 Can you find the right words?

Ziel: Übung des neu eingeführten Vokabulars.

Unterrichtsempfehlungen
Die Übung eignet sich gut als schriftliche Hausaufgabe.

Lösungen: *1. pollution 2. environment 3. recycle 4. petrol 5. waste 6. pollutes 7. saves*

Schülerbuch Seite 65

Step B An article in *Our Earth* magazine

Ziel: Einführung in das Passiv im *simple present* und *simple past*.

Neu: *to cut down, wide, to damage, bulldozer, to pull down, not … anymore; Greendale*

Unterrichtsempfehlungen
Semantisierung: *A motorway often has two or three lines of cars going each way, it's a* <u>wide</u> *road* (Gestik); *when they build new roads they have to take away trees – they* <u>cut down</u> *trees, they have to take houses and walls away, too, they* <u>pull</u> *them* <u>down</u>. *Then they bring along a big machine, a* <u>bulldozer</u>. *It pushes the earth about and makes everything ready for the road. If they hit a tree or a wall and* <u>damage</u> *it, they pull that down too. Everything looks different, it's* <u>not</u> *the same* <u>any more</u>. *Let's read about* <u>Greendale</u> *and find out what happened there.*
Der Text eignet sich zum stillen Lesen aber auch zum Vorlesen, wobei verschiedene S versuchen sollten, die Äußerung von Mavis Brandon mit viel Gefühl vorzutragen.
Aktivsätze werden in einer Liste angeschrieben und die entsprechenden Passivsätze aus dem Text dazu gesucht und zwar unter Verwendung der neu eingeführten Wendung *It says …. (What does it say in the text?)*

Tafelanschrieb bzw. eigene Folie

They destroy the countryside.   *The countryside is destroyed.*
They cut down trees.   *Trees are cut down.*
They build wider roads.   *Wider roads are built.*
They damage our environment.   *Our environment is damaged.*

They destroyed two fields.   *Two fields were destroyed.*
They pulled down some houses.   *Some houses were pulled down.*
They moved the road.   *The road was moved.*
They made lots of other changes.   *Lots of other changes were made.*

Es sollte darauf hingewiesen werden, dass nicht gesagt wird, wer etwas gemacht hat: *It says 'Trees are cut down'. It doesn't say who did it.*

1 Looking at English

Ziel: Bewusstmachung der Form und Verwendung des Passivs.

Neu: *passive*

Unterrichtsempfehlungen

Nach der Benennung des Passivs anhand der Formen in den aufgelisteten Beispielsätzen wird zunächst auf den Gebrauch eingegangen (**Grammar** § 15, 1. Teil auf Seite 111). Mit den Beispielsätzen an der Tafel oder OHP-Folie wird die Satzanalyse der Passivsätze wie im SB vorgeschlagen vorgenommen. Zur Bestätigung der Regelformulierung lesen L und S gemeinsam §15a) und b) (Seite 112).

                         GR §15

                         GR §15 a), b)

Lösungen: *Present simple passive:*
            present tense of 'to be' + past participle
            Past simple passive:
            past tense of 'to be' + past participle

2 New roads

Ziel: Erste Anwendung des Passivs im *present simple*.

Unterrichtsempfehlungen

Die gemeinsam unter *ex. 1* formulierten Regeln bleiben sichtbar, während die S zunächst mündlich dann schriftlich diese und die folgende Übung erarbeiten. Weitere Übungen zum Passiv finden sich im *Workbook*.

                   WB S.44, B1

Lösungen: *2. Tunnels are built. 3. Walls are pulled down. 4. Bulldozers are brought in. 5. Good farm land is destroyed. 6. The countryside is changed. 7. The environment is polluted.*

3 Last year

Ziel: Anwendung des Passivs im *past simple*.

Unterrichtsempfehlungen

Um die Sozialform des Unterrichts zu ändern, kann diese Aufgabe zunächst in Partnerarbeit gelöst und anschließend im Plenum besprochen werden. Vorher sollte L die S darauf hinweisen, dass das Material in ‚Telegrammstil' gegeben wird, sie müssen also auch Artikel ergänzen. Die Übung zum *past passsive* im Workbook bietet weitere Informationen über den *theme park Alton Towers*.

                   WB S.45, B2

Lösungen: *2. Some trees were cut down. 3. The road was made wider. 4. A car park was built. 5. Three houses were pulled down. 6. A service station was built.*

Schülerbuch Seite 66

Step B Saving the environment

Ziel: Erweiterung des Hauptthemas. Einführung des *present perfect passive* und *future passive*.

Neu: *the Stone Age, instead of, to injure, public transport, to improve, law, bottle bank, to pass; Rugby, Birmingham, Bournemouth*

Unterrichtsempfehlungen

Semantisierung: *the Stone Age: a long time ago, men used stones as knives. We call that time the Stone Age; instead of: If you want to write something, you can use a pencil instead of a biro or a felt tip instead of a pencil; to injure: to hurt or damage; public transport: Buses, trams and trains are public transport; anyone can use them; to improve: to make s.th. better; law/to pass a law: A law says you have to do or not do s.th.. The police make sure that people keep the law. Only Parliament can pass laws – make new laws. bottle bank: Don't throw empty bottles away, put them in the bottle bank, then the glass people can make them into new glass and new bottles* (Falls die S den Rap-Reim "*Clap 'n' Rap*" in **Green Line New** Band 2 5C2 kennen, sollte man hier daran erinnern); *Birmingham, Bournemouth:* s. Karte am Anfang des Buches. *Rugby* liegt etwa 15 km südöstlich von Coventry.

Landeskundlicher Hinweis: *Bottle banks* sind in GB überall zu finden, sowie meist an zentralen Orten Container für Altpapier, Blechdosen, und (von der Heilsarmee aufgestellt) für gebrauchte Textilien. Je nach Gemeinde gibt es auch regelmäßige Sammlungen von Altpapier, Blechdosen, Alufolie, Altöl, Autobatterien und Weihnachtsbäumen.

Der gemeinsamen Lektüre der Leserbriefe kann sofort Übung 4 folgen. Dabei hat die inhaltliche Diskussion zunächst Vorrang vor der Erweiterung der Grammatik.

4 What do you think?

Ziel: Zustimmung und Ablehnung äußern.

Unterrichtsempfehlungen

Die Fragen unter a) behandeln jeden Brief einzeln und eignen sich gut für Gruppenarbeit mit anschließender Kontrolle im Plenum. Dabei löst sich die Diskussion jeweils von den Briefvorlagen anhand der Erweiterungsfragen zu jedem Brief, damit die S eine eigene Meinung äußern können. b) erfordert konkrete Vorschläge, die vielleicht zunächst die unmittelbare Umgebung (Schule, Klassenzimmer) betreffen könnten.

Lösungsmöglichkeiten: a) *1. Perhaps Paula Warren is thinking of cars, washing machines and other machines that need energy. 2. Bikes are cleaner than cars but they are not as easy for old people or for going a long way. And in bad weather you get wet and cold. 3. Maybe Ricky Dart is thinking of things like cars and lorries, heavy industry ... 4. Paper and bottle banks are places where you can put old newspapers and magazines or empty bottles so that they can be used again to make new paper or new bottles.*

b) Eigene S-Lösungen

Schülerbuch Seite 67

5 It's up to you

Ziel: Anwendung des *present perfect passive*.

Neu: *It's up to you.*

Unterrichtsempfehlungen

It's up to you: it's your job. L erinnert an die Tabelle zur Struktur des *present und past passive*, die bei *ex. 1* erstellt wurde. Zur Erinnerung wird betont: *passive = a form of 'be' + past participle*. In Partnerarbeit suchen die S in den Leserbriefen nach weiteren Passivformen. In gemeinsamer Arbeit werden dann an der Tafel oder auf Folie zwei weitere Tabellen erstellt. (Siehe nächste Seite.) Anschließend kann Aufgabe a) in Partnerarbeit oder als Hausaufgabe gelöst werden. Als zusätzliche Hilfe weist L auf **Grammar** § 15 c) und d) hin. Eine Kontrolle der Ergebnisse im Plenum schließt sich an.

                   GR §15 c), d)

	present perfect form of 'to be'	past participle
The environment	has been	polluted.
Problems	have already been	found.
Everything	has been	polluted.
	future form of 'to be'	past participle
A clean kind of energy	will be	found.
Public transport	will be	improved.
Our whole environment	will be	destroyed.
When	will (laws) be	passed?

Tafelanschrieb oder eigene Folie

Bevor man dann zur weiteren Übung der *future passive* fortschreitet, empfiehlt sich eine kurze Auflockerung entweder durch die Arbeit mit Bildfolie 15 *"After the burglary"*, durch die *Workbook*-Übung oder durch ein Spiel, z.B. eine Variation auf *'Kim's game'*, die sich gut für Gruppen eignet. Mehrere Gegenstände werden auf einem Tisch ausgebreitet, wobei einzelne Sachen teilweise aufeinander liegen, aber so, dass alles deutlich zu sehen ist. Alle haben 1 Minute Zeit, sich die Gegenstände und ihre Lage einzuprägen. Dann drehen alle den Rücken, bis auf den Spielleiter/die Spielleiterin, der/die die Lage von zwei Gegenständen ändern darf und eine Sache wegnehmen kann. (Die Anzahl kann von Mal zu Mal unterschiedlich festgelegt, sollte aber am Anfang bekannt gegeben werden.) Die übrigen S der Gruppe müssen raten, was sich geändert hat: *I think the ... has been moved. It was on the ... ./I think the .../one of the ...s has been taken away*, etc.

Bildfolie 15
WB S.45, B3

Teil b erfordert eine kurze Vorbereitung, indem der Sachverhalt wieder in Erinnerung gerufen wird. Dazu eignet sich eine Betrachtung des Doppelbildes auf SB S. 67. Eine Bildbeschreibung führt in eine allgemeine Diskussion ein: *The picture shows the earth as a face. The earth face is smiling and looks happy. Its eyes are looking up. It can see that for its hair there are trees and green things. Above it is a blue sky and the sun is shining. If you turn the picture round you can see a different face. It isn't smiling, it's unhappy. The sky above it isn't blue, it's full of dirty black clouds. There are no trees on the earth, only buildings and factories. Perhaps this is what earth will look like one day. All the trees will be dead . ... .*
Die Tabelle mit *future-passive*-Formen bleibt als Hilfe sichtbar..

Lösungsmöglichkeiten: *a) Public transport has been improved. – Special cycle paths have been built. – Bottle and paper banks have been put in the car park. – The town centre has been made into a traffic-free zone. – The pond in the park has been cleaned.*

6 At Alton Towers

Ziel: Anwendung des *future passive*.

Unterrichtsempfehlungen
Die Übung eignet sich für eine Bearbeitung in Gruppen oder als Hausaufgabe.

WB S.46, B4

Lösungen: *2. ... your purse will be found ... it will be sent to you. 3. That ride will be improved next year. 4. The film will be shown in half an hour. The doors will be opened in fifteen minutes. 5. Your group will be collected here in half an hour. 6. ... You will be taken all the way to the top.*

Schülerbuch Seite 68

7 Role play: Cars – or bikes and public transport

Ziel: Rollenspiel als Vorübung zur Debatte.

Unterrichtsempfehlungen
Zunächst stellt L das Thema als Aussage in den Raum: *We should give up cars and use bikes or public transport*. Die Materialsammlung von Argumenten für und gegen das Thema kann vorher als Hausaufgabe gestellt werden und wird anschließend im Unterricht an der Tafel oder auf einer OHP-Folie in 2 Spalten festgehalten. Die Klasse wird in 2 Gruppen aufgeteilt, wobei die eigene Meinung für diese Übung keine Rolle spielt. L: *Group 1 you are <u>for</u> giving up cars, or you pretend you are for it. Group 2 you are <u>against</u> it or you pretend you are against it. It's a role play.*

8 An accident

Ziel: Anwendung des Passivs in verschiedenen Zeiten.

Neu: *owner*

Unterrichtsempfehlungen
Semantisierung: <u>owner</u>: *own* ist als Adjektiv bekannt. L: *Is this your book/..., S1? Is it your own book or is it the school's? If it's your own book/... then you're the owner of it. The owner of a car is not always the person who drives it.*
Diese Übung ist für lernstarke S oder Gruppen gedacht, könnte aber mit entsprechender Vorbereitung mit der ganzen Klasse erarbeitet werden. Zunächst lesen L und S gemeinsam **Grammar** § 15 auf Seiten 111–112 oder schauen nochmals auf die selbst unter *exs. 1* und *5* erstellten Listen. Dabei weist L besonders auf die Stellung des Adverbs beim *present perfect* hin: *Problems have <u>already</u> been found.* Die Situation stellt einen Rundfunkbericht dar und verwendet verschiedene Verbzeiten. S sollten also besonders auf Signalwörter achten.

GR §15

Lösungen: *1. was killed...2. were injured 3. have already been taken 4. was not hurt 5. was damaged 6. will be taken 7. has now been taken 8. has not been found 9. was not hurt 10. was improved*

9 ⟨Just for fun⟩

Ziel: *Fun element*

Neu: *driving licence*

Unterrichtsempfehlungen
L sollte nicht auf diesen kleinen Witz eingehen, sondern den S überlassen, ihn zu entdecken.

Schülerbuch Seite 69

Step C Tomorrow

Ziel: Lesevergnügen. Über eine Utopie sprechen.

Neu: *to enter, model, assembly line, air stream travel, God, Japanese, technology, reason, freedom, biology, section, to touch, to have a baby, human*

Unterrichtsempfehlungen
Bewusst führt der Haupttext dieser *Unit* weg von der Rahmenhandlung mit der Familie Penrose in Alton Towers: Nach und nach lösen sich die Verbindungen zu den handelnden Personen des Lehrwerks.
Es reicht aus, wenn vor dem ersten Hören der Geschichte der Text um vier Begriffe entlastet wird: *section, assembly line, freedom, human.* L schreibt sie an die Tafel und erklärt sie einzeln: *1. A museum has different <u>sections</u> where you can see different things, like a department store with its different departments. 2. In*

car factories the workers put cars together on <u>assembly lines</u>. For example one worker puts on the wheels, the next worker puts the seats in and a third one puts in the windows while the car is moving on. 3. You can give a bird in a cage its <u>freedom.</u> Just open the cage and let it fly and it will be free. 4. Dogs and cats are animals but men and women are <u>humans.</u>

Die Geschichte wird in voller Länge vom Tonträger bei geöffneten Büchern präsentiert. L fragt anschließend nach dem Auto in der Abbildung: *What kind of car is that? - Why is it famous? -They say it was the beginning of everything? What do they mean? What began with the assembly line? - Who are those five people in the picture at the bottom of the page?* Nach Beantwortung dieser Fragen lesen die S die Geschichte noch einmal gemeinsam und klären die restlichen Vokabelfragen.

Landeskundliche Hinweise für L

Ford's Tin Lizzy: The first Model T, which left the Ford factory at Detroit in 1908, was neither the first nor the fastest automobile on American roads. But while other cars sold by the hundred, production of the Model T grew at a fantastic speed ... . During the nineteen years of its production more than 15 million Model Ts were produced and sold - a success story that was to be repeated only years later by the Volkswagen Beetle.
The Model T was an ugly car, ... it couldn't go faster than 40 miles an hour. ... A screwdriver, a few other tools and a piece of wire were about all you needed to get the car going again. ... Thousands of owners, for whom the Model T was far more than just another piece of machinery, used it to pump water, produce electricity or even power vacuum cleaners. It was something almost human. It was their Tin Lizzy and the subject of hundreds of jokes and stories:
A farmer was taking his old tin roof off his barn, when one of his neighbors stopped and asked what he was going to do with the old roof. "Throw it away," he answered. The neighbor suggested that he should send it to the Ford Motor Company. "Your car," the company wrote back, "is one of the worst wrecks we have ever seen, but we'll have it repaired for you in a week or so."
(From: Modern Course, RS 5/6, p.54, Klett Verlag, Stuttgart 1978)

Schülerbuch Seite 70

1 Looking at the story

Ziel: Beschäftigung mit der Geschichte.

Unterrichtsempfehlungen
Für die Beantwortung der Fragen und Lösung der Aufgaben ist Partner- oder Gruppenarbeit am besten geeignet. Schnelle Antworten werden die S u.U. nicht finden. Sie brauchen Zeit zur Aussprache, da der Text mit seinen Andeutungen nicht immer gleich auf den ersten Blick zu deuten ist.

Lösungen: *1. They are in the transport section of the World Museum. 2. They are looking at the famous Model T because it was the first car from an assembly line. They have never seen a real car before. - 3. Because assembly lines were then used to produce other things. They made cars cheaper, so more people could have one, but the car was one of the things that polluted everything and made the environment change. 3. Because Dordy is the best pupil. He always gives the right answers. 5. Models of tigers and elephants, two real cats and a dog and the last five humans. 6. That they are the only ones still alive. Usually they are kept in different places and not even allowed to be together. They are not allowed to have babies, so soon there will be no more people.*

2 Working with the text

Ziel: Detailliertere Betrachtung der Geschichte; über die Zukunft spekulieren.

Unterrichtsempfehlungen
Die S sollten Zeit haben, Material zur Beantwortung der Fragen aus dem Text zu sammeln. Bei der anschließenden Besprechung sollte immer wieder nach Belegstellen gefragt werden, damit alle die Entwicklung des Leserwissens im Laufe der Erzählung verfolgen können.
Als weiterführende Aufgabe bietet es sich an, die S in den Rollen von Miry bzw. Dordy einen Brief *(summary)* über ihren Museumsbesuch schreiben zu lassen. In diesen Briefen sollen sie ihre Gefühle, die sie bei ihren Rundgängen an den zwei Tagen empfanden, zum Ausdruck bringen. L kann verpflichtend vorgeben, folgende Adjektive im Text zu verwenden: *interesting, funny, stupid, great, exciting, dangerous, frightening.*

WB S.46, C1

Lösungsmöglichkeiten: *1. The story takes place in the future. It says in l. 62 that there are only 5 people left. 2. We are not sure until the end that the teacher and the pupils are not humans. Then in line 67 the teacher says "These are the last five humans". 3. The people died. The environment changed because cars and other things (factories) polluted everything (line 30). They couldn't find any other forms of energy (ll. 34-36) and then it was too late. 4. It says that nobody wanted to stop the car industry. People thought that a car meant freedom. I think/don't think people really think that.*

3 Words without plurals

Ziel: Differenzierung von zählbaren und unzählbaren Substantiven.

Unterrichtsempfehlungen
Die S erstellen ihre eigene Liste (1 S schreibt hinter die Tafel oder auf Folie. Bei der anschließenden Kontrolle der Listen stellt L auch die Frage, *How did you decide which have plurals? What questions did you ask yourself?* (S z.B. *I tried to say a/ an ... or three ...* .) Anhand dieser oder ähnliche Antworten kann L den Begriff *countable/uncountable* einführen oder einfach feststellen, *That's right, you can't count them.*

Lösungen: Keine Pluralform bilden: *fun, water, information, luck, petrol, pollution, traffic, air.*

4 How many?

Ziel: Wiederholung von Mengen- oder Stückangaben bei unzählbaren Substantiven

Neu: *phrase, expression*

Unterrichtsempfehlungen
Semantisierung: *'Glass' is a word, 'a glass of' is a <u>phrase</u> or <u>expression</u>.* Zu den Zählmöglichkeiten sollte man *litres* hinzunehmen, da sowohl Milch als auch Mineralwasser und Limonade in Litermengen verkauft werden.
a) Nach einer ersten Übung in der Reihenfolge wie im Buch kann das Zusammenfügen von *phrase* und Wort relativ schnell in Form eines Quiz geübt werden. Zwei Mannschaften werden gebildet. Der Reihe nach ruft ein S von *Team 1* ein *word with no plural*, wobei sie selbstverständlich auch andere Wörter nehmen können als nur die in *ex. 4*. Ebenfalls der Reihe nach muss ein S von *Team 2* eine passende *phrase* dazu geben: *S1: chocolate! S2: two bars of chocolate.* Für jede richtige Antwort gibt es einen Punkt. Für jede falsche Antwort geht ein Punkt an die fragende Mannschaft, aber nur wenn S1 die Antwort selber richtig geben kann.
b) eignet sich als Hausaufgabe.

WB S.47, C2

Lösungsmöglichkeiten: *a) one piece of news – 3 bars of chocolate – 2 cups of coffee – 5 bottles/litres of lemonade – 4 pieces of information – 7 cups/kinds of tea – 6 glasses of water – 3 pints of milk – 2 bars of soap*

Schülerbuch Seite 71

Step C A surprise

a

Ziel: Einführung des Passivs mit *by-agent*.

Unterrichtsempfehlungen
Erst jetzt, nachdem die S mit mehreren Passivzeiten gearbeitet haben, wird der Gebrauch des *by-agent* eingeführt. So haben sich die S erst an die Funktion des Passivs gewöhnen können, als Mittel über eine Aktion sprechen zu können, ohne zu sagen, wer sie ausführt. In diesem Dialog, der die Rahmenhandlung der *Unit* weiterführt, wird der *by-agent* ebenfalls in seiner typischen Funktion eingeführt, nämlich als Zusatz zu einem Passivsatz, in dem es vordergründig um das Ereignis geht. Die kleine Szene sollte von den S mit verteilten Rollen gespielt werden. Dabei ist auf den Ausdruck und die Lebhaftigkeit zu achten, die eine solche Aufregung über einen möglichen Einbruch erfordert. In einer zweiten Phase schreibe die S in Stillarbeit die Passivsätze vollständig aus dem Text heraus (ein S schreibt sie an die Tafel oder auf OHP-Folie): **Tafelanschrieb oder eigene Folie**

Look, that window has been broken.
I hope our TV hasn't been stolen.
That window wasn't broken <u>by burglars</u>.
That window was broken <u>by Robert</u>.

L fragt nach den unterstrichenen *phrases*: *What do they tell us?* (*Who does or did it.*) und geht auf Übung 5 über. Es gibt keinen zwingenden Grund, von der üblichen Aktiv-Passiv-Transformation mit Umsetzung des Subjekts als *by-agent* auszugehen, die u.U. hier nur Verwirrung stiftet.

5 All this happened the same day

Ziel: Bildung von Passivsätzen mit *by-agent*.

Unterrichtsempfehlungen
Auch hier muß die Betonung eher auf *What happened?* als auf *Who/What did it?* liegen, sonst wäre in einigen Fällen ein Aktivsatz die bessere Lösung. Nach gemeinsamer Erarbeitung des Beispiels: L: *What happened?* S: *The window was broken.* L: *Who by?* S: *By Robert.* Tafelanschrieb: *The window was broken <u>by Robert</u>.* legt man zunächst im Unterrichtsgespräch die Passivsätze unter Verwendung der angegebenen Verben fest:
2. A blue car was hit. 3. Someone / A tennis fan was injured. 4. Becky was woken up. 5. Jenny's bag was taken 6. The thief was caught. In Stillarbeit oder als Hausaufgabe beantworten die S unter Verwendung des *by-agent*, die Frage *Who or what by?* **WB S.47, C3**

Lösungen: *2. A blue car was hit by a red van. 3. Someone / A tennis fan was injured by a tennis ball. 4. Becky was woken up by Maxi. 5. Jenny's bag was taken by a boy in a green anorak. 6. The thief was caught by the police.*

b

Ziel: Abschluss der Rahmenhandlung

Unterrichtsempfehlungen
Die S lesen den kurzen Text selbständig.

6 Looking at English

Ziel: Differenzierung der transitiven und intransitiven Verben.

Unterrichtsempfehlungen
Die Liste wird von den S einzeln erstellt und im Plenum kontrolliert (Tafelanschrieb):

Verbs with no object:	*Verbs with an object:*
arrive	open (the door)
smile	take (him)
look	see (Robert)
be	break (your window)
	ask (them)

Kommen S nicht sofort durch *break* in der rechten Liste darauf, dass Passivsätze nur mit *verbs with an object* möglich sind, kann L durch einfache Tafelzeichnungen und die Frage *What has happened in the second picture?* Beispiele für Passivsätze mit Verben aus der rechten Spalte geben:

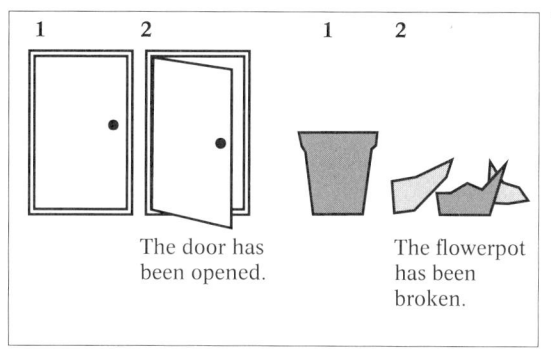

Tafelbild

1	2	1	2
[closed door]	[open door]	[flowerpot]	[broken flowerpot]
The door has been opened.		The flowerpot has been broken.	

Anschließend liest man zusammen den Vermerk am Ende von **Grammar** § 15. Wenn die S eine Erklärung dafür haben wollen, kann man auf die schematische Darstellung unter § 16 eingehen. **GR § 15** **GR § 16**

Schülerbuch Seite 72

7 ⟨A song: 2-4-6-8 Motorway⟩

Ziel: Auflockerung des Unterrichts. Erweiterung des Themas ‚Straßenverkehr'.

Neu: *truck, midway, Fairlane cruiser, headlights, driving rain, window frame, star, to hitch a ride, chorus, whizzkid, two-wheel stallion, ten-ton lorry, Got a bead on you, Ain't no use setting up with a bad companion, Ain't nobody get the better of you-know-who, Ain't no route, Ain't nobody know ..., roadway, Gonna keep on driving, to truck on*

Unterrichtsempfehlungen
Fakultatives Element. Vor dem ersten Hören geht L zusammen mit den S die neue Lexik im Vokabelverzeichnis durch und klärt dabei die Aussprache. Das Lied schildert eine Fahrt auf der *motorway* in einem großen Lastwagen, und erwähnt andere Verkehrsteilnehmer wie den Lastwagen, der versucht links zu überholen (Strophe 1) und den Motorradfahrer auf seinem „Hengst mit zwei Rädern".
Sprachlicher Hinweis: Wie bei vielen modernen Liedern ist die Sprache bewusst salopp gehalten. Dabei werden oft Kontraktionen gebraucht, die einen solchen Text zunächst für deutsche Schülerinnen und Schüler schwer verständlich machen. Mit etwas Übung ist es für die S möglich, die Texte solcher Lieder etwas genauer herauszuhören. An diesem Text fällt auf, dass Pronomen oder Phrasen wie *There's a* oft weggelassen wurden, sodass eine Art Telegrammstil entsteht. Unter den Verbkontraktionen kommt *ain't* besonders häufig vor. *ain't* wird regional unterschiedlich ausgesprochen. Es ersetzt hier *(it) isn't* und ist immer Teil eines doppelten Negativs: *ain't never, ain't no use, ain't nobody, ain't no route, ain't nobody* (in der nächsten Zeile allerdings: *no one knows*). Eine weitere beliebte Kontraktion ist *gonna* for *going to* (3. Str., 4. Zeile).

8 Listening practice: Park-and-ride in Nottingham

Ziel: Hörverstehen. Einer Erklärung folgen und den Sachverhalt durchschauen.

Neu: *park-and-ride, cartoon, multi-storey car park, system*

Text
Police officer:
Parking is always a problem in cities. It's the same in Nottingham. It's possible to park in Nottingham, of course. There are a few multi-storey car parks and there are some other places, too. But the best thing is to use our park-and-ride system. There is a field just outside the city centre. It's where Goose Fair is in October. Well, you can leave your car there. You can park there free. Then you take a bus into town. That doesn't cost very much and you never have to wait very long. Then you can go shopping in town and after that you take another bus back to your car. The park-and-ride system keeps cars out of the city centre. So it isn't as noisy there, it's safer and there isn't as much air pollution. And you don't have to worry about where to park. It isn't a perfect system, but it's a system that works well. A lot of cities use it now.

Unterrichtsempfehlungen
Den Begriff *park-and-ride* sollen sich die S durch die Hörverstehensaufgabe selbst erschließen. Er darf vorher also keinesfalls von L erläutert werden! Der Begriff könnte einigen S bereits geläufig sein, da er auch in Deutschland verwendet wird. Diese S sollten ihr Wissen zurückhalten. *Multi-storey car park: car park* ist den S schon bekannt: *a car park with lots of floors or levels. system* erklärt sich durch das Schriftbild.
Die Aufgabenstellung wird an der Tafel notiert: *Park-and-ride. How does it work in Nottingham? (Four sentences!)* Die S übertragen dies in die Hefte.
Das erste Hören erfolgt ohne anschließende Aussprache. Die S halten in Partnerarbeit ihre ersten Ergebnisse fest. Nach dem zweiten Hören formulieren sie die Lösung in vier Sätzen und tragen sie vor. Anschließend tragen alle gemeinsam mündlich die Vorteile zusammen, die dieses System bietet: *keeps cars out – not as noisy – safer – not as much air pollution – no parking problems.*
Als nette Ergänzung zum sonst ernsthaften Thema Straßenverkehr bietet sich die Arbeit mit Bildfolie 16 an. Hier sind eine Reihe von bekannten Verkehrsschildern abgebildet, allerdings neu gedeutet mit teilweise skurrilen Bezeichnungen. Den S macht es bestimmt Spaß, weitere solche Deutungen zu finden, oder gar neue Schilder z.B. für ihre Schule selbst zu entwerfen, wie das von den Bewohnern eines Altenheims in Aberdare, Wales gemacht wurde. Das übliche Schild des alten gebeugten Menschen mit Stock fanden sie langweilig. So entwarfen sie Schilder mit Senioren auf dem *skateboard*, auf dem Einrad oder auf zwei Rädern im Rollstuhl fahrend, die jetzt die Wände ihres Altenheims schmücken! (Quelle: *The Sunday Times*, 9.9.1996)

WB S.47, C4
WB S.48, C5
Bildfolie

Lösungsmöglichkeiten: *1. You can leave (park) your car in a field outside the city (centre) where Goose Fair is in October. This car park is free. 2. Then you take a bus into town (which doesn't cost very much). 3. Then you can go shopping in town. 4. After that you take another bus back to your car.*

Schülerbuch Seite 73

Step D Let's check

1 A new road

Ziel: Kontrolle der Passiv-Anwendung mit verschiedenen Verbzeiten.

WB S.48, D1
WB S.49, D2

Unterrichtsempfehlungen
L weist auf Signale für die Verbzeiten hin, dann bilden die S die Sätze in Partnerarbeit mit anschließender Kontrolle im Plenum. Bei den Sätzen sind manchmal mehrere Verben möglich.

Lösungen: *1. The environment has been polluted for many years. 2. These trees were cut down last month. 3. A house is built every day.* (auch möglich: *A house is being built/has been built every day.*) *4. A new road will be made/built/finished soon.*

2 An accident report

Ziel: Kontrolle der Passivanwendung im Kontext.

Unterrichtsempfehlungen
Diese Aufgabe verlangt den Einsatz des richtigen Verbs in der Form, die vom Kontext verlangt wird. Sie eignet sich als schriftliche Hausaufgabe. Unsichere S sollten an § 15 der **Grammar** erinnert werden. Inhaltlich ist der kleine Text eine ernsthafte Warnung gegen das sogenannte *"joyriding"*, das für die Jugendlichen selbst und ihre Angehörigen manchmal noch tragischer endet.

Lösungen: *were pulled – was thrown – were taken – will be sent – will be interviewed – was (/had been) stolen – are stolen – are taken*

3 Counting things

Ziel: Kontrolle der Mengenangaben bei unzählbaren Substantiven.

Unterrichtsempfehlungen
Die Übung kann schnell in Partnerarbeit durchgeführt werden. Sie kann zusätzlich als Grundlage einer Aufgabe für Gruppenarbeit dienen, indem jede Gruppe in einer Minute möglichst viele unzählbare Substantive auflisten muss, die zum Wortfeld der abgebildeten Gegenstände gehören:
information: news, paper
milk: water, lemonade, tea, coffee
cake: bread, butter, meat, fish
chocolate: toffee, sugar

Lösungen: *1. three pieces of information 2. Four glasses of milk 3. Two pieces of cake 4. One bar of chocolate*

4 The environment

Ziel: Wortfeldarbeit

WB S.49, D3

Unterrichtsempfehlungen
Alternativ zum *mind-map* können S ein *pollution chart* erstellen, auf dem sie festhalten, was welche Verschmutzung verursacht. Als Überschriften dienen die Bereiche *earth – air – water – noise.*

Schülerbuch Seite 74-75

Workshop D Let's write

Allgemeine Hinweise
In diesem *Workshop* geht es um die weitere Entwicklung der Schreibfähigkeit und die bewusste Schulung des Textaufbaus. Nachdem in *Workshop C* verschiedene Textsorten präsentiert wurden, ist die Arbeit hier der Übersichtlichkeit halber auf eine Textsorte begrenzt, das *review*.

1 Getting ideas together

Ziel: Die Textsorte „Rezension" kennenlernen.

Neu: *review, graphics*

Unterrichtsempfehlungen
Oben auf dieser Doppelseite wird die Textsorte *review* zunächst schülerorientiert über ihren Zweck im Sprechblasendialog vorgestellt. Anhand von Kritiken zu Computerspielen, die vielen S vertraut sein dürften, werden Beispiele der Textsorte dann in den ersten zwei Übungen der Doppelseite präsentiert. Zur Einstimmung: Gespräch über Computerspiele, dabei wird relevanter Wortschatz auch aus Übung 1 und 2 eingeführt: *Do you use a computer? Play games? Your favourite games? Why? What's important in a computer game? – graphics: pictures on a computer or in a book; colourful: colour* ist bekannt; *screen: a TV has a screen, so does a computer. You see words and pictures on it. to click on: You use the mouse to find something on the computer screen, then you click on it when you want the computer to do something; violence: hitting, hurting or killing people or animals; dragon* (u.U. aus *Workshop A* oder *Unit 3* bekannt.) *There's a red dragon on the Welsh flag; you can see one on page 13 and page 44, too; How do you choose a new computer game? – Read the review.*
Evtl. sollte bereits hier zu Beginn der Unterrichtseinheit den S das Ziel, eine eigene Kritik zu erstellen, vorgestellt werden und zusammen überlegt werden, wie man die Ergebnisse der Arbeit veröffentlichen kann, z.B. in der Schülerzeitung, als Klassenheft oder als Wandzeitung. Dadurch wird die Motivation der S, brauchbare Texte zu erstellen, erhöht.

1 A model text

Ziel: Eine Kritik eines Computerspiels lesen.

Neu: *not only ... but also, dragon, level, colourful, especially, on the whole, introduction, opinion*

Unterrichtsempfehlungen
Semantisierung des Wortschatzes wie oben; der Rest wird nach Lektüre des Textes erschlossen. Über bekannte Wörter/Wortfamilien: *not only ... but also, on the whole*, über das Deutsche: *level, especially;* über den Kontext: *introduction, opinion.* Anschließend Erarbeitung des Inhaltes anhand von Übung 3 oder über Fragen: *What is the game about? How do you win? What does Mike Jenkins like about it? What doesn't he like? Would you buy the game? What do you / don't you like about it?* Anschließend Besprechung des Textaufbaus, evtl. werden die Bezeichnungen für die Abschnitte *(title, introduction, main part, ending)* kurz auf deutsch besprochen und mit dem Aufbau aus dem Deutschunterricht bekannter Textsorten abgeglichen (z.B. Beschreibung, Bericht, Erzählung): was ist gleich - was ist anders?

2 Becky's review

Ziel: Den Aufbau einer „Kritik" üben.

Neu: *lipstick, in my opinion, It's worth buying. boyfriend, to click on s.th., motorbike, violence, screen*

Unterrichtsempfehlungen
Semantisierung des Wortschatzes wie oben, der Rest durch Erschließen. Über Wortfamilie: *boyfriend, motorbike*; über das Deutsche: *lipstick;* über den Kontext: *it is(n't) worth buying.*
Erarbeitung des Textaufbaus in Partner- oder Stillarbeit, Vortrag des fertigen *review*. Dabei werden die Teile benannt: *The title is: ...; The introduction says / goes like this: ...; etc.*
Anschließend Besprechung der Kritik wie in Übung 1 über Fragen: *What is the game about? How do you win? What does Becky like about it? What doesn't she like? Would you buy the game? What do you / don't you like about it?* Hier wird evtl. die Frage der Gewalt angesprochen, die Becky erwähnt. Gewalt spielt in vielen *computer games* auch sogar in seriösen Lernspielen eine Rolle, indem ein Gegner besiegt/abgeschossen/getötet werden muss, um Punkte zu gewinnen und im Spiel weiterzukommen. Aus erzieherischen Gründen sollte L die Diskussion nicht abschneiden, auch wenn sie auf Deutsch geführt werden muss.
Dass man ein *review* nicht nur über *computer games* schreiben kann, wird in **Workbook** Übung 1.1 anhand von verschiedenen *review*-Auszügen demonstriert.   WB S.51, 1.1

3 Good or bad?

Ziel: Auswertung der Kritiken.

Unterrichtsempfehlungen
Beim Übertragen des Rasters gleich eine evtl. zwei weitere Spalten anlegen lassen für Übung 6. Außerdem kann an dieser Stelle die Anordnung der Kriterien besprochen werden (vgl. Box mit *tip*), evtl. weitere Kriterien ergänzen, z.B.: *price, graphics, sound effects, etc.*
Erarbeitung evtl. in Gruppen zu *review 1* bzw. *review 2*. Abgleichen der Ergebnisse in der Klasse.

Lösungen:

Title:	Merlin's pupil:	Girl meets boy
Kind?	–	on CD for girls who want to find a boyfriend
Where?	In the past	–
What?	–	Play role of Tammy or Candy and follow boys
Win?	Complete all five levels	When boy says "I love you"
Good?	colourful graphics, great sound effects	..., great songs
Bad?	puzzles and quizzes difficult	silly game
Buy?	Yes, you get a lot for your money.	No, too silly.

4 Review words

Ziel: Wortschatzarbeit.

Unterrichtsempfehlungen
Neben den Wörtern und Wendungen der vorliegenden Texte können S ihre Listen durch bekannten Wortschatz ergänzen, z.B.: *to find s.th. good, wonderful, great, fun, exciting, bad, terrible, boring, interesting, OK, all right; easy, difficult; cheap; to like / to hate s.th., to enjoy s.th., to be pleased with s.th., surprised about s.th.,(not) to agree with s.o., to be sure, to believe; drama, fantasy, role play, quiz.*
Ergänzt wird diese Arbeit durch eine Aufgabe über *prepositions* und eine über nützliche *phrases* im **Workbook**.   WB S.51, 1.2   WB S.52, 1.3

5 Brainstorming

Ziel: Ideensammlung zur Vorbereitung der eigenen Textproduktion.

Neu: *brainstorming, etc.*

Unterrichtsempfehlungen
Semantisierung von *etc:* über ein Beispiel: *Fruit means apples, bananas, etc., vegetables are potatoes, carrots, etc.* Besondere Beachtung sollte L der Aussprache des vollständigen Wortes *etcetera* [ɪtˈsetərə] schenken; *brainstorming* durch Erklären der Arbeitstechnik. Dann moderiert L die Brainstorming-Phase. Wichtig dabei ist, dass die Ideen nicht bewertet werden, sondern nur gesammelt, da sicherlich unterschiedliche Vorstellungen bei den S existieren. Um jegliche Bewertung zu vermeiden, können die S auch aufgefordert werden, in Stillarbeit innerhalb von ca. 3 Minuten alles zu der Abbildung aufzuschreiben, was ihnen einfällt. Anschließend Sammeln der Ideen in der Klasse.

6 Organizing ideas

Ziel: Eine Gliederung erstellen.

Unterrichtsempfehlungen
Zusammenstellung der Informationen in Partner- oder Einzelarbeit. Die Gliederung kann anhand von Übung 1.4 im **Workbook** geübt oder die Tabelle von Übung 3 kann als Ordnungsmodell genutzt werden. Zu diesem Zeitpunkt soll das *review* noch nicht geschrieben werden: Vor der endgültigen Fertigstellung des *review* empfehlen sich die vorgeschlagenen Stilübungen von Seite 76.

WB S.52, 1.4
WB S.52, 1.5

Schülerbuch Seite 76

2 Writing the text

1 Conjunctions

Ziel: Strukturierung eines Textes mit Konjunktionen.

Unterrichtsempfehlungen
Erarbeitung der Konjunktionen als Hausaufgabe oder mündlich in der Klasse. In einer anspruchsvolleren Aufgabe im **Workbook** müssen die Konjunktionen verwendet werden, um die Reihenfolge der Sätze im Text zu bestimmen.

WB S.53, 2.1

Lösungen: 1. *because* 2. *but* 3. *so* 4. *Although* 5. *When* 6. *and* 7. *but.*

2 Putting ideas together

Ziel: Festigung des Gebrauchs der Konjunktionen.

Unterrichtsempfehlungen
Teil a) in Einzelarbeit durchführen, Teil b) entweder durch Nebensitzer oder bunt gemischt in der Klasse erarbeiten lassen. Auch in der entsprechenden **Workbook**-Übung geht es um die Verbindung von Satzteilen und Sätze durch Konjunktionen.

WB S.53, 2.2

Lösungsmöglichkeiten: a) 2. *... I find them very dangerous.* 3. *... he went to town by bus.* 4. *... it's raining cats and dogs.* 5. *... I had to climb through a window.* 6. *... we telephoned our parents to tell them everything.* 7. *... I'll finish reading my book.*

3 Interesting words

Ziel: Wortschatzarbeit.

Unterrichtsempfehlungen
Erstellen der Wörterlisten als Hausaufgabe oder in Gruppenarbeit: je ein Wortfeld z.B. auf Folie, anschließend Besprechung und Ergänzung der Wörterlisten.

Lösungsmöglichkeiten:
Characters: alone, angry, boring, brave, calm, clever, crazy, false, famous, happy, lazy, lonely, lucky, miserable, nasty, nervous, old, polite, royal, scared, silly, small, surprised/surprising, strong, stupid, terrible, thin, tired, trapped, upset, weak, wild, worried, young;
A story: all right, bad, the best of all, better, boring, clear, different, exciting, fantastic, frightening, funny, possible, readable, serious, strange, typical, (un-)predictable, the worst;
Pictures or graphics: careful, careless, colourful, lovely, nice, perfect, pretty, professional, sweet, tidy, wonderful;
A game: cheap, complete, expensive, fast, interesting, slow;
Tips: difficult, easy, free, hard, missing, safe, simple, understandable, useful, useless.

WB S.54, 2.3
WB S.54, 2.4

4 Writing the text

Ziel: Anfertigen eines *review*.

Unterrichtsempfehlungen
Erstellen des *review* im Computerraum oder aber als Hausaufgabe, möglichst am Computer, damit der Text später problemlos überarbeitet werden kann.

WB S.55 2.5

5 ⟨Just for fun⟩

Ziel: Auflockerung des Unterrichts; bildliche Vorlage deuten.

Unterrichtsempfehlungen
Cartoon beschreiben und Äußerung des Vaters erklären lassen: *Why is the father worried?* Evtl. kann sich ein Gespräch über Leseverhalten der S anschließen. Zusammen mit der Aussage des *Cartoon* von Übung 4, Seite 77 könnte, wenn ausreichend Zeit zur Verfügung steht, auch ein *questionnaire* zum Einsatz und Umgang mit elektronischen und Printmedien angefertigt und durchgeführt werden.
Für die S, die Fantasievolleres schreiben möchten, bietet das *Workbook* die Möglichkeit, selber ein *computer game* zu schreiben.

WB S.55, 2.6

Schülerbuch Seite 77

3 Checking the text

1 Collecting tips for a checklist

Ziel: Kriterien zur Selbstkontrolle entwickeln.

Neu: Unterrichtsempfehlungen
Semantisierung: *punctuation:* Folgender Satz wird angeschrieben und bearbeitet: *that game the one I bought yesterday is very exciting I not think – What does this sentence need? Commas* (eintragen) *and a full stop, that's punctuation. And it needs a capital letter, at the beginning. The negative isn't right, the word 'do' is missing and the negative 'not' is missing after 'is' Can someone correct it? Now the sentence reads: That game, the one I bought yesterday, isn't very exciting, I don't think. – It's correct, but is it good style?* (anschreiben). *Not really, because the relative clause is too long and 'I don't think' should come at the beginning, then you don't need two negatives. It would be better to write: I don't think that game I bought yesterday is very exciting.* Siehe dazu auch **Workbook**-Übung 3.1.
Die S können Karteikarten zu den „Tipps" anlegen, auf denen sie für Teil a) die Beispiele für jeden Tipp dazu schreiben. In Teil b) könne die zusätzlichen Tipps auf der jeweiligen Karte mit Beispiel ergänzt werden, z.B.:
Spelling and punctuation: Look up difficult words in a dictionary/the alphabetical wordlist.

WB S.55, 3.1

Grammar: right preposition?
present of past tense?
Style: good explanations?

Evtl. weist L die S darauf hin, dass eine solche Überprüfung nicht nur beim *review*-Schreiben sondern auch bei Klassenarbeiten und Tests ganz nützlich sein kann.

WB S.55-56, 3.2

2 Checking your review

Ziel: Überarbeiten des *review*.

Neu: *clear*

Unterrichtsempfehlungen

Semantisierung: *If glass is clear you can see through it. When something isn't clear you can't see what it is or understand it. Is that clear?* Nachdem Teil a) in Stillarbeit durchgeführt wurde, wird für Teil b) ein Wechsel der Sozialform in Partnerarbeit vorgenommen, wobei die S den Partner selbst bestimmen sollen, um ein positives Arbeitsklima zu gewährleisten. Teil c) ggf. im Computerraum bzw. als Hausaufgabe am Computer. Evtl. anschließend ein Heft mit den gesammelten Reviews von Computerspielen erstellen, als Klassenheft auflegen oder der Schülerzeitung zur Veröffentlichung anbieten.

WB S.56, 3.3

3 Practising your skills

Ziel: Festigung der gelernten Texterstellung.

Neu: *skill, about* (ungefähr)

Unterrichtsempfehlungen

Semantisierung: *skills* deutsch erklären; *about:* not exactly. Auch hier sollte für Öffentlichkeit gesorgt werden, z.B. kann man Referate für ein wöchentliches Review verteilen, eine Wandzeitung im Klassenzimmer einrichten, oder eine regelmäßig erscheinende Spalte in der Schülerzeitung anregen. Gibt es ein Schülerradio, bietet sich natürlich auch das an. Dann sollte man allerdings daran erinnern, dass die Texte gesprochen bzw. vorgelesen werden sollen, d.h. lieber etwas kürzere Sätze enthalten sollen, oder solche, die man durch Atempausen gut gliedern kann.

Eine andere Erweiterungsmöglichkeit wäre die Erstellung eines narrativen Textes, etwas, was die S schon längst können, aber jetzt mit den *skills*, die sie in *Workshop D* dazugelernt haben. Eine Handlung bieten die zwei Bildfolien 17a und 17b. Da die ganze Geschichte relativ lang ist, kann man im Klassengespräch vorher die Namen der handelnden Personen festlegen und dann entweder in Gruppen oder von den S einzeln nur den ersten Teil (Folie 17a) oder nur den zweiten Teil (Folie 17b) der Geschichte erzählen lassen. Nach dem Vorlesen einiger Versionen erfolgt eine gemeinsame Besprechung der Titelfrage: Will man bei *Adventure in London* bleiben oder einen anderen Titel suchen?

Bildfolien 17a, 17b

4 ⟨Just for fun⟩

Ziel: Auflockerung des Unterrichts.

Neu: *Congratulations, to reach*

Unterrichtsempfehlungen

Semantisierung: *Congratulations* ist u.U. schon von Geburtstagen usw. bekannt, sonst die deutsche Entsprechung geben. *to reach:* to get to. Beschreiben des *cartoon*, anschließend evtl. Diskussion über die Aussage, dass Mädchen nicht mit Computern umgehen können. Vgl. außerdem Hinweise zu S. 76, Üb. 5.

Schülerbuch Seite 78

Unit 5 Great Britain and the sea

Step A An island country

Ziel: Aus Texten und Bildern Stimmungen entnehmen und beschreiben; Revision: *Conditional sentences type I.*

Neu: *lonely, fever, oil, flat, cliff, close to, unpredictable, calm, wave, rough, tide, coastguard, lifeboat; the North Sea*

Unterrichtsempfehlungen

Semantisierung: *lonely:* alone and with nobody to care for you; *fever:* a temperature; *oil:* machines need oil so that they run well. Some kinds of oil are used for cooking (olive oil); *flat:* with no hills, not steep; *cliff:* Tafelzeichnung; *close to:* near; *unpredictable:* not able to say what will happen next; *calm:* quiet, not dangerous; *rough:* opposite of 'calm'; *wave:* in a rough sea there are dangerously high waves (Tafelzeichnung); *tide:* At the seaside the water comes in and leaves again in a 6-hour-rhythm. There is high tide and low tide; *coastguard: coast* und *guard* sind bekannt, daher direkt verständlich; *lifeboat:* a boat used to help people who are in trouble at sea; *the North Sea:* the sea between Britain and Denmark/Schleswig-Holstein.

Tafelbild

Nach der Vokabeleinführung Vorspiel vom Tonträger des ganzen Textes bzw. L-Vortrag desselben. Die Bücher bleiben geschlossen. Arbeitsauftrag: *Try to remember as much information as possible about Britain and the sea.* Dann Abruf des Auftrages und Erstellung eines Tafelanschriebs. Evtl. Lenkungsfragen durch den L, etwa: *How long is Britain's coastline? What is especially dangerous there …* .

Öffnung der Bücher. Das Turner-Bild wird zunächst die Aufmerksamkeit auf sich ziehen. Daher Start hier:

1 A picture and a poem

Ziel: Bildbeschreibung; Stimmungen definieren.

Unterrichtsempfehlungen

Es wäre von Vorteil, wenn L das Bild J.M.W. Turners (*'Lifeboat and Manby apparatus going off to a stranded vessel'*) großformatiger präsentieren könnte (Dia, Poster, Projektor, Bildband). Die größte Sammlung von Turner-Malereien ist die Clore-Sammlung in der *Tate Gallery*, London. Dort sind auch Reproduktionen (Poster, Dias) von Turner-Bildern erhältlich:
Tate Gallery Publishing Ltd.,
Millbank,
London SW1P 4RG, GB (Tel.: 0044-171-887 8869)
Das abgebildete Gemälde ist im *Victoria & Albert Museum*, weitere Turner-Bilder hängen in der *National Gallery*, London. Joseph Mallord William Turner (1775–1851) gehört zu den großen Malern des 19. Jahrhunderts. Anfangs malte er Aquarelle, seit 1796 auch in Öl. Er reiste viel und machte Tausende von Skizzen. In seinen Bildern sind Szenen oft in Licht und Atmosphäre fast aufgelöst. Neben den vielen Meeresszenen ist sein berühmtestes Bild vielleicht *"Rain, Steam and Speed"* (1844), das eine Dampflokomotive der *Great Western Railway* zeigt. S beschreiben zunächst spontan das Bild. Situation: Rettung eines gestrandeten Schiffes / Rettungsboot / Pier / dunkler Himmel / rauhe See / Farben. Dann den Eindruck schildern, den das Bild von der See vermittelt, etwa: *dangerous, fantastic, strong …*
Arbeitsauftrag: *Let's collect adjectives and verbs that*

can help to describe the sea. S arbeiten entlang der *alphabetical word list* (S.156ff) bzw. ihrer Vokabelhefte und verwenden die Wortlisten zur Charakterbeschreibung, die sie in *Workshop D* erstellt haben. S schreiben ihr so entstehendes Wortfeld *(dangerous) sea* in ihre Vokabelhefte. Anschließend im Plenum (Tafel) Abruf. (Mögliches Wortmaterial: *angry, beautiful, cold, dead, great, deep, terrible, wonderful, to drown, to swim, to die, to kill, to need help, to rescue, to row, to shout, to warn ...*

SB S. 156 ff

WB S.57, A1

Aufmerksamkeitslenkung dann auf die Zeilen aus Masefields Gedicht. L liest vor, so dass der Wellenrhythmus gut deutlich wird. Im Sinne des *Workshop C* (S. 56) L: *How do you expect this poem will go on? What will it tell us about the sea?* S arbeiten in Partnerarbeit, gebrauchen evtl. *beautiful, great, blue, deep, friendly, wonderful, to enjoy, to be excited, to hope, to watch ...* Im Plenum dann L: *What were your ideas, how will it go on?* Gespräch über die Vorschläge. Besprechung der tatsächlichen 2. Zeile:

I must down to the seas again, to the lonely sea and the sky,
And all I ask is a tall ship and a star to steer her by: ...

Gesprächslenkung auf die Verschiedenartigkeit der See-Darstellung bei Masefield und Turner. Möglichkeiten dann:
– Den gehörten Einführungstext lesen und detaillierte Erarbeitung der Information.
– Leseübung
– Masefields Gedicht *Sea-Fever* komplett behandeln (sehr lohnend).
– L zeigt noch weitere Turner-Bilder, etwa: *The Shipwreck* (1805) oder ‚Fischer in stürmischem Wetter, an einem schützenden Ufer' (1802).
– S sammeln Bilder von der See (Postkarten, Zeitschriften ...) und beschreiben sie im Unterricht.
– Im norddeutschen Raum ist es sicher auch möglich, Strömungskarten von GB und Tideninformationen zu bekommen (interessant, besonders relevant für den Text *Sea Rescue*).

2 Listening practice: People and the sea

Ziel: Die Haltung verschiedener Leute zur See kennenlernen; Hörverstehenstraining.

Neu: *blood, to be into s.th.*

Text
1.
Man (Scottish east coast accent):
The sea is in my blood. We've always been fishermen in my family – my grandfather and father – and now me. Fishing has always been a hard life. The sea can be a friend – but an enemy, too. We get terrible storms here on the east coast of Scotland. I lost one of my best friends two years ago when his boat went down. And now we have more problems. There aren't enough fish for all the fishing boats – and there are so many rules about what we are or aren't allowed to do. I don't know what the future is for people like me. Maybe there is no future.

2.
Woman (Birmingham accent):
I love the seaside! Actually, I live in Birmingham – about as far as you can get from the coast in Britain. But my cousins live here in Cornwall, and I visit them in the school holidays. For me Cornwall is the place for a holiday. Well, OK – it isn't always as sunny as Spain or Italy. But I don't just want to lie on the beach. I'm really into water sports – swimming, surfing, windsurfing – I love them all. And the waves here are great!

3.
Woman (Irish accent):
People always ask me what a girl from Belfast is doing on a channel ferry. Well, in fact my first job was on a ferry across the Irish Sea – so all I've done is to change ferries! In summer the cafeteria is a crazy place – the ferries are always full, and everyone wants to eat at the same time! I know it sounds funny – but although I work on the sea, I don't see much of it. Sometimes I feel it, of course – when it's rough. That's the only time when I'm not so busy. Suddenly most people don't feel hungry any more.

Unterrichtsempfehlungen
Semantisierung: *blood:* If you hurt yourself badly with a knife, drops of red blood will come out of you. *to be into s.th.:* to like doing s.th. very much.
a) Kurzes Unterrichtsgespräch. S finden z.B. *hard work/job/fun/holidays/...*
b) L bereitet S darauf vor, dass die Sprecher auf dem Tonträger mit Akzent sprechen (schottisch, Birmingham, irisch). Hörauftrag: Vergleich der Erwartungen aus a) mit den Hörtexten.
c) In Partnerarbeit finden S die Lösung und diskutieren insbesondere die Aussagen des Fischers: 'no future'. Danach: *What role does the sea play in your life? Which of the three people did you think was the most interesting?*

Schülerbuch Seite 79

3 Sea words

Ziel: Erweitern des in *ex. 1* begonnenen Wortfeldes *the sea.*

WB S.57, A2

Neu: *description*

Unterrichtsempfehlungen
a) S arbeiten zunächst in Partnerarbeit in ihren Vokabelheften, später Erarbeitung eines Tafelbildes und Ergänzung der Eintragungen im Vokabelheft. S nutzen, was sie in *ex. 1* begonnen haben, dann auch die Vokabelliste auf S. 156ff., evtl. 'Sea-Fever' von John Masefield, das sie aus den Hörtexten *ex. 2* erinnern und Material von Bildfolie 20.

SB S. 156ff.
Bildfolie 20

b) Semantisierung: *description:* noun of 'to describe'. Vgl. Vorschlag zu *ex. 1.* Zusatzaufgabe hier: Verschriftlichung: S schreiben Text zu einem Bild. Bilder dann gut sichtbar im Raum verteilen. S bewegen sich frei im Raum, verlesen ihre Beschreibungen bei mehreren Mit-S, diese müssen das jeweils dazugehörige Bild identifizieren. Aufgabe: Jede(r) S muss mindestens 3x vorlesen und 3x die Bilder anderer S erraten.

4 If you think about it, you won't do it!

Ziel: Wiederholung der *conditional sentences, type I.*

WB S.57, A3

Unterrichtsempfehlungen
L erläutert die *seaside*-Situation. Beispielsatz als Tafelanschrieb und kurze Wiederholung der Zeitenfolge bei diesem Satztyp. Gemeinsames Lesen von **Grammar** § 17, 1. Teil (Monnys Sprechblase und dazugehörigen Text). In Partnerarbeit erstellen S die Sätze. Diese Übung kann auch durch jeweils 2 S szenisch dargestellt werden. Hinzufügung dann: ein Schlußsatz darüber, wie sich der gewarnte S entscheidet. Evtl. auch ein paar in die Situation einführende Sätze durch einen dritten S.

GLN2 GR § 13
GR § 17

Lösungen: *2. She won't come back, if she is too scared. 3. And if the eggs become cold, the little birds in them will die. 4. Anyway, you will hurt yourself, if you try to climb that cliff. 5. And if the cliff is not strong enough, it will fall away. 6. If you fall with it, you will break a leg or worse. 7. And then you will be sorry, if you don't listen to me.*

5 ⟨Just for fun⟩

Ziel: *fun element.*

WB S.58, Tandem Activity 5

Neu: *stormy, lifeboatman, extra-ordinary, thing about the sea.*

Unterrichtsempfehlungen
Semantisierung: *stormy: with a lot of strong wind; lifeboatman: man who helps people in trouble at sea; extra-ordinary: very special* (normale Schreibweise natürlich ohne Bindestrich; hier als Wortspiel um die Supernormalität zu betonen, nicht das Ungewöhnliche); *(the) thing about the sea is ...: it is like this with the sea:...*
Die S nehmen den *cartoon strip* zur Kenntnis. *Just for fun* sollte wörtlich genommen werden. Beschreibungen, *summaries, comments ...* hätten eher demotivierende Wirkung. Mit Ausnahme von *thing about the sea* sind alle Vokabeln zum Bildverständnis bereits eingeführt. 'Extra-ordinary' im Titel kann zum Schluß semantisiert werden (bzw. auf S-Nachfrage). Die in der Einleitung zum *cartoon strip* erwähnte *lifeboat service* ist das *Royal National Lifeboat Institution*, weshalb Stan die Buchstaben RNLI auf dem Pullover trägt. Für weitere Informationen siehe Kommentare zu SB-Seite 82.

Schülerbuch Seite 80

Step B Out in the North Sea

Ziel: Einführung in die *conditional sentences type II*; Ratschläge geben können; Einblick bekommen in das Leben auf einer Bohrinsel.

Neu: *oil rig, helicopter*

Unterrichtsempfehlungen
Semantisierung: *oil rig: 'oil'* ist bekannt. *A factory built into the sea where people try to get oil from under the ground; helicopter:* wird durch das Laut- und Schriftbild klar. Zum Einführungstext: Vokabeleinführung ist nicht nötig. Im Sinne des Workshop C: *Look at the picture, the headings and guess what the text will be about.* Dann Textpräsentation über Tonträger (oder L-Vortrag). L stellt einige Verständnisfragen, die sich aus den weißen Interview-Fragen ergeben.
Bewusstmachung I : L lässt 1-2 *if-clauses* aus dem Text an die Tafel schreiben, z.B. [Tafelanschrieb]

If you worked on the rig,   you would find out just how hard.
If you had a job on land,   you would see your family more often.

Zunächst nur die Bildung (Zeitenfolge) und Terminologie bewusst machen (Farbkreide!):

If- clause	Main clause
past tense	would + infinitive = Conditional tense

1 Would you like it?
Ziel: Analogiebildungen zu den *conditional sentences type II* WB S.59, B1

Unterrichtsempfehlungen
Die S üben hier die Bildung der oben bewusst gemachten Form. Zunächst 2–3 Beispiele zur Sicherung im Plenum, dann Partnerarbeit. Zuletzt noch einmal Plenum. L verweist immer wieder auf den Tafelanschrieb oben.
Zum Schluss Identifizierung aller *if-clauses* im Eingangstext und Verweis auf die Bildung der *negatives* und die Möglichkeit der Umstellung von *if-clause* und *main clause*.

2 Important work
Ziel: Weitere Festigung der *conditional sentences type II*

Neu: *fisherman*

Unterrichtsempfehlungen
Semantisierung: *fisherman: a man whose job it is to catch and sell fish.*
a) Die Übung ist einfach und kaum fehleranfällig. Sie sollte daher von allen S gleichermaßen ohne Hilfe gemacht werden. Vorschlag: schriftlich (zur besonderen Festigung), dann verlesen.
b) Gleichermaßen schriftlich anfertigen lassen.
Lösungen: *a) 2. If there were no fishermen, we wouldn't have any fish to eat. 3. If all the ferries stopped, everyone would have to use the Channel Tunnel. 4. If we didn't have any lifeboats, more people would die at sea. 5. If nobody made weather forecasts, we wouldn't know when to expect bad weather.*
Lösungsmöglichkeiten: *b) 1. ...life would be more exciting./...life would be one long holiday 2. ... I would buy a boat and sail to the Bermudas./...*

Schülerbuch Seite 81

3 Looking at English
Ziel: Bewusstmachung der Zeitenfolge im *conditional sentence type II*; Bewusstmachung des Gebrauchs der *conditional sentences type II*.

Neu: *conditional tense*

Unterrichtsempfehlungen
conditional tense: 'would' + 'infinitive' to express s.th. that will probably not happen. a) Diese Aufgabe ist oben bereits teilweise gelöst. Hier: Ergänzung der Satzsammlung aus dem *report* an der Tafel (insgesamt 4 Sätze). Wiederholung der Zeitenfolge und der Möglichkeit der Umstellung von Konditional- und Hauptsatz. Siehe auch **Grammar § 17.**   GR § 17
Bewusstmachung II: Kontrastierung mit dem Deutschen: Einer der Sätze an der Tafel wird übersetzt, etwa: Wenn du auf der Plattform arbeitetest (arbeiten würdest), fändest du heraus (würdest du herausfinden), wie schwer es (das Leben) ist. Identifizierung: Konditional im Bedingungssatz <u>und</u> im Hauptsatz. Eintragung des Ergebnisses am oben begonnenen Tafelbild.
b) Im Sinne der Aufgabe einen Satz des Typs I (S.79) an die Tafel bringen, z.B.   [Tafelanschrieb]
  If the eggs become cold, the little birds will die.
Vergleich mit :
  If the eggs became cold, the little birds would die.
S finden mit Hilfe der Lenkungsfragen im SB, dass
– in Typ I die Situation *more real* ist,
– in Typ II die Situation *imagined, not very probable* ist.
Insgesamt entwickelt sich dann etwa folgendes Tafelbild: [Tafelbild]

If the eggs <u>become</u> cold, the little birds <u>will die</u>.
If the eggs <u>became</u> cold, the little birds <u>would die</u>.

		If- Clause	Main Clause	
E	Type I	present tense	future tense	'real' situation
D	Typ I	Präsens	Futur	
E	Type II	past tense	conditional (would + inf.)	situation 'not very probable'
D	Typ II	Konditional	Konditional	

L verweist auf die Entsprechungen englisch-deutsch und besonders auf den anfälligen Unterschied (Farbkreide!).   WB S.59, B2

4 Just imagine   WB S.60, B3
Ziel: Transfer des Gelernten: Anwendung von *conditional sentences type II*.

Unterrichtsempfehlungen
L erläutert die Übung: *If*-Satz mit Hilfe der 6 Bilder und Verben bilden, Hauptsatz aus dem Verb-Angebot links. Ein Beispiel durchgehen. Verweis auf die Bildungsregeln.

S arbeiten in Partnerarbeit oder Gruppenarbeit. Später, zur Kontrolle, Sätze im Plenum.

Lösungsmöglichkeiten: *2. If I found £1,000,000 I would take it to the police/invite all my friends to a big party/buy a big house for my family. 3. If I won a dream holiday for two, I would take my best friend to Hawaii/.../give it to my parents/ ... . 4. If I met a knight, I would run away/ fight with him against bad people/ ... . 5. If I got stuck in a lift, I would go crazy/ shout for help. 6. If I became King/Queen, I would live in a big palace/buy lots of nice clothes/ ... .*

5 If I were you

Ziel: Ratschläge erteilen; *were* statt *was* bei Personen im *conditional sentence type II*. GR § 17

Unterrichtsempfehlungen
a) Obwohl heute die Form *If I was you ...* bereits gängige Sprachpraxis ist, sollten die S in diesem frühen Lernstadium die Form *were* als feststehende Wendung in dieser Funktion lernen.
Am Beispielsatz 1 wird das Phänomen *was/were* beschrieben. Im Sinne des *tip* arbeiten die S die Übung zunächst jede(r) für sich still durch. Danach Partnerarbeit und 2–3 ‚Stichproben' im Plenum durch den L
b) Es wäre wohl hilfreich, wenn zu Beginn einige *problem situations* gemeinsam an der Tafel gesammelt würden. Dann Partnerarbeit im Sinne der Aufgabe.
Vorschläge für *problem situations*: *rough sea, stranded ship, rescue? – dark wood, take a short cut through it to get home earlier? – knee trouble, go skiing in winter? – write a vocabulary test tomorrow, watch two films on TV tonight?*

Lösungen: *a) 2. If I were you, I wouldn't take my boat out tomorrow/I'd listen to the weather forecast. 3. If I were you, I would go somewhere where the weather is always nice. 4. If I were you, I wouldn't go to France by ferry./I'd use the Channel Tunnel. 5. If I were you, I wouldn't go to that dangerous cliff. 6. If I were you, I wouldn't lie in the hot sun all day.*

Schülerbuch Seite 82

Step B The lifeboat service

Ziel: Tipps für ein Flugblatt zusammenstellen; *passive infinitive/passive of verbs with prepositions*.

Neu: *crew, to inform s.o. about s.th., safety*

Unterrichtsempfehlungen
Semantisierung: <u>crew</u>: *group of people who work together on a ship or plane*; <u>to inform s.o. about s.th.</u>: *to give information*; <u>safety</u>: *noun of 'safe'*. Einstieg möglich über die ‚Deutsche Gesellschaft zur Rettung Schiffbrüchiger' (DGzRS) L zeigt evtl. die bekannte schiffsrumpfförmige Sammelbüchse herum – oder schreibt den Namen der Gesellschaft an und übersetzt ihn ins Englische. S sprechen über Aufgaben, Erfolge, Finanzierung, Personal etc. Es könnte konkret auch eine Sammlung in der Schule für die Gesellschaft initiiert werden.
L liest dann den Text S.82 oben vor *(The coast... in boats)*. S formulieren jede(r) schriftlich drei Fragen zur Information, die der Text bereitstellt, etwa: *How much money do the crews get for their work? ...* Abruf der Fragen und Beantwortung. Dann Aufnahme des Vorschlags: ‚Vorbeugung/ Sicherheit auf Booten' (Nr.6).

Landeskundlicher Hinweis: Das britische Gegenstück zur DGzRS, die *Royal National Lifeboat Institution* (RNLI) wurde 1824 als *National Institution for the Preservation of Life from Shipwreck* gegründet. Schon vorher waren an einigen besonders gefährlichen Stellen der britischen Küste einzelne Boote von Städten und Gemeinden zum Zweck der Lebensrettung gestellt worden.

Es gab im Laufe der Jahre dann mehrere Wettbewerbe, um ein unversinkbares, sich wieder aufrichtendes Boot zu entwickeln. Obwohl alle *lifeboatmen* in den 219 *lifeboat stations* an der britischen Küste (inkl. *Republic of Ireland*) diese Tätigkeit freiwillig und unbezahlt ausüben und ihren Lebensunterhalt als Briefträger, Rechtsanwalt, Hotelmanager usw. verdienen, hat die RNLI ca. 600 Angestellte, die sich hauptsächlich um den Unterhalt der Boote und der weiteren Ausrüstung kümmern. Dieser Unterhalt kostet (1997) £194 000 pro Tag, allein die Ausrüstung für eine Person im *lifeboat* kostet über £300. Finanziert wird alles über Schenkungen und Geldsammlungen. Seit 1824 sind über 129 000 Menschenleben gerettet worden. Im Durchschnitt wird Tag für Tag alle anderthalb Stunden nach einem *lifeboat* gerufen. Ein Drittel der Rettungsaktionen findet bei Dunkelheit statt. Weitere Informationen (auch interessante Hefte gegen eine kleine Gebühr):
RNLI,
West Quay Road,
Poole,
Dorset BH15 1HZ, GB

6 Tips for people in boats

Ziel: Tipps für ein Flugblatt zur Sicherheit auf Booten erstellen.

Neu: *instructions, radio, to slip, darling, tide table, lifejacket*

Unterrichtsempfehlungen
Semantisierung: <u>instructions</u>: *information about what you have to do*; <u>radio</u>: klar durch das Schriftbild; <u>to slip</u>: *you slip on slippery ground*; <u>darling</u>: *somebody you like or love very much*; <u>tide table</u>: *a leaflet with information about when there is high or low tide*; <u>lifejacket</u>: *life* und *jacket* sind bekannt, daher direkt verständlich. a) Das Motivationspotential der *cartoons* nutzen: S betrachten die Bilder und ordnen die dazugehörigen Tipps und zu. Wenn die S Neigung zeigen, kann verbalisiert werden, was an den *cartoons funny* ist.

b) Durch die sprachlichen Hilfen und das *pattern*-System ist die Übung recht leicht durchführbar. Bewusstmachung: Es ist lediglich nötig, an die Passivbildung (siehe *Unit 4*) zu erinnern. Beispiel an der Tafel: GR § 15

	Form von to be	+	past participle
The trip	is		planned.
The trip	must be can should		planned

Regel: *In passive sentences a passive infinitive (be + past participle) follows the auxiliary (can, must, ...)* GR § 19

Danach werden die Beispielsätze 1 und 2 gemeinsam mit Hilfe der Regel durchgesprochen, dann schreiben alle S in Einzelarbeit jeweils 4-5 *tips* auf, die dann in der Klasse verlesen werden. Zusätzliche Hilfen für *tips: carry lamps; take along life-boats; not forget drinking-water; watch traffic at sea carefully; listen to weather forecast.* Weitere Übungsmöglichkeiten ergibt Bildfolie 18 WB S.60, B4

Bildfolie 19

Lösungen: *a) A: use signals safely; B: carry extra petrol and a rope; C: A radio can be useful.*

Schülerbuch Seite 83

7 All for the lifeboats

Ziel: *passive of verbs with prepositions.*

Unterrichtsempfehlungen
Zunächst ohne Buch: S finden (mit Tafelanschrieb) als

Vokabelwiederholung zu den hier vorkommenden Verben die dazugehörigen Präpositionen:

L schreibt: to pay   S sagen und schreiben: for
           to look   after, at, down, for, round
           to think   of
           to laugh   at
           to write   about, down
           to speak   to
           to hear   of

Tafelanschrieb

Die S bilden dann Aktivsätze mit diesen *verbs + prepositions*, z.B.: *My mother pays for my clothes, etc.* Dann Übung 7 gemeinsam mündlich mit Hilfe des Tafelbildes. Bewusstmachung: L lenkt die Aufmerksamkeit auf *verb + preposition*. S formulieren die einfache Aussage: *In active and in passive sentences verb + preposition always stay together.*

WB S.62, C1
GR § 114

Lösungen: *1. for; 2. after; 3. of; 4. at; 5. about; 6. to; 7. of*

8 A big oil problem

Ziel: *passive infinitive in the past tense.*

Neu: *tanker*

Unterrichtsempfehlungen

Semantisierung: *tanker: a big ship that carries oil.* Anhand der Bilder erkennen S (*Workshop C!*), worum die Übung inhaltlich gehen könnte. Ein S liest dann den Eingangstext (*In February ...polluted*) vor. Zur Lösung der 7 Aufgaben verweist L noch einmal auf die Bewusstmachung in Übung 6b (Tafelbild) und lässt die S den dortigen Satz: *The trip must be planned* in die Vergangenheitsform setzen: *The trip had to be planned.* Hiernach bereitet die Übung 8 keine Schwierigkeiten mehr. S arbeiten in Partnerarbeit. L macht dann 3–4 Kontrollen im Plenum.

GLN2 GR §23, § 24
WB S.61, B5
WB S.61, B6

Lösungen: *2. The beach had to be cleaned. 3. All the sand with oil on it had to be taken away. 4. The oil on the rocks had to be collected. 5. The poor seabirds had to be helped. 6. The live birds had to be caught and washed. 7. All the thousands of dead birds had to be picked up.*

9 A song: Sloop John B.

Ziel: Auflockerung des Unterrichts.

WB S.61, B7

Neu: *sloop, We did roam ..., broke-up, to hoist up, sail, mainsail, to set, ashore, to get drunk, to break into s.th., captain, trunk, constable; Nassau*

Unterrichtsempfehlungen

Die S lesen in Stillarbeit die Vokabelerklärungen auf S. 154. Beim ersten Hören des Liedes bleiben die Bücher auf S. 154 offen. Den Song vom Tonträger vorspielen / oder: L mit Gitarre o.ä. Beim 2. Vorspiel, summen S mit. S lesen Text und schlagen notfalls noch einmal im Vokabular S. 154 nach. 3. Vorspiel, S singen mit.
Ergänzung des Wortfeldes *the sea* um einige Wörter aus dem Song.
Evtl Miniprojekt : *Songs of the Sea.*

Schülerbuch Seite 84-85

Step C Sea Rescue

1 Before you read the story

Ziel: Über den möglichen Verlauf einer Geschichte spekulieren; Erwartungen an einen Text formulieren.

Neu: *rescue, to get trapped, to be on patrol, otherwise, to dial, maritime, emergency, to co-ordinate, to search for s.th., red flare,*

Unterrichtsempfehlungen

Semantisierung: <u>rescue:</u> *noun of 'to rescue'*; <u>to get trapped:</u> *not to be able to escape*; <u>to be on patrol:</u> *a Roman wall-soldier had to be on patrol: he walked on the wall and protected Roman Britain*; <u>otherwise:</u> *if not, then ...*; <u>maritime:</u> *having to do with the sea*; <u>emergency:</u> *a very dangerous situation*; <u>to co-ordinate:</u> *to organize things so that they work well*; <u>to search for s.th.:</u> *to look for s.th.*; <u>red flare:</u> *a red light shot at sea to show that there is an emergency.* a) Die S erinnern, was sie im *Workshop C* gelernt haben: Stilllesen des *leaflet*-Textes. Zeitvorgabe ca. 1 Minute, dann:
b) S schreiben mit oder ohne Hilfe der Buchhinweise hier auf, was er/sie aufgrund von a) erwartet und um welche Textsorte es sich handelt. Einige Vorschläge werden vorgelesen und stichwortartig an der Tafel festgehalten.

2 Now read the story

Ziel: Hörverstehensübung; Reaktionen auf einen Text formulieren (*while- and post-reading activities*).

Neu: *kid, engine, onto, serious, nightmare, one by one, to turn s.th. over, might, hold on, brave, medal; Broad Haven, Nolton Haven, Druidston, Milford Haven*

Unterrichtsempfehlungen

Semantisierung: <u>kid:</u> *child*; <u>engine:</u> *motor*; <u>onto:</u> *on s.th., compare 'into'*; <u>serious:</u> *not funny*; <u>nightmare:</u> *a very bad dream*; <u>one by one:</u> *one after the other*; <u>to turn s.th.over:</u> *to turn s.th. so that the bottom is up*; <u>might:</u> deutsch 'könnte'; <u>hold on!:</u> *do not let go!*; <u>brave:</u> *not scared*; <u>medal:</u> wird durch das Schriftbild klar. *'Gold medal' at Olympic Games*; Vokabeleinführung (Alternative: S erhalten 3 Minuten Gelegenheit, die Vokabelliste S.155 zu studieren).
Zur Kenntnisnahme der *map* in Verbindung mit der Karte vorne im SB oder der Wales-Karte auf Seite 44; L liest Textanfang vor (Z. 1-13). S spekulieren anhand des Tafelanschriebs aus 1b), welche der Erwartungen wohl erfüllt werden. Wie könnte die Geschichte weitergehen? L spielt die nächsten Abschnitte des Textes (Z. 14-36, 37-65: CD *tracks* 40 und 41) über Tonträger vor (Alternative: L liest vor). L: *Where are Mary and the children now? Where did Sam and his father go? Where are they now? What has the coastguard done?* Anschließend wird der Rest der Geschichte vorgespielt (Z. 66-120, CD *tracks* 42 und 43) bzw. vorgelesen. S reagieren spontan, voraussichtlich: *I liked the story because .../ I didn't like it .../ It was a bit boring because .../ That day must have been a nightmare... etc.*
Die S lesen dann die Geschichte noch einmal still. Auftrag: jeder S schreibt eine Frage an den Text auf, die sich ihm/ihr beim Lesen stellt. Dann Abruf der Fragen und Beantwortung/ Diskussion in der Klasse. Fragen etwa:
– Z. 9: *Why did they wait on the beach until it was too late? That was stupid!*
– Z. 27: *How could Tom leave his wife and the younger children alone on that dangerous beach? Couldn't the parents have carried the children?*
– Z. 43: *Wasn't it unprofessional of the coastguard to let Tom and Sam walk back again? They could not help anyway – and later they had to be rescued by the Cliff Rescue team, too!*
– Z. 120: *Will the Jacksons have to pay for all the stupid trouble they caused?*

Post-reading activities:
– Write about Mrs Jackson's feelings when she and the children were left alone by her husband.
– Interview mit Tom Jackson. Ein S in der Rolle des Tom wird von den anderen S befragt, etwa: *How could you leave ...? Why did you walk back ...? What did you think when ...? Why didn't you leave Sam in Druidston at least? etc.*
– Wortfeld '*the sea*' (s.o.) ergänzen durch Vokabeln aus dem Text.

- Selektives Lesen: Zeit, Ort, Dauer der Rettungsaktion genau ausmachen.
- Tidenhub und Strömungen in der Gegend von Milford Haven erkunden und die Gefahr erkennen, in der die leichtsinnigen Jacksons waren.

Schülerbuch Seite 86

3 The map

Ziel: Weitere *post-reading activities*/Selektives Lesen

Unterrichtsempfehlungen
a) S lösen die Aufgabe in Partnerarbeit.
Lösungen: *Nolton Haven: That's where the Jacksons went and were trapped. – Druidston: It's where they went for help and where they were taken after the rescue. – Milford Haven: That's where the coastguard was.*
b) Siehe Hinweise zu *ex.2*. Hier zusätzlich: *What do you think, why did he go back and why did he take Sam along?*

4 Writing a newspaper report

Ziel: Umsetzung eines Textes in eine andere Textsorte: *report*.   WB S.62, C2

Neu: *to leave out.*

Unterrichtsempfehlungen
Semantisierung: *to leave out: opposite of 'to add'.*
a), b), c) sind gut geeignet als Hausaufgabe. S fertigen ihre *reports* an und stellen sie in der Klasse zur Diskussion. Vorschlag: in Gruppenarbeit: Jede(r) S verliest seinen/ihren *report*. Die Gruppe stellt ihren 'Favoriten' den anderen Gruppen vor.
Zur Textsortencharakteristik *newspaper report* gehört der häufige Gebrauch von Passivkonstruktionen. L sollte zum Schluss darauf verweisen. S unterstreichen dann die selbst gebrauchten Passive in ihren Texten und verlesen sie (als Grammatikfestigung) im Unterricht.

5 What would you do?

Ziel: Übung der *conditional sentences type II*.

Unterrichtsempfehlungen
In Partnerarbeit. Weitere Vorschläge für *dangerous situations: a car accident/a broken leg on a skiing tour /hearing a strange noise in a dark house/house on fire/...*

6 Looking at English: Special nouns

Ziel: *collective noun*s kennenlernen.

Unterrichtsempfehlungen
a) Die Beispielsätze werden im Unterrichtsgespräch diskutiert. Feststellung der Möglichkeiten *singular* und *plural* für *family. Is there a difference?* S sollten finden: *singular = family as a whole (one family) – plural = all the different members (7 members of the Jackson family).*
b) S schreiben in Einzelarbeit die 4 Sätze und diskutieren/vergleichen dann ihre Ergebnisse mit dem Nachbarn. Ein von L und S gleichermaßen kommentierter Durchgang im Plenum ist hier wichtig.

Lösungen: *1. live/ is; 2. was/ were; 3. is / speak; 4. lose / needs.*

Schülerbuch Seite 87

Step D Let's check

1 You know

Ziel: Wortschatzübung   WB S.62, C4

Unterrichtsempfehlungen
Da es sich hier um eine Lernzielüberprüfung handelt, sollten alle Übungen individuell (evtl. als Hausarbeit) angefertigt werden.

Lösungen: *1. flat; 2. nightmare; 3. unpredictable; 4. helicopter; 5. calm; 6. cliffs 7. lifeboatmen.*

2 All around Britain

Ziel: Überprüfung und Festigung der *conditional sentences type II*   GR § 113 WB S.63, D2

Unterrichtsempfehlungen
Als Hausaufgabe eignet sich eine intensivere Bearbeitung von nur 2 Themen, da den S mehrere mögliche Aktivitäten in jeder Gegend bekannt sind.

Lösungsmöglichkeiten: *2. If I visited North Wales, I would go to Snowdonia National Park. 3. If I went to Caerleon, I would visit the old Roman camp and I would also try to find Camelot. 4. If I were in Nottingham, I would look for places that have to do with Robin Hood. 5. If I had a holiday in Cornwall, I would try to get to Land's End. 6. If I spent a week in London, I would visit the Tower and Mme. Tussaud's.*

3 A fantasy school

Ziel: Festigung des *passive infinitive*.   GR § 114 WB S.63, D1

Unterrichtsempfehlungen
Am besten sind diese Sätze als *List of rules* aufzustellen.

Lösungsmöglichkeiten: *Pupils should be paid for their work. – Reports about teachers should be written. – A TV must be put into every classroom. – Homework needn't be done. – Exams should be made easier. – Games can be played in lessons. – A school trip to Caernarvon should be organized. – Pets can be taken to school – ...*

4 ⟨Just for fun⟩

Ziel: *Unit*-Ausklang   WB S.64

Neu: *diet*

Unterrichtsempfehlungen
Semantisierung: *diet:* wird über das Schriftbild klar. *You are on a diet if you only eat things that don't make you fat or ill.*
S nehmen den Dialog zur Kenntnis und erkennen das Wortspiel *sea – see*.

⟨Extra Line⟩

Wie in den beiden vorangegangenen Bänden von **Green Line New** handelt es sich hier um ein Angebot von Zusatzmaterialien zu einigen der *Units* bzw. *Workshops*. Ihre Behandlung ist absolut in das Belieben der jeweiligen Lehrkraft – und der Schülerinnen und Schüler – gestellt. Wortschatz und Strukturen gehören nicht zu dem Lernstoff, dessen Nichtkenntnis die Arbeit mit dem Folgeband **GLN 4** erschweren würde.

Andererseits handelt es sich um ein Angebot, dessen große Motivationskraft genutzt werden sollte:
1. Es werden für die Schülerinnen und Schüler dieser Altersstufe interessante landeskundliche Informationen vermittelt.
2. Variable Textsorten wecken jeweils neues Interesse und eröffnen verschiedene Zugangsmöglichkeiten.
3. Möglichkeiten für handlungsorientierte, auch fächerübergreifende, Arbeit sind in den Materialien angelegt.
4. Auch die Intensität der Behandlung der Materialien ist freigestellt: vom bloßen kursorischen 'Zur-Kenntnis-Nehmen' bis zur umfangreicheren Kleinprojektarbeit sind alle Formen denkbar.

Im Folgenden werden zu den einzelnen Texten Vorschläge gemacht und Anregungen gegeben, die im Wesentlichen nach dem Prinzip ,vom Einfachen zum eher Aufwendigen' geordnet sind. Zeitfaktor und Schülerinteresse werden bei der Auswahl für den konkreten Unterricht entscheidend sein.

Schülerbuch Seiten 88-90

Reading Corner

The Gunpowder Plot
(Didaktischer Ort: nach *Unit 1*)

Geschichtlicher Hintergrund
Der Text beantwortet im Wesentlichen die Fragen: *Why do the British celebrate the 5th of November?* und *Who was Guy Fawkes?*.
Einige Erläuterungen zum Text sind evtl. hilfreich:
1. Die Charaktere Catesby, Percy, Wright, Winter, Guy Fawkes und Lord Monteagle sind historisch.
2. Z. 6: *'one group of people hated him...'* = *Roman Catholics*, die seit der Zeit Heinrich VIII unterdrückt wurden (anti-katholische Gesetze). Die Gruppe versuchte durch ihren Gewaltakt gegen König und Regierung für sich und ihre Glaubensgenossen Bürgerrechte zurückzugewinnen.
3. Z. 14-17: Fawkes, 1570 geboren, war 1593 in die spanische Armee in Flandern eingetreten. Im Krieg gegen Heinrich IV von Frankreich nahm er an der spanischen Eroberung von Calais teil. Nach Jahren kehrte er nach England zurück und wurde in das *Gunpowder Plot* verwickelt.
4. Z. 58-65: Die Frage, wieso es 36 Fässer sein mussten und woher Fawkes diese Menge Sprengstoff bekam, ist ungeklärt.
5. Z. 77: Man sagt, der Verräter sei einer der Verschwörer gewesen, der seinen Verwandten Monteagle *(Member of the House of Lords)* vor dem Tode bewahren wollte.
6. Z. 85: Nur Fawkes war dort unten. Er war ausgesucht worden, die Sprengladung zu zünden.
7. Z. 90: Unter starker Folter verriet Fawkes die Namen seiner geflohenen Mitverschwörer. Am 31. Januar 1606 wurde er vor dem Parlamentsgebäude hingerichtet. Der Anschlag hatte auch politisch keinen Erfolg. Erst 1829 *(Catholic Emancipation Act)* erhielten die Katholiken in Grossbritannien volle politische und bürgerliche Rechte.

Unterrichtsempfehlungen
L erzählt den S von den Vorgängen am 5. Nov. heute in Grossbritannien (die Inflation hat schon längst vom traditionellen *"a penny for the Guy"* zu *"10p for the guy"* geführt; *burning of effigies; bonfires; fireworks; searching of the cellars of the Houses of Parliament ...*), stellt den Reim vor (vgl. Buch: *Remember ...*), fordert S auf, Fragen zu stellen (Sammlung an der Tafel bzw. am OHP, etwa: *Why do they burn the figures/guys? Why do they search the cellars?*). L verspricht Antworten durch den Text S. 88–90.

S finden auf S. 14–15 die *Houses of Parliament* und auf S. 18 die nächstgelegene U-Bahn-Station. Wenn aus *Unit 1* noch nicht bekannt, wäre ein Bild (Dia, Poster) dieses berühmten *sights* motivierend.

Da der Text eine Reihe unbekannter Vokabeln enthält, empfiehlt sich an dieser Stelle ein kurzer, gemeinsamer Durchgang durch die Vokabelangaben der Seiten 88–90. Alternativ: L semantisiert die Vokabeln, die er/sie zum Hörverständnis für unbedingt notwendig hält. Die restlichen werden von den S erschlossen bzw. später geklärt.

Die S hören den Text vom Tonträger; dann evtl. zweites Hören: S lesen mit.

Es ist auch möglich, das Stück selber als Hörspiel vorzubereiten und aufzunehmen. Dann sollte das Vorspielen vom Tonträger ausschnittsweise im Rahmen der Vorbereitungen erfolgen, z.B. als Intonationshilfe an kniffligen Stellen. Siehe auch Angaben unter b).

Aktivitäten:
a) Die Fragen (s.o.) werden im Unterrichtsgespräch aus dem Text heraus geklärt. L gibt bei Bedarf Zusatzinformationen.
b) Die S lesen den Text mit verteilten Rollen. Damit in diesem Stück, in dem die Hauptpersonen alle Männer sind, Mädchen auch Rollen bekommen, sollten die *Speakers*, der Chor, der die Reime spricht, und die Rolle der *House owner* in *Scene 2* mit Mädchen besetzt werden.
c) Die S lernen den *Remember*-Reim auswendig.
d) Die S schreiben ein persönliches Urteil über die Geschichte / über den Verrat des *plot* / über Fawkes. Dabei Nutzung der *helpful phrases* S. 183.
e) Die S sprechen/schreiben über die Gewissensbisse des Verräters und über Fawkes' Gedanken nach der Gefangennahme.
f) Die S erzählen die Geschichte aus der Sicht Monteagles.
g) Diskussion offener Fragen im Text: Wer hat das *plot* verraten und warum? / Wie konnten die Soldaten nach diesem Briefinhalt (Z. 78-79) wissen, dass sie im *cellar* suchen mussten? / Wer gab Fawkes so viel Sprengstoff?
h) L gibt mögliche Zeitungsüberschriften zum Thema. Die S suchen jeweils eine aus und schreiben dazu einen Artikel (etwa: *Plotters caught in attempt to blow up the King / King and Parliament saved / Catholic terrorists disturb London / Was Fawkes framed? etc)*.
i) Die S schreiben Stichworte zur Geschichte auf (vgl. *Workshop A*, S. 12) und erzählen dann mit Hilfe ihrer *notes* die Geschichte des *Gunpowder Plot*.
j) Die S bauen zum 5. Nov. selbst einen *Guy*.
k) Die S besorgen sich Zusatzinformationen zum Thema (Befragung von L der Schule, Lexika etc.). Hilfreich ist das Internet. Unter
http://www.bcpl.lib.md.us/~cbladey/guy/html/main.html
http://www.fas.harvard.edu/~cpowell/church/guyfawkes.html
http://ezinfo.ucs.indiana.edu/~shyde/guyhome.html
finden sich hinreichend Materialien zu Unterthemen wie: *The route of the conspirators as they fled Lon-*

don / How the Plot changed History / Guy Fawkes' Day Liturgy (bis ins 19. Jh. üblich), *etc.*
l) *The Plot: an act of terrorism:* Die S besorgen Zusatzmaterial (s.o.), finden Beispiele von Terrorismus heute (N. Irland, Israel, Deutschland, ...), sammeln Zeitungsmeldungen etc., diskutieren die Zeilen 31-32 im Text: Tötung Unschuldiger?! Gewalt als Mittel der Problemlösung? (natürlich nur auf deutsch möglich).

Schülerbuch Seite 91

Religious festivals in Britain
(Didaktischer Ort: nach *Workshop B*)

Unterrichtsempfehlungen
Diese Seite kann zu einem effektiven Beitrag zur Völkerverständigung werden. Sie ist eine direkte Ergänzung des auf S. 16 begonnenen Themas: *Britain as a multicultural society* und stellt verschiedene Glaubensrichtuungen anhand ihrer Feiertage dar. Eine umfassende Behandlung des jeweiligen Glaubens ist nicht beabsichtigt und in diesem Rahmen gar nicht möglich. Dieses Material passt in die Vorweihnachtszeit
– L erinnert an Samiras Familie (S. 16); evtl wird diese Seite noch einmal zusammen angesehen. L: *We're going to learn more about diffferent people in Britain and their festivals.*
– In Stillarbeit lesen die S die Texte der Seite 91, benutzen dabei die Vokabelerläuterungen. L liest die Texte dann vor.
– Tafelarbeit. *What do we learn about the festivals of ...?*
    Jews   Hindus   Muslims
    –   –   –
– Alternativ: Die Klasse in 3 Gruppen aufteilen, jede Gruppe erarbeitet einen Text und gibt die gewonnenen Informationen anschließend an die Klasse weiter.
Im Folgenden: *Let's try to find more information:*
a) Sollten S einer der angesprochenen Glaubensrichtungen vorhanden und dazu bereit sein (auch Parallelklassen, Austauschschüler/innen, Fremdsprachenassistent/innen, die Schule insgesamt nutzen), können sie ihre Feiertage persönlich darstellen. Fakten werden gesammelt. Evtl. sind hier auch die Eltern dieser S bereit, im Unterricht zu helfen.
b) Sollte a) insgesamt nicht in Frage kommen, sammeln S selbst Informationen über ihnen unbekannte Festtage. L stellt entweder Material zur Verfügung oder die S suchen selbst in der elterlichen Bibliothek, der Schulbücherei bzw. im Internet. (Über die Suchmaschinen http://altavista.digital.com/ und http://www.yahoo.com ist bei Eingabe der jeweiligen Suchbegriffe (Diwali/ Hannukah/ Chinese New Year/ St. Patrick's Day/ Thanksgiving/ etc.) umfassend Material erhältlich.
– *Ethnic food:* S sammeln Rezepte und stellen sie vor.
– S schreiben über eigene Festtage (wie im Buch mit jeweils 50-70 Wörtern): *Easter, Christmas ...*
– Fächerübergreifend: S sprechen im Religionsunterricht über andere Glaubensrichtungen, und bringen dies im Englischunterricht ein.
– An den erwähnten Festtagen (Hannukah etc.) entwerfen, schreiben und senden die S jeweils *greetings-cards* an Mitschüler/innen der jeweiligen religiösen Zugehörigkeit.

Schülerbuch Seiten 92-93

Nathan and Lara
(Didaktischer Ort: nach *Workshop C*)

Unterrichtsempfehlungen
Eine Anbindung ist inhaltlich an *Unit 1*, S. 16 und arbeitstechnisch an den *Workshop C Let's Read* möglich und sinnvoll.

S öffnen das Buch. Nach einem kurzen Blick auf den Titel, die Bilder und das Erscheinungsbild des Textes formulieren sie ihre Erwartungen bezüglich des Inhalts und stellen Vermutungen über die Textsorte an. L gibt evtl. anhand der Postkarte noch einige Zusatzinformationen über Shakespeare und Stratford (die Postkarte unten auf S. 93 zeigt u.a. typische Straßen in Stratford, die Avon, und [Bild unten Mitte] das Shakespeare Memorial Theatre, das direkt am Fluß liegt und das Zuhause der *Royal Shakespeare Company* ist), um die Wichtigkeit von Laras Teilnahme an der Fahrt dorthin allen S deutlich zu machen.
Textpräsentation entweder:
a) S lesen den Gesamttext still und mit Hilfe der Vokabelliste, oder
b) L oder Fremdsprachenassistent/in macht auf einige wichtige neue Vokabeln aufmerksam, liest dann Gesamttext vor, die S lesen mit, oder
c) L oder Fremdsprachenassistent/in liest jeweils Teile des Textes vor (Vorschlag: bis Z. 56; bis 89; bis 111), S lesen mit, dann Diskussion der jeweiligen Sachlage, z.B. *What do you think? What could Lara say? What are her feelings when she goes to the football match? Did she make any mistakes? What's going to happen now? etc.*
Die S formulieren ihre Reaktion auf die Gesamtgeschichte.
Gemeinsame Erstellung eines Tafelbildes: *What exactly is the situation?* Diskussion. — Tafelbild

Nathan	Lara
likes Lara	likes Nathan
is needed in important football match	wants to spend last day with Nathan
wants to spend last day with Lara	must join her group to Stratford
hates getting up early and Lara's bus leaves early Sunday morning	must fill in worksheets
	really wants to learn about Shakespeare
	school is important, doesn't want trouble
	never misses lessons
	not interested in football

Danger	
team might lose the game	punishment at school
team might throw him out	parents might be notified
	she must lie

Adjektivsammlung an der Tafel: S füllen die Tafel mit Hilfe ihrer Vokabelhefte oder des Vokabulars S. 156ff. Frage: *Which adjectives say best how Lara and Nathan feel in some of the situations in the text?*
Rollenspiele:
a) Gespräch mit dem Fußballtrainer und Spielern über eine Wiedereinstellung Nathans.
b) Gespräch mit Nathan über seine Gefühle, als er in Stratford bemerkte, dass Lara nicht dabei war.
c) Gespräch mit Lara: *What did you think when you realized that Nathan was not on the field?*
Nathan formuliert eine schriftliche Entschuldigung und bittet um Wiedereingliederung ins Team.
Lara schreibt einen versöhnlichen Brief als Antwort auf die Karte von Nathan.

Schülerbuch Seiten 94-95

The killing of a god
(Didaktischer Ort: nach *Unit 5*)

Unterrichtsempfehlungen
Der Text behandelt die letzten 10 Lebenstage Cooks zwischen dem 4.2. und 14.2.1779. Dies ist für die S im

3. Lernjahr Englisch eine spannende Geschichte. Sicher haben einige von ihnen auch Vorkenntnisse aus Abenteuerbüchern, die vom L eingeholt und nutzbar gemacht werden können. Die S können dann den Auftrag erhalten, aus Lexika (zu Hause oder in der Schule) mehr Informationen über das Leben Cooks herauszuholen. Besonders interessant sind seine 3 Reisen:
1. 1768-1771: Entdeckung der Südinsel Neuseelands und der Ostküste Australiens. Große kartographische Leistungen Cooks.
2. 1772-1775: Entdeckung der New Hebrides, New Caledonias, Fidjis, Tongas, der Society Islands. Umschiffung von Antarctica.
3. 1776-1780: Entdeckung der Marquesas Islands, der Cook Islands, Hawaiis. Fahrt entlang der Westküste Amerikas von Kalifornien nach Alaska, Bering Strait. Tod am 14.2.79 in Kealakekua Bay, Hawaii.

Auch die berühmte Sauerkraut-Anekdote taucht vielleicht auf: *Cook knew that on a long trip everyone would get scurvy* (Skorbut). *He wanted the sailors to eat sauerkraut because fruit and vegetables stop people getting scurvy. But the sailors didn't like it. So Cook said that only the officers could have sauerkraut. Then, of course, all the sailors wanted it, too.*

Lohnend und motivierend wäre auf jeden Fall ein Nachvollzug der Reisen auf einer Landkarte. Danach:
– kurze Semantisierung nur der allerwichtigsten neuen Vokabeln.
– L oder Fremdsprachenassistent/in sollten den Text gut studieren und lebhaft (als spannende Abenteuergeschichte) vortragen. S-Bücher bleiben geschlossen.
– S klären die Fragen (Z. 13): *Why did the priests for a long time think of Cook as of a god?* – (Z. 55): *Why didn't they treat him like a god any more when he returned to the island a few days later?*
– S lesen den Text in Stillarbeit noch einmal unter Benutzung der Vokabelhilfen im Buch.
– Mögliche Aktivität zum *close reading*: Tafelbildentwicklung: *Show the increasing unfriendliness of the natives.* **Tafelbild**

Diskussion über das Benehmen und Verhalten der Weißen auf der Insel.
Die S schreiben entweder eine Zeitungsmeldung oder einen persönlichen Kommentar über den Tod Cooks.
Wenn mehr Zeit investiert werden kann, wären Projekte lohnend über: *Hawaiian legends;* – *Other famous sea-captains* (V. da Gama; Magellan, Columbus, Cabot, etc.).

Schülerbuch Seite 96

Christmas
(Didaktischer Ort: nach Workshop B / Weihnachten)

Unterrichtsempfehlungen
Aus den Vorbänden **GLN** 1 und 2 haben die S bereits einige Vorkenntnisse zum Thema *Christmas in Britain*. Insbesondere kennen sie *mince pie, turkey, Christmas pudding*.
Das *gingerbread*-Rezept sollte in jedem Fall von den S real ausprobiert werden: Entweder nutzt L die Schulküche (S bringen Zutaten) oder S backen zu Hause und bringen ihre Ergebnisse mit. Im Sinne der Seite 91 (*Religious festivals ...*) könnte Festtagsgebäck anderer Kulturen auch vorgeführt werden. Dann: Verzehr bei Kerzenschein im Klassenzimmer.
Wiederholen: *How do British people celebrate Christmas?* (**GLN** 1, S. 114 / **GLN** 2; S. 98f.).
Wiederholen des Liedes aus **GLN** 1 (S. 114): *We wish you a merry Christmas.*
Lernen des neuen Liedes *The Little Drummer Boy*:
a) Vorspiel von Tonträger (oder L-vortrag), S summen mit.
b) 2. Vorspiel, S summen mit singen die pa rumpa pum pum-Teile mit.
c) Buch S. 96: gemeinsamer Durchgang durch den Text, Semantisierung von Vokabeln, wo nötig, kurze Leseübung zur Sicherung der Aussprache.
d) Vorspiel von Kassette, S singen mit.
e) S singen das Lied ohne Hilfe.

| treated like a god paradise on their knees respect | often stole things | happy that ships are sailing away no pigs left whites have red blood too | give all their food, nothing much in return stay too long 2nd visit not in the legends pigs more expensive | take largest boat hold King back throw stones kill with knives and stones | crowd kills Cook cut body into pieces |

Schülerbuch Seite 97

Translation Practice (Lösungen)

Unit 1 A trip to London
a) – Wie kommen wir von hier zum Tower?
– Wir können die U-Bahn nehmen. In Victoria müssen wir in die Circle Line umsteigen und dann Tower Hill aussteigen.
– Vielleicht könnten wir am Nachmittag/nachmittags in den London Dungeon gehen?
– Ja, das fände ich schön. Es ist nur ein kurzer Weg zu Fuß vom Tower. Oder möchtest du nicht mehr laufen?
– Nein, es ist OK. Ich gehe gern zu Fuß.

b) *What's that in English?*
1. – *What do you enjoy doing in your free time?*
– *I like reading. And I like playing table-tennis.*
– *Do you also like swimming?*
– *No, I'm not so good at swimming!*
2. – *Look at this recipe. 'Indian chicken with curry and bananas'. That sounds good.*
– *Maybe it tastes good, too.*

Unit 2 Trouble at school
a) *Edward:* Möchte jemand meine Fotos sehen?
David: Sind das Fotos von Indien?/die du in Indien gemacht hast?
Edward: Nein, ich dachte nur, ihr würdet gern ein paar

Bilder von der Internatsschule sehen, auf die ich gegangen bin. Hier, das ist ein Foto, das mein Vater am Semesterende gemacht hat.
David: Mann! Ist das die Uniform, die du tragen musstest? Die sieht ja noch schlechter aus als unsere!– Hey, und wer ist das Mädchen da?
Edward: Das ist ein Mädchen, dessen Bruder in meiner Klasse war. In St. John's gab es keine Mädchen.
David: Keine Mädchen? Eine merkwürdige Schule!

b) *Becky:* Mein Portemonnaie ist weg! Was soll ich tun?
Edward: Mach dir keine Sorgen. Ich bezahle deine Chips für dich. Soll ich dir auch was zu trinken kaufen?
Becky: Bitte! – Meinst du, Wayne könnte mein Portemonnaie genommen haben? Du weißt, wie er ist!

c) *Jenny:* Was machst du heute Abend, Edward?
Edward: Ich mache nichts Besonderes.
Jenny: Na ja, vielleicht würdest du gern zu mir kommen. Becky und Robert kommen auch. Robert bringt sein Video von ‚Romeo und Julia' mit.
Edward: Ja, na klar komme ich. Danke!

d) *What's that in English?*
1. *Have you read the book that I lent you last week?*
2. *Do you know the girl who is talking to Edward?*
3. *I like teachers who tell jokes in the lessons.*
4. *I can't stand people who lie.*

Schülerbuch Seite 98

Unit 3 Welcome to Wales

a) – Guten Abend. Haben Sie noch zwei Doppelzimmer frei? Wir haben nicht reserviert.
– Einen Augenblick. Ah ja, Sie haben Glück. Jemand hat abgesagt.
– Liegen die Räume nebeneinander?
– Nein, aber sie sind beide auf derselben Etage. Hier sind die Schlüssel. Der Fahrstuhl ist gleich dort drüben.
– Vielen Dank …Wir sind sicher schon zu spät für ein Abendessen, nicht wahr?
– Aber nein. Das Restaurant ist bis halb zehn geöffnet.

b) – Was ist los? Du siehst heute nicht sehr fröhlich aus.
– Ich weiß nicht, was ich tun soll. Ich habe Sam verloren! Frau Lees Hund! Ich habe dir von Frau Lee erzählt, nicht wahr. Sie besucht ihre Schwester in Amerika, und ich kümmere mich seit einer Woche um Sam. Gestern gingen wir in der Nähe des Flusses spazieren, und plötzlich war er weg.
– Mach dir keine Sorgen! Ich helfe dir beim Suchen.
– Aber ich weiß nicht, wo ich suchen soll! Ich mache mir schon den ganzen Tag Sorgen, und ich bin schon überall gewesen.

c) *What's that in English?*
1. *Why are you so late? I've been waiting for you for 20 minutes now.*
2. *How long have you been living in Wales? Since February.*
3. *"A miracle has happened!" Merlin said. "For many years I've been dreaming of this day. Now Arthur has shown us all that he is our true king."*

Unit 4 : The environment

a) – Dieser langsame Verkehr ist furchtbar. Vielleicht war da ein Unfall.
– Nein, guck, da vorne ist eine Baustelle.
– Was zum Teufel machen sie diesmal mit der Straße? Erst letztes Jahr haben sie diesen Teil verbreitert und all die schönen alten Bäume abgeholzt. Erinnerst du dich?

– Ja!
In dieser Gegend hat sich so viel verändert, dass ich fast vergessen habe, wie es war, als wir hierher zogen!

b) *How to help the environment*
1. Lass dein Auto stehen und benutze öffentliche Verkehrsmittel. Sollte das nicht möglich sein, benutze dein Auto nur, wenn unbedingt nötig.
2. Spare Energie und lass die Heizung nicht die ganze Nacht laufen.
3. Kaufe keine Getränke in Plastikflaschen. Hebe Plastiktüten auf – du kannst sie wieder benutzen.
4. Bringe alte Zeitungen und Zeitschriften in einen Papiercontainer. Wenn sie wiederverwertet werden, rettet das Wälder.
5. Iss Obst und Gemüse, die in deiner Gegend wachsen. Denk daran, wieviel Energie verschwendet wird, wenn Nahrungsmittel von der einen Seite der Welt zur anderen geschickt werden.

c) *What's that in English?*
1. *I have just heard an interesting piece of news.*
2. *Some pieces of information are wrong.*
3. *Every day energy is wasted. New roads are built. The environment is polluted and our beautiful landscape is changed. If nothing is done to improve the situation, our world will slowly be destroyed.*

Schülerbuch Seite 99

Unit 5 Great Britain and the sea

a) – *was trapped:* war gefangen; saß in der Falle
– *Black Dog Rocks:* die „Schwarzer Hund"-Felsen
– *when the tide was out:* bei Ebbe
– *changed into a nightmare:* wurde zum Alptraum
– *was coming in fast:* kam schnell herein
– *how serious:* wie ernst
– *they wondered whether:* sie fragten sich, ob …
– *too rough:* zu rauh, zu schwer
– *bravely:* tapfer
– *steep and dangerous in that area:* steil und gefährlich in dieser Gegend
– *coast path:* Küstenweg
– *they were in trouble:* sie waren in Schwierigkeiten

b) *What's that in German?*
1. Wenn das Wetter gut ist, gehen wir morgen an den Strand.
2. Wenn wir dicht an der See lebten, würden wir ein Boot kaufen.
3. Ich würde in dem Teich nicht schwimmen, wenn ich du wäre.
4. Die Küste um Britannien herum muss von der Küstenwacht bewacht werden.
5. Wenn Leute auf See in Not sind, müssen Rettungsboote geholt werden.

c) *What's that in English?*
1. *If the summer is nice this year, I'll go swimming every day.*
2. *If Peter had more free time, he wouldn't have so much money!*
3. – *Don't you have life-jackets?*
– *No, but the weather forecast is good. I don't think anything will go wrong, if we sail out in the boat.*
– *I wouldn't do that if I were you!*

Grammar revision

Zusatzübungen für Schülerinnen und Schüler, die nach **Orange Line New** Band 1 und 2 mit **Green Line New** 3 anfangen. Diese Übungen dürfen für den Schulgebrauch vervielfältigt werden.

1 Can / could / be able to GR Rev 1 SB S. 100

Can you do these things? Put in different phrases for the ... .

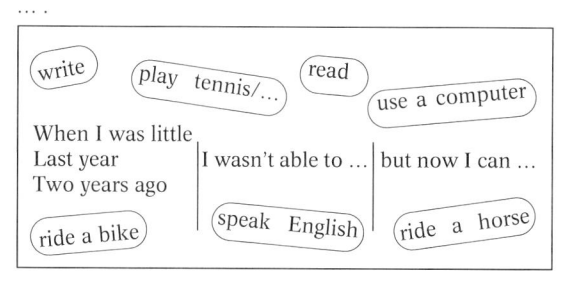

> (write) (play tennis/...) (read) (use a computer)
> When I was little
> Last year I wasn't able to ... but now I can ...
> Two years ago
> (ride a bike) (speak English) (ride a horse)

2 Adverbs of manner GR Rev 2 SB S. 100
Siehe auch SB Seite 114

These sentences need an adverb. Choose the right adjective and use its adverb form.

(careful) (hard) (easy) (quiet) (fast) (good)

1. *Sarah:* Our German homework is very difficult.
   Jenny: Oh, but I can do it ... .
2. *Sarah:* Mum, can I use your bike today?
   Mrs Dixon: Yes, OK, but don't ride too ... .
3. *David:* Can I play my guitar in here, Dad?
   Mr Penrose: OK, but do it ..., I'm writing a letter.
4. *Robert:* Do you want to play football?
   Jenny: No, you always kick the ball too ... .
5. *Simon:* Do you know this song?
   Becky: Yes, it's great! I know it very ... .
6. *Sarah:* Can I write in your diary, Becky?
   Becky: OK, but write ... .

Lösungen: *1. easily 2. fast 3. quietly 4. hard 5. well 6. carefully*

3 Comparison of adverbs GR Rev 3 SB S. 101

Make sentences about these people – they all do something best.

Example:
1. Robert – play cards – clever
   Robert plays cards **most cleverly.**
2. Sarah – ride her bike – fast.
3. David – play the guitar – beautiful.
4. Becky – do puzzles – quick.
5. Jenny – speak German – good   *(Be careful!)*

Lösungen: *2. fastest 3. most beautifully 4. most quickly 5. best*

4 Comparisons with adverbs GR Rev 4 SB S. 101

Who's the winner? Who does it best?

1. All the animals eat quickly. But Maxi eats most quickly. She eats ... than Mini and Tabby.
2. All the girls run fast. But Sarah runs ... . She runs ... than Becky and Jenny.
3. All the boys write untidily. But little Mark writes ... . Robert and David.
4. All the fathers sing very badly. But Mr Leinert ... . Mr Dixon and Mr Penrose.

Lösungen: *1. more quickly 2. fastest – faster 3. most untidily. He writes more untidily than ... . 4. sings worst. He sings worse than ... .*

Lösungen zu den Spielwiesen: Let's play with words

> Schülerbuch Seite 129

2 What can you say about people

a) **Lösungen:** *nervous, scared, surprised, happy, angry, tired, glad, unhappy*

Hinweis auf Vorlagen für Zeichnungen: Eine Fundgrube für Strichzeichnungen für den Einsatz im Fremdsprachenunterricht ist: Andrew Wright. *1000 Pictures for teachers to copy.* Walton-on-Thames: Nelson, 1993

b) **Lösungen:** *terrible, crazy, famous; boring, busy, clever; happy, silly, rich, polite; interesting, stupid, excited; upset, poor, careful, worried.*

> Schülerbuch Seite 143

1 Change one letter only

Mögliche Lösungswege:

W A L L	R A C E	H O L D
F A L L	L A C E	H O L E
F E L L	L A K E	R O L E
F E E L	T A K E	R U L E

Bei Bedarf können folgende zwei Folgeaufgaben als Hausaufgabe gestellt werden:
FALL → WELL, TELL → SALE, HOT → SIT

Mögliche Lösungswege:

F A L L	T E L L	H O T
F E L L	T A L L	H A T
T E L L	T A L E	S A T
W E L L	S A L E	S I T

2 Which words sound the same?

Lösungen: *hear – here, one – won, rode – road, write – right; nose – knows, their – there, sea – see, where – wear; by – buy, red – read, meat – meet, our – hour; no – know, two – too, whole – hole, weigh – way*

3 Add or take away letters

Lösungen: live (– 3); car (– 2); nose (– 2); drive (+1); palace (+ 1); feet (– 5); blue (– 3); shot, shut (– 1); brown (+2); cat (– 2); lose (– 3); cream (– 1); snow (+ 1); seal (– 3); market (+2); near (– 3); train (+ 1); dive (– 1)

> Schülerbuch Seite 150

1 Opposite pairs

Lösungen: (Die jeweils fehlenden Wörter sind in Klammern gesetzt)
stupid – clever; new – (old); find – (lose); whisper – shout big – small; different – same; save – spend; slow – (fast); dead – (alive); back – front; remember – forget; cry – laugh; rich – (poor); answer – question; inside – outside; close – open; wife – husband; hate – love; bad – good; first – last; friend – enemy; empty – full; difficult – easy; day – night; hot – cold; careful – careless; worst – best; before – after; leave – arrive; never – always; together – alone; well – badly; (late) – early; (sell) – buy; (fat)) – thin; (pull)) – push; (quiet) – noisy.

Vertiefungsübungen

Diese Übungen dürfen für den Unterrichtsgebrauch kopiert werden.

Workshop A

1 Countries and nationalities *(brainteaser)*

A group of reporters arrived in Brussels on the EUROJET. One of the reporters has left a camera on the plane. Find out where everybody sat, and where the the camera is. (Seats A and B are Row 1, seats B and C are Row 2, and so on.)

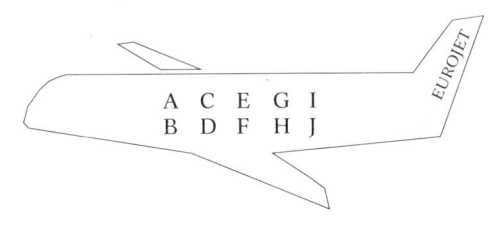

```
        A C E G I
        B D F H J     EUROJET
```

The reporter from Denmark sat in the fourth row.
The reporter who left the camera is from Scotland.
The Danish reporter sat next to the Greek reporter .
The Dutch reporter sat in the front row.
The English reporter sat in the second row.
The German reporter sat on the left of the English reporter.
The reporter from Turkey sat behind the Danish reporter.
The reporter from France sat on the right of the reporter from the Netherlands.
The reporter from Spain sat behind the reporter from Germany.
The Italian reporter sat in front of the Danish reporter.
The Turkish reporter is talking to a British reporter.
The Spanish reporter sat next to the Italian reporter.

New: *reporter*

2 What would you say? *(speaking)*

a) Find the pairs. They make little dialogues.
b) What other answers could you give?

1. I'm sorry I'm late!
2. Thank you for the birthday present!
3. Could you carry my bag for me, please?
4. Do you mind if I open the window?
5. Have a nice weekend.
6. I'm not feeling well.
7. Would you like to come to the disco with me?
8. Would you like another piece of cake?
9. Hello, how are you?
10. Have you got the time?

a) No, not at all.
b) No, thanks. I've already had two.
c) Never mind/It doesn't matter.
d) It's half past eleven.
e) Of course.
f) Yes, I'd love to.
g) I'm pleased you like it!
h) Oh dear. What's the matter?
i) Thanks. Same to you!
j) Fine, thanks.

Weiterführende Übung: *Schreiben Sie die Stimuli auf Kartensätze. Jeder Schüler/Schülerin bekommt ein Kärtchen. A liest seinen/ihren Stimulus B vor. B liest seinen/ihren Stimulus für C, und so weiter.*

Vorschläge für Stimuli (3 Sätze für eine Klasse mit 30 S):

I'm sorry that I lost your CD.
Could you lend me some money, please?
Thanks for helping me with my homework.
Do you mind if I use your dictionary?
Happy Birthday!
I've got some bad news.
Would you like to come to my party?
Would you like some more pizza?
You look grumpy. What's the matter?
What's the time?

3 Telephone language *(speaking + writing)*

a) Put the phrases into two groups: 'Making a call' and 'Taking a call'.

No-one of that name lives here. – When can I call again? – Would you like to leave a message? – Please speak after the long tone. – Yes, of course. What's the message? – Oh, sorry, I've got the wrong number. – Scarborough Youth Hostel. The warden speaking. – Can I speak to Simon, please? – Oh well, can I leave a message? – Please tell him I'll phone back this evening. – Oh no! I hate talking to these machines! – Hello, this is Kim here. – Who's calling, please? – Could you give her a message? – I'm afraid he isn't at home. – Oh hello, Yasmin. What can I do for you?

b) Work in pairs. Imagine a funny situation and write a telephone dialogue. You can use phrases from (a) if you like. Practise your dialogue and act it to the class.

4 Telephoning role plays *(speaking)*

<u>Jackie:</u> You have just come back from a fantastic holiday. You visited lots of countries and did lots of interesting things. Call your friend William and tell him about it.

<u>William:</u> You are giving your cat some milk when you drop the bottle on the kitchen floor. There is milk and broken glass everywhere. You want to clean up the mess before anyone else sees it. The phone rings.

<u>Jerry:</u> An argument with a friend has upset you. Call Emma and tell her all about it. Emma is a good listener. Talking to her usually makes you feel a lot better.

<u>Emma:</u> You are getting ready to go to a disco You have to leave in twenty minutes, and you still want to wash your hair and have something to eat. The phone rings.

<u>Mildred:</u> You are 77 years old, and you have just won a holiday – your first in 20 years! The only problem is your budgie Zebedee. Maybe Liam, the nice boy next door, can look after him while you are away. Phone him and give him your good news – and don't forget to ask about Zebedee.

<u>Liam:</u> You have invited all your friends to a spaghetti party. The food is ready to eat now, and your guests are waiting for you at the table. The phone rings.

Unit 1

1 Cockney Rhyming Slang *(vocabulary)*

'Plates of meat' (feet), and 'Dicky Dirt' (shirt) are examples of Cockney Rhyming Slang. This special language started in London in Victorian times, and some people still speak it today. Usually, the second word in the pair (meat, dirt) rhymes with the 'real' word (feet, shirt). When you leave out the first word, rhyming slang becomes a kind of secret code.

Can you work out what this rhyming slang means?

1. Talking with your north and south full is not polite.
2. How about a nice cup of Rosie Lee?
3. I'll call you on the dog and bone.
4. I'm tired. I'm going to go to Uncle Ned.
5. Didn't you get enough Bo Peep last night?
7. I eat spaghetti with a fork and a man on the moon.
8. His hair is so long, you can't even see his boat race.
9. Looking at the sun is bad for your mince pies.

2 Christoph's diary (adjectives and adverbs)

Choose the right word.

I had my first Indian curry today. It didn't taste too *(bad/badly)* and I even tried some of Darren's Vindaloo. I've never eaten anything so *(hot/hotly)*.
Darren has got a cold, so he can't taste and smell very *(good/well)*.
We were feeling *(hungry/hungrily)* after walking around London all day, and I think he ate his Vindaloo too *(quick/quickly)*.
He looked *(terrible/terribly)* after the meal, and I don't think he'll sleep *(good/well)* tonight. Even my tummy feels a bit *(strange/strangely)*.
Tomorrow we're going to go to the British Museum. Mrs Grant has given us some worksheets. I've already looked at mine *(careful/carefully)*, but Darren doesn't seem *(interested/interestedly)* in his.
I think he's going to rest *(quiet/quietly)* at home tomorrow anyway !

3 Questionnaires (writing, speaking)

Teilen Sie die S in Gruppen ein. Jede Gruppe bekommt ein unterschiedliches Thema, z.B. pop music, TV, food and drink, hobbies, holidays. Sagen sie ihnen, daß sie eine Umfrage zu ihrem Thema machen werden. Die erste Aufgabe der S ist es, einen Fragebogen zu entwickeln, der die folgenden Fragen enthält.

Do you enjoy ...? Do you like ...?
Are you good at ...? Are you interested in ...?

Nachdem sie die Umfragen gemacht haben, schreiben die S ihre Ergbebnisse auf (z.B. 45% of the class enjoy going to museums). Danach stellen sie der Klasse die Ergebnisse vor. Diese können auch mit Bildern, Postern usw. im Klassenzimmer ausgestellt werden.

4 Something isn't quite right (all skills)

Write a summary of the story "A trip to the British Museum", but change five facts. Read your story to the class. They must tell you when they hear a 'wrong' fact.

Example: They travelled to the British Museum by bus. *(It should be* by train.*)*

Workshop B

1 Queen of the court (reading)

a) Pre-reading questions:

- Can you name any young tennis stars? How old were they when they became famous?
- Do you think it's a good thing to become famous when you're young? What would you like or not like?

b) *Don't look up any of the words while you are reading the text. (You'll be able to guess most of them anyway.) Then do the exercises below. They will help your vocabulary to grow.*

Martina Hingis has, in her 16 years, achieved more than most people can manage in a lifetime. She's earned millions of dollars as the best tennis-player on the women's tour. She's made history as the youngest ever Grand Slam winner, taking the Australian Open Title in January 1997, and five months later she won the Wimbledon women's title, overtaking the great Steffi Graf for the number-one spot in the world. And Martina loves to win.
 But still, she is only 16. Most of us imagine our first car will be a second-hand mini or a rusty 2CV – anything with wheels that provides freedom – but Martina has a shiny new Porsche Boxter in her mother's garage in Switzerland. It was part of her winnings from her first tournament victory in Filderstadt last year, but she's still too young to drive it. And when she is old enough to sit behind the wheel, it will be her mother who teaches her to drive just as it was she who taught her to be a tennis champion.
 "Life doesn't change just because you win another $100,000," she says. "I still can't drive, I still can't go out, because I'm underage wherever I go. But the money just gives you more freedom, you can go to more places. It makes you free."
 However, Martina is beginning to realise that the more famous you are, the less you need to spend. In Melbourne, she tried to buy a handbag, but in the end she got the bag and a leather jacket for free. In New York her fame went before her. "They knew me when I was walking down Broadway and even when I was in the All Star Café," she says. "I didn't have to pay for anything. The bigger you are and the richer you are, the less you have to pay."
 The good life is exactly what her mother Melanie was thinking of when she first gave the two year-old a sawn-off racquet to play with. Melanie lived under the old Communist regime in what was then Czechoslovakia. Those with supreme talent – like Martina Navratilova – could escape. Melanie was a good player but not a great one, and she wanted to give her daughter every chance to be free. For Melanie, tennis spelled freedom.

(388 words)

1. Your lifetime is not just a small part of your life, but your w_ _ _ _ life.
2. Does earn mean (a) you work for your money, or
    (b) you get money for nothing?
3. F_ _ _ cars overtake s_ _ _ cars.
4. If something is rusty, is it (a) red-brown, or
    (b) green-blue?
5. Free means *frei* so what does freedom mean?
6. Money or a present someone gets as a p_ _ z _ is that lucky person's winnings.
7. Martina will use this wheel to make the car t_ _ _ left and right. (She won't need to sit under the car!)
8. If someone is underage, they are too y_ _ _ _ to drive.
9. Wool comes from sheep, and leather from _ _ _ s.
10. Fame is a noun and fam_ _ _ is the adjective.
11. sawn-off: Martina was very small, so her mother cut off part of her racket to make it sh_ _ ter.
12. If you have supreme talent, is it (a) something everybody has, or (b) something really special?

c) *Try to guess the other new words or look them up in the alphabetical word list in your book. (Tip:* shiny *comes from the verb* shine.*)*

2 An interview (role play; writing a report)

Work in groups of three or four. Read your role cards and act out the TV interview. Make a recording of yourselves on a cassette and write a report of the interview.

Tennis star: You will be the star guest of a TV interview. Before the interview starts, think about what the interviewer might ask, and plan what you will answer.

Parent(s): You are the proud parent(s) of a young tennis star. You and your child will be the star guests of a TV interview. Before it starts, think about what the interviewer might want to know, and what you will say.

Interviewer: You are going to interview a young tennis star and his/her proud parents. Before the interview starts, make notes of some questions to ask them.

Unit 2

1 Limericks (vocabulary)

Complete the limericks.

1. There once was a p _ _ _ _ called W _ _ _ _
   Whose reports said again and again
   He doesn't revise,
   He plays t _ _ _ _ _, he tells l _ _ _
   What a terrible waste of a br _ _ _.

2. There once was a clown from Tashkent
   Whose b _ _ _ _ _ _ wheel was all b _ _ _
   He got into a panic
   And called a m _ _ _ _ _ _ _
   Who just laughed at the wheel and then went.

3. There once was a g _ _ _ from the Nile
   Who wanted a pe _ crocodile.
   But a big alligator
   Caught her and _ _ _ her
   It always had d _ _ n _ r in style.

4. I once had a teacher of s _ _ _ _
   Who gave me an awful r _ _ _ _ _.
   I was not an athl _ _
   As I had two left _ _ _ _
   I could not do the things that he taught.

2 Quiz: Go and find out (relative clauses)

Can you find out the answers to these questions?
Use relative clauses or contact clauses in your answers.

Example: What was the Titanic? – It was the ship that went
down after it hit an iceberg.

Who or what is /was …
1. Rip van Winkle? 2. The Pathfinder? 3. a double decker? 4. Buckingham Palace? 5. a shuttlecock? 6. a Francophile? 7. a philatelist? 8. an emu? 9. Kitty Hawk? 10. an amphibian?

3 My ideal school

a) *Some pupils wrote about their idea of a perfect school. Put the parts of the sentences together.*

1. It kills you walking up the stairs to most lessons, so
2. It is important that you feel relaxed and at home while you work, so
3. People who do their homework to music find it easier to concentrate, so
4. At school we just learn about the past, but
5. We should have laptops, not exercise books. Then
6. We shouldn't have lazy pupils who don't work, or bullies who upset people because

A … the classrooms would have comfortable chairs and your own posters on the walls.
B … there should be music in the background during the lessons.
C … in my ideal school we should have escalators to make life much easier for everybody.
D … they make school life miserable for the rest of us.
E … we will be able to save the rainforests, and writing will be much easier for us.
F … really we should learn about things that will help us for the future.

b) *Collect new words that are useful to you, and write them down them in a way that makes them easier to learn.*

c) *Write a report about your ideal school. (Tip: Before you start, make a mind map of school words.)*

Unit 3

1 Which tense? (pres. perf. vs. pres perf. prog.)

a) *Which sentence answers the question 'How many …?', and which answers the question 'How long?' What are the tenses in each sentence called?*

1. Mr Pritchard has been painting walls all morning.
2. He has only painted three so far.

b) *Now look at the sentences below. Which tense do we use when the result is more importat? Which tense is better when the activity is more important?*

3. I've been practising the piano.
4. I've passed my piano exam!

c) *Complete the gaps with the best form of the verb.*

1. Gwen … four letters to Michelle this month. *(write)*
2. Hugh … for his German test for an hour. *(revise)*
3. He … all the irregular verbs, so he'll be OK. *(learn)*
4. Sorry I'm late. I hope you … long. *(not wait)*
5. The Walkers … just … at the Snowdon Hotel. *(arrive)*
6. They've … lots of bags with them. *(bring)*
7. The Pritchards … in North Wales since August. *(work)*
8. Mr Walker … Snowdon twice already. *(climb)*

2 Marcel's questions (interpreting)

Florian and his family are staying at a farmhouse in Wales. Florian's little brother Marcel doesn't speak much English. He wants to ask the farmer some questions, and Florian is helping him.
What does Florian say? Start with He wants/He'd like to know *or* He's wondering.

1. Ich will ein Kuh melken. Aber wie macht man das?
2. Ich weiß nicht, welches Pferd ich reiten soll.
3. Ich will draußen spielen. Wann muss ich zurückkommen?
4. Gibt es wirklich Frösche hier? Wo finde ich sie?
5. Darf ich den Traktor selbst fahren?
6. Falls ich King Arthur treffe, was soll ich ihm sagen?
7. Warum legen Hühner Eier? Kannst du ihn fragen?

3 Write a story (creative writing)

Here are some new words from Units 1–3.
Work in small groups. Write a story with all of these words. (It's a story, so use the simple past form of the verbs.) Then read your story to the other groups.

danger – lie to fetch – luck – true – farmer – useless – jealous – whether – to smell – huge - village – prince – million – alive – promise – lazy – mend – afterwards – to notice – to be tired of – prison – ugh! – thief – pigeon – queen – to lose – phew!

Workshop C

1 London's beginnings (authentic text)

The earliest prehistoric settlers in the London area lived along parts of the Thames valley. At this time it was mostly wild forested countryside. In later prehistoric times the settlers became more organized. They lived in villages of huts, and they hunted, fished and farmed.

Roman soldiers arrived to conquer Britain in AD 43, and founded Londinium, now called London. They built a bridge over the Thames, and there has been a "London Bridge" in the same area ever since.

Roman Londinium grew up on the north side of the bridge. The Romans brought olive oil, wine and other products by ships from different parts of the Roman Empire and unloaded them onto wooden quays along the river.

In AD 61 the <u>native</u> Iceni tribe, led by Queen Boudicca, rebelled against the Romans. They burned Londinium to the ground and killed all its <u>inhabitants.</u> You can see a statue of Boudicca by Westminster bridge.

In the end the Roman armies <u>defeated</u> Boudicca. The Romans <u>rebuilt</u> Londinium and also built a wall of stone and brick around it which was there for many centuries.

The houses inside the Roman wall had <u>bright</u> red <u>roof tiles</u>. There were probably temples, bath houses, shops and market stalls. You can still walk along part of the route of the old wall. The area that was inside it is now the <u>business district</u> of modern London, called the City.

Reproduced from BOOK OF LONDON by permission of Usborne Publishing Ltd. © 1996, Usborne Publishing Ltd.

Difficult to guess: to found: *gründen;* wooden: *aus Holz;* quay [ki:]: *Kai;* unload: *aus-, ent-, abladen;* native: *einheimisch;* inhabitants: *Einwohner;* to defeat: *besiegen;* bright: *hell oder leuchtend;* roof tiles: *Dachziegel;* business district: *Geschäftsviertel*

a) Match the headings to the paragraphs

A The Iceni Rebellion
B A Roman quayside
C Inside the wall
D Early prehistoric settlers
E Roman London Bridge
F Rebuilding London

● *b) What do these words mean? How did you guess?*

> prehistoric olive oil products settler forested to rebuild to hunt to farm to rebel

c) True or false?

1. The earliest prehistoric settlers lived in villages.
2. The Romans built a bridge over the River Thames.
3. They bought wine and olive oil while they were in Londinium.
4. The Iceni tribe killed everyone who lived in London.
5. Boudicca won her battle against the Romans.
6. The wall the Romans built around London is still standing.

Unit 4

1 Which sounds better? *(active/passive)*

● *Look at these pairs of active and passive sentences. Which do you think is the better sentence in each pair?*

1. a) Mark loves Alton Towers.
   b) Alton towers is loved by Mark,
2. a) The Romans didn't build Rome in a day.
   b) Rome wasn't built in a day.
3. a) Kim has taken her driving test.
   b) Kim's driving test has been taken by her
4. a) These sweatshirts are made in Japan.
   b) The Japanese make these sweatshirts.
5. a) David is reading a copy of Our Earth.
   b) A copy of Our Earth is being read by David.

2 Choosing the right form *(active/passive)*

Put in the verb in the right form (active/passive, simple present/simple past).

1. Every year more of our countryside … . (destroy)
2. Cars … pollution. (cause)
3 Last year they … three houses. (pull down)
4. A bottle bank … near our flat two days ago. (put)
5. Mr Jones's letters often … in Our Earth (appear)
6. Samual Jones… in a car accident yesterday. (injure)
7. Most of the earth … by water. (cover)

3 Project: What happens to the plastic?

Find out what happens to the plastic we throw away, and write a report. Try to answer these questions:

– In the area where you live, what do people put their plastic into? (yellow sacks? green bins?)
– How often is the plastic collected where you live.?
– Who is it collected by, and how?
– Where is it taken to?
– What is done with it?

Start like this: In our area people put their plastic into yellow sacks. Every two weeks, the full sacks are put by the side of the road, and the sacks are … Then … , After that …

Show the different steps in a FLOW CHART like this. Draw pictures in boxes that show what happens, and connect the boxes with arrows.

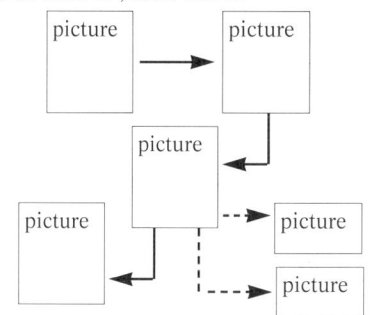

Workshop D

1 The woman in white *(creative writing)*

Write a story from these notes. You can add or change details if you like.

American tourists Paul and Debbie – holiday in Scotland – Youth Hostel – near castle on hill – Paul interested in old castles – Debbie finds them boring – decides to look for souvenirs in village – Paul climbs hill alone – at top hears music and laughing in castle – goes inside – big party in ballroom – people dancing in historical costumes – woman in long white dress – most beautiful woman Paul has ever seen – asks her to dance – they waltz for hours – wonderful time – angry young man appears – hits Paul – woman frightened – runs away – Paul follows – woman gone – Paul remembers Debbie – goes back to Youth Hostel – Debbie waiting – asks about Paul's black eye – Paul explains – Debbie jealous – next morning they climb hill together – castle a ruin – ballroom gone – just grass – was it a dream? – warden explains – ghost of Moira McKellan – killed by jealous boyfriend on day of big dance exactly 100 years ago.

New: ballroom; to waltz, grass

Example: Two American tourists, Paul and Debbie, were on holiday in Scotland. They were staying in a Youth Hostel that was near ….

2 Project: Class magazine

Write a class magazine. First brainstorm for ideas.

– What can you put in your magazine? (ideas below!)
– Who will do what?
– Where and how often will you meet to plan things?
– How many pages will your magazine have?
– How will you write it (by hand? on a computer?)
– Who will check for mistakes?
– Do you want photos, graphics? Who will do this?
– Will you sell it? For what price? What will you do with the money?

Ideas: recipes (see example on page 96 of your book) – articles about sport – hobbies – interesting things to do in your town – interviews – problem page – quizzes – jokes – crossword puzzles – horoscope – stories – reviews

Unit 5

1 What does it mean? *(passive infinitive, vocabulary)*

wearable = If something is **wearable** it **can be worn**.

Explain these words in the same way. Use it can *or* it cannot.

1. usable
2. undrinkable
3. washable
4. unbelievable
5. breakable
4. untranslatable
5. understandable
6. unpredictable
7. untouchable
8. bendable

2 Man overboard! *(listening and reacting)*

L liest der Klasse eine wahre Geschichte vor und unterbricht das Vorlesen an bestimmten Stellen, um Fragen zu stellen.

New: ship, South Africa, equator, announcement, loudspeaker, to fall overboard, shark, boots

"I was about 9 years old. My family was travelling from South Africa to England on a big ship. When we crossed the equator there was a huge party on the ship, but my sister and I weren't allowed to go to the party. Mum and Dad said we were too young.

How would you feel if you couldn't go to the party?

We were upset because we wanted to go, too. The party went on all night, and we couldn't sleep because it was so noisy.

If you went to the party, how might you feel the next morning?

The morning after we went down to breakfast. The man who usually sat at the next table wasn't there. "He probably had too much wine," said my mother. Then we heard an announcement over the loudspeaker. "Ladies and gentlemen, this is your captain speaking. One of the passengers is missing. We think he has fallen overboard, so we are going to turn back and look for him."

How would you feel if you heard this announcement?

Some of the passengers got angry. One woman said "We'll never find him! The captain must be crazy." Someone else said "That's right! Just think of all those sharks! He'll be eaten alive!" Then a man stood up and said to everyone "Yes, he hasn't got a chance, so we shouldn't waste time. And we don't want to the ship to be a day late, do we?

What would you say to these passengers?

Not all of the passengers were angry. Some of us were hopeful. My sister and ran up onto the deck where people were trying to catch sight of the man. We watched and waited all morning. At one o'clock some people went for lunch, but we stayed. A few minutes later a man shouted "There he is!" We all ran to the side of the ship to look, and the rescue began. But now there was a big crowd of people, and my sister and I couldn't see anything.

How would you feel if you couldn't see anything? What would you do?

We were lucky. My father ran to fetch his video camera and filmed the whole rescue operation. After we got back to England he showed us the video. The man was fished out of the water by the lifeboat crew and then the lifeboat was pulled onto the ship.

What do you think the man looked like after he was rescued?

The man wasn't wearing any clothes – only his boots – and after 11 hours in the water the sun had burnt his skin badly. He was drunk when he fell overboard, and when he was rescued he was still holding a wine bottle. Maybe the bottle saved his life. Or maybe it was the captain's hope.

3 A lonely island *(ranking; finding concensus)*

Work in pairs. You are going to spend a week together on a lonely island. Your boat is very small, so you can only take things you really need. Discuss which of these things below you would need most, and say why. Add two other things you think are important. Then write a new list. Put the things in order where 1 = the most important.

radio	signal flares
drinking water	pocket knife
life jacket	matches
lucky mascot	good book
food for one week	map
diary	medicine

Find another pair and compare your lists. Decide together which are the five most important things to take.

4 Which word is wrong? *(vocabulary)*

Find the wrong words and put them in the right groups.

1. helicopter, plane, kite, cliff
   Example: 'Cliff' is wrong because the other things can fly.
2. coastguard, captain, tanker, fisherman
3. serious, lonely, swim, rough
4 ferry, lifeboat, lifeboatman, hovercraft
5 play, dive, drown, bird
6. beach, calm, sea, rocks

5 Grammar quiz

1. What is the past form of 'be able to'?
2. In which of these two sentences is the gerund the object?
   a) Dancing is good for you.
   b) I love dancing.
3. Translate these sentences:
   a) *Der Radfahrer sah ärgerlich aus.*
   b) *Der Radfahrer sah Christoph ärgerlich an.*
4. Which of these verbs are not reflexive in English?
   cut – concentrate – remember – sit down – hurt – meet
5. In which sentence can you leave out the relative pronoun to make a contact clause?
   a) That's the pullover which I gave you for your birthday.
   b) Robert is the boy whose mother is a reporter.
6. Explain when you use 'since' and when you use 'for' in sentences in the present perfect. *(You can do this in German if you like.)*
7. I'm not sure whether I should go by train or bus. Say it another way.
8. 'The Pritchards live in Wales, <u>*don't they?*</u>'
   What do we call this part of a sentence?
9. 'The church bells wake me up every morning'.
   Change this active sentence to the passive.
10. Complete the rule for conditional sentences:
    (I) If clause: simple present; main clause: (?)
    (II) If clause: (?); main clause: would + infinitive

Lösungsvorschläge

Workshop A

1 French reporter A, Dutch reporter B, English reporter C, German reporter D, Italian reporter E, Spanish reporter F, Danish reporter G, Greek reporter H, Turkish reporter I, Scottish reporter (and camera) J

2 What would you say?
1. c 2. g 3. e 4. 1 5. i 6. h 7. f 8. b 9. j 10. d

3 Telephoning
a)
Making a call
Oh, sorry, I've got the wrong number.
Hello, this is Kim here.
Can I speak to Simon, please?
Could you give her a message?
Oh well, can I leave a message?
Please tell him I'll phone back this evening.
When can I call again?
Oh no! I hate talking to these machines!

Taking a call
Scarborough Youth Hostel. The warden speaking.
Who's calling, please?
I'm afraid he isn't at home.
Oh hello, Yasmin. What can I do for you?
No-one of that name lives here.
Would you like to leave a message?
Yes, of course. What's the message?
Please speak after the long tone.

Unit 1

1 Cockney rhyming slang
1. mouth 2. tea 3. phone 4. bed 5. sleep 6. spoon 7. face 8. eyes

2 Christoph's diary
1. bad 2. hot 3. well 4. hungry 5. quickly 6. terrible 7. well 8. strange 9. carefully 10. interested 11. quietly

Workshop B

1 You understand more than you think!
1. whole 2. (a) 3. fast – slow 4. red-brown 5. *Freiheit* 6. prize 7. turn 8. young 9. cows 10. famous 11. shorter 12. (b)

Unit 2

1 Limericks
1. pupil, Wayne, tricks, lies, brain 2. bicycle, bent, mechanic 3. girl, pet, ate, dinner 4. sport, report, athlete, feet

2 Quiz: Go and find out
1. Rip van Winkle is the story about a man who slept for 20 years. He woke up to find the world had changed. 2. The Pathfinder was the spaceship that landed on Mars. 3. A double decker is a bus that has two decks/floors/levels. 4. Buckingham Palace is the place where the Queen lives/the place the Queen lives in. 5. A shuttlecock is the thing you hit over the net in Badminton. 6. A Francophile is somebody who loves France and things that are French 7. A philatelist is somebody who collects stamps. 8. An emu is a bird that cannot fly. /EMU = European Monetary Union 9. Kitty Hawk is the place where the Wright Brothers made their first flight. 10. An amphibian is a creature/animal that lives on land and in water.

3 My ideal school
1. C, 2. A, 3. B, 4. F, 5. E, 6. D

Unit 3

1 Present perfect or present perfect progressive?
a) How many? 2 *(present perfect)* How long? – 1 *(present perfect progressive)*
b) Result : 4 *(present perfect)* Activity: 3 *(present perfect progressive)*
c) 1. has written 2. has been revising 3. has learnt 4. have not been waiting 5. have just arrived 6. have brought 7. have been working 8. has climbed

2 Marcel's questions
1. He wants to know how to milk a cow. 2. He's wondering which horse to ride. 3. He wants to know when to come back. 4. He wants to know where to find frogs. 5. He'd like to know whether he can drive the tractor himself. 6. He's wondering what to say if he meets King Arthur. 7. He wants to know why chickens lay eggs.

Workshop C

1 London's beginnings
a) A 4th paragraph   D 1st paragraph
   B 3rd paragraph   E 2nd paragraph
   C 6th paragraph   F 5th paragraph
b) –
c) 1. false, 2. true, 3. false, 4. true, 5. false, 6. false

Unit 4

1 Active or passive?
1. a, 2. b, 3. a, 4. a, 5. b

2 Choosing the right form
1. is destroyed 2. cause 3. pull down 4. was put 5. appears 6. was injured 7. is covered

Unit 5

1 What does it mean?
1. It can be used.
2. It cannot be drunk.
3. It can be washed.
4. It cannot be believed.
5. It can be broken
6. It cannot be translated.
7. It can be understood.
8. It cannot be predicted.
9. It cannot be touched.
10. It can be bent.

4 Which word is wrong?
2. tanker (the others are people) 3. swim (the others are adjectives) 4. lifeboatman (the others are forms of transport that go on water) 5. bird (the others are verbs) 6. calm (the others are 'geography words' that you find at the sea)

5 Grammar quiz
1. could 2. b) 3. a) The cyclist looked angry. b) The cyclist looked angrily at Christoph. 4. concentrate, remember, sit down, meet 5. a) 6. 'since' when you give an exact time, and 'for' when you give a period of time. 7. whether to go 8. question tag 9. I am woken up by the church bells every morning. 10. (I) will + infinitive, (II) simple past

Hinweise zu den Übungen im Workbook

Workbook Seite 1

Workshop A Let's talk

1 New friends

1 International dialogues

Ziel: Ländernamen in Europa; gehörte Informationen zuordnen.

Text

1.
(Background noises – beach sounds)
Emma: Excuse me! Your T-shirt!
Conchita: Que?
Emma: Here's your T-shirt. It's just fallen out of your beach bag.
Conchita: Oh, I – thank you. You're English, yes?
Emma: Well, I'm British – Welsh. My name is Emma.
Conchita: And I'm Conchita.
Emma: It's good that you speak English. I don't understand Spanish.
Conchita: Are you on holiday here?
Emma: Yes, I am. Are you on holiday, too?
Conchita: No, I live here.
Emma: You're lucky! Living near a beach like this must be fantastic. And the weather in Spain is so beautiful and sunny, too. It's … .*(fade out)*

2.
(Background noises – ferry engine etc.)
Cameron: Oh, sorry. Did you want to sit at this table?
Andrea: I – er – we can sit together.
Cameron: If that's OK with you – thanks. I think it's the only free table, anyway.
Andrea: Yes, the restaurant is very full.
Cameron: Everywhere on this ferry is so full! Where are you from? France?
Andrea: No, I come from Italy. From Milano – Milan, I think you say in English.
Cameron: Aha! A.C. Milan football team!
Andrea: Right! Where are you from?
Cameron: Scotland. I live in Glasgow.
Andrea: (in same tone as Cameron before) Aha! Glasgow Rangers football team!
Cameron: Ha ha. So you're a football fan, too, eh? Do you know … *(fade out)*

Lösungen: a) 1. Wales 2. Germany 3. Italy 4. Scotland 5. Spain 6. England
b) Picture 1 (ferry): Cameron, Andrea Picture 3 (beach): Emma, Conchita
c) Anke, Mike
Dialoge: eigene S-Lösung

2 Brainteaser

Ziel: Sprachrätsel lösen.

Lösung: *Dutch*

Workbook Seite 2

2 The right words

1 How can you call it that?!

Ziel: Übung von Sätzen mit *object complement*.

Lösungsmöglichkeiten: *1. I don't call this a wonderful hotel. The beds are too hard./How can you call this hotel wonderful? It's awful. 2. How can you call this meal lovely?/How can you call this a lovely meal? It's so hot. 3. You can't call this an interesting area!. There are only trees./How can you call this area interesting? It's so boring. 4. Why do you call me Mr Miserable? Because you always say bad things./How can you call me Mr Miserable? Because you never say nice things.*

2 Travel situations

Ziel: selbständige Bildung von *subordinate clauses*.

Lösungsmöglichkeiten: *1. It makes my sister nervous when the train stops in a tunnel. 2. It makes my parents angry when the buses are late. 3. It makes our dog happy when we take him for a ride. 4. It makes me excited when I sit in a plane.*

3 What can you say?

Ziel: Übung von *formal* und *informal speech* in der Anrede.

Lösungsmöglichkeiten: *1. You idiot! That was my CD player! 2. Excuse me, but I think it's my turn. 3. Oh dear! Now I must wash my anorak. 4. Hey! What are you doing there?*

Workbook Seite 3

4 Polite words

Ziel: Differenzierung zwischen *formal* und *informal speech*.

Lösungen:
a) <u>Polite:</u> *Excuse me … – Do you mind if … ? – Can you please … ? – I'd like … – Thank you.*
<u>Not so polite:</u> *No! – Give me … – Hey! – I want … – Help me …*

b) Individuelle S-Lösungen

5 When you don't know a word …

Ziel: Lösungen üben zur reellen Situation, ein Wort in der Zielsprache nicht zu wissen.

Lösungsmöglichkeiten: *2. cheap hotel for young people. 3. I must phone a friend/my parents. 4. I think they are very different. 5. I can't open the door without it./ I need it to open the door 6. I like how Scottish people sound when they speak.*

Workbook Seite 4

Ziel: Kenntnisse über die britischen Inseln anwenden.

6 The British Isles
Lösungen: b) *1. The Republic of Ireland is not part of the UK. 2. The British Isles are the UK and the Republic of Ireland. 3. The UK has got four parts. 4. England is the biggest part of the UK. 5. Scotland lies north of England. 6. Northern Ireland is the smallest part of the UK. 7. Wales is the smallest part of Great Britain. 8. Great Britain is only England, Scotland and Wales.*

3 On the telephone

1 Telephone language

Ziel: Wendungen fürs Telefonieren üben.

Lösungen: *a) (Telephone sentences): Hello. This is Becky. – Can I speak to Sarah, please? – Oh well, can I leave a message? – Please tell her I'll call again after tea.*
b) Kim: Kim Dixon here. Who's speaking, please?
Becky: Hello. This is Becky.
Kim: Oh hello, Becky. What can I do for you?
Becky: Can I speak to Sarah, please?
Kim: I'm sorry. She isn't at home.
Becky: Oh well, can I leave a message?
Kim: Yes, of course. What's the message?
Becky: Please tell her I'll call again after tea.
Kim: OK. I'll tell her. Bye.

Workbook Seite 5

2 Robin Hood's answering machine

Ziel: die richtige Präposition verwenden.

Lösungen: *to – on – at – at – on – in – for – on – to*

3 Careful with the sounds!

Ziel: stimmhafte und stimmlose Konsonanten unterscheiden können.

Lösungen: *b) 2. riding, fan 3. came, very 4. bag, pick 5. town, pair*

4 What the other person says

Ziel: aus sprachlichen Vorgaben schlussfolgern.

Lösungsmöglichkeiten: *Hello, Yasmin, this is Mike. – No, I don't. Have you heard the news? – Sarah is angry with David and isn't talking to him. – Robert told me. I thought you should know. – Maybe you can think of something we can do.*

Workbook Seite 6

4 A short talk

1 Which one is different?

Ziel: Üben von regelmäßigen und unregelmäßigen Verbenformen.

Unterrichtsempfehlungen
Es wird sehr viel Zeit zum Lernen der unregelmäßigen Verbformen aufgewendet, sodass die S gelegentlich die regelmäßige Bildung der *past tense form* aus dem Blick verlieren. Diese Übung soll wieder daran erinnern.

Lösungen: *1. happened – stopped – opened – cycled – arrived 2. brought – bought – thought – caught – sang 3. walked – watched – counted – stopped – booked 4. showed – flew – threw – grew – knew 5. spent – meant – went – did – lent 6. started – wanted – stayed – needed – visited*

2 Your talk will sound better!

Ziel: erkennen, was Konjunktionen zum Textfluss und Textverständnis beitragen; diese Kenntnisse praktisch anwenden.

Lösungen: *a) when, while, suddenly, at first, because, so, and then, but when*
Lösungsmöglichkeiten: *b) Let me tell you what happened when we were on holiday in Ireland. While we were walking in the hills, we saw a group of men far away. They walked towards us and then they stopped. Suddenly they started to shoot with bows and arrows. I wanted to run away because it was so frightening. But my father just laughed. I couldn't understand why, but when I saw a big film camera, I started to laugh, too!*

Workbook Seite 7

Unit 1 A trip to London

Step A Famous sights

1 Funny London names

Ziel: Namen vom Londoner Stadtplan zuordnen.

Lösungen: *a) Trafalgar Square, Big Ben, Buckingham Palace, Notting Hill, London Dungeon, Covent Garden, Waterloo Station, Madame Tussaud's*
b) 1. The Queen lives in Buckingham Palace. 2. The big clock there is Big Ben. 3. Because they want to see Madame Tussaud's. 4. Trains for Paris leave from Waterloo Station. 5. You can feed the pigeons in Trafalgar Square. 6. The carnival is in Notting Hill. 7. The most frightening sight in London is in/at the London Dungeon. 8. You can listen to music in the street in Covent Garden.

Step A The exchange visit

2 Listening practice: Londoners

Ziel: gezielt nach bestimmten Informationen hören.

Text
Sue:
Hello, my name is Sue, that's S-U-E, and I'm 14 years old. I live in South London quite close to Waterloo Station. My parents are from Hong Kong but they came to London 20 years ago. I'm Chinese and British! My favourite time of the year is the Chinese New Year in January or February. It's always fantastic and there's music and lovely food.

Angelo:
Hi, I'm Angelo. I'm 15 years old and I come from Italy. I came here with my parents two years ago. They are working in my uncle's restaurant in Camden, That's where we live. We're only going to stay here for another year, then we're going back to Italy. London is great, and I really like the double-decker buses!

Val:
I'm Val, V-A-L, and I'm 14 years old. I live in North London with my grandparents. They came from the West Indies, but my brother and I were born in London. I like London: it's always so noisy and busy. The best time of the year is August. That's Notting Hill Carnival, and I always go there with my family and friends.

Lösungen: *1. Name: Sue. Age: 14 years old. Family from: Hong Kong. Lives in: South London (quite close to Waterloo Station). Likes: the Chinese New Year in January or February.*
2. Name: Angelo. Age: 15 years old. Family from: Italy. Lives in: Camden. Likes: the double-decker buses.
3. Name: Val. Age: 14 years old. Family from: West Indies. Lives in: North London. Likes: Notting Hill Carnival in August.

Workbook Seite 8

Step A What you can see in London

3 On the underground

Ziel: Fragen zu einem authentischen Fahrplan verstehen und beantworten können.

Lösungen: *1. You will need 18 minutes. 2. A ticket to Ham-*

mersmith is 70p. 3. Piccadilly Circus is before Covent Garden. 4. A ticket to Heathrow costs £1.80. 5. Yes, the Piccadilly Line train stops at Northfields.
b) 6. Piccadilly Circus or Leicester Square. You will need 17 or 18 minutes to get there. 7. Yes, you can. You need Knightsbridge station. The ticket is £1.30.

4 Brainteaser

Ziel: mit dem Londoner U-Bahn-Plan arbeiten, Routen beschreiben.

Lösungen: a) 1B – 2A – 3C.
b) D: Take the Bakerloo Line to Piccadilly Circus. Then change to the Piccadilly Line (eastbound). The next station is Leicester Square.

Workbook Seite 9

Step A At the Tower

5 The Tower is London

Ziel: Informationen aus einer schriftlichen Vorlage entnehmen.

Lösungen: 1. The Tower is in the City of London. It's on the River Thames, next to Tower Bridge. 2. Yes, you can get there by underground. You can take the Circle or District Lines to Tower Hill station. 3. Yes, you can go in at 9:30 on Saturday morning. 4. Yes, there are cafés there. 5. You need at least two hours for your visit.

Lösungsmöglichkeit: I would like to see the Crown Jewels, the prisons and dungeons ...

Step B What do you like doing?

1 Doing things is great

Ziel: gerund als Subjekt anwenden.

Lösungen: 2. Oh, isn't swimming in the sea dangerous? 3. Watching TV is a good idea. 4. Looking at the waxworks will be fun. 5. Oh no, reading history books is interesting.

Workbook Seite 10

2 Your turn: What about you?

Ziel: Eigene Vorlieben ausdrücken unter Verwendung des gerund als Objekt.

Lösungsmöglichkeiten: individuelle S-Lösungen

Step B Going places

3 London dialogues

Ziel: gerund nach Präpositionen üben.

Lösungen: 1. Mum, I'm tired of looking at the Egyptian things. 2. Are you interested in going to the theatre at the weekend? 3. Oh, I'm tired of walking round London. 4. We're lost! Are you good at reading maps? 5. And I'm not very good at dancing.
1E – 2B – 3D – 4C – 5A

4 A letter

Ziel: gerund-Strukturen verwenden, um schriftliche Informationen zu eigenen Person zu geben.

Lösungen: individuelle S-Lösungen

Workbook Seite 11

Step B Going out for a meal

5 What do you think?

Ziel: Üben von Adjektiven nach Verben der sinnlichen Wahrnehmung.

Lösungsmöglichkeiten: individuelle S-Lösungen

Step C A trip to the British Museum

1 Word power

Ziel: fun element: puzzle; Wörter definieren

Lösungsmöglichkeiten: → 2. _husband:_ Mr Penrose is Mrs Penrose's husband. 3. _copy:_ Don't copy each other's homework. 4. _pardon:_ Pardon? What did you say? 5. _talk:_ Please speak to us about London. Give us a short talk. ← _across:_ The bike shop is opposite, just across the road. 7. _upset:_ Jane is upset, because her cat has just died. 8. _shout:_ I can hear you. You needn't shout. ↓ _stupid:_ That wasn't clever, it was really stupid. 10. _normal:_ He's not unusual, he's just a normal person. ↑ 11. _steps:_ You have to go up 13 steps to get upstairs. 12. _worksheet:_ Please fill in your worksheets and hand them in at the end of the lesson! 13. _scarf:_ Oh, my neck is cold. I haven't got a scarf. 14. _cyclist:_ A cyclist should always wear a helmet when he or she's on his or her bike.

Workbook Seite 12

2 Are you a good exchange partner?

Ziel: Situationsschilderungen verstehen.

Lösungen: individuelle Schülerantworten

Step D Let's check

1 Word power

Ziel: fun element: puzzle.

Lösungen: 1. De(=u)n~~mark~~ + ~~p~~igeon = Dungeon
2. under + grou~~p~~ + ~~a~~nd = underground

Workbook Seite 13

2 After the exchange visit

Ziel: Verwendung des gerund als Objekt kontrollieren.

Lösungsmöglichkeiten: 2. He liked going by underground. 3. He loved visiting the Tower. 4. He didn't like walking in Hyde Park. 5. He didn't like going round the shops. 6. He couldn't stand waiting in queues. 7. He hated going out with his partner. 8. He liked making new freinds. 9. He enjoyed practising his English. 10. He loved eating English food.

3 Using the underground

Ziel: phrasal verbs: get.
Lösungen: 1. get on 2. go to 3. get to 4. get off

Workbook Seite 14

Tandem Activity 1

Ziel: Informationen über Vorlieben und Neigungen austauschen.

Hinweis: Die Bilder stellen folgende Aktivitäten dar: *reading (books), taking photos, cooking, watching TV.*

Workbook Seite 15

Workshop B Working with words

1 Understanding new words

1 Understanding from the context

Ziel: Erschließung unbekannter Vokabeln mit Hilfe des Kontexts

Lösungen: *1. C 2. A 3. B 4. D*

2 Can you guess?

Ziel: Anwendung und Bewusstmachung der verschiedenen Techniken zur Bedeutungserschließung.

Lösungen:
jungle – Dschungel – *It sounds like the German word.*
insects – Insekten – *It looks like the German word.*
half-time – Halbzeit – *I know 'half' and 'time'.*
brilliant – glänzend – *It's the same word in German.*
score – Spielstand – *The context helped me: 'at the end of the match' and '46-39'.*
captain – Kapitän – *It looks like the German word.*
puzzles – wundert – *I know the noun 'puzzle'.*
put on – anziehen – *The context helped me.*
boots – Stiefel – *The context and the picture helped me.*

3 Listening practice

Ziel: Entnahme von Erschließungshilfen aus Bild und Kontext.

Text

1.
Samira: Are you ready to go, Jane?
Jane: Yes, I'm ready.
Samira: Don't you want to dry your hair first? It's still wet.
Jane: No, let's go to the snack bar. I'm hungry.
Samira: Me too. Wasn't it crowded today? And wasn't the water cold?
Jane: Yes, terrible.

2.
(Phone rings, sound of receiver being picked up.)
Man: Good morning, Sutton Sports. Can I help you?
Lee: Yes, are you open on Sundays?
Man: Yes, we are. We're open all day, from ten in the morning to ten in the evening.
Lee: Oh, good. And can we hire skates there? We haven't got our own.
Man: Yes, of course. It costs two pounds an hour and three pounds to get into the rink.
Lee: Right then, thanks very much.
Man: You're welcome.
Lee: Bye.
(Click of receiver being replaced)

3.
Darren: Hey, Tony, stop! Wait for me! TONY!
Tony: What's wrong?
Darren: I think I've got a flat tyre. It was probably that broken glass in the road.
Tony: Oh yes, it is a flat tyre! We'll just have to mend it here. I don't want to walk home.
Darren: Don't worry. I'm good at repairing bikes. Just give me the kit, please

Tony: I haven't got it! I thought you had it!
Darren: And I thought you had it... *(Groan. Fade out.)*

4.
Teacher: Right, let's practise our funky hip-hop dance from last week. Remember how it goes?
Harry: No!
Jane: I wasn't here last week!
Teacher: OK, I'll go through the steps again quickly. Start with your back to the mirror, cross your right foot in front. When the music starts count to seven. On eight turn quickly to the front like this. No, Harry! Turn to the left! That's it.

Lösungen: a) freie Schülerlösungen z.B. A: jazz dance, gym, B: swimming, changing room C: bikes, to mend D: ice rink, skating

b) *Text 1: picture B; Text 2: picture D; Text 3: picture C; Text 4: picture A*

Workbook Seite 16

2 Organizing words

1 Organizing and learning words

Ziel: Erkennen und Bewusstwerden von verschiedenen Möglichkeiten, ein Vokabelheft zu führen. Abwägen von Vor- und Nachteilen der einzelnen Verfahren.

Lösungen: a) *Tobias Metzger: B; Jens Piatzer: C; Anja Maier: D; Nicole Hermann: A*
b) 1. B, D – 2. A, D – 3. B – 4. A, B, D – 5. B, D – 6. C – 7. A – 8. individuelle S-Lösung

2 Using a vocabulary book

Ziel: Anwendung der in der Vorgängerübung gezeigten verschiedenen Möglichkeiten, Vokabeln zu notieren.

Lösungsmöglichkeiten: <u>size:</u> how big or small something is; <u>to upset:</u> to make somebody unhappy or angry; <u>however:</u> but;; <u>husband:</u> Mr Burton is Mrs Burton's husband; <u>key:</u> You need a key to open a door (if it is locked).

3 Word groups

Ziel: Wortarten erkennen und benennen.

Lösungen: *1. adjectives: terrible, lucky 2. nouns: bat, football 3. verbs: jump, run 4. adverbs: fast, cleverly 5. prepositions: over, under, beside, in*

Workbook Seite 17

4 Word partners: verb + noun

Ziel: Festigung von Kollokationen.

Lösungen: *1. did homework – made mistakes 2. did the washing-up – went for a walk 3. spent all day – had a great time – 4. made sandcastles – went swimming 5. had ... rides on – spent ... money*

5 Verbs with two parts

Ziel: Aufgabe zu *phrasal verbs.*

Lösungen: *1. I'll take ... off. 2. I won't fall over. 3. I'll pick ... up. 4. Put ... down, Mum! 5. I'll put ... on.*

6 Writing a text: When I was little

Ziel: Impulsgesteuerte Schreibaufgabe zu *creative writing.*

Lösungen: individuelle S-Lösungen

Workbook Seite 18

3 Saying things in different ways

1 Sports quiz

Ziel: Zusammenstellung von Sportbegriffen.

Lösungen: *1. SWIMMING 2. RACKET 3. TABLE TENNIS 4. HOCKEY 5. ATHLETICS 6. MATCH*

2 I'm looking for a ...

Ziel: Umschreibung als Hilfsmittel bei Nichtkenntnis der entsprechenden Vokabeln.

Lösungsmöglichkeiten: *2. sun cream: You put it on your body so that the sun can't hurt your skin. 3. suitcase. A large bag to carry your clothes in when you travel. umbrella: 4. You hold it over your head so that you can't get wet in the rain. 5. toothbrush: You clean your teeth with it.*

4 Words in grammar

1 Jane's diary

Ziel: Gebrauch der *reflexive pronouns*

Lösungen: *–/myself/ – / – /ourselves/ourselves/ – / – / –*

2 What is happening, or what has happened?

Ziel: Unterscheidung zwischen *reflexive* und *reciprocal pronoun*.

Lösungen: *1. The man has cut himself. 2. The children are drawing each other. 3. They are shooting (arrows) at each other. 4. The elephants are washing each other. 5. The girls are looking at themselves. 6. The boy has hurt himself.*

Workbook Seite 19

5 Wordbuilding

1 Beginnings and endings

Ziel: Bildung von Adjektiven mit der Vorsilbe *un-* und den Nachsilben *-ful* und *-less*.

Lösungen: *2. unlucky 3. untidy 4. useless 5. helpful 6. careful 7. careless 8. useful*

2 Making nouns from verbs

Ziel: Bildung von Substantiven aus Verben mit der Nachsilbe *-er*.

Lösungen: *2. winner 3. writer 4. runner 5. singer 6. dancer*

Workbook Seite 20

3 One word from two words

Ziele: Hinweis auf bekannte *compounds* und ihre drei möglichen Schreibweisen.

Lösungen: (Reihenfolge beliebig) *flowerpot – post office – tea-cosy – football – fire brigade – hot dog – ghost train*

4 Map isn't "Mappe"

Ziel: Hinweis auf die Wortgruppe der sogenannten *false friends*.

Lösungen: *1. folder* (und nicht *map*) *2. skirt* (und nicht *rock*) *3. husband* (und nicht *man*) *4. three years ago* (und nicht *for three years*) *5. happy* (und nicht *lucky*) *6. needn't* (und nicht *mustn't*) *7. quiet* (und nicht *still*)

5 Brainteaser

Ziele: Denksportaufgabe zur Auflockerung des Unterrichts und erinnernder Hinweis, dass viele Berufsbezeichnungen anders als im Deutschen geschlechtsneutral sind.

Lösungen: *1st: Ben – shop assistant. 2nd: Melanie – vet. 3rd: Colin – teacher. 4th: Anna – mechanic. 5th: Charlie – police officer*

Workbook Seite 21

Unit 2 Trouble at school

Step A The video conference

1 Listening practice: Questions and answers

Ziel: Hörverstehensübung, Überprüfung der landeskundlichen Kenntnisse zum Thema ‚Schule'.

Text
Becky: Have you got the questions, Jenny?
Jenny: Yes, I'll read them, and everyone else can answer them, right?
Becky: Yes, we'll take turns. Ready, everyone? I'm starting the cassette … now!
Jenny: The first question is from Markus. When do you use the library? Robert, you answer that.
Robert: Well, we can come here in the lunch break or when we haven't got a lesson. I sometimes do my homework here or I work on one of my projects.
Jenny: Thank you. Here are two questions for David. They're from Sebastian. The first one is: How much are the school meals?
David: Well, they cost between one and five pounds. If your parents haven't got much money, you get free meals.
Jenny: And here's the other question. Can you choose between different meals?
David: Oh, yes. I usually choose things like sausages and chips. But if you don't eat meat, or you want something healthier, you can get meals with different vegetables. Yuk!
Jenny: There's a question here about tests from Daniel. He asks: Do you get a lot of tests? Sarah, can you answer that one, please?
Sarah: Do we get a lot of tests? Well, not really. We get a lot of short ones, like vocabulary tests. The most important tests are at the end of the school year. They're about what we've learned that year. We do a lot of projects, too – they're important.
Jenny: There's one more question, from Amelie. Her class is doing a project on British schools. They'd like some more information about Haywood. What can we send them?
Robert: That's easy! The Haywood Herald! That's our school magazine. There are lots of old ones in the library cupboard because we never sell all of them. We can send them to you.
Jenny: Yes, you'll get lots of useful information about school life from the Haywood Herald. Well, that's all for today. If you have any more questions, please write to us again.
All, in unison: Auf Wiedersehen!

Lösungen: *1. ✘ Robert does his homework in the library. 2. ✔ 3. ✘ You can get meals without meat. 4. ✔ 5. ✔*

2 Word power

Ziel: Wortschatzarbeit als Vernetzungsübung, *Writing practice.*

Lösungsmöglichkeiten: *You have <u>English lessons</u> in a <u>classroom</u>. You find <u>books</u> in a <u>library</u>. The pupils go to the <u>gym</u> for their <u>P.E. lesson</u>. They have <u>lunch</u> in the <u>canteen</u>. They go <u>swimming</u> in a <u>pool</u>. They're in the <u>playground</u> at <u>break</u>. They meet in a <u>hall</u> for <u>assembly</u>.*

3 Your turn: School life

Ziel: Einbringen eigener Erfahrungen zum Thema ‚Schule'.

Lösungen: individuelle S-Lösungen.

> Workbook Seite 22

4 School subjects

Ziel: Partneraufgabe mit Sprechanlässen.

Lösungen: individuelle S-Lösungen.

Step B The new boy

1 The stories Edward told

Ziel: Bildung von *contact clauses*.

Lösungen: *2. A monkey took a banana Mum was eating. 3. They got lost on a mountain they were climbing. 4. Mum caught a snake she found under the bed. 5. They fell into a river they were crossing. 6. They were sick after they ate a curry Dad cooked.*
(**Sprachlicher Hinweis:** Es ist auch denkbar, jeweils den unbestimmten Artikel in einen bestimmten zu ändern: *The monkey took <u>the</u> banana Mum was eating,* etc.)

> Workbook Seite 23

Step B Wayne gets into trouble

(In der 1. Auflage vom *Workbook* war die Nummerierung der folgenden Übungen leider falsch. **Step B Wayne gets into trouble** sollte wie in den folgenden Angaben mit Übung 2 anfangen. In späteren Auflagen wurde dieser Fehler korrigiert. Anm. der Redaktion)

2 Mr Stuart's lesson

Ziel: Vervollständigen von Sätzen unter Anwendung von *who* und *which*.

Lösungen: *1. ... which was climbing up her teacher's leg. 2. ... who was writing on his desk. 3. ... who was sitting in front of her. 4. ... which flew in through the window. 5. ... who were fighting in the playground. 6. ... which had some very exciting stories in it.*

3 Wrong words

Ziel: Unterscheidung des Gebrauchs der drei Relativpronomen *which / that / who*.

Lösungen: zu streichen sind: *2. which 3. which 4. who 5. which 6. who 7. which*

Step B A meeting on the stairs

4 Interesting people

Ziel: Relativsätze mit *who* und *whose*.

Lösungen: *2. ... whose wife works in a circus. 3. ... who saw a ghost in Nottingham castle. 4. ... whose son is the world skateboarding champion. 5. ... who cook the meals at Haywood School. 6. ... whose budgie can sing the alphabet song.*

> Workbook Seite 24

Step B A busy week

5 I'm very sorry, but ...

Ziel: Anwendung *present progressive* mit Zeitangabe der Zukunft.

Lösungen: individuelle S-Lösungen unter Verwendung des *present progressive*

6 How do you say it?

Ziel: Betonung von mehrsilbigen Wörtern, deren Betonung oft von ähnlichen deutschen Formen abweicht.

Unterrichtsempfehlungen
Die S können darauf hingewiesen werden, dass das alphabetische Wörterverzeichnis bei Ungewissheiten zu Rate gezogen werden kann. (Hinweis auf die Betonungszeichen für Hauptbetonung und Nebenbetonung.)

Lösungen: ['- - -]: *interesting, sandwiches;* ['- -]: *progress, teacher;* [- ' -]: *mistake, report;* [- ' - -]: *detention, assembly*

Step B Emma

7 What can you say?

Ziel: Vorschläge und Wünsche erfragen *Shall ...?* / Wunsch oder Bitte aussprechen mit *Will you?* / Ratschläge erteilen mit *you should / shouldn't*

Lösungsmöglichkeiten: *1. Shall I close/shut the window? 2. You should change/wash your socks. 3. Would you open the door for me, please? 4. You shouldn't smoke, it's bad for you. 5. Shall I help you? Shall I carry some of the books/dictionaries for you?*

> Workbook Seite 25

Step C A thief in the school

1 Story puzzle

Ziel: Training des Leseverstehens.

Lösungen: a) 1C – 2E – 3B – 4F – 5G – 6D – 7A

b) individuelle S-Lösung

2 Seen this, been there, done that

Ziel: Anwendung von *contact clauses* mit Superlativen.

Lösungen: Im Sinne der nicht ganz ernst gemeinten Aufgabenstellung sollten auch entsprechende Antworten akzeptiert werden.
2. Yes, she's the most interesting person I've ever met. 3. Yes, it's the most exciting book I've ever written. 4. Yes, it's the most expensive car I've ever had. 5. Yes, but it isn't the highest mountain I've ever climbed. 6. Yes, but it isn't the longest tunnel I've ever been through. 7. Yes, but it isn't the most dangerous animal I've ever fought. 8. Yes, but he isn't the richest husband I've ever had.

> Workbook Seite 26

3 Who are they?

Ziel: Unterscheidung zwischen Sätzen mit notwendigem Relativpronomen und *contact clauses*.

Lösungen: *who* kann in den Sätzen 2, 5 und 7 gestrichen werden.

4 Brainteaser

Ziel: Sprachliche Knobelaufgabe.

Lösungen: *Monday: play tennis with Jackie. Tuesday: lunch with Helen. Wednesday: go to the cinema with Sophie. Thursday: go ice-skating with Sandra. Friday: take Annabel to the disco. Saturday: go on a boat trip with Yasmin. Sunday: go to the Adventure Centre with Jessica.*

Step D Let's check

1 Word Power

Ziel: Finden von Kollokationen.

Lösungen:
to take a test – to get into trouble – to ring a bell – to get a good mark

Workbook Seite 27

2 Mark goes to school now, too!

Ziel: Unterscheidung der Relativpronomen *who*, *which* und *whose*.

Lösungen:
a) 1. *who* 2. *which* 3. *whose* 4. *whose* 5. *which*
b) sentences 1, 2 and 5
c) sentence 5

3 Plans for next week

Ziel: Anwendung des *present progressive* zur Wiedergabe der Zukunft mit Zeitangabe der Zukunft.

Lösungsmöglichkeiten: 1. Sarah is going ice-skating on Saturday morning. 2. David is cooking an easy recipe on Thursday evening. 3. Edward is having/going to a party on Friday evening. 4. Wayne is playing football on Wednesday afternoon. 5. Robert and Jenny are reading/acting/practising Romeo and Juliet/a play on Tuesday.

4 Choosing clothes for the school play

Ziel: Ausdruck von Vorschlägen, Wünschen und Bitten

Lösungen: 1. B; 2. A; 3. C; 4. E; 5. D

Workbook Seite 28

Tandem Activity 2

Ziel: Partneraufgabe zur Wiederholung des *Unit*-Wortschatzes

Workbook Seite 29

Unit 3 Welcome to Wales

Step A Country and people

1 A quiz about Wales

Ziel: Übung einiger neuen Vokabeln.

Lösungen: 1. *King* 2. *Cardiff* 3. *North* 4. *rugby* 5. *castles* 6. *railway* 7. *industry* 8. *sheep* 9. *museums* 10. *breakfast* 11. *King Arthur*

2 Word power: Town and countryside

Ziel: Wortfeldarbeit

Lösungsmöglichkeiten: a) *street, cars, buses, shops, ...*
b) *hills, trees, sheep, horses, grass, bushes, cows, ...*

3 Sounds and spelling

Ziel: Rechtschreibübung.

Lösungen: *high – buy; key – sea; who – threw; said – bread; mine – sign; last – passed; city – pretty; court – bought; killed – build*

Workbook Seite 30

Step B The Pritchards

1 In the evening

Ziel: Üben des *present perfect progressive* mit *for* und *since* und entsprechenden Zeitangaben.

Lösungen: 2. Mrs Pritchard has been reading a book since 8.00. In other words, she has been reading a book for an hour. 3. Hugh has been doing the washing-up since 8.50. In other words, he has been doing the washing-up for 10 minutes. 4. Gwen has been listening to her walkman since 8.40. In other words she has been listening to her walkman for 20 minutes. 5. Foxy, their dog, has been sleeping since 7.00. In other words, Foxy has been sleeping for 2 hours.

2 The Walkers in Wales

Ziel: Üben des *present perfect progressive* und Erkennen des Kontextes für *for* und *since*.

Lösungen: 1. ... has been raining – since 2. ... have been looking – for 3. ... have been climbing – for 4. ...have been sitting – since 5. ... have been watching – for 6. T... have been getting – for

3 Your turn: All about you

Ziel: eigene Gewohnheiten ausdrücken.

Lösungen: individuelle S-Lösungen

Workbook Seite 31

Step B Tips for visitors

4 Yes, but ...

Ziel: Üben des Infinitivs nach Fragewörtern.

Lösungen: 2. ... *which to buy.* 3. ... *don't know how to play tennis.* 4. ..., *I don't know where to put it.* 5. ..., *I don't know when to practise.* 6. ... *I don't know whether to go with him or not.*

5 Asking for help

Ziel: Bildung von Sätzen mit Infinitiv nach Fragewort.

Lösungen: 2. ... *where to go?* 3. ... *how to spell 'Piccadilly'?* 4. ... *which to see.* 5. ... *what to give her?*

Workbook Seite 32

Step B The Celts and their language

6 Word partners

Ziel: Erkennen von Wortpaaren als stehende Wendungen

Lösungsmöglichkeiten: 2. Angles and Saxons: The Angles and Saxons invaded Britain after the Romans left. 3. England and Wales: England and Wales are part of the UK. 4. park and ride: There's a park and ride service in Caernarvon for Snowdonia. 5. TV and radio: You can hear weather forecasts every day on TV and radio. 6. walkers and climbers: Lots of walkers and climbers go up Snowdon every year. 7. fish and chips: There are takeaway shops for fish and chips in Britain. 8. physics and chemistry: We do physics and chemistry in Science lessons at school. 9. India and Pakistan: India and Pakistan are both countries in Asia. 10. thunder and lightning: You shouldn't stand under a tree if there's thunder and lightning.

Step B Plans for the weekend

7 King Arthur and his knights

Ziel: Üben von *question tags*.

Lösungen: 2. ... didn't he? – Yes, he did. 3. <u>don't tell:</u> ... do they? – No, they don't. 4. <u>there are:</u> ...aren't there? – Yes, there are. 5. <u>was:</u> ...wasn't it? – Yes, it was. 6. <u>were:</u> ...weren't they? – Yes, they were. 7. <u>had:</u> ...didn't they? – Yes, they did. 8. <u>didn't have:</u> ...did he?

8 Only you can answer these!

Ziel: Bilden von *question tags* und Antworten darauf.

Lösungen: 2. ... can't you? 3. ... don't you? 4. ... have you? 5. ... did you? 6. ... aren't you?
Weitere Lösungen: individuelle S-Lösungen.

> Workbook Seite 33

Step C The sword in the stone

1 How Arthur became King

Ziel: Ablauf der Erzählhandlung rekonstruieren; Gründe für bestimmte Ereignisse versprachlichen

Lösungen: a) 1.C; 2. E; 3. B; 4. F; 5. D; 6. A
Lösungsmöglichkeiten: b) 1. Arthur wanted to learn how to be a knight. 2. Sir Ector wanted Arthur to pull the sword out of the stone but he wanted it to be a surprise. 3. Sir Kay was jealous. He thought the knights were silly. It was only his younger brother Arthur.

2 Listening practice: The Round Table

Ziel: Hörverstehen.

Text
Narrator: One of the first people who wrote about King Arthur told the story of the Round Table.
It all started at Christmas time one year. Soon after Arthur became king, some of his knights had a terrible argument. You see they all wanted to sit in the most important place – at the head of the table. Listen to their argument ...

1st knight: Hey, you can't sit here, Kay! this is my seat!
Sir Kay: No, it isn't. This is where I want to sit. I'm King Arthur's brother, so it's only right that I sit at the head of the table.
2nd knight (indignantly): No! Just because you're the King's brother, that doesn't mean you're the "first knight"! You needn't think you're better than the rest of us!
1st knight: Well, I'm going to sit here now. And if you don't like it, Sir Kay, you'll have to fight me for it –
(Sound of sword being drawn)
Sir Kay: I'll fight you, if that's what you want –
(Sound of another sword being drawn, and fighting, shouting, etc.)
Narrator: When King Arthur came in and saw his knights were fighting, he was very angry. Four weeks later, a very big oak table stood in the castle at Camelot. It had seats for a hundred and fifty people – and it was round.
Now listen to what King Arthur said to his knights ...

King Arthur: Sit down, my good knights! From now on, there will be no arguments about who sits where. As you see, this beautiful new table is round. That means there is no head of the table! You are all my knights. You are here to help each other, not to fight against each other! No knight is more important that the other knights. This is our Round Table. And from today you will be the Knights of the Round Table!
(Cheering and clapping, moving of chairs)
Now you have all found seats – Let us drink to the future!
Knights (several together): To the future! To our good King!
(Clinking of cups and goblets)
Knights (all together): To our good King! To King Arthur!

Lösungen: 1. a young man 2. "first knight" 3. the King's brother 4. was angry with the knights. 5. 150 people 6. more important than the others.

> Workbook Seite 34

3 Big Pit

Ziel: Präpositionen nach dem Kontext gebrauchen.

Lösungen: in – from. For – for. in – in. At – of – in – of. in – as. down – on. in – of – into. in – on. in – to – for. at – of – to. to – on – of – of – of – of – in – at. to – in.

4 Brainteaser

Ziel: *fun element*; Vokabelübung.

Lösungen: 1. railway 2. strong 3. valley 4. Welsh 5. prince 6. ride 7. cow 8. racket 9. play 10. foot
Welsh castle: RNVENRCAAO = Caernarvon

> Workbook Seite 35

Step D Let's check

1 How to guess more about people ...

Ziel: Kontrolle der Bildung vom *present perfect progressive*.

Lösungen: 2. She has been playing tennis for many years. 3. They haven't been living here for long. 4. He has been waiting there for a long time. 5. She has been talking for a long time.

2 Caerleon

Ziel: Kontrolle der Bildung von *question tags*.

Lösungen: 1. ... aren't we? 2. ... didn't they? 3. ... did they? 4. ... won't we? ... didn't they? 5. ... will we?

3 Difficult situations

Ziel: Kontrolle der Bildung von Infinitivsätzen nach Fragewörtern.

Lösungen: 1. I don't know when to go to the station. 2. I don't know whether to believe her. 3. I don't know who to invite. 4. I don't know what to say. 5. I don't know where to put it.

> Workbook Seite 36

Tandem Activity 3

Ziel: Partnerübung. Informationen austauschen um gemeinsam ein Ziel zu erreichen.

> Workbook Seite 37

Workshop C Let's read

1 Starting off

1 Looking at different texts

Ziel: Informationen aus verschiedenen Textsorten erkennen lernen.

Lösungen: 1. B – ... left Britain (because) Rome was in danger. 2. D – Roman – ... unhappy/lonely (when) he thinks of home/the weather is bad (and) he remembers his mother and sister/he remembers the warm summer evenings in Italy. 3. A – Latin – ... difficult 4. D – film/programme – ... Roman soldier (who) is in Britain/goes to London. 5. C – tour/trip – ... the English countryside/the north of England – ... Hadrian's wall (and) Corbridge Roman Town and Museum.

> Workbook Seite 38

2 Do you like reading?

Ziel: sich zu verschiedenen Textsorten äußern.

Lösungsmöglichkeiten: individuelle S-Lösungen

3 A puzzle: What the Romans brought to Britain

Ziel: Vokabelübung.
Lösungen: 1. towns 2. cities 3. theatres 4. baths 5. toilets 6. carrots 7. cabbages 8. cats 9. streets 10. roads

> Workbook Seite 39

2 How to read a text

1 Understanding the main ideas

Ziel: aus einem Text und Illustration mit zum Teil unbekannten Vokabeln Informationen gewinnen; sich nicht durch unbekannte Wörter abschrecken lassen.

Hinweis: Es ist ratsam, vor der Bearbeitung des Textes gemeinsam mit den S den *tip*-Kasten zu lesen. In dieser Übung geht es nämlich darum, trotz unbekannter Vokabeln bestimmte Informationen aus Text und Illustrationen zu ermitteln. Die unbekannten Wörter werden <u>nicht</u> erklärt.

Lösungsmöglichkeiten: *1. The Romans used the fort at Housesteads for three centuries – T 2. No, there were houses outside the south gate of the fort – Ph 3. There were shops and inns in the "civil settlement" outside the south gate of the fort. – T 4. Yes, there were four gates into the fort: north, south, east and west. – P 5. I think so, there was a hospital. – P 6. There are hills and the wall and open countryside. – T*

> Workbook Seite 40

2 Looking for details

Ziel: Wortbedeutungen aus dem Kontext erschließen.

Lösungen: individuelle S-Lösungen

> Workbook Seiten 41-42

3 Reacting to a text

Caratacus – a British hero

Ziel: bei der Textbesprechung die Tatsachen und die Gefühle des Erzählers erkennen können.

Unterrichtsempfehlungen
Seite 41 bietet das Material für die Übungen auf Seite 42, bei denen es um eine detailliertere Textbetrachtung geht. Der Text unter a) auf Seite 41 gibt den historischen Hintergrund (so weit er bekannt ist) zum britischen Helden Caratacus (auch Caractacus oder walisisch Caradog). Der Text in Teil b) ist ein erfundener Tagebucheintrag, in dem Caratacus selber seinen Empfang in der Hauptstadt des römischen Reichs etwas salopp schildert.

1 Facts

Ziel: die tatsächliche Aussage eines Textes erkennen.

Lösungsmöglichkeiten: *1. The leaders of many of the British tribes made friends with the Romans, but Caratacus fought against them. 2. In AD 48 he escaped to the mountains. They only caught him three years later. 3. In Rome, he was in chains but he spoke in front of the people.*

2 Feelings

Ziel: die im Text zum Ausdruck gebrachten Gefühle erkennen.

Lösungsmöglichkeiten: *1. ... seen a city like this before. 2. Caratacus expects to see a big man, but the emperor is so small and looks awful. 3. He can't believe that the emperor of the world talked to him, the leader of one British tribe. 4. Caratacus can't believe that his chains are off and he is really free. 5. Caratacus sees how big the Empire is and how beautiful everything in Rome is. There are no towns in Britain as beautiful as Rome.*

3 Can you read between the lines?

Ziel: *creative writing:* einige Situationen aus dem Text weiterführen.

Lösungen: individuelle S-Lösungen

> Workbook Seite 43

Unit 4 The environment

Step A A trip to a theme park

1 Word power: Traffic words

Ziel: Üben einiger neuen Vokabeln.

Lösungen: 2. heavy ... 3. slow ... 4. ... jam 5. ... accident 6. ... news

2 Visiting a friend

Ziel: einen Weg beschreiben.

Lösungsmöglichkeiten: *1. ... she must turn right, and go on until she gets to the end of the road. Then she must turn right. After that she must take the third road on the left and go on round the corner. When she gets to the service station she should turn left. She should go along that road and my friend's house is on the right, just before the next road to the right.*

2. You go along this road and turn left. Go along to the end and turn right. Then take the second road on the left and go past the school. Take the second road on the right after the school, then turn left. Take the first road on the right, turn left, then right and go past the hospital. After the hospital the road turns right. Go to the end of that road and turn left. My friend's house is on the right.

3. She should go along this road and turn left. Then she must go along to the end and turn right, take the second road on the left and go past the school. After the school she must take the second road on the right, then turn left. At the end of that road she should turn right, take the first road on the left, then the first road on the right. Go along that road and turn right. There's a road to the left. My friend's house is on the left after that.

Workbook Seite 44

Step A In the car

3 What should or shouldn't they do?

Ziel: Üben von *should/shouldn't*.

Lösungsmöglichkeiten: *She should turn off the water. She can't listen to the radio and watch TV: she should turn off the TV or the radio. She should turn the heating down and close/shut the the window. She should recycle as much as possible, not put things in the rubbish bin. They shouldn't take the car for short trips, they should walk/ leave the car in the garage. She shouldn't throw rubbish out of the window.*

Step B An article in Our Earth magazine

1 Old neighbourhoods

Ziel: Bildung von Passivsätzen mit *simple present*.

Lösungen: *1. Sometimes houses are painted. 2. Sometimes walls are built. 3. Sometimes new windows are put in. 4. Sometimes rubbish is picked up. 5. Sometimes streets are repaired.*

Workbook Seite 45

2 Alton Towers

Ziel: Bildung von Passivsätzen mit *simple past;* weitere Informationen über Alton Towers erfahren

Lösungen: *was built – was given – was built – was made – were made – was added – was put up – was made – was built*

Step B Saving the environment

3 An accident

Ziel: Bildung von Passivsätzen mit *present perfect*

Lösungen: *1. The car has been hit. 2. The tree has been damaged. 3. The house has been destroyed. 4. Somebody has been injured. 5. The windows have been broken.*

Workbook Seite 46

4 At a garage

Ziel: Bildung von Passivsätzen mit *will-future*.

Lösungen: a) *will be collected – will be repaired – will be sprayed – will be put in – will be changed and checked – will be brought – will be washed – will be cleaned*

Lösungsmöglichkeiten: b) *Yes, I've had an accident. I've hurt my leg and the car needs some repairs – No, it won't start. – Can you collect it from my house? – The front needs to be repaired. – Can you spray it, too? – It needs a new window at the side. – Could you put new/summer/winter tyres on and check them, please? ... When will it be ready? – Sorry, I can't come after 4. – Oh, one more thing ... – Could you wash the car and clean the inside, too? – OK, thanks. See you at 10.*

Step C Tomorrow

1 Diary

Ziel: eine Geschichte erzählen unter Verwendung von verschiedenen Verbzeiten im Passiv.

Lösungen: *were caught – were brought – was taken – have been examined – was done – are put – are not hit – won't be taken*

Workbook Seite 47

2 Plurals

Ziel: Gebrauch von unzählbaren Substantiven: Pluralbildung.

Lösungen: *2. kinds of petrol 3. piece of information 4. bottles of lemonade 5. kinds of pollution 6. pieces of toast 7. cups of tea*

3 A new bridge between England and Wales

Ziel: Bildung von Passivsätzen mit *by-agent*.

Lösungen: *2. In 1996 a new bridge was opened by Prince Charles. 3. It was built by a British and a French firm. 4. The old bridge was used by many people. 5. The new bridge is used by more people. 6. The first cars were led across the bridge by police.*

4 Listening practice: Life without a car

Ziel: Hörverstehen; nach bestimmten Informationen hören.

Text
Mr Nelson is a guest on Mrs Croft's radio show. He is talking about the environment and what he and his family have done.

Mrs Croft: Can you tell us what you and your family have done, Mr Nelson?
Mr Nelson: Yes, you see, we wanted to do something for the environment. Everybody always talks about it but nobody ever does anything. Well, we wanted to do something. So we talked about it in the family and in the end we sold our car and started using bikes for everything in our area, and public transport when we had to go on a longer trip – you know – we used buses and trains.
Mrs Croft: I'm sure that was very difficult at first.
Mr Nelson: Not really. At first it was fun, like an adventure. And we were able to save a lot of money. That was good. But then, after a while, the children – we've got two girls: 12 and 14 – well, the children weren't so happy. You see, our world has been made for cars – and if you haven't got one, you have a lot of problems.

Mrs Croft: What problems do your girls have?
Mr Nelson: They do a lot of activities – sports and clubs and things like that. So they often have to ask other people to take them there or to bring them home, because public transport doesn't always take you where you want to go – or when. They don't like that very much.
Mrs Croft: Yes, I can understand that.
Mr Nelson: Then we sometimes have problems with shopping. It's not the weather, really. You can put on a raincoat or warm clothes, that's not the problem. It's heavy things like a big bag of potatoes or a lot of big bottles.
Mrs Croft: Yes, I see. That must be very difficult.
Mr Nelson: We often don't feel safe in heavy traffic. My wife was injured last month. She was hit by a car.
Mrs Croft: I'm sorry about that. Is she all right now?
Mr Nelson: Yes, she's fine. It wasn't very bad, but now we're all a bit scared when there's a lot of traffic. Another thing is that some people think we're crazy – but we're still doing it. We still don't want to have a car, but I don't know how much longer we'll be able to go on like this.

Lösungen: *1. The Nelsons have sold their car and they have started using bikes for everything in the area, and public transport when they have to go on a longer trip. They have done this because they want/wanted to do something for the environment. 2. It's good that they are doing something for the environment. And they have saved a lot of money. 3. The girls often have to ask other people to take them to clubs or things like that. Public transport doesn't always take you where you want to go – or when. The world is made for cars. There are problems with shopping. It is difficult to take heavy things on a bike. Another problem is the heavy traffic: Mrs Nelson was injured last month.*

Workbook Seite 48

5 Brainteaser: At Alton Towers

Ziel: *fun element.*

Lösungen: *1. Kevin, 16, hamburgers, Germany
2. Andy, 11, hot dogs, France
3. Petra, 13, cheese sandwich, USA
4. Nina, 14, fish and chips, Italy
5. Chris, 9, ham sandwich, England*

Step D Let's check

1 Alton Towers

Ziel: Kontolle der Passivbildung bei verschiedenen Verbzeiten.

Lösungen: *was taken – have been taken – were driven – is changed – are improved – was built – will be added*

Workbook Seite 49

2 Yesterday

Ziel: Kontrolle der eigenständigen Bildung von Passivsätzen mit *present perfect*.

Lösungen: *1. The sausages have been eaten by the dog. 2. The flowerpot has been broken by the window. 3. A purse has been found/picked up by a little girl. 4. The bike has been destroyed by a bus. 5. A house has been built by Wilson & Son.*

3 A word box

Ziel: Wortschatzübung zu den Wortfeldern *environment, traffic.*

Lösungen: → *factories, roadworks, freedom, bike, cars, petrol, environment, science, technology;* ↓ *experiment, traffic, earth;* ↑ *energy, nature;* ↘ *bus, map, pollution, air*

Workbook Seite 50

Tandem Activity 4

Ziel: Partnerarbeit; Weg beschreiben/Anweisungen geben.

Workbook Seite 51

Workshop D Let's write

1 Getting ideas together

1 Reviews

Ziel: Testauszüge lesen und den Gegenstand der Besprechung feststellen.

Lösungen: *2. a TV programme 3. a game 4. a film 5. a restaurant 6. a book/story*

2 Word power: Prepositions

Ziel: Präpositionen nach Kontext einsetzen.

Lösungen: *2. You play the role of one of Emperor Hadrian's best soldiers. 3. You have to escape from your enemies, the Celts. 4. You can click on objects; then facts about them appear on the screen. 5. The puzzles are too difficult, in my opinion, for most people. 6. But if you're good at Roman history you won't have any problems. 7. You have fun while you're learning, on the whole.*

Workbook Seite 52

3 Word power: Phrases for reviews

Ziel: *phrases* ihren Definitionen zuordnen.

Lösungen: *1. It's full of action. 2. You don't learn anything. 3. In my opinion, ... 4. The worst thing about it was ... 5. It was better than I expected. 6. It's really exciting. 7. They weren't very interesting. 8. She was great in the role.*

4 Organizing ideas

Ziel: eine Textgliederung ordnen

Lösungen: *Title: D; Introduction: K; Main Part: what you do: C, I; good points: A, E, G, J, M; bad points: B, F, H; Ending: L*

5 Writing notes for a review

Ziel: eine Gliederung selber erstellen; Notizen dazu machen

Musterlösung
*Title: "The Middle of Nowhere", film
Main part:* <u>What happens:</u> *a girl, Sally, and her dog Huggles run away from home get lost in the Welsh mountains – bad weather – Sally hurt – dog fetches parents.* <u>Good points:</u> *brave dog – Nicola Flanders wonderful as Sally – beautiful music.* <u>Bad points:</u> *some scenes frightening – too long.* <u>Ending:</u> *worth watching – makes you cry.*

Workbook Seite 53

2 Writing the text

1 Using connecting words

Ziel: Konjunktionen erkennen; ihre Funktion zur Gliederung eines Textes erkennen.

Lösungen: <u>conjunctions:</u> *in this film, then, and, on the whole, when, but, But, although, because, so.*

1.c 2.e 3.g 4.a 5.k 6.l 7.b 8.h 9.j 10.f 11.i 12.d

2 Connecting ideas

Ziel: Konjunktionen im Satz verwenden.

Lösungsmöglichkeiten: *1. She thought he was a waxwork until he smiled at her. 2. Although my computer checks my spelling, it doesn't notice all my mistakes. 3. There were road works on the M6, so the Penroses decided to go by train. 4. I didn't do my homework because there was a fire in our flat. 5. Our neighbour has given up his boring job and now he's travelling around the world. 6. When you're in Great Britain, cycle on the left. 7. Some people never revise for exams, but they do well anyway.*

> Workbook Seite 54

3 Sounds and spelling

Ziel: Homophone erkennen und gebrauchen.

Lösungen: *a) right – write; road – rode; know – no; one – won; week – weak; their – there*

b) buy – by; hear – here; meet – meat; knew – new; where – wear; threw – through; night – knight; your – you're

c) individuelle S-Lösungen

4 Word power: Adjectives

Ziel: a) Wortfeldarbeit: Adjektiv + Substantiv; b) Adjektive kontextgerecht in einen Text einsetzen.

Lösungen: *a) 2. lunch 3. bag 4. boy 5. car/bike 6. people 7. story 8. book 9. adventure 10. enemy*
b) individuelle S-Lösungen

> Workbook Seite 55

5 Writing the review

Ziel: ein eigenes *review* schreiben.

Musterlösung: (vgl. „notes" unter Workshop D, 1,5 oben.)
"The Middle of Nowhere":
It's a film about a girl and a dog who get lost in the Welsh mountains.
The girl, Sally, has an argument with her parents. So she runs away from home and takes her dog Huggles with her. Because of the bad weather Sally and Huggles soon get lost in the mountains. Sally is hurt so Huggles goes to fetch her parents and they come and rescue her.
Some scenes are too frightening for children but Nicola Flanders is wonderful in the role of Sally and the music is beautiful. Although the film goes on too long at the end, it's worth watching if you enjoy films that make you cry.

6 The statue game

Ziel: eine Erzählung nach Vorgaben schreiben.

Lösungsmöglichkeiten: *1. You go into a strange room. The walls are red, and there are lots of small windows. 2. There is a huge white statue with only one arm. 3- Suddenly the statue says: "Can you find my second arm for me?" 4. I feel sorry for the statue and I ask her: "Where did you lose it?" 5. She doesn't answer me but she gives me an old book. I have to read the book and find out about the tricks of ten different levels. In the end I'm able to find the arm and bring it back to her.*
Andere individuelle Schülerlösungen möglich.

3 Checking the text

1 Using punctuation

Ziel: Interpunktion in einen Text einsetzen.

Lösungen:
Dear Mum, Dad and Sarah,
 We're having a lovely time here in Italy. The youth hostel is huge and we've already met lots of interesting people. It's raining now, so we're sitting in a nice, dry café and drinking capuccino. We love the Italian food but we think it's making us fat. If the weather gets better tomorrow we may go to the beach. I miss you.
 Love, Kim

2 Looking at mistakes

Ziel: Fehleranalyse und -korrektur.

Lösungen: *2. wrong preposition 3. wrong verb form 4. small instead of capital letter 5. wrong negative verb form 6. wrong apostrophe 7. wrong word 8. wrong plural form 9. wrong spelling (comparative) 10. wrong pronoun 11. wrong relative pronoun 12. wrong plural 13. wrong choice of verb 14. wrong form: should be adverb 15. wrong tense 16. wrong spelling of pronoun*

> Workbook Seite 56

3 Word power: Zany Zoos

Ziel: Vokabelübung.

Lösungsmöglichkeiten: *takes place in – play the role of – levels – win – lose – teaches – click on – screen – graphics – In my opinion – on the whole*

> Workbook Seite 57

Unit 5 Great Britain and the sea

Step A An island country

1 A word puzzle

Ziel: Übung einiger neuen Vokabeln.

Lösungen: *1. storm 2. tide 3. coast 4. weather 5. close 6. fishing 7. calm*
Puzzle (von oben): *coast – close – calm – storm – fishing – tide – weather*
Lösungswort: *seaside*

2 Words from the same family

Ziel: Wortbildung

Lösungen: *2. wind – windy 3. to live – life 4. safe – safety 5. Britain – British 6. especially – special*

3 Beach talk

Ziel: Wiederholung der Bildung von Konditionalsätzen Typ I.

75

Lösungen: *2. If the dog throws sand over the sandwiches, we won't be able to eat them. 3. If it rains again tomorrow, we'll take the next train home. 4. If those people don't switch off their radio, I'll throw it into the water. 5. If you eat another ice-cream, you'll be sick. 6. If you children don't stop fighting, we'll never take you to the beach again.*

Workbook Seite 58

Tandem Activity 5

Ziel: Partnerarbeit zum kreativen Umgang mit der Sprache.

Workbook Seite 59

Step B Out in the North Sea

1 Your choice

Ziel: Üben der Konditionalform *would*.

Lösungen:
individuelle S-Lösungen

2 Different ways to react

Ziel: Bildung von Konditionalsätzen Typ II.

Unterrichtsempfehlungen

Nach der Bearbeitung der 4 Fragen durch die S lohnt sich ein Unterrichtsgespräch über die Antworten. Es ist denkbar, dass die S mit den vorgegebenen Antworten nicht zufrieden sind und noch weitere Reaktionsmöglichkeiten anbieten möchten.

Lösungen:
individuelle S-Lösungen

Workbook Seite 60

3 Jobs and other people

Ziel: Bildung von Konditionalsätzen Typ II.

Lösungen: *1. Lifeboatman: If people understood more about the sea, they wouldn't need the lifeboat service so often. 2. Teacher: If people talked to their children about homework, it would help them to do better at school. 3. Bus driver: If people used buses instead of cars, they would not cause so many traffic jams. 4. Doctor: If people looked after their bodies better, they would be much healthier. 5. Police officer: If people locked their doors and windows, they would make life more difficult for thieves. 6. Bank clerk: If people saved a little money every month, they would always have something in the bank.*

Step B The lifeboat service

4 What must be done?

Ziel: Anwendung des *passive infinitive* nach *must / should*; Gebrauch von formaler Sprache in schriftlichem Kontext.

Lösungen: *2. A broken leg must be kept very still. 3. The patient's shoe shouldn't be taken off. 4. The leg can be held in place with clothes. 5. The patient must be watched for signs of shock. 6. Someone should be sent for help.*

Workbook Seite 61

5 Cliff problems

Ziel: Anwendung des *passive infinitive* nach *could/ couldn't/had to*

Lösungen: *couldn't be saved – couldn't be used – had to be put up – couldn't be rescued – couldn't be sold – had to be built*

6 All kinds of situations

Ziel: Bildung von Nebensätzen mit *when*.

Lösungsmöglichkeiten: 2. *When I'm shouted at by my parents, I talk to my friend. 3. When I'm smiled at by someone I don't know, I smile back. 4. When I'm spoken to by a police officer, I listen carefully. 5. When I'm laughed at by my friends, I start to cry.*

7 Fun with words

Ziel: *fun element;* Wortschatzübung.

Lösungsmöglichkeiten: *able, act, air, and, at, aunt, bad, band, bar, bat, bean, bear, beard, bed, been, bend, , bird, bit, blue, brain, build, builder, burn, but, can, candle, car, card, care, cat, Celt, centre, clap, clean. clear, club, clue, crab, cup, cut, dance, dancer, date, dear, deep, detail, dial, dice, die, diet, drop, ear, eat, end, enter, ice, idea, in, it, lace, land, late, lead, learn, lend, let, lie, line, near, need, nice, pair, part, pen, pence, pencil, pet, picture, piece, pint, plan, plane, plate, prince, put, race, rain, react, read, real, recipe, red, ride, rule, run, table, tale, tea, ten, tide, tip, tired, train, tree, trip, true, tunic, under, unit, until, up,*

Workbook Seite 62

Step C Sea rescue

1 'On', 'out' and 'up'!

Ziel: Üben von *phrasal verbs*.

Lösungen: *1. Come on! 2. Cheer up! 3. Hold on! 4. Wake up! 5. Watch out! 6. Get out!*

2 Listening practice: The story behind the news

Ziel: a) Hörverstehen; *note-taking;* b) *creative writing.*

Text
Newsreader:
… And finally: the rescue services in Cornwall had a busy day today. A brother and sister were taking their dog for a walk when the dog ran after a rabbit and fell over a cliff. He landed near the bottom of the cliff just above the sea. The girl tried to climb down to her trapped pet, but before she could get down to the dog she got trapped on the cliff, too. So her brother had to run to the nearest village to call the rescue services. A lifeboat and a coastguard helicopter arrived on the scene at the same time. The girl was very happy to be rescued by the helicopter, but the dog decided that he didn't need the lifeboat after all. He suddenly jumped into the sea, swam along the coast to a place where the cliff wasn't so high – and climbed back up again himself. Oh well, all's well that ends well.

Lösungen: individuelle S-Lösungen

3 Fun with words

Ziel: *fun element;* Wortschatzübung

Lösungen: *1. ask 2. sun 3. beach 4. rope 5. water 6. team 7. medal*

4 Brainteaser

Ziel: Knobelaufgabe; Wortschatzübung

Lösungen: *A. mile – mine – mind – wind B. wave – save – same – some C. life – line – fine – find D. calm – call – wall – well*

Workbook Seite 63

Step D Let's check

1 Scenes from a seaside town

Ziel: Kontrolle des Gebrauchs von *should/shouldn't*.

Lösungen: *1. Dogs shouldn't be left in cars on hot days. 2. Motor boats shouldn't be used where there are swimmers. 3. Rubbish shouldn't be dropped on the beach. 4. Swimming things shouldn't be worn in restaurants.*

2 Good advice

Ziel: Kontrolle der Bildung von *if*-Sätzen Typ II.

Lösungen: *1. You wouldn't feel so tired if you went to bed earlier! 2. Your money wouldn't go so fast if you spent it more carefully! 3. Your room wouldn't seem so small if you kept it tidier! 4. You wouldn't do so badly at school if you worked harder! 5. Your cooking wouldn't be so terrible if you used a recipe book!*

Workbook Seite 64

A Green Line New 3 game

Ziel: *fun element*; Wortschatzübung

Lösungen: *3. The 13th century (SB S. 44). 4. The Romans (SB S. 58). 7. A theme park (SB S. 62). 9. Big Ben (SB S. 15). 11. The White Tower (SB S. 19). 12. The Angles (SB S. 50). 14. A racket has got strings (SB S. 29). 15. 999 (SB S. 84). 18. The New Zealand rugby team (SB S. 27). 19. Camelot (SB S. 45). 21. An old wizard (SB S. 52). 24. Baker Street (SB S. 15). 25. Cardiff (SB S. 45). 27. Hull (SB S. 7). 29. West Indians (SB S. 16). 31. England, Scotland and Wales (SB S. 9). 32. Dutch (SB S. 7). 35. GCSE (SB S. 33). 39. Bed and breakfast (SB S. 44-45). 40. The left (SB S. 22).*

Hörverstehenstexte

Materialien zur Freiarbeit

Workshop A

Kevin and Judy's travel story

Part 1

Judy: Hurry, Kevin. I'm cold!
(telephone dialling)
Kevin: I am hurrying.
(number rings, receiver is picked up)
Warden: Ambleside Youth Hostel. The warden speaking.
Kevin: Good morning. My name's Kevin McNeil. I'd like to book – er – two beds for tonight, please.
Warden: Sorry, we're full tonight.
Kevin: Oh, no! Do you know anywhere else we can stay in Ambleside?
Warden: Hmm ... you could try the Kendall Guest House, down by the lake. Would you like the number?
Kevin: Oh, yes, please. Just a minute. I'll get a pen ... OK, I'm ready. The Kendall Guest House, right? How do you spell 'Kendall'?
Warden: K-E-N-D-A-L-L. The owner is a Mrs Roberts, and the number is Ambleside 3-0-double 2-7.
Kevin: Roberts ... 3-0-double 2-7. OK, I'll call her right away. Thanks very much.
Warden: That's all right. Bye!
(sound of receiver being put down)

Part 2

Kevin: A guest house right by the lake, Judy! Sounds good, eh?
Judy: Lovely, but don't take all day, Kevin! It's going to rain soon!
Kevin: OK, OK.
(telephone dialling, ringing tone)
Kevin: It's ringing!
Man with Indian accent: Taj Mahal, good afternoon.
Kevin: Er – isn't that the Kendall Guest House?
Man: No, it isn't. This is Ambleside 3-0-double 2-1, the Taj Mahal Indian Takeaway.
Kevin: Oh, I wanted 3-0-double 2-7. I'm sorry!
(sound of receiver being put down)
Kevin: Wrong number, Judy! That was my last 20p.
Judy: Here, I can give you one. Oh, look! It's raining now!
(telephone dialling)
Kevin: I'm doing my best, Judy. *(Ringing tone)* Ah ... it's ringing!
Recorded message: This is the Kendall Guest House. There is no one here to answer your call at the moment, but if you leave your name and number after the tone, we'll call you back as soon as possible.
(sound of receiver being put down)
Kevin (gruffly): I hate those machines!

Part 3

Kevin: The map says the Kendall Guest House should be right here.
Judy: Well, all I can see is a field of sheep. This is the last time I come on a walking holiday!
Kevin: Look – there's a phone here. Let's call the guest house again and ask for the way.
Judy: OK, but I'll call this time, Kevin. I've got one 20p piece.
(telephone dialling, ringing tone; receiver is picked up)
Little girl: Hello.
Judy: Hello? Is that the Kendall Guest House?
Little girl: Um, yes ... *(proudly)* My name's Melissa Jane Roberts and I'm three!
Judy: Really? That's nice. Can I speak to your mum, please?
Little girl: OK. Mum! MUM! ... *(muffled shout: "I'm having a bath")* My mum's having her bath.
Judy: Well, is your dad at home? Will you go and get him for me, Melissa! There's a good girl!
Little girl: My dad? All right. Bye bye!
(sound of receiver being put down)
Judy: Argh!!! There goes my last 20p!

Part 4

Judy: I'm cold, tired and hungry. I can't walk another step. Can't you carry me, Kevin?
Kevin: Very funny, Judy.
(sound of car approaching)
Kevin: Hey, a car's coming! Stop! STOP!
(sound of car stopping)
Warden: Hello. Is anything wrong?
Judy: We're lost, and we can't find anywhere to stay tonight.
Warden: What about the Youth Hostel? It's only a short walk up the hill.
Kevin: The Youth Hostel's full. We phoned this morning.
Warden: Well, it isn't full now. We've had some cancellations, so we've got some beds now.
Judy: Hey, that's great! So you work there, do you?
Warden: Yes, I'm the warden. Can I take you to the hostel? You look tired.
Kevin: Oh, wow, thanks!
Warden: Just be careful with all those boxes in the back. That's my lunch.
Judy: Your lunch? *(sniffs)* Oh yes – there's a nice smell of curry! Mmm!
Warden: I've just collected it from the Indian Takeaway. It's much better than hostel food!

Unit 1

London by underground

Part 1

Driver: In a few moments we'll be at Paddington Station. This is the end of the line, so all passengers must get off at Paddington. Thank you for travelling with Thames Turbo trains.
Philip: Wake up, Craig!
Craig: Huh? What? Oh, are we at Paddington already? Hey – where's my scarf?
Philip: Under your seat. And don't forget your anorak! You'll forget your head next.
Craig: Ha ha. OK – I've got everything now. Let's hurry – I don't want to miss the game!

Part 2

Philip: Which line is Wembley Park on, Craig?
Craig: Let's look at the map.
Philip: There's Wembley Park. It's on the Metropolitan Line. So we need to take the Bakerloo Line and change at Baker Street. Easy!
Craig: Quick, Phil – the train's waiting! Run!

Part 3

Driver: Warwick Avenue. Next station Maida Vale.
Philip: Huh? Warwick Avenue? This can't be right, Craig.
Craig: Oh, no! We're going the wrong way, Phil! Look at the map!
Philip: You're right, we're going west, not east.
Craig: Let's get off at Willesden Junction. We can get a train to West Hampstead, and then take the Jubilee Line to Neasden – it's right next to Wembley Park.
Philip: No – that's a British Rail train, Craig. It'll take too long, and we should stay on the underground anyway. Let's just get off at Kilburn Park and go back to Baker Street. It'll be faster.
Craig: OK, back to Baker Street.

Part 4

Driver: Finchley Road. Next stop, Wembley Park.
Philip: Good – we're going the right way. We mustn't forget to get off at the next stop.
Woman: Excuse me, but are you two going to watch a game at Wembley Stadium?
Craig: Yes. Why?
Woman: Well, you're going the wrong way. You want Wembley Central, not Wembley Park.

Philip: What? Are you sure?
Woman: Yes, the stadium is at Wembley Central. It's on the Bakerloo line.
Driver: Wembley Park. Next stop, Preston Road.
Woman: Get off here and go back to Baker Street. Then change onto the Bakerloo Line, and go west!

Part 5
Driver: Wembley Central. Next stop, North Wembley.
Philip: Wembley Central. At last!
(Background noises: 'Mind the gap' announcement, boisterous fans)
Craig: Wow! Look at all those fans. This must be right.
Philip: It's a good thing we've already got our tickets, isn't it?
Craig: Yes. But where did I put them? Oh no!
Philip: Craig! You idiot! Don't tell me you didn't bring them!
Craig: Oh, I brought them all right. But I think I left them on the train at Paddington.

Workshop B

Clowns! Episode 3

"I want to go to the toilet!"
"I told you not to drink all the lemonade, Pip!" said Colin. "Come on, we'll try to find it."
Colin and Pip left their seats and walked through the Big Top. Pip still had the poster of Charlie the clown in his hand. Tigers ran around the ring and made a terrible noise. Outside the Big Top it was very dark. A large box said "Tigers". There were lots of caravans, all dark and quiet. But no toilets. Suddenly, Pip wasn't next to Colin. He ran behind one of the caravans. It said "Manager's Office". The caravan door opened and someone came out.
"Charlie!" shouted Pip. The clown looked at the little boy. "I like how you took the rich man's money!"
The clown looked down at Pip. "What ...?" he asked in a quiet voice. "You saw?" He put his hand in the pocket of his yellow coat.
"Yes, we all loved the show, Charlie!"
"Ah ... the show!" said the clown.
"Can I have your autograph?" asked Pip. "I've got your poster, look!"
Suddenly, the clown laughed. "My autograph? Later..."
"I want it now!" said Pip and started to cry.
"OK, OK! But don't make so much noise!" The clown smiled and wrote "Best wishes from Charlie!" and then left.
Colin was very angry when he found Pip. "But I met Charlie!" said Pip. "And he gave me his autograph, look!"
After the show, there was a long queue near the exit. Hundreds of kids waited to get the famous clown's autograph. Charlie wrote in big letters "Best wishes from Charlie!" Suddenly, a group of police officers pushed through the crowd. With them was the circus manager and his assistant. There was blood on the assistant's head. The manager's eyes were almost crazy. He looked at Charlie.
"There he is! That's the thief! He took all the money! He tried to kill my assistant!" he shouted.
Two of the officers took Charlie's arms. The crowd started to shout "Hey, you can't do that to Charlie!" A large officer shouted "It's all right everybody, please, don't worry!"
"Charlie Watson?" The large officer asked the clown.
"Y-yes," Charlie started. "That's me..."
The officer had something to say to Charlie: "You're under arrest!"

Unit 2

Wayne's school report

Mr Dobson: 34 pupils! That's a big class!
Wayne: No, that's 34 for the tutor group, Dad. Most of our classes are smaller.
Mrs Dobson: Oh, Wayne! An 'E' for History! This is worse than last term! "Wayne shows no interest in the subject, and his last project was not complete. He must work harder." Who is your teacher?
Wayne: We've got Mrs Percy for History. She hates me, just because of that snake.
Mrs Dobson: I'm sure that's not true, Wayne! But she's right. You really must work harder.
Mr Dobson: And look, Religion isn't too good – only a 'D'. "He can be noisy and difficult sometimes. I hope he will show more interest in the subject next term." And a 'D' for music. "I'm a bit disappointed."
Wayne: Well, I hate singing, and the lessons are always so boring, so I was disappointed, too!
Mr Dobson: I don't want to hear it, Wayne. You're too lazy, and you know it! Look – your Science teacher says that you should concentrate more, and that you're careless. You can do better than a 'D' in Science!
Wayne: Well, I did get a few good marks! Look – I even got two 'A's!
Mrs Dobson: Oh yes, an 'A' in P.E. Ooh – and one in French, too, Wayne!
Wayne: I always get an 'A' in P.E.. It's my favourite subject, and I'm in all the teams.
Mr Dobson: Good – football and hockey ... Oh, and the under-15 swimming team, too! But you've never had an 'A' in French before.
Mrs Dobson: Maybe our holiday in France helped! And what did your German teacher think? "He often makes careless mistakes in his tests, but I am very pleased with his ..." – what's this word? I can't read it. Prowess?
Wayne: No, Mum, he's pleased with my progress!
Mrs Dobson: Oh ...
Mr Dobson: Your English teacher is Mrs Taylor, right? She's very nice, I think.
Wayne: Well, she never writes nice things about me.
Mr Dobson: "Wayne's stories are interesting, but his spelling is very weak." Well, she gave you a 'C'. That isn't too bad. Better than the 'D' you got in English last term.
Mrs Dobson: A 'C' for Geography. "I was very pleased with Wayne's project on London, but he did not do well in his last test."
Wayne: That was after I was ill, don't forget. Hey – what do you think of my 'B' for Art?
Mr Dobson: So you won first prize for your statue of Friar Tuck! You never told us!
Wayne: Yeah – they're going to give it to me on prize day! Want to come?
Mr Dobson: Of course! Hey, I got a 'B' in Maths! Look – it says "He did very well this term." Not bad, eh?
Wayne: What do you mean, you got a 'B'?
Mr Dobson: Well, I helped you with all that Maths homework, remember? I hope you're all proud of me!
Mrs Dobson: Oh, Wayne! Have you really had detention four times this term? That's too much!
Wayne: Yeah, but I'm getting better. I had detention six times last term.
Mrs Dobson: What does Mr Stuart mean by 'class clown' anyway?
Wayne: No idea. Maybe the teachers just don't find my jokes funny.

Unit 3

Clowns! Episode 5

That evening the kids were watching Kincaid's house.
"I think we should tell the police now," said Mandy. "We can't do this ourselves."
"First we must be sure Kincaid is the thief," said Colin. "He's probably thrown the clown costume in the rubbish already. If we can find the nylon wig, we'll have what we need!"
Just then Kincaid's front door opened and he came out. He was carrying a large rubbish bag.
"The costume must be in that bag!" whispered Simon.
Kincaid looked at his watch and then walked to the rubbish. But he didn't stop. He got in his car, put the bag on the front seat, and drove away.
"Come on!" said Colin.
They jumped on their bikes and followed the car. It stopped outside a house in a dark street. Kincaid got out with the bag.

"What do you kids want?" asked Kincaid in an annoyed voice.
"We saw you at the circus ... on Saturday!" was Colin's answer.
"Oh really?" asked Kincaid.
"We know you left before the end of the show," said Simon. "And we know where you went!"
"I wasn't feeling too good ..." said Kincaid. "So I went home early – but wait a minute! Why am I telling you this – what are you kids doing here, huh?!"
"You're telling lies! You didn't go home early: you stayed at the circus – in a clown costume!" shouted Colin.
"We know you bought a clown costume, just like Charlie's!" Mandy added. "That's what you've got in the bag! You went to the circus manager's office and hit his assistant with a stick and stole the money! They arrested poor Charlie, but it should be you!"
"And now you want to throw the costume in the rubbish!" said Simon.
"Don't be silly!" Kincaid laughed.
Just then, something fell out of the bag. It rolled on the ground. They all looked at it. It was a red clown's nose! But then, suddenly, a little girl of six opened the front door of the house and shouted, "Grandpa! Have you got the clown costume?! Hurry, all my friends are waiting!"
Later that evening they were sitting in Colin's bedroom. They were all very disappointed.
"Great detectives we are!" said Mandy. "Poor old Kincaid was only a clown for his granddaughter's birthday party! Have you got any more great ideas, Colin?"
"Well, yes, I have ..." he answered. "That handwriting on Pip's poster – I've just remembered where I've seen it before ... ."

Workshop C

A listening crossword
These are the clues across.
1 across is an adjective. It means 'the most important'.
3 across is an adjective. It is the opposite of 'strong'.
5 across is a noun. It is made of glass and built into a wall.
7 across is an adjective. It means 'wrong' or 'not real'.
8 across is a noun. You should have one when you're dirty.
10 across is a noun. You can't taste things without it. It is also another word for 'language'.
11 across is a noun. You give it when you say how old you are.
13 across is a verb. The wind does it.
14 across is a verb. It means to 'choose to do something'.
15 across is a noun. It is the title of a paragraph or a newspaper article.
18 across is an adjective. It means the opposite of 'cold'.
20 across is a noun. It is in the sky and you see it when there aren't any clouds.
22 across is a verb. You do this when you change the words from one language into another.
23 across is a noun. Atishoo! *(groaning in a congested nasal voice)* Oh, I think I've got one ... A-a - a -TISHOO!!
24 across is a noun. It is very expensive and you get it from mines. It is also a colour.
25 across is an adjective. It means the opposite of 'fat'.
26 across is a verb. You do it when you lie, or act in a way which is not how you feel.
27 across is a verb or an adjective. If you say to a guest,"Hello, it's nice to see you," you are doing it.
30 across is a noun. A group of sentences that make part of a text.
32 across is a verb. It means 'to think that something will happen'.
33 across is a verb. It is the past form of 'shine'.

These are the clues down.
2 down is a verb. An army does it when it marches into another country and tries to conquer it.
4 down is a verb. It means 'to end someone's life'.
5 down is a question word. If you don't understand something, you can ask this little word.
6 down is a noun. It is a word for 'false hair'.
7 down is a noun. Farmers work in them.
9 down is a noun. When armies fight, they are having one.
10 down is a noun. You have more than one in your mouth.
12 down is a verb or a noun. As a verb it means 'to want'.
13 down is a verb. It is what fire does.
16 down is a noun. It is another word for 'writer'.
17 down is a noun. It means 'the main ideas of a text'.
19 down is a preposition. It means the opposite of 'inside'.
20 down is a noun. This person is the member of an army.
21 down is a verb. You do it when you want someone to remember something.
23 down is a verb or an adjective. As a verb it means 'to finish' or 'to fill in something'.
28 down is a verb. The most important person in a team must be good at this.
29 down is an adjective or a verb. It means the opposite of 'closed' or 'to close'.
31 down is a noun. Maybe you are writing with one at the moment.

Unit 4

Two stories in one
Radio announcer: It's time now for the six o'clock news.
(Time signal)
Newsreader:
An accident between a milk van and a police car caused a traffic jam in Blackport early this morning. Milkman Paul Harvey was putting out milk bottles when two young men jumped into his milk van and drove away. Mr Harvey stopped a taxi and tried to catch up with the van, which cannot go faster than 20 miles an hour. While they were following the van around a roundabout, the thieves began to throw milk bottles into the path of the taxi. They later caught up with the van at some traffic lights. A police car was waiting for the green light, and the milk van drove right into the back of it. Nobody was injured, but there was a lot of damage.
A member of the group that has been living in the forest near Blackport for over two months was taken to hospital by ambulance last night. Mrs Nora Oakley is expecting her third child. The Oakley family is part of a group of environmentalists who are living in tree houses they have built in the forest. The group hope to stop the plan to build a motorway through Blackport. The motorway, they say, will do too much damage to the environment. Mrs Oakley says that as soon as her baby is born, she will go back to the rest of her family in the tree house. Although the road builders are starting work next week, the Oakley family will not move. Mr Oakley said they will lie down in front of the bulldozers if they have to.

Workshop D

Brainstorming
David: What should we call our report, Jenny?
Jenny: Hmm – what about something like 'Saving the Environment'?
David: Yeah, that sounds good. I'll put that in the middle. Saving ... the... environment.
Jenny: OK, so what should we write about?
David: I think one part should be the problems of the environment.
Jenny: Yes, that can be the first part. But what sort of problems are you thinking of?
David: Well, what about pollution?
Jenny: Yes, we can talk about the different kinds of pollution.
David: That's right, like water pollution.
Jenny: And air pollution, and noise pollution.
David: And pollution of the earth itself.
Jenny: OK, so that's different kinds of pollution. What other problems can we write about?
David: Um – how about the way we are losing the countryside. You know, like when people destroy fields and cut down trees to put up shopping centres – or build more roads.
Jenny: OK, so put down, ...erm..., 'losing our countryside'. Then add examples, like 'roads' and 'shopping centres'.
David: Roads ... shopping centres ...
Jenny: Hey, we should also talk about what pollutes the environment. That can be the second part.

David: Oh, yes, I'll write 'things that pollute'.
Jenny: Like factories and cars and ... people!
David: People? What do you mean?
Jenny: Well, you know, people who are careless with rubbish, or who ...er ...
David: Oh, I see. Right, so we've got 'things that pollute', and then cars, factories and people as examples.
Jenny: And the third part should be about what we can do about the problems.
David: Yes, that's very important. *(writing)* What we can do.
Jenny: Then we can give examples, like saving energy.
David: And then we say how we can save energy. You know, turn off lights, turn down the heating.
Jenny: Yeah – and another thing is that we shouldn't throw things in the rubbish that we can use again.
David: Yes, like bottles and plastic cups. Then there won't be so much waste.
Jenny: People should give up their cars. I think they should walk more, and use public transport.
David: Not so fast! What was that? Give up cars. Walk more. Use public transport. Oh, and I can add 'build more cycle paths' ... *(writing)*
Jenny: Wow – where are we going to stop?

Unit 5

All in a day's work

Judy: We shouldn't leave the path, Kevin. Look – there's a sign. 'Danger: Do not leave the path'.
Kevin: I just want to look down at the beach. Wow! This cliff is really steep!
Judy: Don't go too close, Kevin! You'll fall!
Kevin: No, I won't. Come and look, Judy. It's great!
Judy: I can't! Oh, please come back, Kevin. It's dangerous!
Kevin: Ooh, it's a long way down to the bottom. Hmm, the tide's coming in.
Judy: Be careful, Kevin!
Kevin: Don't worry, I'm all r... ! *(screams as he tumbles down cliff)*
Judy: Kevin!
Kevin: Help!
Judy: Oh, Kevin! Are you all right?
Kevin: No!
Judy: Have you hurt yourself?
Kevin: No, but I can't move. I'm scared that I might fall again!
Judy: I'll climb down and help you!
Kevin: No, Judy. Stay where you are! Just get someone – quickly!
Judy: But there isn't anyone. Oh – wait a minute. I think someone's coming. Kevin, just hold on, right?
Kevin: I am holding on. Help!
Judy: He's running towards us. Yes ... it's a coastguard! Thank God!
Coastguard: Has someone fallen over the cliff?
Judy: Yes, he tripped and...
Coastguard: Don't worry, we'll get him up safely.
Kevin: Please hurry! I can't hold on ...
Coastguard: Now, listen carefully. I'm going to throw down a rope for you.
Kevin: A rope? OK!
Coastguard: Ready?... Here! ... Got it?
Kevin: Yeah, got it!
Coastguard: Now, young lady. You take this bit of the rope. We're going to pull him up. When I count to three, you start climbing, and we'll pull, OK?
Kevin: OK.
Coastguard: One, two, three!
(grunts all round as Kevin is hoisted up)
Judy: Oh, Kevin!
Kevin: Judy! *(to coastguard)* Oh, and thanks so much. You should get a medal. I mean, you've saved my life.
Coastguard: Oh, that's all right. It's all in a day's work.
Kevin: What a nightmare! It's a good thing you were up here.
Coastguard: You were really lucky! The last person who fell down this cliff never got up again.

Kevin: Really? Ugh! Well, the cliff is very slippery, and those rocks ...
Coastguard: That's why we put up that sign. Look – 'Danger. Do not leave the path'. Didn't you see it?
Kevin: Well, um ... ...*(fade)*

Kontrollaufgaben

Workshop A

Phone messages

1.
Sarah: 967 2506, Sarah speaking.
Boy: Oh, is Kim there?
Sarah: No, she's gone out. I'm not sure where. Who's speaking, please?
Boy: It's Peter. Can you give her a message, please? It's really important.
Sarah: Yes, I'll just write it down.
Boy: Tell her to meet me at the cinema at 8 o'clock this evening ... not St Peter's Church at 7.30. Will you tell her?
Sarah: Yes, the cinema at 8 o'clock.
Boy: Thanks! Bye!
Sarah: Bye!

2.
Sarah: 967 2506, Sarah speaking.
Girl: Hi, Kim is that you?
Sarah: No, it's her sister Sarah speaking. Who is it?
Girl: It's a friend. Do you know when she'll be back?
Sarah: Well, she's just gone to the library so she should be back soon. Do you want to leave a message?
Girl: Yes, please. Tell her to ring Avrina.
Sarah: Sorry, who?
Girl: Avrina, that's A-V-R-I-N-A.
Sarah: OK. Does she know your number?
Girl: I don't think so. It's 3-1-9-6-7- double 4. I must talk to her.
Sarah: OK, don't worry. I've written the message down and I'll put it on her bedroom door.
Girl: Oh, thanks! Bye!

3.
Sarah: 967 2506, Sarah speaking.
Woman: Hello. Can I speak to Kim Dixon, please?
Sarah: I'm sorry, she isn't in at the moment. Who is it please?
Woman: It's Music World here. Do you now when she'll be in?
Sarah: She won't be long, but I can take a message if you like.
Woman: Well, I'm just phoning to tell her that her CD has arrived.
Sarah: Oh, good. She'll be glad to hear that. I'll tell her when she comes in!
Woman: Thank you. Goodbye!

Unit 1

A London bus tour

Welcome to London, the capital of the United Kingdom where over 7 million people live. More than 9 million visitors come to London each year and every year the number is bigger. Today we are going to take you to London's most famous sights.

On your left is Buckingham Palace. I'm sure you know the Queen lives there. The palace has 600 rooms and some of them are open to visitors, but only in July and August. You won't be alone because seven thousand people visit the palace every day when it's open.

Here we are at Speakers' Corner just next to London's largest park, Hyde Park. Here anyone and everyone can stand and talk to the crowd about anything. Sometimes people talk about really strange things but the crowd is polite and will listen even if they think the speaker is a bit crazy!

We are now passing 221b Baker Street, the home of the famous Sherlock Holmes. Of course, Sherlock Holmes didn't really live here because he was only someone in a book. Many Sherlock Holmes fans come from all over the world to visit this house. Some of them are very disappointed when they find out that he never lived here! And just up the road is the famous Madame Tussaud's waxwork museum. Look at the queue! It's the longest in London. Madame Tussaud's is one of London's most popular places for visitors. About two and a half million people visit it every year. Now we're going to look at … *(fade)*

Workshop B

Jackie and Gabi

Gabi: I like your shorts, Jackie!
Jackie: What – these? These are my football shorts! We've got a match this afternoon.
Gabi: Really? Do you play in a club or something?
Jackie: No, I play for the school. I'm goalkeeper in the first eleven.
Gabi: The school team? You must be good!
Jackie: Well, there isn't much competition, really. Some of the other girls say I'm crazy.
Gabi: I think they're right. I mean, you must be crazy if you like running up and down a pitch on a day like this. In shorts!
Jackie: Well, I think it's fun.
Gabi: Yes, but if you're just the goalkeeper, that's boring, isn't it?
Jackie: No! The goalkeeper is the most important person.
Gabi: Can girls play hockey at your school, too?
Jackie: Can? We must play hockey at our school. I can't stand the game.
Gabi: What about rugby? Don't tell me girls also play that at English schools!
Jackie: No, usually only boys play it.
Gabi: It's really dangerous, isn't it?
Jackie: Yeah. The accidents can be terrible!
Gabi: Well, I'm not surprised. I mean, the size of some of those players – they're like bears!
Jackie: Yeah, but I must say, I like watching rugby matches. All those nice boys! *(giggles)* And the matches are a thousand times more exciting than say, cricket matches. Have you ever watched a cricket match, Gabi?
Gabi: No, not a live one. I saw one on TV once, but not much happened, until …
Jackie: That's right! Nothing happens! The players just stand around and wait for hours until someone throws a ball! It's so boring and so complicated. Well, I think so, anyway.
Gabi: There was one exciting bit, Jackie. A man ran across the pitch, and *(whispers conspiratorially)* he didn't have any clothes on! *(giggles)*
Jackie (feigning shock): Well, really! *(primly)* Well, Gabi, cricket isn't usually like that.

Unit 2

Romeo and Juliet

(sound of phone ringing, receiver being picked up)
Jenny: Nottingham 961 4735.
Robert: Hello Jenny. This is Robert.
Jenny: Oh, hi Robert … *(teasingly)* Romeo. You are coming tonight, aren't you?
Robert: Well, I'm sorry, but I can't Jenny. I'm going to the doctor's at 4.30.
Jenny: Oh, no! And I've just learnt all my lines.
Robert: Well, what about tomorrow? We can meet after school!
Jenny: I'm starting piano lessons tomorrow! But Wednesday is OK. There's no Bird Watcher's Club this week.
Robert: Well, I can't on Wednesday. I'm going to youth club with Edward.
Jenny: With Edward? To the youth club?
Robert: Yeah, it was his idea.
Jenny: Well, why not? Maybe he'll make some new friends there.
Robert: Yeah, I hope so. Do you have time this week at all, Jenny?
Jenny: Let me think … hm … What about Thursday?
Robert: Thursday is bad for me. I'm playing volleyball. What about Friday?
Jenny: Becky and I are going to see 'Dracula's Castle' at the Odeon. Want to come?
Robert: Thanks, but Mum and I are going to a concert.
Jenny: Hey, are you taking part in the bike ride on Saturday?
Robert: Yeah, it'll be fun, won't it? But Jenny, what about the play? When are we going to practise?
Jenny: Well, there's always Sunday.
Robert: But Emma's party is on Sunday.
Jenny: Oh, so Emma's having a party is she? Well, she never sent me an invitation. Do you really want to go?
Robert: No, not really. OK, Jenny, let's meet on Sunday.
Jenny: Great. What time on Sunday?
Robert: Um … four o'clock.
Jenny: Why not earlier? Let's make it three.
Robert: OK. Right. *(writing)* Sunday … three o'clock. Oh, and don't forget to bring your book.
Jenny: I don't need it. I've learnt my lines, remember?

Unit 3

Living in North Wales

Friend: You've been here for a long time now, haven't you, Gwen?
Gwen: We moved here to North Wales last summer. So I guess we've been here for 6 months now.
Friend: Yes, I remember when you first came. Do you like it here?
Gwen: I do now. Well, I've always liked it. I liked all the little villages and the beautiful valleys right away. But I didn't want to come here because we didn't know anybody here – I had to leave all my friends in the south.
Friend: Yes, that's always the problem when you move.
Gwen: You know, when we first came here, it was very exciting. We wanted to see everything – the seaside, all the castles and the sights.
Friend: Have you ever been to Snowdon – all the way to the top?
Gwen: Yes, we went up last September. It was wonderful. We even had good weather.
Friend: Did you walk up?
Gwen: Well, the men in the family – Dad and my brother *(ironic)* wanted to test themselves. They wanted to conquer the mountain. So they walked. But Mum and I took the little railway. It was great. You know we were sitting on the train and riding to the top when we saw the 'boys' – and *(amused)* they looked very tired.
Friend (laughing a bit): So now you really feel at home here, don't you?
Gwen: Yes – the only problem is Welsh. In the South not so many people speak it. We didn't and now we often have to use it – and it isn't easy. It's so different from English.
Friend: But you have lessons at school.
Gwen: Yes, I do. I've been learning it for 3 years. You see, I had it in South Wales, too, but I still don't know how to speak it very well.
Friend: Well, everyone here speaks English, too, don't they?
Gwen: Yes, but many people here don't like speaking it – and Mum and Dad have big problems with Welsh, too. They need it for their jobs. So they've been having lessons in the evening for 5 months now. We even try to speak it to each other sometimes now.
Friend: Good. I'm sure it's only a question of time. It'll be normal for all of you soon.

Workshop C

Professor Johnson and the Roman remains

Interviewer: Here we are at the remains of a Roman fort just outside Dover. With me is Professor Johnson. Well, Professor, what have you found?

Professor: Well, it's very exciting! We think about three thousand Roman soldiers lived in this fort and they've left many interesting things from their lives. The stones you can see here are the corner of a pool. So, this could be where the baths were. The Romans loved their baths, you know ...

Interviewer: And what's this?

Professor: We think it's part of an old sandal *(laughs)* ... and here ... this is very exciting ...

Interviewer: It's Roman money!

Professor: Yes, we think this could be from a shop or the market square. We found this pot here, too

Interviewer: A pot?

Professor: Yes, if you put all these bits together, they make a big pot. We think it was for wine. And ...yes, look, this is interesting ... it's part of a small statue.

Interviewer: Oh, there's a bit missing!

Professor: Yes, but we can see it's a statue of a man ... maybe a Roman god. They had many gods, you see. We found it over there so we think that might be the temple.

Interviewer: Anything else, Professor?

Professor: Yes, this is probably the best one! It's part of a wonderful Roman sword! It's very dirty but when we clean it up it'll be the most interesting thing we've found at this fort. There's even some writing on it, look ... *(fade)*

Unit 4

The environment

Mrs Croft: My guest today on Tea and Talk is Mr Arthur Woodthorpe. He has come to talk to us about the environment. Mr Woodthorpe.

Mr Woodthorpe: The environment – er – well, let me tell you about something that I did last week. I went to Newstead, the village where I lived as a boy. Newstead was a lovely green healthy place then. But a lot of things have changed since I lived there. For example, many of the nice old houses have been pulled down, and new offices have been put there. And the river, the beautiful river, where I went swimming as a boy. That has been polluted by the factories that were built there a few years ago.

Mrs Croft: Yes, I've heard about that. Terrible, isn't it? I've also heard that a new road has been built.

Mr Woodthorpe: That's right. It goes to the motorway. Now, some people think that's a good thing, because travel has been improved, but I don't. The traffic in Newstead is very heavy now.

Mrs Croft: Let's hope that the new road will at least be good for all the shops.

Mr Woodthorpe: I don't think it will. Newstead is very noisy and dirty now. No one wants to live there any more. Some of the shops have already closed. Also, a lot of trees were cut down for the new road and that wasn't very good for the air. It's terrible what is done to so many of our lovely little towns. When you go to Newstead now, everything looks grey and dirty – and cars are parked everywhere.

Mrs Croft: Perhaps a new car park will still be built.

Mr Woodthorpe: I'm sure you're right. And that means that more fields will be destroyed and that will be even worse for the environment. We really must start doing something before it's too late. *(fade)*

Workshop D

A concert in London

Lucy: Hi, Dad! We're back!

Father: Good! So how were the Backstage – um – Brothers, then?

Lucy: The Backstage Boys, Dad. They were fantastic!

Steve: They were terrible! I hate that sort of music.

Lucy: Well, it's better than the rap you listen to. Look at this, Dad, I bought a Backstage Boys T-shirt.

Steve: Guess how much it cost?

Father: £10.99

Steve (surprised): Hey, that's right! How do you know?

Father: It says £10.99 on the back – look. So tell me all about the concert.

Lucy: There were hundreds of fans. I've never seen so many!

Steve: I felt silly. All the girls were screaming their heads off *(mimics hysterical squeals)*. Lucy was the loudest.

Lucy: Well, it was exciting – we couldn't wait! Before they came on stage there was a video about their family. I wanted to buy it after the concert, but my dear brother wouldn't lend me any money.

Steve: I didn't have any more money! Not after I bought you that candle – dear sister.

Father: A candle? What did you want a candle for?

Lucy: Oh, when they sang the slow songs we all held candles. It was so beautiful! Some of the girls started to cry. But I didn't, I just sang.

Steve: Well, I nearly cried. The music was so awful!

Lucy: Shut your mouth, Steve!

Father: Now, Lucy, you're lucky to have a brother like Steve who takes you to concerts.

Lucy: Thanks for paying for us, Dad. It was a lovely birthday present. And thanks for coming with me, Steve.

Steve: That's OK, Lucy.

Lucy: Um, Steve?

Steve (warily): Yes?

Lucy: There's another Backstage Boys concert soon. I thought – maybe, well, do you think you could ...?

Steve: No, I couldn't.

Unit 5

The lifeboat service

Lifeboatman:

I'm Jack Miller. I'm a newsagent. I live near the coast and I have been a lifeboatman for a long time. And, you know, if I were young again, I would do the same thing. I would join the service again. Rescues can be very exciting, and I've always liked helping people.

You know, people sometimes do really silly things. Boat trips have to be planned, but people don't know how to do that or what to take – like lifejackets, something to eat and drink and a warm sweatshirt. They just jump into a boat and row out to sea. They don't worry about the weather. It can change quite suddenly. It can be sunny one minute and stormy the next. Well, if the sea becomes rough, a small boat can be turned over very easily. And then they can be in big trouble, and we have to go out and help them. The boat should also be checked first. Sometimes boats aren't used for a long time – and then people just go out in them. They can have some bad surprises that way. And another thing, if I wanted to go out, I would always tell somebody about it. Then if I'm not back later, they can get help.

And, you know, if I couldn't swim, I would never go out in a boat. But people just aren't careful. They don't think that anything can happen to them, but that's not true. The sea can be very dangerous.

Even if you don't go out in a boat, you can be trapped on a beach when the tide comes in. Last year that happened to a lady – but she was very lucky. You see, she had one of those little telephones you can take with you, and she just called us and asked for help, and we sent out a helicopter to rescue her. That was all. Saved by technology.

But we've had some very difficult rescues, too. One time ... *(fade)*

Alphabetische Wortliste

In dieser alphabetischen Wortliste ist das Vokabular von *Green Line New 1, 2* und *3* enthalten. Namen werden in einer gesonderten Liste nach dem Vokabular aufgeführt.

Der Wortschatz aus Übungen und Texten, die in Spitzklammern ⟨ ⟩ stehen, ist wahlfrei. Die Liste enthält den wahlfreien Wortschatz aus *Green Line New 3*. Das Zeichen * nach einem Verb bedeutet: unregelmäßiges Verb.

Die mit einem ° gekennzeichneten Wörter zeichnen den rezeptiven Wortschatz aus. In Bundesländern, in denen nicht ausdrücklich rezeptiver Wortschatz verlangt wird, werden diese Wörter genauso behandelt wie der übrige Wortschatz. Die rezeptiv gekennzeichneten Wörter können innerhalb der *Unit*, in der sie erstmalig vorkommen, eigenständig von den Schülerinnen und Schülern angewandt werden. Falls sie in späteren *Units* auftauchen, werden sie nur mit Hilfe von Vorgaben verlangt.

Die Zahlen verweisen auf das erstmalige Vorkommen der Wörter, z. B.
again I 2D 33 = Band 1, Unit 2, Step D (Text), Seite 33
ago II 4A 33b) = Band 2, Unit 4, Step A, Seite 33, Text b)
to **answer** I 6C 70,3 = Band 1, Unit 6, Step C, Seite 70, Übung 3
about III WSD3 77,3 = Band 3, Workshop D, Teil 3, Seite 77, Übung 3

A

'A' level III 2A 33,2
a I LS2 9,d)
to be **able to** II 8B 73
about I 2C 35,2
 to talk about I 2C 35,2
 to write about I 2D 37,3
 What about …? I 2D 37,5
about III WSD3 77,3
above II 5A 42
accent III WSA2 9,4
accident I 7 77
across III 1C 22
to **act** *sich verhalten* III 1C 23; *spielen, nachspielen* °I 3C 45,5
to **act normal** III 1C 23
action °II 9B 81
activity I 4UK 53
actor II 5D 49
AD °III 3B 50
to **add** II 5D 49
address II 7A 63
adjective II 3A 25
adult II 5UK 47
adventure II 2A 15
adverb II 9B 83,8
advice (*no pl*) III 2C 40,1
to **affect** ⟨III WSC2 59,3⟩
African °III 1A 16,3
after I 6B 68
 after all III 2C 40,2
 after a time II 7D 67
afternoon I 2B 32,b)
afterwards III 1C 22
again I 1B 23,5
against III 2C 40,2
age II 2C 20
 the Middle Ages II 2C 20
travel **agent's** II 7A 63
ago II 4A 33
 a long time ago II 7B 65
to **agree** III 1B 20,2
Ain't no route. ⟨III 4C 72,7⟩
 Ain't no use setting out for the bad companion. ⟨III 4C 72,7⟩
 Ain't nobody get the better of you-know-who. ⟨III 4C 72,7⟩
 Ain't nobody know … ⟨III 4C 72,7⟩

I ain't gonna lose. ⟨III WSB3 29,3⟩
air III 4A 64
 air stream travel °III 4C 69
airport I 3A 40,a)
alive III WSA1 7
all *alle/alles* I 2D 37,5; *ganz, völlig* I 5A 58
 all over I 6D 74
 all right II 4D 39
to be **allowed to** II 8B 74,a)
almost II 6B 53
alone II 3D 31
along I 1C 23
alphabet I 4A 49
alphabetical II 4A 33,2
already I 10D 111
although II 7D 67
always I 6B 69,b)
ambulance °I 7UK 82
American II 3A 25,1
an I 1C 26,a)
and I LS2 8,b)
 and so on II 5D 50
angry I 4D 55
animal I 9B 100,3
anorak I 5C 62,6
another I 5D 64
answer I LS4 12,3
 answering machine III WSA3 10,1
to **answer** I 7D 84
any I 6C 73,b)
anybody II 5B 45
anyone II 5D 49
anything I 6C 73,a)
anyway II 3B 26
anywhere II 5B 45
to **appear** III 2C 40,2
appendix II 8D 76
apple I 1C 26,a)
April I 5A 58,1
area III 3A 46,4
arm I 6C 72
army III 1A 19,9
around II 2UK 19
arrangement °III 2B 38,11
to **arrive** °I 8UK 91,2
arrow II 2A 15
Art II 1A 8
article III WSB5 31

as *in der Rolle von, als* II 4B 34; *während* II 9D 87
 as … as II 3B 26
 as soon as II 2C 20
ashore ⟨III 5B 83,9⟩
to **ask** I 1B 24
 to ask for I 3A 40,3
assembly I 6UK 71
Assembly Hall II 10D 95
assembly line °III 4C 69
assistant I 2A 31,a)
 shop assistant I 7A 77,b)
 vet's assistant I 2A 31,a)
at *an* I LS2 9,c); *beim Arzt* II 8C 75; *um (bei Zeitangaben)* I 3C 44
 at first II 2B 17
 at home I 1 21
 at last I 10B 108
 at least II 8D 76
 at lunchtime II 1C 11
 at night II 9A 80
 at once I 1D 12
 at the bottom of I 10B 108
 at the top of … I 2D 36
athletics III WSB1 26,1
attraction °III 1A 14
August I 5A 58,1
aunt I 3A 40,c)
 aunty I 3B 41
author III WSC3 60,1
autograph II 5B 46
autumn I 9C 102
away I 10A 106

B

baby I 9D 103
 to have a baby III 4C 69
babysitting II 9D 88,2
back *hintere/hinterer/hinteres, Hinter-* III 2B 36; *zurück* I 5D 64
 back door I 7D 84
bad I 1B 24
badminton I 4UK 53,3
bag I LS3 10,a)
bagpipes II 7B 65
ball I LS3 10,1

banana I LS3 10,1
band II 10A 90
   brass band II 10A 90
bank I 2A 31,a)
   bank clerk I 2A 31,a)
bar I 6C 73,a)
to bark I 8D 95
bat III WSB3 29
bath I 5UK 63,1
   bubble bath I 6D 74
   to have a bath I 5UK 63,1
bathroom I 5UK 63
battle III 1A 19,9
BC °III 3B 50
to be* I LS8 18
   to be able to II 8B 73
   to be allowed to II 8B 74,a)
   to be annoyed III 2C 40,2
   to be called II 2UK 19
   to be careful I 2D 36
   to be excited I 10B 108
   to be excused ⟨III 2A 33,4⟩
   to be finished °I 9D 103
   to be fun I 6B 70
   to be going to I 10B 107
   to be good at … I 4D 55
   to be in a hurry III 2C 40,2
   to be in use ⟨III WSC2 59,3⟩
   to be into s.th. III 5A 78,2
   to be lucky I 3B 41
   to be on I 4B 50
   to be pleased with III 2A 34,6
   to be quiet I LS8 18
   to be right II 7D 67
   to be scared of II 2B 17
   to be sure I LS7 16,a)
   to be surprised °I 10D 111
   to be tired of s.th. III 1B 21
beach I 8A 88
bean II 6A 52
bear II 9UK 84
beard II 4A 33
beautiful II 7UK 62
because I 8B 90
to become* III 1A 19,9
bed I 1A 21,b)
   B&B (= bed and breakfast) III 3A 45,1
   bed and breakfast place II 7A 63
   to get out of bed on the wrong side II 10D 95
bedroom I 5UK 63
beef II 6A 52
   roast beef II 6A 52
beetle I 6C 72,2
before *bevor* II 2C 20; *vor (zeitlich)* I 5C 61,a)
to begin* II 1A 7,2
beginning II 2D 22,2
behind I 5C 60
   from behind II 3D 30
Belgian III WSA1 7,2
to believe III 3C 53
bell °III 2C 41
bench III WSB5 31
to bend* III 1C 22
   to bend down II 9D 87
best °I 5C 61,b)
best of all °I 10B 108
better °I 7C 83
   Ain't nobody get the better of you-know-who. ⟨III 4C 72,7⟩
between I 5C 60
big I 1A 21,b)

Big Wheel II 3C 28,5
bike I 1D 28
biology III 4C 69
bird II 1C 11
   bird watcher II 1C 11
biro I LS3 10,2
birthday I 5 58
biscuit I 1A 21,a)
   dog biscuit I 1A 21,a)
bit III 1A 14
   a bit I 7C 83
black I 2A 31,b)
blood III 5A 78,2
to blow* III WSC1 56
blue I 2A 31,b)
blues ⟨III WSC1 56⟩
board III WSB2 27,3
   notice board II 1B 9
boarding school III 2A 33,2
boat °I 8A 88
boating lake I 8A 88
body I 6C 72,2
book I LS3 10,1
   bookshop II 6B 55,5
   exercise book II 2D 22,3
to book III WSA3 11,4
border °III WSC2 58,1
boring I 4A 49
She was born … III 1A 16,3
both II 1A 8,5
to bother s.o. II 10D 95
bottle I 6C 73,4
   bottle bank °III 4B 66
at the bottom of I 10B 108
bow II 2A 15
I've taken my bows. ⟨III WSB3 29,3⟩
box I 2B 32,a)
   lunch box I 2B 32,a)
boy I LS4 12,a)
boyfriend °III WSD1 75,2
brain ⟨III 2A 33,4⟩
brainstorming III WSD1 75,5
brass band II 10A 90
brave III 5C 85
bread I 3C 45,4
break II 1A 8
to break* II 8A 71,1
   to break a horse ⟨III WSC3 60,1⟩
   to break into s.th. ⟨III 5B 83,9⟩
breakable III WSB5 31,4
breakfast I 6B 68
   to have breakfast II 9B 81
brick ⟨III WSC3 60,1⟩
bridge III 1A 14
fire brigade I 7UK 82
bring-and-buy sale II 10A 90
to bring* II 6A 52,2
   to bring here °I LS8 18
British I 3A 40,c)
brochure II 7UK 62
broke-up ⟨III 5B 83,9⟩
broken I 1C 26,a)
brother I 1A 21,a)
brown I 2A 31,b)
bubble bath I 6D 74
bucket °I 8C 92
budgie II 9A 80
to build* III 1A 19
bulldozer °III 4B 65
bully II 1D 12
to bully II 10D 96,3
burglar °I 7D 85,2
to burn* III WSC2 58,1

bus I 3C 44
   bus shelter III WSA4 12,2
   bus stop I 10D 111
busy II 5B 44,3
but I 1A 21,a)
butter I 3C 45,4
to buy* I 5C 60
by I 3UK 43
by heart II 4C 38

C

cabbage II 6A 52
cage II 9A 80
cake I 5B 59,a)
   fruit cake I 7D 69,4
calf, calves (*pl*) I 9A 98
call III WSA3 10,1
   to make a call III WSA3 10,1
to call *nennen* III WSA2 8; *rufen, anrufen* I 7UK 82
   to be called II 2UK 19
calm III 5A 78
camcorder II 9B 81
camera I 3D 46
camp °III 3A 45,1
to go camping I 10A 106
can I 3B 41
   Can't buy me love. ⟨III 2C 41,6⟩
to cancel °III WSA3 11,4
candle I 5D 64
canteen I 6UK 71
capital III 3A 45,1
capital letter III WSD3 77,1
captain ⟨III 5B 83,9⟩
car I 1A 21,b)
   car park II 5A 42
   car wash II 10UK 92
   multi-storey car park °III 4C 72,8
caravan I 10A 106
card I 7C 83,3
to care for ⟨III 2C 41,6⟩
to be careful I 2D 36
carefully II 9D 87
careless III WSB5 31
carnival °III 1A 14
carrot II 6A 52
to carry II 10D 95
cartoon III 4C 72,8
case III 2B 36
   pencil case I 2A 31,b)
cassette III 3A 25,1
castle °I 8C 92
cat I 2A 31,a)
to catch* II 2A 15
   to catch up with s.o. III 1C 23
cathedral III 1A 14
to cause III 4A 64
'cause (= because) ⟨III WSB3 29,3⟩
cave II 2UK 19
CD I 1B 22,b)
   CD player I 1B 22,a)
Celtic °III 3B 50
centre I 3C 44
   city centre I 3C 44
   shopping centre II 5A 42
   sports centre II 1C 11
century °III 3A 45,1
certificate °III 2A 33,2
chair I LS5 14
challenge ⟨III WSB3 29,3⟩

champion II 8A 71
chance III 2B 36
change III WSC3 60,1
to change (sich) ändern,
　　verändern II 7D 67; umsteigen,
　　wechseln III 1A 18,7
changeable III WSB5 31,4
changing room III WSB3 29,2
character I 8C 93,3
charity II 10A 90
cheap II 3A 25
to check °I LS9 20
to check in III WSA3 11,4
checklist III 1C 24,4
cheer III 3C 53
Cheer up! III 1C 22
cheese I 3C 45
chemist's II 8C 75
chicken I 9A 98
child, children (pl) I 2A 31,a)
Chinese II 6A 52
chips I 6A 67,a)
chocolate I LS7 16,a)
choice III 3B 49
choir °III 3A 45,1
to choose* II 6UK 58
chorus ⟨III 4C 72,7⟩
Christmas II 4A 33
　　Christmas Day III 1A 19,9
church °I 10C 109,1
cinema I 10C 109,1
circus III 1A 14
city I 3C 44
　　city centre I 3C 44
　　City Information Centre I 10C 109
to clap II 4D 39
class I LS3 11,8
classroom I LS4 13,c)
clause °III 2B 37,6
to clean II 6D 59
clean II 4A 33
clear III WSD3 77,2
clerk I 2A 31,a)
　　bank clerk I 2A 31,a)
clever I 1B 24
to click on s.th. °III WSD1 75,2
cliff III 5A 78
to climb up I 7D 85,2
climbing II 1C 11
clock II 5A 42
to close I 7D 84
close to III 5A 78
closed II 9A 80
clothes (pl) I 5C 62,6
cloud II 10D 95
clown °III 1B 21
club II 1C 11
clue III 2C 40,2
to co-ordinate ⟨III 5C 84,1⟩
coach II 7A 63
coal III 3A 45,1
coast III 1A 19,9
coastguard III 5A 78
coat II 2D 21
coconut II 3C 28,5
　　coconut shy °II 3C 28,5
coffee II 6C 57,1
　　coffee shop II 5A 43
cold I 4C 54
to have a cold III WSC1 56
to collect abholen °I 6B 69,a); sammeln,
　　einsammeln I 9A 98
colour I 2A 31,b)

to colour in I 2A 31,3
colourful III WSD1 74,1
to come* I 3B 42,b)
　　Come on. I 2D 36
　　to come in I 4B 51
　　to come off II 4D 39
comic I LS8 18
comma III WSD3 77,1
comment III 2A 34,6
to commit a crime ⟨III WSB3 29,3⟩
to compare II 3B 26,2
to compete in s.th. III WSB1 26,1
competition I 6A 67,a)
complete III WSC1 56,1
to complete II 5B 46,9
compound II 5B 45,4
comprehensive school °III 2A 33,2
computer I 1B 22,b)
to concentrate III WSB4 30,b)
concert II 10A 90
conditional °III 5B 81,3
conference III 2A 32
Congratulations! ⟨III WSD3 77,4⟩
conjunction II 7D 69,5
to conquer III 3A 45,1
to consider ⟨III WSB3 29,3⟩
constable ⟨III 5B 83,9⟩
context III WSB1 26,2
to cook II 6A 52
copy III 4A 64
to copy III 1C 23
corner II 5B 44
cornflakes I 6B 69,a)
correct II 9B 83,8
to correct I LS8 19,1
corridor II 1D 12
to cost I 8C 94
costume II 4A 33
cottage I 10A 106
could II 2B 18
to count I 4A 49
counter °I 5C 60
country II 10UK 92
countryside III 3A 45,1
course III 2A 32
　　of course I 4A 49
court °III WSB1 26,1
cousin I 3A 40,c)
to cover ⟨III 3B 50,8⟩
cow I 9A 98
crab I 8B 90
Crash! III 3D 30
crayon I 2A 31,b)
crazy I LS3 10,a)
cream II 6D 59
creature ⟨III 2B 37,8⟩
crew °III 5B 82
cricket I 4UK 53
crisps (pl) I 6A 67,a)
critic ⟨III WSC2 58,1⟩
Croak! I 1D 28
to cross III 1C 22
crossing III WSA1 7
crowd II 2D 22
crown °III 1B 21
　　They are crowned. °III 1A 17,5
to cry III 2C 40,2
cup Pokal, Becher III WSB2 28,6;
　　Tasse II 6C 57,1
cupboard II 4A 33
curry II 6D 59
curtain ⟨III WSB3 29,3⟩
　　I've taken my curtain

calls. ⟨III WSB3 29,3⟩
customer II 5B 44,1
to cut* II 6B 53
　　to cut down III 4B 65
　　to cut out II 8A 71,2
to cycle III WSA4 12,2
cyclist III 1C 22

D

dad I 1A 21,a)
to damage III 4B 65
to dance III 1B 20
dancer III WSB5 31,3
danger III 3C 53
dangerous II 7B 65,3
Danish III WSA1 7,2
darling ⟨III 5B 82,6⟩
date II 1C 11
daughter II 4B 36
day I 5A 58,2
　　in those days II 2C 20
　　one day ⟨III WSA5 13,3⟩
　　the day after tomorrow II 7C 66
　　the day before yesterday II 7B 65
Day Rider Ticket °I 10 110
dead °I 9D 103
dear I 5A 58
　　Oh dear! I 4D 55
December I 5A 58,1
to decide III WSC1 56
deck III WSA2 8
　　on deck III WSA2 8
deep II 7C 66
to defend s.th./s.o. III WSC1 56
definition III 2C 42,8
department store II 5A 42
to describe II 3C 29,6
description III 5A 79,3
desk I LS4 13,c)
to destroy III 4A 64,3
detail II 1C 11
detention °III 2A 32,1
to dial III 5C 84,1
dialogue °I 2C 35,1
diamond ⟨III 2C 41,6⟩
diary °II 7B 64
dice I 6C 72,2
dictionary II 6B 55,5
to die °I 9D 103
diet ⟨III 5D 87,4⟩
difference III WSA2 9,3
different I 7UK 82,3
　　in different ways II 10UK 92
difficult II 3B 27
dining-room I 9B 100
dinner III 2C 40,2
　　dinner lady °III 2C 40,2
dirty I 6C 72
disappointed III 1A 17
disco II 10UK 92
to dive III WSB3 29,2
to divide III WSA4 12,3
to do* I 3B 41
　　to do the washing-up I 6B 70
　　to do well III 2A 34,6
doctor I 7UK 82,2
　　at the doctor's II 8C 75
the dodgems II 3A 25
dog I LS2 8,b)
　　dog biscuit I 1A 21,a)
　　dog-free I 8B 89

door I 4B 51
　back door I 7D 84
　front door I 7D 84
double I 1C 27,7
　double decker bus III 1A 14
down I 10B 108
downstairs I 5UK 63
downward ⟨III WSC3 60,1⟩
dragon ⟨III WSA5 13,3⟩;
　°III WSD1 74,1
drama °I 6UK 71
to draw* I 2A 31,3
dream II 2B 18
dress II 4A 33
to drink* I 9B 99
to drive* I 9D 101
driver I 7UK 82,2
driving licence ⟨III 4B 68,9⟩
driving rain ⟨III 4C 72,7⟩
drop II 10D 95
to drop II 6D 59
to drown II 9D 87
dry II 10D 95
duck I 8D 95
dues (pl) ⟨III WSB3 29,3⟩
during II 10A 90
Dutch III WSA1 7

E

e-mail (= electronic mail) °III 2A 33,2
each II 2D 23,9
each other III WSB4 30,a)
eagle ⟨III WSC3 60,1⟩
ear II 8A 71,2
early I 6B 69,a)
earth II 5D 49
　What on earth ...? II 5D 49
east II 7UK 62
eastbound °III 1A 18,6
Easter II 7A 63
easy I LS6 15,3
to eat* I 8A 88
egg I 1C 26,a)
Egyptian III 1A 15
elephant II 9UK 84
else °I 6C 73,a)
emergency III 5C 84,1
emperor ⟨III WSC1 56⟩
empire ⟨III WSC1 56⟩
empty I 9B 99
end °I 6D 74
　in the end II 7B 64
ending °I 7D 85,2
enemy II 2A 15
energy III 4A 64,3
engine III 5C 84,2
English I LS3 10,2
　in English I LS3 10,2
to enjoy II 7UK 62
enough I 9B 99
to enter III 4C 69
environment III 4A 62
escalator II 5A 42
escape II 9C 85
to escape II 9C 85
especially III WSD1 74,1
etc °III WSD1 75,5
even II 10UK 92
　even more II 4D 39
evening I 4C 54

in the evening I 4C 54
event °III WSB2 27,3
ever II 7B 65
every I 6B 68
on every hand ⟨III 3B 50,8⟩
everyday life III WSC3 60,1
everyone I 5D 64
everything I 2B 34,9
everywhere II 5D 49
exam III 2A 33,2
to examine °I 9D 103
example I LS7 17,3
　for example I 2B 32,2
exchange visit III 1A 16
to be excited I 10B 108
excitedly II 9D 87
exciting I 4B 51
to excuse I 10C 109
　Excuse me. I 10C 109
exercise I 4E 57,2
　exercise book II 2D 22,3
exile ⟨III WSC3 60,1⟩
to exist III 3B 50
to expect III WSC1 56,1
expensive II 3A 25
experience III WSA4 12
experiment III 2A 34,6
to explain II 6D 60,2
express III WSB2 27
expression III 4C 70,4
extra °I 6D 74
　extra-ordinary ⟨III 5A 79,5⟩
eye I 6C 72

F

face II 4D 39
　face to face III WSA3 10,1
　pointed face ⟨III WSC3 60,1⟩
fact III WSB2 27,2
factory III 3A 45,1
fair II 2UK 19
to fall* °I 6D 74
　to fall off s.th. III 1C 22
　to fall over II 9B 81
false III WSC2 58,1
fame ⟨III WSB3 29,3⟩
family I 2A 31,a)
famous II 3A 25
fan II 1C 11
fantastic II 5B 44
fantasy III 2B 38,12
far I 10C 109
farm I 9 98
farmer III 3B 49,6
fast II 9B 83
fat I 9B 99
father I 1A 21,a)
favourite I 5C 61,b)
feature ⟨III WSC2 59,3⟩
February I 5A 58
to feed* I 9A 98
to feel* I 7C 83
　to feel sorry for s.o. III WSC3 61,3
　to feel well II 8B 72
feeler I 6C 72,2
feeling III 3C 54,1
ferry °I 3UK 43
festival °III 1A 16,3
to fetch III 3C 53
fete II 9D 88

fever ⟨III 5A 78⟩
a few II 10UK 92
field III WSC2 58,1
to fight* III 1A 19,9
to fill in s.th. III 1B 21,4
film II 2A 15
to film II 9B 81
to find* I LS3 10,3
　to find out II 5A 43,3
to be fine II 4B 34
finger II 8A 71,2
to finish I 6B 68
　to be finished °I 9D 103
fire brigade I 7UK 82
fireman I 7UK 82,2
firm I 7D 84
first erste/erster/erstes I 5A 58;
　zuerst I 9B 101
fish I 7D 84
　fish finger I 7D 84
　fish tank II 9A 80
to fish III 3B 49
fisherman III 5B 80,2
flame ⟨III WSC2 58,1⟩
red flare ⟨III 5C 84,1⟩
flat flach III 5A 78; Wohnung I 1UK 25,2
flaw ⟨III 3B 50,8⟩
flight III 1A 16
floor Boden, Fußboden I 4D 55;
　Stockwerk II 5A 42
flower III 2B 38,11
flowerpot I 4D 55
fly III 1B 21
to fly* II 9A 80
folder I LS3 10,1
to follow III 3C 52
food I 10A 106
　Food Court II 5A 42
foot I 10D 111
　to go on foot I 10D 111
football I 1B 22,a)
for I 1D 28
　for example I 2B 32,2
　for sale II 9D 87
weather forecast II 7C 66
forest II 2A 15
to forget* II 4B 34
fork II 6D 59
form I 6B 69,3
formal °III WSA2 8,1
fort °III WSC2 58,1
fortune ⟨III WSB3 29,3⟩
Frankly, ... ⟨III WSD2 76,5⟩
free frei I 4 49; gratis III 2C 40,2
　free time I 4 49
freedom III 4C 69
French °I 10A 106
Friday I 5C 61,b)
friend I LS2 9,d)
friendly II 3D 31
frightening II 4A 33
frog I 1D 28
from I LS2 8,a)
　from behind II 3D 30
　from ... to von ... bis I 3C 44,1; von ...
　nach I 3UK 43,2
front III 1C 22
　front door I 7D 84
　front seat II 10D 95
　in front of I 5B 59,a)
fruit (sg/pl) II 6A 52
　fruit cake II 7D 69,4
frying pan ⟨III 3B 50,8⟩

full III WSA4 12,1
  full of II 1D 12
fun I 4C 54
  great fun II 10A 90
  to be fun I 6B 70
  to have fun I 4C 54
to **function** °III WSC2 59,3
funny I LS2 8,b)
future II 4D 40,4

G

gallows II 2D 21
game I LS5 14,2
garage I 4D 55
garden I 1B 23,b)
GCSE (= General Certificate of Secondary Education) °III 2A 33,2
general °III 2A 33,2
Geography II 1A 8
German I LS4 12,b)
gerund °III 1B 20,1
to **get*** *bekommen* I 4B 52; *fangen, auffangen* I 4D 55; *holen, erwischen* II 2D 36
  Get out! I 6C 72
  Get well. I 7C 83,1
  to get better III 2A 34,6
  to get drunk ⟨III 5B 83,9⟩
  to get into trouble III 2B 36
  to get lost °I 8D 95
  to get off I 10D 111
  to get on I 8A 88
  to get out of bed on the wrong side II 10D 95
  to get rid of s.th. III 2B 36
  to get s.th. right III WSC2 59,2
  to get stuck °I 7D 85,2
  to get the gist °III WSC2 58,1
  to get there I 3UK 43
  to get up I 6B 68
  to get ... ready I 4B 51
ghost II 3A 25
  ghost train II 3A 25
girl I LS3 11,b)
to **get the gist** °III WSC2 58,1
to **give*** I 3B 42,a)
  to give a talk III WSA4 12
  to give away II 10A 90,2
  to give s.th. up III 4A 64,3
glad I 8D 95
glass II 6C 57,1
go II 3C 28,1
  a go II 3C 28,1
  to have a go II 3C 28,1
to **go*** I 3B 41,3
  Go away! II 8A 71
  to go camping °I 10A 106
  to go crazy III WSA2 8
  to go for a walk I 4C 54
  to go home I 5C 62,7
  to go inside III 1C 22
  to go on I LS2 9,5
  to go on foot I 10D 111
  to go on for II 2UK 19
  to go out for a meal III 1B 21
  to go sight-seeing III 1A 19
  to go swimming I 8A 88
  to go to I 3B 41,3
  to go to the shops I 6B 70
  to go with III 3A 45,1

to go wrong *schief gehen* II 3D 30; *sich verfahren* II 7B 64
goal I 4D 55
goalkeeper °III WSB1 26,1
God III 4C 69
to be **going to** I 10B 107
gold III WSC1 57
golf III 3B 49
Gonna keep on driving. ⟨III 4C 72,7⟩
good I LS3 10,a)
  Good morning. I LS4 12,a)
  to be good at ... I 4D 55
Goodbye. I LS3 10,a)
goose, geese (*pl*) II 2UK 19
Gosh! II 9B 81
have **got** I 1B 23,a)
Got a bead on you. ⟨III 4C 72,7⟩
graffiti III 2B 36
grammar school III 2A 33,2
grandma I 7B 81
grandpa I 9A 98
graphics (*pl*) °III WSD1 74
great I LS2 9,c)
  great big II 9C 86,6
  great fun II 10A 90
  great uncle II 5D 49
Greek I 3A 40,3
green I 2A 31,b)
ground III WSB5 31
group I LS2 9,c)
  youth group II 10UK 92
to **grow*** II 6A 52
grumpy II 10D 95
guard III 1A 19
to **guess** III WSB1 26,2
guest I 9A 98
  guest house I 9A 98
guitar I 3B 42,b)
gym (= gymnasium) III WSB1 26,1

H

hair (*sg/pl*) II 5D 49
haircut II 5D 49
half II 10A 90
  half an hour II 5D 49
  half past (eleven) I 3A 40,b)
hall °I 5UK 63
ham I 3C 45
hammer ⟨III 3B 50,8⟩
hamster II 9A 80
hand I 6C 72
handle III 3C 52
hangman II 2D 21
to **happen** II 2D 21
happy I 5D 64
hard II 6D 59
hat II 2D 22
to **hate** III 1B 20
to **have*** I 3C 45,5
  have got I 1B 23,a)
  to have a baby III 4C 69
  to have a bath I 5UK 63,1
  to have a go II 3 28
  to have a look I 5D 64
  to have a ride on II 3A 25
  to have breakfast II 9B 81
  to have fun I 4C 54
  to have lunch I 6UK 71
  to have on II 7D 67
  to have to II 8B 72

he I LS2 9,d)
head I 6C 72
headache II 8B 72
heading III WSC2 58,1
headlights (*pl*) ⟨III 4C 72,7⟩
headteacher I 6D 74
healthy I 6A 67,a)
  healthy living I 6A 67,a)
to **hear** I 10C 109,2
heart II 4C 38
  by heart II 4C 38
to **heat** ⟨III 3B 50,8⟩
heather ⟨III WSC1 56⟩
central **heating** ⟨III WSC2 58,1⟩
heavy III 3A 45,1
helicopter III 5B 80
hello I LS1 7
  to say hello to I 7D 84
helmet II 8A 71
help I 7UK 82
to **help** I 3C 45
helper II 8D 76
helpful III WSB5 31
helpless III WSB5 31,2
her *ihr/ihre* I LS4 12,a); *ihr/sie* I 3B 42,a)
here I LS2 8,a)
  Here you are. I 1C 27,5
hers II 8B 74,b)
herself III WSB4 30,a)
Hey! I LS2 9,c)
Hi! I LS2 8,a)
to **hide*** II 1D 12
high II 7C 66
  high jump III WSB1 26,1
hill I 10UK 110
him I 3B 42,a)
himself III WSB4 30,a)
Hindu °III 1A 14
to **hire** II 5UK 47
his *sein/seine* I LS4 12,a); *seine/r/s* II 8B 74,b)
History II 1A 8
to **hit*** II 3D 30
to **hitch a ride** ⟨III 4C 72,7⟩
hobby II 9B 81
hockey I 6UK 71
  hockey stick III WSB3 29
to **hoist up** ⟨III 5B 83,9⟩
to **hold*** II 9D 87
Hold on! III 5C 85
hole I 1B 24
holidays (*pl*) I 10A 106
  on holiday I 10A 106
home I 1UK 25,2
  at home I 1 21
  to go home I 5C 62,7
homework (*no pl*) I LS8 18
hood II 2D 21
to **hope** I 9D 103
horse II 7UK 62
  horse-breeder ⟨III WSC3 60,1⟩
hospital I 7B 79
hot *heiß* I 10B 108; *scharf (gewürzt)* III 1B 21
  hot dog II 3A 25
hotel I 10A 106
hour II 5D 49
  half an hour II 5D 49
house I 1UK 25,1
housekeeper II 4D 39
housework °I 6B 70
hovercraft I 3UK 43
how I LS3 11,b)

How are you? **I 5A** 58
How many? **I 8C** 94
How much? **I 6A** 67,a)
however **III 1A** 19,9
huge **III 3A** 46,5
human **III 4C** 69,3
the human race ⟨**III WSB3** 29,3⟩
Humanities (*pl*) **II 1A** 8
hungry **I 1A** 21,a)
hunter ⟨**III WSC3** 60,1⟩
to **hurry** **II 7D** 68
Hurry up! **III 1C** 22
to **hurt*** *verletzen* **II 7D** 67; *weh tun, schmerzen* **I 7C** 83
husband **III 1C** 23
hut ⟨**III WSC1** 57,2⟩

I

I **I LS1** 7
ice cream **I 7D** 84
ice rink **II 5UK** 47
idea **I 1B** 24
idiot **II 2D** 22
if **II 4B** 35
ill **II 4C** 38
to **imagine** **III WSA1** 7,1
important **II 3A** 25
to **improve** **III 4B** 66
in **I LS1** 7
  in different ways **II 10UK** 92
  in front of **I 5B** 59,a)
  in my opinion **III WSD1** 75,2
  in the end **II 7B** 64
  in the evening **I 4C** 54
  in the middle of **II 5A** 42
  in those days **II 2C** 20
  in time **II 6D** 59
Indian **II 6UK** 58
industry **III 3A** 45,1
infinitive **II 6B** 54,3
to **inform s.o. about s.th** **III 5B** 82
information (*sg/pl*) **II 4C** 38,2
to **injure** **III 4B** 66
inn **III 3C** 52
inside *drinnen* **I 2D** 36; *hinein, in(nerhalb von)* **III 3A** 46,5
instead of **III 4B** 66
instructions (*pl*) **III 5B** 82,6
instrument **III 3B** 48,4
interest in s.th. **III 2A** 34,6
to be **interested in s.th.** **III 1B** 21
interesting **II 3B** 27
international **III WSA1** 7
to **interview s.o.** **III 3B** 48,4
into **I 5D** 65,3
introduction **III WSD1** 74,1
to **invade** **III 3B** 50
invitation **I 5B** 59,a)
to **invite** **II 6B** 53,1
Irish **III WSA2** 9,3
iron ⟨**III 3B** 50,8⟩
irregular **I 6B** 69,3
is **I LS1** 7
island **II 7UK** 62
it *er/sie/es* **I LS5** 14,a); *es/ihn/sie/ihm/ihr* **I 4B** 52
Italian °**I 3A** 40,3
its *sein/seine, ihr/ihre* **I 2B** 32,b); *seine/r/s, ihr/e* **II 8B** 74,b)
itself **III WSB** 30

J

jacket **II 4A** 33
January **I 5A** 58
Japanese °**III 4C** 69
jazz dance **III WSB1** 26,1
jealous of s.th/s.o. **III 2C** 41
jeans **I 5C** 62,6
job **I 4B** 51
to **jog** °**III WSB1** 26,1
to **join** **II 1C** 11
joke °**I 7B** 79
July **I 5A** 58,1
jump **II 10D** 96,3
to **jump** **I 3D** 30
June **I 5A** 58,1
junior **II 1B** 9
just **I 4B** 51
  just the thing **II 10B** 91
  just then **II 10D** 95

K

to **keep*** **II 9A** 80
  to keep on doing s.th. ⟨**III WSB3** 29,3⟩
key **III WSA4** 12
to **kick** °**I 4D** 55
kid **III 5C** 84,2
to **kill** **II 6A** 52
kilo **III WSB2** 27
kilt **II 7B** 65
kind **II 6UK** 58
king **III 1A** 17,5
kingdom **III 3C** 52
kitchen **I 1A** 21,a)
kite **I 4A** 49
knee **II 8A** 71,2
knife, knives (*pl*) **I 2B** 32,a)
knight °**III 3B** 51,10
to **know*** **I 7A** 77,b)
  Ain't nobody know … ⟨**III 4C** 72,7⟩
knuckle **II 3C** 28,5
  white knuckle ride **II 3C** 28,5

L

lace **II 5UK** 47
lad ⟨**III 3B** 50,8⟩
ladder **I 7D** 84
lady **II 8D** 76
lake **I 8A** 88
lamb **I 9A** 98
land **III 3B** 50
to **land** **III 1A** 16,2
language **III WSA1** 7,2
last **I 4A** 49
  at last **I 10B** 108
late **I LS3** 10,a)
  to work late **I 4B** 51
Latin ⟨**III WSC2** 58,1⟩
laugh **II 4B** 34
to **laugh** **I 4D** 55
  to laugh at **II 3D** 30
law **III 4B** 66
to **lay*** **I 9A** 98
lazy **III 2A** 34,6
to **lead*** **III WSC2** 58,1
leaflet **II 2A** 15
to **learn*** **I 4B** 50

learner **III WSB5** 31,3
to **leave*** **I 8UK** 91,2
  Leave me alone! **II 3D** 31
  to leave free **III 2B** 38,12
  to leave out **III 5C** 86,4
left **I 10C** 109
  on the left **I 10C** 109,1
leg **I 3D** 46
legion ⟨**III WSC3** 60,1⟩
lemonade **I 6C** 73,b)
to **lend*** **I 6A** 67,a)
lesson **I LS8** 18
to **let*** **II 8A** 71
letter *Brief* **I 5A** 58,a); *Buchstabe* **I 4A** 49
letterbox **I 5C** 60
level °**III WSD1** 74,1
library **III 2A** 32,1
lice (*pl*) ⟨**III WSC1** 56⟩
lie **III 2C** 41
to **lie*** °**I 8D** 95
  to lie down **II 8A** 71
life **II 2C** 20
lifeboat °**III 5A** 78
lifeboatman ⟨**III 5A** 79,5⟩
lifeguard ⟨**III 5C** 84,1⟩
lifejacket °**III 5B** 82,6
lift **II 5A** 42
light *leicht, gering* **III 4A** 63,2; *Licht* **III 4A** 64,3
lightning **II 4D** 39
to **like** **I 7A** 77,b)
  I'd like … **II 5C** 48,1
like **I 1A** 21,b)
  like this **I 3D** 46
limerick ⟨**III 2B** 37,8⟩
line **II 4D** 40,1
lion **II 9UK** 84
lipstick °**III WSD1** 75,2
list **I 5B** 59,1
  shopping list **II 6D** 59
to **listen** **I LS3** 10,4
listening practice **I LS7** 17,5
little **I 1A** 21,b)
a **little** **II 8D** 76
to **live** **I 8B** 90
live **II 7B** 65
living-room **I 2D** 36
local ⟨**III WSC2** 59,3⟩
loch **II 7B** 64
to **lock** **III WSA4** 12
locked **I 7D** 84
lonely **III 5A** 78
long **I 10A** 106
  a long time ago **II 7B** 65
  a long way **II 10UK** 92
look **III 3C** 53
  to have a look **I 5D** 64
to **look** *aussehen* **I 7A** 77,b); *sehen, ansehen* **I LS2** 9,d)
  to look after **II 9D** 88
  to look at **I LS7** 16,b)
  to look down **II 9D** 87
  to look for **I 6B** 70
  to look round **II 5B** 45
to **lose*** **III WSA4** 12
  I ain't gonna lose. ⟨**III WSB3** 29,3⟩
loser ⟨**III WSB3** 29,3⟩
to get **lost** °**I 8D** 95
lots of **III WSA1** 7,2
a **lot of** **I 5C** 61,a)
loud **II 4D** 39
love *alles Liebe, Herzliche Grüße (als Briefschluss)* **I 5A** 58; *Liebe* **I 5A** 58

to love **I 10A** 106
lovely **II 4A** 33
lower **II 5A** 42
luck **III 3C** 52
  What a piece of luck! **III 3C** 52
lucky **I 6D** 74
  to be lucky **I 3B** 41
lunch **I 2B** 32,a)
  lunch box **I 2B** 32,a)
  to have lunch **I 6UK** 71

M

machine **III WSA3** 10,1
  answering machine **III WSA3** 10,1
magazine **I 7A** 77,a)
maiden 〈**III WSC3** 60,1〉
main **III WSC2** 58,1
mainsail 〈**III 5B** 83,9〉
to make* **I LS2** 9,6
  to make a request **I 7D** 86,7
  to make money **II 10UK** 92
  to make s.o. do s.th. 〈**III WSC3** 60,1〉
man, men (*pl*) **I 2A** 31,a)
to man 〈**III WSC2** 59,3〉
many **I 8C** 94
  How many? **I 8C** 94
map **I 3UK** 43
March **I 5A** 58,1
to march 〈**III WSC1** 57,2〉
maritime 〈**III 5C** 84,1〉
mark **III 2A** 33,2
market square **I 10C** 109
mascot **I 6E** 76,5
match **III WSB1** 26,1
to match **II 10C** 93,2
Maths **II 1A** 8
It doesn't matter. **II 5UK** 47
May **I 5A** 58,1
may **I 9B** 99
maybe **I 1B** 23,a)
me **I 3B** 42,a)
meal **II 6A** 52
to mean* **II 5UK** 47,1
meaning **II 9B** 83,9
meat **II 2C** 20
mechanic **I 7A** 77,b)
medal **III 5C** 85
medicine **II 8C** 75
to meet* (*sich*) *kennen lernen*
  III WSA1 7; (*sich*) *treffen* **I 8B** 89
meeting **II 1B** 9
member **II 10A** 90
memory **II 9B** 81,3
to mend **III WSB1** 26,1
mess °**I 6B** 70
message **III WSA3** 10,1
metre **III WSB1** 26,1
middle **II 2C** 20
  in the middle of **II 5A** 42
  the Middle Ages **II 2C** 20
midway 〈**III 4C** 72,7〉
might **III 5C** 85
mile **III 4A** 62
military 〈**III WSC2** 59,3〉
milk **I 3C** 45,4
to milk **III 3B** 49,6
milkman **II 9B** 81
million **III 3A** 45,1
mince **II 6D** 59
mind **III 3A** 46,3

mind map °**III 3A** 46,3
to mind **II 9D** 88
  Never mind. °**I 8A** 88
mine *Bergwerk, Mine* **III 3A** 45,1;
  meine/meiner/meines **II 8B** 74,b)
minute **I 3C** 44
miracle °**III 3C** 52
mirror **II 5D** 50
miserable **II 3D** 30
to miss *vermissen* 〈**III 3B** 50,8〉;
  verpassen **III 3C** 53
missing **III 1C** 24,5
mistake °**II 10D** 96,2
model **III 4C** 69
moment **I 5D** 64
Monday **I 5C** 61,b)
money **I 6A** 67,b)
  pocket money **I 7A** 77,a)
  to make money **II 10UK** 92
monkey **II 9UK** 84
monster °**I LS2** 8,2
month **I 5A** 58
monument 〈**III WSC2** 59,3〉
more **I 1D** 28
  one more **I 5D** 64
morning **I LS4** 12,a)
  Good morning. **I LS4** 12,a)
most **II 2C** 20
  most of them **III 1A** 16,3
mother **I 1A** 21,a)
motorbike **III WSD1** 75,2
motorway **III 4A** 63
mountain **I 10A** 106
  mountain rescue **II 7D** 67
mouse, mice (*pl*) **II 9A** 80
mouth **I 6C** 72
to move *sich bewegen* **III WSB2** 27;
  umziehen **III 3B** 47
Mr **I LS4** 12,b)
Mrs **I LS4** 12,a)
Ms °**III WSB5** 31
much **I 5C** 61,5
  How much? **I 6A** 67,a)
  very much **I 5C** 61,5
muddle **I 2B** 34,9
multi-storey car park °**III 4C** 72,8
mum **I 1B** 24
mummy °**III 1C** 22
murgh **III 1B** 21
museum **I 5UK** 47
music **I 4UK** 53
  pop music **I 4UK** 53
Muslim **III 1A** 16,3
must **I 3B** 42,b)
my **I LS1** 7
myself **III WSB4** 30,a)

N

name **I LS1** 7
nasty **II 8C** 75
national **III WSB2** 27
nationality **I 3E** 48,5
near **I 10A** 106
nearly **II 5B** 45
'neath (= beneath) 〈**III 3B** 50,8〉
to need **I 7A** 77,b)
negative **III WSD3** 77,1
neighbour **I 2B** 34,9
neighbourhood **I 2B** 34
nervous about **II 3D** 30

never **I 6B** 69,b)
  Never mind. °**I 8A** 88
New Year's Day **III 3C** 52
new **I LS2** 8,a)
news (*no pl*) **II 2A** 15
newsagent's **II 1D** 12
newspaper **III WSB5** 31
next **I 3C** 44
  next door **III WSC3** 60,1
  next time **I 6D** 74
  next to **II 5A** 42
nice **I LS2** 9,d)
night **I 9C** 102
  at night **II 9A** 80
nightmare °**III 5C** 84,2
no *kein/keine* **I 4D** 55; *nein* **I LS3** 11,b)
  No, thank you. **I LS8** 18
no-one **III WSC1** 57
nobody **I 4B** 50
to nod 〈**III WSC3** 60,1〉
noise **I 2D** 36
noisy **III 2B** 39,14
non-swimmer **II 5UK** 47
none 〈**III 3B** 50,8〉
normal **III 1C** 23
Norman **III 1A** 19,9
north **II 7UK** 62
northbound °**III 1A** 18,7
nose **II 8A** 71,2
not **I LS3** 10,a)
  not only ... but also **III WSD1** 74,1
  not ... any more **III 4B** 65
  not ... yet **I 1D** 28
note **I 9D** 104,3
nothing **I 2D** 36
notice **II 1B** 9
  notice board **II 1B** 9
to notice **III 1C** 23
noun **II 10D** 96,3
November **I 5A** 58,1
now **I LS3** 10,3
number **I LS3** 11,b)
nurse **II 8B** 74,7
nursery school °**I 6B** 69,a)

O

oak **II 2UK** 19
object **III WSA2** 8
occupation 〈**III WSC2** 59,3〉
at ... o'clock **I 3A** 40,b)
October **I 5A** 58,1
of **I 3C** 45,5
  of course **I 4A** 49
off **II 2D** 22
  Off you go! **II 1D** 12
office **I 7B** 81
police officer **I 7UK** 82,2
official **III 3B** 50
often **I 6B** 69,b)
Oh ... **I LS2** 8,b)
oil **III 5A** 78
  oil rig °**III 5B** 80
OK **I LS4** 12,b)
old **I LS3** 11,b)
on *an* **II 7B** 64; *auf* **I LS5** 14
  on (Radio Nottingham) **I 4B** 51
  on holiday **I 10A** 106
  on the left **I 10C** 109,1
  on the right **I 10C** 109
  on the seventh of ... **I 5B** 59,a)

on the telephone **I 2B** 33,5
on the whole **III WSD1** 74,1
to be on **I 4B** 50
to go on **I LS2** 9,5
to have on **II 7D** 67
one more **I 5D** 64
  one by one **III 5C** 85
  one in five **III 3A** 45,1
only *einzige/einziger/einziges* **II 7D** 67;
nur, erst **I 3D** 46
onto **III 5C** 84,2
open **I 7D** 84
to open **I 7D** 84
operation **II 8D** 76
opinion **III WSD1** 74,1
  in my opinion **III WSD1** 75,2
opponent °**III WSB2** 27
opposite *Gegenteil* **I 4E** 57,1;
gegenüber **II 5A** 42
or **I LS3** 10,5
  or so **II 10D** 95
order **I 6B** 69,4
to organize **II 10UK** 92
other **I 8B** 89,2
otherwise ⟨**III 5C** 84,1⟩
Ouch! **II 8C** 75
our **I LS4** 13,c)
ours **II 8B** 74,b)
ourselves **III WSB4** 30,a)
out **I 4B** 52
  out of **II 1D** 12
  out of the way **II 10D** 95
  out of work **III 3B** 47
outlaw **II 2A** 15
outside *außerhalb von* **III WSC3** 60,1;
draußen **I 2B** 33
over *über* **I 3C** 44,1; *vorbei, zu
Ende* **II 1D** 12
  over there **I 1C** 26,b)
own **III WSA4** 12,3
  children of her own ⟨**III WSC3** 60,1⟩
owner **III 4B** 68,8

P

packed lunch **III 2A** 32,1
packet **I 6A** 67,a)
page **I 1UK** 25,2
to paint **III 1B** 21,5
pair **I LS3** 10,3
palace **III 1A** 14
paper **II 5D** 50,3
paragraph **III WSC2** 58,1
Pardon? **III 1C** 22
parents (*pl*) **I 2B** 33
park **I 1D** 28
  car park **II 5A** 42
to park **III 3B** 49
part **II 2D** 22,6
past participle **II 6B** 54,4
partner **I 1B** 23,4
party **I 5B** 59,a)
to pass (*Gesetze*) *verabschieden;
vorbeigehen an* **III 4B** 66; *reichen,
weitergeben* **I 3C** 45,5
passive °**III 4B** 65,1
past **III 1B** 20
  past participle **II 6B** 54,4
  past progressive **II 9B** 82
  simple past **II 2D** 22,3
past *an ... vorbei* **III WSB2** 27; *nach*

(*bei Uhrzeiten*) **I 3A** 40,b)
path **II 7D** 67
patient **II 8B** 73
to be on patrol ⟨**III 5C** 84,1⟩
to patter down ⟨**III WSC1** 56⟩
to pay* **II 5B** 44
  to pay s.o. back **III 2C** 40,2
PE (= Physical Education) **II 1A** 8
pen **I LS3** 10,a)
pence (= p) **I 6A** 67,a)
pencil **I LS3** 10,1
  pencil case **I 2A** 31,b)
penfriend **III 3B** 47
people (*pl*) **I 3A** 40,a)
present perfect **II 6B** 56,10
perfect **III WSA1** 7,2
person **II 2D** 22,8
personal **III WSC2** 59,3
pet °**I 8D** 95
  pet shop **II 9D** 87
petrol **III 4A** 63
Phew! **III WSA1** 7
to phone **I 3B** 42,a)
photo **I 3UK** 43,3
  to take a photo of **I 3D** 46
phrase **III 4C** 70,4
piano **II 1C** 11
to pick out **III WSC2** 59,3
to pick up **II 6D** 59
picnic °**III WSA4** 12,2
picture **I LS6** 15
  in the picture **I LS6** 15
piece **II 5D** 50,3
  What a piece of luck! **III 3C** 52
pig **I 9A** 98
pigeon **III 1A** 14
pillow **II 4D** 39
pink **II 5D** 49
pint **I 6C** 73,a)
pipe ⟨**III 3B** 50,8⟩
pitch °**III WSB2** 27
pitcher ⟨**III 3B** 50,8⟩
pizza **II 5A** 42
place **I 2B** 32,b)
plan **I 5UK** 63,2
to plan **II 5B** 46,9
plane **I 3A** 40,b)
plastic **III 4A** 64,3
plate **II 6D** 59
play **II 1B** 9
  role play **I 3C** 45,3
to play **I LS5** 14,2
player **II 1C** 11
playground **I LS7** 16,a)
  in the playground **I LS7** 16,a)
please **I LS2** 9,5
to be pleased with **III 2A** 34,6
pleasure cruise ⟨**III WSB3** 29,3⟩
pocket **I 7A** 77,a)
  pocket money **I 7A** 77,a)
pointed face ⟨**III WSC3** 60,1⟩
poison ⟨**III WSC2** 58,1⟩
police **I 7UK** 82
  police officer °**I 7UK** 82,2
Polish **III WSA1** 7,2
polite **II 5C** 48,1
to pollute **III 4A** 64
pollution **III 4A** 64
pond **I 1B** 24
pony **II 9A** 80
pool **II 5UK** 47
poor **I 1D** 28
pop music **I 4UK** 53

popcorn **II 3A** 25
popular **II 3A** 25
porridge **II 7B** 65
possible **III 2C** 41,5
post office **I 5C** 60
postcard **I 5C** 60
poster **I LS2** 9,6
pot ⟨**III 3B** 50,8⟩
potato, potatoes (*pl*) **II 2C** 20
  roast potatoes °**II 6A** 52
pound (= £) **I 6C** 73,a)
pound (= lb) **I 5C** 60
word power **I 1C** 26,2
practice **I LS3** 10,4
  listening practice **I LS7** 17,5
  sound practice **I LS3** 10,4
to practise **I 6B** 56,10
preposition **II 4B** 36,8
prescription **II 8C** 75
present **I 1D** 28
present perfect **II 6B** 56,10
  present perfect progressive °**III 3B** 47,2
simple present **II 3D** 31,2
to pretend **III WSC3** 60,1
pretty **II 4A** 33
primary school **III 2A** 33,2
prince **III 3A** 45,1
prison **III 1A** 17,5
prisoner **II 2D** 21
  to take prisoner **II 2A** 15
prize **I 6A** 67,a)
probably **II 1D** 12
problem **I 1B** 22,c)
professional **II 4UK** 37
programme **II 10UK** 92
progress (*no pl*) **III 2A** 34,6
progressive (form) **II 3D** 31,4
  past progressive **II 9B** 82
project **III 2A** 34,6
promenade **I 8C** 92
to promise **III 2C** 40,2
prompter **II 4A** 33
to protect **III WSC1** 57
to be proud of **II 6D** 60
public **III 4B** 66
  public transport **III 4B** 66
to pull **II 9D** 87
  to pull down **III 4B** 65
pullover **I 5C** 62,6
pump **I 2B** 33
punctuation °**III WSD3** 77,1
pupil **I 6UK** 71
puppet **II 4UK** 37
purse **II 1D** 12
to push **III 2C** 40,2
to put* **II 2D** 36
  to put down **II 9B** 81
  to put in **I 2B** 32,3
  to put the telephone down **II 7D** 68
  to put work into s.th. **III 2A** 34,6
puzzle **I 1B** 24,8

Q

quarter **I 3A** 40,b)
queen **III 1A** 14
question **I LS3** 11,8
  question tag °**III 3B** 51,10
questionnaire **I 7B** 80,7
queue **III 1A** 14
quick **II 1D** 12

quiet I LS8 18
quite III 1C 22
quiz I LS4 12,2

R

rabbit II 9A 80
race I 10D 111
racket III WSB3 29
radio *Funkgerät* III 5B 82,6; *Radio* I 1B 22,a)
railway III 3A 45,1
rain II 10D 95
to rain I 4C 54
rainstorm III WSA4 12,2
rainy III WSA4 12,2
RE (= Religious Education) °II 1A 8
to reach ⟨III WSD3 77,4⟩
to react to s.th. III WSC3 60
to read* I 4A 49
readable III WSB5 31,4
reader III WSB5 31,3
ready I LS3 10,a)
real III 3C 54,4
really I 7C 83,1
reason III 4C 69
rebellion III WSC2 58,1
recipe II 6A 52
recording III WSA2 9,4
to recycle III 4A 64,3
red I 2A 31,b)
reduced in size I 6A 67,b)
referee °III WSB3 29,2
reflexive verb °III WSB4 30,1
refrain ⟨III WSB3 29,3⟩
relative clause III 2B 37,6
   relative pronoun °III 2B 36,4
religion III 1A 19,10
remains (*pl*) °III WSC2 59,4
to remember °I 5A 58,1
to remind s.o. of s.th. III WSC3 61,4
to repair I 4A 49
to repeat III 2A 33,2
   to repeat a year III 2A 33,2
report II 8D 77
request I 7D 86,7
   to make a request I 7D 86,7
rescue III 5C 84
   mountain rescue II 7D 67
to rescue II 7D 68
to rest II 8B 74,a)
restaurant II 5A 42
review III WSD1 74
to revise III WSA1 7,1
rhyme I LS3 11,b)
rhythm II 5C 48,2
rich II 2C 20
That rids me of Rome. ⟨III WSC3 60,1⟩
ride II 3A 25
   to have a ride on II 3A 25
   white knuckle ride II 3C 28,5
to ride* II 7UK 62
rider III WSB5 31,3
riding school II 9A 80
right I LS4 12,b)
   Right? I LS4 12,b)
   to be right II 7D 67
right I 10C 109
   on the right I 10C 109
right away °I 3D 46
ring I 2D 36

to ring* *klingeln* II 6D 59; *läuten* III 2C 41
river II 2C 20
road (= Rd.) I 1UK 25
roadside III 3B 49
roadway ⟨III 4C 72,7⟩
roadworks °III 4A 63
We did roam ... ⟨III 5B 83,9⟩
roast beef II 6A 52
   roast potatoes II 6A 52
rock I 8B 90
role play I 3C 45,3
Roman °III 1A 15
room *Platz* III WSC3 60,1; *Raum, Zimmer* I 1B 22,a)
rope II 2D 21
rose ⟨III WSB3 29,3⟩
rough III 5A 78
round *rund, durch ganz ...* III WSA2 8; *um ... herum* I 4B 52
roundabout *Karussell* II 2C 28,5; *Kreisverkehr* III 4A 63
route III 3B 49
   Ain't no route. ⟨III 4C 72,7⟩
row II 4D 39
to row II 7B 65
royal °III 1A 17,5
rubbish I 8D 95
rugby III WSB1 26,1
rule II 7D 68,2
to run* I 10B 108
   to run off II 3D 30
runner III WSB5 31,3
Russian III WSA1 7,2

S

saddlebag I 2B 33
safe III 2C 41
safety III 5B 82
sail ⟨III 5B 83,9⟩
salad I 3C 45,4
for sale II 9D 87
   bring-and-buy sale II 10A 90
the same I 2D 38,6
sand I 8C 92
sandal ⟨III WSC2 58,1⟩
sandcastle I 8C 92
sandwich I 8D 95
satisfied ⟨III 2C 41,6⟩
Saturday I 4D 55
sauerkraut II 6B 55,6
sausage I 6A 67,a)
to save *retten* I 9D 103; *sparen* I 7A 77,a)
to say* I LS3 10,4
   It says ... III 4A 64
   to say hello to I 7D 84
scared °I 1D 28
   to be scared of II 2B 17
scarf, scarves (*pl*) III 1C 23
scene II 4D 39
   behind the scenes II 4D 39
school I LS2 9,c)
   nursery school I 6B 69,a)
   school report III 2A 34,6
Science II 1A 8
Scottish III WSA2 9,3
to scream III WSB4 30,b)
screen III WSD1 75,2
sea I 8B 89
seal II 9UK 84

search III 5C 84,1
at the seaside I 8A 88
season I 9C 102
seat I 8A 88
   front seat II 10D 95
second III WSB2 27
secondary school III 2A 33,2
section III 4 69
to see* I 2D 36
   You see ... ⟨III WSC3 60,1⟩
   See you tomorrow! III WSA2 8,1
to seek* ⟨III 3B 50,8⟩
to seem II 9D 87
to sell* I 7A 77,b)
to send* II 7D 68
sentence I LS6 15,1
September I 5A 58,1
serious III 5C 84,2
service III 3B 49
   service station III 4A 63
to set ⟨III 5B 83,9⟩
   The sun was setting. ⟨III WSC1 57,2⟩
to settle III 3B 50
   to settle s.th. III 2B 36
shall III 2B 39
share ⟨III WSB3 29,3⟩
she I LS2 9,c)
sheep (*sg/pl*) I 9A 98
sheepdog I 9A 98
shelf, shelves (*pl*) I 2B 32,a)
sheriff °II 2A 15
to shine* III WSC1 57
shirt II 4A 33
shock II 2B 18
shoe I 4A 49
to shoot* II 2A 15
shop I 2B 33
   shop assistant I 7A 77,b)
   to go to the shops I 6B 70
shopping centre II 5A 42
shopping list II 6D 59
short II 4A 33
   for short III 3A 45,2
short cut II 7D 68
should II 10C 93
to shout I 10D 111
show-off °III 2B 35
to show* I 9A 98
to shut* III 2B 36
Shut up! III 2B 36
side II 4D 39
sight III 1A 14
sign II 5UK 47
signal II 2D 22,3
silly I 2D 36
simple II 2D 22,3
   simple past II 2D 22,3
   simple present II 3D 31,2
since III 3B 47
to sing* I 5D 64
singer II 10B 91,1
sir III 3B 48,5
sister I 1B 23,a)
to sit* I 5UK 63,1
   to sit down I LS8 18
   to sit up II 8B 73
situation II 10C 93,2
size III WSB2 27
skate I 5UK 47
skateboard I 1B 22,a)
skater II 8A 71
to ski III 1B 20
skill III WSD3 77,3

skin I 9D 104,1
skirt II 4A 33
sky III WSC1 56
to sleep* I 8D 95
sleepless III WSB5 31,2
to slip ⟨III 5B 82,6⟩
slippery II 7D 67
sloop ⟨III 5B 83,9⟩
slow II 9B 83
slung ⟨III 3B 50,8⟩
small I 8C 92
to smell* III 1B 21
smile II 10D 96,3
to smile II 5D 50
to smoke II 5UK 47
snack bar I 8B 89
snake I LS5 14
snow I 9C 102
to snow III WSA4 12,2
so I LS4 12,a)
So do you! III 2B 39
soap I 6D 74
sock II 5A 43
solder ⟨III 3B 50,8⟩
soldier III WSC1 56
some I 6A 67,b)
somebody II 5B 45
someone II 6A 52
something II 1A 7,2
sometimes I 6B 69,b)
somewhere II 5B 45
son II 4B 36
song I 7D 86,7
soon I 5B 59,a)
sore throat II 8C 75
Sorry. I LS3 11,b)
   Sorry about … II 3D 31
sound I LS3 10,4
   sound effects II 4D 39
   sound practice I LS3 10,4
to sound II 10C 93
soup III 1B 21
south II 7UK 62
souvenir I 8C 94
spade I 4B 52
Spanish I 3A 40,3
to speak* I 3B 41
   to speak to I 3B 42,a)
special I 9A 98
special help III 2A 33,2
to spell* I 4A 49,1
to spend* ausgeben I 7A 77,a);
   verbringen I 10A 106
Splash! ⟨III 5A 79,5⟩
spoon I 2B 32,a)
sport °I 6UK 71,1
Sports Day III WSB1 26,1
   sports centre II 1C 11
sportsfield III WSB1 26,1
spot °I 2B 34,9
spray III 2B 36
to spray III 2B 36
spring I 9C 102
spy °III 1A 19,10
to spy II 1A 7,2
   I spy (with my little eye …) °II 1A 7,2
square III 1A 14
stage II 4B 34
stairs (pl) III 2B 37
stall II 3D 30
stamp I 5C 60
to stand* I 4B 51
   I can't stand … II 6A 52

to stand up °I 6D 74
star III WSB2 27,1
to start I LS3 12,9
   to start off III WSC1 56
statement III 3C 54,2
station I 8B 89
statue I 10UK 110
status III 3B 50
stay II 10D 96,3
to stay I 9A 98
to steal* III 2B 37
steep II 7D 67
step °I 1A 21,a)
still noch I 9B 99; ruhig I 10B 108
stomach-ache II 8C 75
stone I 4B 52
   the Stone Age °III 4B 66
stop III 1A 18,6
to stop aufhören, anhalten II 1D 13;
   halten I 10B 108; verhindern,
   stoppen II 2B 16
   Stop it! II 1D 13
department store II 5A 42
stormy ⟨III 5A 79,5⟩
story I 4C 54,2
straight II 2D 22
strange II 2B 18
street I 8B 89
to strike s.o. ⟨III WSC3 60,1⟩
string III WSB3 29
strong III 3A 45,1
to get stuck °I 7D 85,2
student II 7B 65
stupid III 1B 20
style III WSD3 77,1
subject Fach II 1A 8; Subjekt III 1B 20,1;
   Thema III WSC1 56,1
suddenly II 1D 12
sugar I 3C 45,4
summary °II 3D 31,2
summer I 9C 102
   summer fete II 9D 88
sun III WSC1 57
Sunday I 5C 61,b)
sunny I 4C 54
sunroof II 10D 95
super I 1B 23,a)
supermarket I 6C 73,6
I'm (not) supposed to … ⟨III WSC3 60,1⟩
to be sure I LS7 16,a)
surprise I 5B 59,a)
to be surprised °I 10D 111
sweatshirt I 5C 62,6
sweet (n.) I 7A 77,a)
sweet (adj.) II 8D 76
to swim* II 9A 80,1
swimmer III WSB5 31,3
to go swimming I 8A 88
   swimming pool II 5UK 47
   swimming things I 8A 88
Swiss III WSA1 7,2
to switch off III 4A 64
sword °III 3C 52
system III 4C 72,8

T

T-shirt I 4UK 53,3
table I 1D 28
   table tennis II 1C 11
to tackle °III WSB2 27

to take* I 10A 106
   to take a message III WSA3 10,2
   to take a photo of I 3D 46
   to take an exam III 2A 33,2
   to take for a walk II 9D 87
   to take notes I 9D 104,3
   to take off II 2D 22
   to take over III 3C 52
   to take part in s.th. III 1A 16,3
   to take place III 1A 16,3
   to take prisoner II 2A 15
   to take s.o. home I 6B 69,b)
takeaway II 6UK 58
tale II 2A 15
talk III WSA4 12
to talk about I 2C 35,2
tall III WSB2 27
tanker °III 5B 83,8
to taste II 6A 52
taxi III 1A 14
tea Mahlzeit am frühen Abend
   (Abendbrot) I 3C 45; Tee I 3C 45,4
   tea-cosy II 5D 50
   tea shop II 5A 43
to teach* III 3B 47,1
teacher I LS4 12,a)
team I 4D 55
Technology Computerunterricht,
   technisches Werken II 1A 8;
   Technologie, Technik III 4C 69
teddy II 3A 25
telephone I 1C 27,7
   on the telephone I 2B 33,5
to tell* I 4C 54,2
   to tell lies III 2C 41
temperature II 8C 75
temple °III 1A 14
ten-ton lorry ⟨III 4C 72,7⟩
tennis I 4UK 53
   table tennis II 1C 11
tense III WSA1 7,1
term II 1C 11
terrible I 3B 42,a)
test II 8B 73
to test s.b. on s.th. III 2A 33,2
text I LS8 19,1
than II 3B 26
Thanks. I 2A 31,b)
   No, thank you. I LS8 18
   Thank you very much. I 5C 61,5
   Thank you. I LS3 10,a)
that das (da) I LS2 8,b); dass II 4D 39
the I LS4 12,a)
theatre II 4UK 37
their I LS4 13,c)
theirs II 8B 74,b)
them I 4B 52
theme park °III 4A 62
themselves III WSB4 30,a)
then I 4A 49
   just then II 10D 95
there I 1B 24
   over there I 1C 26,b)
these I 2C 35
they I LS4 12,b)
thief, thieves (pl) III WSB5 31
thin III WSC3 60,1
thing I 1C 26,a)
   just the thing II 10B 91
Thing about the sea is … ⟨III 5A 79,5⟩
to think* I 7D 85,2
   to think of II 9D 87
   to think of s.th. III 2B 37,7

93

thirsty **II 6C** 57,1
this **I 1UK** 25
  this afternoon **I 3B** 42,b)
those **I 2C** 35
though (= although) **III WSC3** 60,1
thousand **I 5C** 61,3
throat **II 8C** 75
through **I 3UK** 43
throw **II 3D** 30
to **throw*** **II 2D** 21
thunder **II 4D** 39
thunderstorm **II 7B** 65,3
Thursday **I 5C** 61,a)
ticket **I 8A** 88
tide °**III 5A** 78
  tide table **III 5B** 82,6
tidy **I 1A** 21,b)
to **tidy up** **I 6B** 70
tiger **II 9UK** 84
tights (*sg/pl*) **III 4A** 33
till (= until) ⟨**III WSB3** 29,3⟩
time *Zeit, Uhrzeit* **I 3A** 40,b);
  Mal **II 5D** 49
  after a time **II 7D** 67
  a long time ago **II 7B** 65
  free time **I 4** 49
  in time **II 6D** 59
  It's time for … **I 4A** 49
  next time **I 6D** 74
  time after time ⟨**III WSB3** 29,3⟩
timetable *Fahrplan* **I 8UK** 91,2;
  Stundenplan **II 1A** 8
tinker ⟨**III 3B** 50,8⟩
tip **III WSA1** 7,2
tired °**I 9D** 103
title **II 4D** 40,1
to *nach* **I 3UK** 43,2; *vor (bei Uhrzeiten)* **I 3A** 40,b)
  from … to *von … bis* **I 3C** 44,1; *von … nach* **I 3UK** 43,2
today **I 2B** 32,a)
toga ⟨**III WSC2** 58,1⟩
together **I 1E** 30,3
toilet **I 5UK** 63
tomato, tomatoes (*pl*) **III 2C** 40,2
tomorrow **I 5D** 65,4
  the day after tomorrow **II 7C** 66
tone °**III WSA3** 10,1
tongue **III WSC3** 60,1
tonight **III 2B** 38
too *allzu, zu* **I 7C** 83; *auch* **I LS2** 9,d)
tooth, teeth (*pl*) **III WSC2** 58,1
top **II 5B** 45
  at the **top of** … **I 2D** 36
to **touch** **III 4C** 69
tourist **II 7C** 66,2
tournament **III 3C** 52
towards **II 1D** 12
tower **III 1A** 14
town **I 7B** 81
  in town **III 2A** 32
  twin town °**I 7B** 81
toy **II 10B** 91
tractor **I 9B** 101
traffic **III 4A** 63
  traffic jam °**III 4A** 63
  traffic lights (*pl*) **III 4A** 63
train **I 3UK** 43
  ghost train **II 3A** 25
to **train** **III WSB1** 26,1
trainers (*pl*) **II 5B** 44
to **translate** **III WSC2** 59,2
transport **III 4B** 66

public transport **III 4B** 66
trapped **III 5C** 84,1
travel agent's **II 7A** 63
to **travel** **II 7UK** 62
tree **I 1B** 24
tribe ⟨**III WSC2** 58,1⟩
trick **II 2B** 16
to **trick** °**I 9D** 103
trifle ⟨**III 3B** 50,8⟩
trip **III 1A** 18,8
to **trip** °**I 6D** 74; **II 8A** 71
trouble **III 2A** 32
trousers (*pl*) **I 5C** 62,6
truck ⟨**III 4C** 72,7⟩
to **truck on** ⟨**III 4C** 72,7⟩
true **III 3C** 52
trumpet **II 10B** 91
trunk ⟨**III 5B** 83,9⟩
to **try*** **II 1C** 11
  to try hard **II 9B** 83
  to try harder **III WSB2** 28,6
  to try on **II 4A** 33
Tuesday **I 5C** 60
tummy **I 2D** 36
tunic ⟨**III WSC1** 56⟩
tunnel °**I 3UK** 43
Turkish °**I 3A** 40,3
to **turn** **I 10C** 109,1
  to turn back **II 7D** 67
  to turn round **II 1D** 12
  to turn s.th. over **III 5C** 85
  Your turn. **I LS2** 8,1
tutor **I LS2** 9,c)
  tutor group **I LS2** 9,c)
TV **I 4A** 49
twice **II 7B** 64
  twice a week **II 9A** 80
twin town **I 7B** 81
typical **III WSA1** 7,1

U

Ugh! **II 9B** 81
uncle **I 3A** 40,c)
  great uncle **II 5D** 49
under **I LS5** 14
underground **III 1A** 17,5
underneath ⟨**III WSC3** 60,1⟩
to **understand*** **I 8D** 95
understandable **III WSB5** 31,4
uniform **I 3B** 42,b)
unit **I 1** 21
unpredictable °**III 5A** 78
untidy **I 2B** 32,b)
until **II 7D** 68
up **II 2B** 18
  It's up to you. **III 4B** 67,5
  up here **III 3B** 47,1
  up to **II 2D** 21
upper **II 5A** 42
to **upset*** s.b. **III WSA2** 8
upstairs **I 5UK** 63
us **I 4B** 52
Ain't no **use setting out for the bad companion.** ⟨**III 4C** 72,7⟩
to **use** **II 5D** 50
useful **II 4A** 33
useless **III WSB5** 31,2
usually **I 6B** 70,6

V

valley **III 3A** 45,1
van **II 7D** 69,4
to **vanish** ⟨**III 3B** 50,8⟩
vegetable **II 6A** 52
verb °**I 6D** 75,3
very **I LS3** 11,b)
  very much **I 5C** 61,5
vet **I 2A** 31,a)
  vet's assistant **I 2A** 31,a)
video **I 5C** 62,7
  video recorder **III 3A** 45,1
village **III 3A** 45,1
violence **III WSD1** 75,2
V.I.P. (= very important person) °**III 2B** 38,12
visit **II 8B** 73
to **visit** **II 3A** 25
visitor **III 3A** 45,1
vocabulary **III WSB2** 27,1
voice **II 4B** 34

W

to **wait** (for) **I 7E** 87,4
waiter **III 1B** 21
to **wake up*** **II 2B** 18
walk **I 4C** 54
  to go for a walk **I 4C** 54
  to take for a walk **II 9D** 87
to **walk** **I 6B** 68
wall **III 2B** 36
to **want** **I 7A** 77,b)
ward **II 8D** 76
warden °**III WSA3** 11,4
warm **I 4C** 54,1
to **warn** **II 7D** 67
wash **II 10D** 96,3
  car wash **II 10UK** 92
to **wash** **II 2C** 20
washable **III WSB5** 31,4
washing machine **III WSB5** 31,4
washing-up **I 6B** 70
  to do the washing-up **I 6B** 70
to **waste** **III 4A** 64,3
to **watch** **I 4A** 49
  Watch out! **I LS3** 10,5
water **I 8B** 90
wave **III 5A** 78
waxwork °**III 1A** 17,5
way *Art und Weise* **III 2B** 39; *Weg* **I 7D** 84
  all the way **III 1C** 22
  in different ways **II 10UK** 92
  out of the way **II 10D** 95
  She's on her way **I 7** 84
  that way **II 7D** 68
we **I LS4** 12,b)
weak **III 2A** 34,6
to **wear*** **I 5C** 62,6
weather **I 4C** 54
  weather forecast **II 7C** 66
Wednesday **I 5C** 61,b)
week **I 5C** 61,4
  twice a week **II 9A** 80
weekend **II 2A** 15
to **weigh** **III WSB2** 27
Welcome to … °**I 3A** 40,c)
  to make s.o. welcome ⟨**III WSA5** 13,2⟩
  to welcome s.b. **III WSC2** 58,1
well *gut* **II 9B** 83; *nun, na ja* **I 4A** 49,2

to feel well **II 8B** 72
Well done. **I 6B** 70
Welsh III WSA2 8
west II 7UK 62
West Indian °**III 1A** 16,3
West of the Sunset ⟨**III WSC3** 60,1⟩
westbound °**III 1A** 18,6
wet I 4C 54
what I LS2 8,a)
What a … **I 2B** 32,a)
What about …? **I 2D** 37,5
What colour is/are …? **I 2A** 31,2
What on earth …? **II 5D** 49
What time is it? **I 3A** 40,b)
What's … like? **I 4C** 54
wheel II 3C 28,5
when *als* **I 10D** 111; *wann* **I 5B** 59,a); *wenn* **II 2B** 17
where I LS5 14
whether III 3B 49
which II 1A 8
while *während* **II 6D** 59; *Weile* **III 2C** 41
whiskers ⟨**III 3B** 50,8⟩
to **whisper III 1C** 22
white I 6A 67,1
whizzkid ⟨**III 4C** 72,7⟩
who *wen/wem* **I 9B** 101; *wer* **I LS4** 12,a)
whole III 1A 17
whom ⟨**III 2B** 37,8⟩
whose I 9B 100
why I 8B 90
wide III 4B 65
wife III 3C 53
wig II 5D 49
wild III 3A 45,1
will II 4B 34
to **win* I 6C** 72
wind III WSC1 56
window I 7D 84
window frame ⟨**III 4C** 72,7⟩
windy I 4C 54
wine II 2D 21
winner °**I 6C** 72,2
winter I 9C 102
to **wish III WSC3** 60,1
with I 1A 21
And with that … **II 10D** 95
without I 5A 58
wizard °**III 3C** 52
woman, women (*pl*) **I 2A** 31,a)
to **wonder III 3B** 49
wonderful II 5D 49
word I LS6 15,3
word building °**III WSB5** 31
word power **I 1C** 26,2
work II 2C 20
to **work I 1B** 23,4
to work late **I 4B** 51
worker III WSB5 31,3
worksheet III 1C 22
workshop III WSA1 7
world II 3B 26
World Cup **III WSB2** 27
to **worry I 9B** 99
worried about II 1D 12
worse II 3B 26
(the) **worst II 3B** 26
It's **worth buying. III WSD1** 75,2
Would you like …? **II 5C** 48,1
Wow! °**I 4B** 51
to **write* I LS6** 15,3
to write about **I 2D** 37,3
to write down **I 4UK** 53,3

writer III WSB5 31,3
writing III 2B 36,3
wrong I LS8 19,1
to get out of bed on the wrong side **II 10D** 95
to go wrong **II 3D** 30
What's wrong? **II 8C** 75

Y

year I LS6 15
yellow I 2A 31,b)
yes I LS2 8,a)
yesterday II 2B 16
the day before yesterday **II 7B** 65
yet *noch* **I 1D** 28; *schon* **II 6B** 55,5
not … yet **I 1D** 28
you *dir/dich/euch/Sie/Ihnen* **I 4B** 52; *du/ihr/Sie* **I LS3** 10,a)
young II 3A 25
your I LS2 8,a)
Your turn. **I LS2** 8,1
yours II 8B 74,b)
yourself III WSB4 30,a)
yourselves III WSB4 30,a)
youth group II 10UK 92
youth hostel **III WSA3** 11,4

Z

zone °**I 8B** 89
zoo II 5UK 47

Boys' names

Alan °**I 9D** 103
Arthur °**II 5D** 49
Asim III WSA2 9,4
Barry II 1D 12
Charles III 4B 66
Clive °**I LS3** 11,b)
Colin I 3C 45
Dafydd ⟨**III 3B** 50,8⟩
Daniel III 2B 37,9
Darren III 1A 16,2
David I LS2 9,d)
Eddy °**I 2A** 31,a)
Florian III WSA1 7
Gavin III 3B 51,10
Harold III 1A 19,9
Harry II 5D 50,4
Hugh III 3B 47
Jack °**I 9A** 98
Jeff °**II 4D** 40,2
John II 1B 10
Jonah III WSB2 27
Kay III 3C 52
Ken °**I 7B** 81,12
Kevin °**I 7B** 79,5
Lee °**II 6A** 52
Lenny °**I 9A** 98
Marcus ⟨**III WSC3** 60,1⟩
Mario III 2B 37,9
Mark I 3A 40,a)
Michael °**I 7D** 86,7
Mike II 1D 12
Owen III 3B 47,1

Pete III 5B 80
Peter °**I 2B** 34,9
Richy III 4C 69
Ricky III 4B 66
Robert I LS1 7
Ryan III WSA2 9,4
Sam I 9A 98
Samuel III 4B 66
Simon I 1A 21,a)
Stan ⟨**III 5A** 79,5⟩
Steve III 3A 46,5
Thomas III 2B 37,9
Tim I 1C 27,8
Tom II 9A 80
Washington °**II 4B** 36
Wayne III WSB4 30,1

Girls' names

Amy III 5B 80
Anna °**I 7D** 86,7
Annabel °**I 6D** 74
Audrey I 4D 55
Becky I LS2 8,a)
Camilla ⟨**III WSC3** 60,1⟩
Candy III WSD1 75,2
Cottia ⟨**III WSC3** 60,1⟩
Ellen III WSA1 7
Emma II 6A 52
Fiona III 2B 38,11
Gwen III 3B 47
Helen I 5D 64
Jackie III WSB1 26,1
Jane III WSB1 26,1
Janet °**I 2A** 31,a)
Jenny I 2B 37,9
Jill III 2B 38,11
Judy II 7D 67
Julie III WSB4 30,1
Kate III WSA2 9,4
Kim I 2A 31,a)
Lucy III 4C 69
Maggie III 2B 37,9
Mary °**I 9D** 103
Mavis III 4B 65
Megan III WSA2 9,4
Michelle III 3B 47
Nina °**II 9A** 80
Nora III WSB5 31
Pat °**I 3B** 41
Paula III 4B 66
Sally I 2B 34,9
Samira III 1A 16,2
Sarah I LS1 7
Shabina II 4A 33
Sue °**II 5A** 43
Susan °**II 9A** 80
Suvina I 6D 74
Tammy III WSD1 75,2
Valaria ⟨**III WSC3** 60,1⟩
Victoria III 1A 18,7
Virginia II 4B 36
Yasmin °**II 9A** 80

Surnames

Adib °**I 6D** 74
Anderson III 5B 80

Barker °I 6D 74
Benson °I 6D 74
Blackwell °II 4B 36
Bloggs °II 9A 80
Brandon III 4B 65
Broadwood °II 5A 43
Brown °II 6A 52
Burton I LS2 8,a)
Cameron III 5B 80
Campbell °II 7C 66
Clark III 2A 34,6
Cooper I LS4 12,b)
Croft I LS2 8,a)
Dane I LS4 12,a)
Dart III 4B 66
Davis II 8D 78,5
Dickens II 4D 40,2
Dixon I LS3 11,b)
Duncan III WSB5 31
Grant III 1C 22
Greenwood °I 9D 104,3
Gwynn ⟨III 3B 50,8⟩
Hilton °I 7D 86,7
Hunt °I 7D 86,7
Ismaili °II 4A 33
Jackson III 5C 84,2
Jenkins II 1D 12
Jessop °II 5A 42
Jones III WSB1 26,1
Jonker III WSA3 11,4
Lee II 2C 20
Lomu III WSB2 27
MacTavish II 7B 64
Martin °II 6A 52
Mason II 4B 34,1
Matthew °II 8C 75
Mc Carthy III WSB1 26,1
Miller °I 2B 32,2
Muddle °I 2B 34,9
Otis II 4B 36
Parker III WSB1 26,1
Patel II 8B 73
Patterson °II 1C 11
Penrose I LS2 9,d)
Price °II 6A 52
Pritchard III 3A 46,5
Richards °I 9A 98
Ripple °II 5B 46
Sheikh III 1A 16,2
Singh °II 1C 11
Smith °I 9D 103
Stevenson II 1B 10,6
Stuart II 10D 95
Taylor III 1A 16,2
Umney II 4D 39
Underwood II 4B 36
Walker III 3A 46,5
Wall °I 6D 74
Warren III 4B 66
White °I 6A 67,1
Wood °I 2B 32,2

Geographical names

Aberystwyth III 3A 44
Africa II 9UK 84,2
the Alps (*pl*) II 7D 67
Ambleside III WSA3 11,4
America II 1B 10
Angel Row °I 10C 109,1
Antarctica II 9UK 84,2
Arndale Road I 1UK 25
Arnot Hill Park I 1D 28
Ashbourne III 4A 63,1
Asia II 9UK 84,2
Australia II 9UK 84,2
Austria III WSA1 7,2
Baker Street III 1A 14
Beastmarket Hill °I 10C 109,1
Belfast °II 6A 52
Belgium °I 3UK 43,2
Ben Nevis II 7C 66
Berlin I 1UK 25
Bethnal Green III 1A 16,3
Birmingham III 4B 66
Bournemouth III 4B 66
Britain II 7UK 62
Britannia ⟨III WSC2 58,1⟩
the British Isles III WSA2 9,3
Broad Haven III 5C 84,2
Caerleon III 3A 44
Caernarvon III 3A 44
Cardiff III 3A 44
Caribbean °III 1A 16,3
Castle Road °I 10C 109,1
Channel Tunnel °I 3UK 43
the Channel °I 3UK 43
Chicago °II 1B 10
China III WSA1 7,2
Cornwall °I 10A 106
Coventry III 1A 16,3
Denmark III WSA1 7,2
Derby III 4A 63,1
Druidston III 5C 84,2
East Cheam III WSB5 31
Edinburgh III WSA2 8
Edward's Lane I 2B 34,7
Elf Row III WSB5 31
Ellastone III 4A 62,1
Embankment III 1A 18,8
England I 3A 40,c)
Europe II 9UK 84,2
Exchange Walk °I 10C 109,1
Fishguard III 3A 44
Fort William °II 7C 66
France °I 3UK 43,2
Friar Lane °I 10C 109,1
Germany I 1UK 25
Glenarm III WSA2 9,4
Great Britain III WSA2 9,3
Greece III WSA1 7,2
Green Park III 1A 18,7
Greendale III 4B 65
Hastings III 1A 19,9
Heathrow Airport °I 3A 40,a)
the High Street °I 8B 89
Holyhead III 3A 44
Hull III WSA1 7
Hyde Park III 1A 14
India III 1A 16,3
Ireland III WSA2 9,3
the Isle of Wight II 7UK 62
Italy III WSA1 7,2
Kent III WSC1 56
King Street °I 10C 109,1
Knightsbridge III 1A 14
Lake Windermere III WSA3 11,5
the Lake District III WSA3 11,4
Larwood Grove I 2B 33
Leeds °II 6A 52
Leicester Square III 1A 18,8
Loch Lomond II 7B 64
Loch Ness II 7C 66
Londinium ⟨III WSC2 58,1⟩
London I LS2 8,a)
Long Row °I 10C 109
Luton III WSA2 9,4
M6 °II 7B 64
Maid Marian Way °I 10C 109,1
Malham III WSA3 11,5
Mansfield Road I 1UK 25
Market Street °I 10C 109,1
Mayfield III 4A 63,1
the Mediterranean Sea ⟨III WSC1 57,2⟩
Milford Haven III 5C 84,2
Mount Street °I 10C 109,1
Nassau ⟨III 5B 83,9⟩
the Netherlands °I 3UK 43,2
New Zealand III WSB2 27
Nolton Haven III 5C 84,2
Normandy III 1A 19,9
North America II 9UK 84,2
the North Sea I 3UK 43,2
Northallerton °I 9B 101,8
Northern Ireland III WSA2 9,3
Nottingham I LS1 7
Notting Hill Gate III 1A 14
Old Market Square °I 10C 109
Paddington III 1A 18,7
Pakistan III 1A 16,3
Paris °I 10B 108,4
Parliament Street °I 10C 109,1
Piccadilly Circus III 1A 14
Poland °I 3A 40,3
Regent's Park III 1A 14
the Republic of Ireland III WSA2 9,3
River Thames III 1A 14
Rome III WSC1 57
Rotterdam III WSA1 7
Rugby III 4B 66
Russia III WSA1 7,2
Scarborough III WSA3 11,5
Scotland °I 10A 106
Shadwell III WSB5 31
Sherwood I 1UK 25
Sherwood Forest II 2A 15
Skegness I 8A 88
Smithy Row °I 10C 109
Snowdon III WSA2 9,4
Snowdonia National Park III 3A 44
South Africa III WSB2 27
South America II 9UK 84,2
South Parade °I 10C 109,1
Spain III WSA1 7,2
St Peter's Gate °I 10C 109,1
Sudbury III 4A 63,1
Swansea III 3A 44
Switzerland III WSA1 7,2
Tenby III 3A 44
Tonga III WSB2 27
Trafalgar Square III 1A 14
Truro °II 6A 52
Turkey III WSA1 7,2
Twycross Zoo II 5UK 47
the UK (= the United Kingdom) I 1UK 25
Uttoxeter III 4A 63,1
Wales II 7UK 62
the West Indies III 1A 16,3
Wheeler Gate °I 10C 109,1
York III WSA3 11,5
Yorkshire °I 9 98